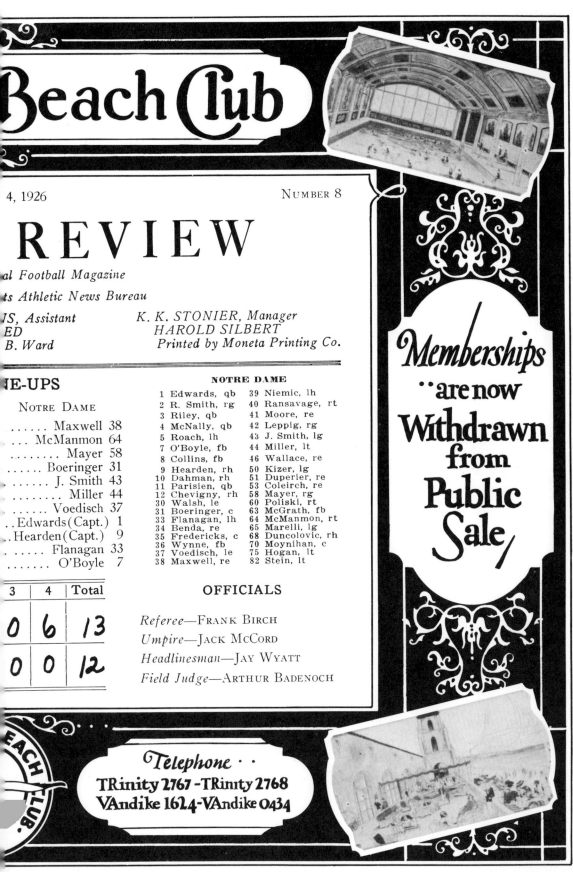

Beach Club

4, 1926   NUMBER 8

REVIEW

al Football Magazine

ts Athletic News Bureau

JS, Assistant   K. K. STONIER, Manager
ED   HAROLD SILBERT
B. Ward   Printed by Moneta Printing Co.

NE-UPS

NOTRE DAME

..... Maxwell	38
... McManmon	64
.... Mayer	58
..... Boeringer	31
...... J. Smith	43
.... Miller	44
.... Voedisch	37
..Edwards(Capt.)	1
..Hearden(Capt.)	9
...... Flanagan	33
.... O'Boyle	7

NOTRE DAME

1	Edwards, qb	39	Niemic, lh
2	R. Smith, rg	40	Ransavage, rt
3	Riley, qb	41	Moore, re
4	McNally, qb	42	Leppig, rg
5	Roach, lh	43	J. Smith, lg
7	O'Boyle, fb	44	Miller, lt
8	Collins, fb	46	Wallace, re
9	Hearden, rh	50	Kizer, lg
10	Dahman, rh	51	Duperier, re
11	Parisien, qb	53	Coleirch, re
12	Chevigny, rh	58	Mayer, rg
30	Walsh, le	60	Poliski, rt
31	Boeringer, c	63	McGrath, fb
33	Flanagan, lh	64	McManmon, rt
34	Benda, re	65	Marelli, lg
35	Fredericks, c	68	Duncolovic, rh
36	Wynne, fb	70	Moynihan, c
37	Voedisch, le	75	Hogan, lt
38	Maxwell, re	82	Stein, lt

	3	4	Total
	0	6	13
	0	0	12

OFFICIALS

Referee—FRANK BIRCH

Umpire—JACK McCORD

Headlinesman—JAY WYATT

Field Judge—ARTHUR BADENOCH

Reprint From 1926 PIGSKIN REVIEW

NOTRE DAME vs. USC

Perhaps a Matter

Keeper of the Trojan Horse

COACH HOWARD JONES has been called "The Henry Ford of Football," because in his system of playing the gridiron game there is an incessant demand for specialization. Only two of his backfield men carry the ball and they alternate in these duties. The other two do nothing but lead interference. A player is not only either a guard or a tackle but is either a left tackle or a right tackle, a running guard or a standing guard, etc. A man cannot be a "jack of all trades" for Jones. This system is purely Jones's, evolved by the crafty coach through 18 years of mentorship beginning in 1908 and served at Yale, Iowa, Syracuse, Ohio State, Duke University and Southern California. In 1921 his system proved better than Rockne's when Jones was at Iowa and Rockne was then with the Irish.

of Horsemanship

Trainer of
the
Four Horsemen

Knute Rockne

Reprint From 1926 PIGSKIN REVIEW

COACH KNUTE ROCKNE has for many
seasons been heralded as one of the vogue-
setters in the intricate game of football.
Like Jones, he has his own individual system which has brought his teams to the lime-
light annually and to one national championship.
For instance, in 1924 Rockne had a team com-
prising 17 seniors. In order to build up for coming years, the foxy mentor started his second
team in every game to give them needed experience. Again it was Rockne who inaugurated the
idea that it is utterly foolish to cripple or wear
out a team with hard scrimmages during the
active season. Rockne used the huddle system
long before the East took it up. Neither Rockne
nor Jones built their teams on the "star system,"
but both have developed long lists of stars and
"All-Americans" as bi-products of their football.

Bert Heiser
half

Don Williams
quarter

Morley Drury
half

Hersh Bonham
full

Jesse Hibbs
tackle

Howard Elliot
quarter

Harold Wheeler
half

Thomas Bros
Lloyd - Max
half *full*

John Fox
center

Bill Ford
quarter

T WENTY-TWO gridiron battlers return from the present squad of 37 players to form the nucleus for the 1927 football aggregation at the University of Southern California. Upon the shoulders of these fellows and those of the most stalwart of the 1926 freshman outfit will fall the duties of filling in the holes left when 15 seniors hang up their moleskins this evening.

With the probable exception of one or two men, every one of the 22 returning members of the present varsity squad has done some actual playing this season. They have tasted the thrill of pigskin action. To fill the shoes of 15 seasoned men is no small task, but there is little cause for fear among Trojan fans that Southern California will not have a presentable team next year.

Only six of the 22 men who return will be in their third season of football next fall, but eight of the 22 will be playing their last years. Bert Heiser, half; Morley Drury, half; Howard Elliott, quarter; Jim Moser, end; Lyle Baldridge, center; and Al Scheving, tackle, will all have turned in a couple of varsity seasons at the end of today's game. Heiser played his first year in 1924 and was out of competition last year. All of the others played in 1925 and 1926 and every one of the six athletes were lettermen at the start of the present season.

Troy's 1927

The two other men who will be in their last season of football next season are Max Thomas, fullback; and Harold Wheeler, halfback. Both lost a year of competition because of transferring to Southern California from other universities, so have but one more year of play. Thomas came from Chicago University where he played freshman football and had to remain out of athletics in 1925. Wheeler came directly from Phoenix Junior College but was eligible without loss of time.

Working with these eight seniors will be fourteen juniors who went through their first seasons of football this year.

These men are Lloyd Thomas, half; Jesse Hibbs, tackle; Alvin Schaub, guard; John Fox, center; Oliver White, guard; Eugene Beatie, tackle; Marion Morrison, tackle; Don Williams, quarter; Lowry McCaslin, end; Leslie Lavelle, end; Herschel Bonham, full; Bill Ford, quarter; Larry Dihel, end; and Hilton McCabe, tackle.

Lowry McCaslin
End

Oliver White
Guard

Jim Moser
End

Marion Morrison
Tackle

Lyle Baldridge
Center

Al Sheving
Tackle

Al Schaub
Guard

Leslie Lavelle
End

Gene Beatie
Tackle

Larry Dihel
End

Hilton McCabe
Tackle

Team Nucleus

With the exception of Don Williams, who was on the 1924 freshman team and out of competition in 1925, all of these men were members of the 1925 yearling outfit.

Of the entire list of 22 men only three were considered as first string starters, and only six played enough football to be termed regulars. On the first string Hibbs always started at tackle. He is the only starting lineman to return for next season. In the backfield Morley Drury was given first call at right half until he sustained a knee injury. His duties then fell to Lloyd Thomas, a sophomore, who filled in the gap satisfactorily. Bert Heiser started at left half throughout the early part of the season, but beginning with the O. A. C. game, Wheeler got the starting call here. Moser played considerable football at end, taking up the work left by Al Behrendt when the big flankman hurt a leg. Don Williams did a lot of early season playing at quarterback, but beginning with the California game became only one of the subs. Howard Elliott became a late season regular when Morton Kaer was injured and he played most of the Idaho and Montana games.

All of the others played only at times throughout the season.

Next season there may have to be considerable shifting to get a first string line-up. It looks like Morley Drury is certain of a right half position if his knee injury does not come back. Lloyd Thomas will remain his first sub. Bert Heiser and Harold Wheeler will battle over the other halfback position. Howard Elliott and Don Williams will alternate at quarterback. Max Thomas will probably be the starting fullback with Hersh Bonham his relief man.

On the line Jesse Hibbs is the only veteran. He will probably play at tackle although there has been some talk of him being converted into a running guard. Al Scheving or one of the many sophomore tackles of this year will be at the other tackle position. Al Schaub, who started at running guard in earlier games this year may be in that position next season. Oliver White is a strong candidate for the standing guard place. John Fox has an edge at center with Baldridge a second choice. Moser will be one end with Lavelle or McCaslin as the other.

Just what sort of season these men will have to play through will be known to the fans today for Pacific Coast managers, faculty representatives and coaches are meeting here this week to decide those questions.

Reprint From 1926 PIGSKIN REVIEW

The Fighting Irish

Tom Hearden
Right Half

Ray Dahman
Right Half

Christy Flanigan
Left Half

Harry O'Boyle
Fullback

Jack Chevigney
Right Half

Johnnie Niemier
Left Half

Fred Miller
Left Tackle

Art Parisien
Quarterback

John Fredericks
Center

John McMannon
Right Tackle

Notre Dame Gridders

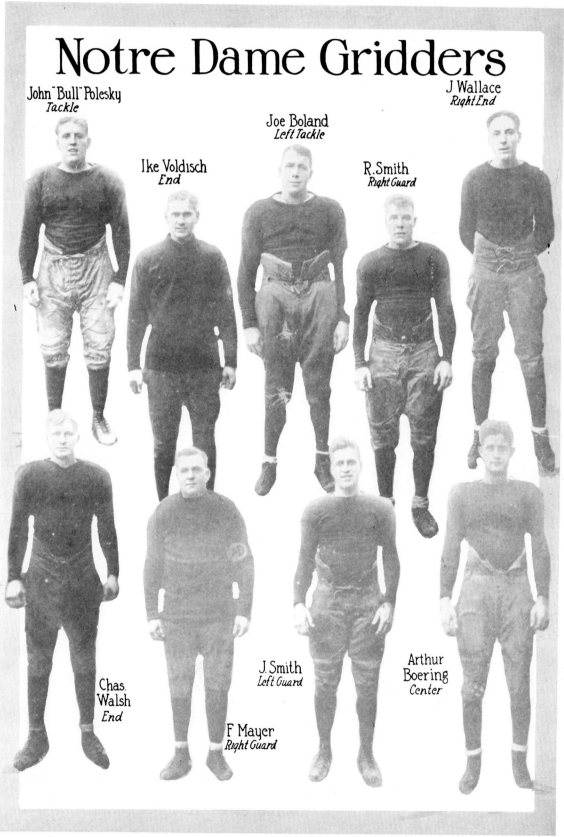

John "Bull" Polesky
Tackle

J Wallace
Right End

Ike Voldisch
End

Joe Boland
Left Tackle

R. Smith
Right Guard

Chas.
Walsh
End

J. Smith
Left Guard

Arthur
Boering
Center

F Mayer
Right Guard

Reprint From 1926 PIGSKIN REVIEW

John McKay   John Robinson

Photo by
Arnold Frankel

OJ Simpson

Ricky Bell

Rod Sherman   Mike Garrett

8

USC

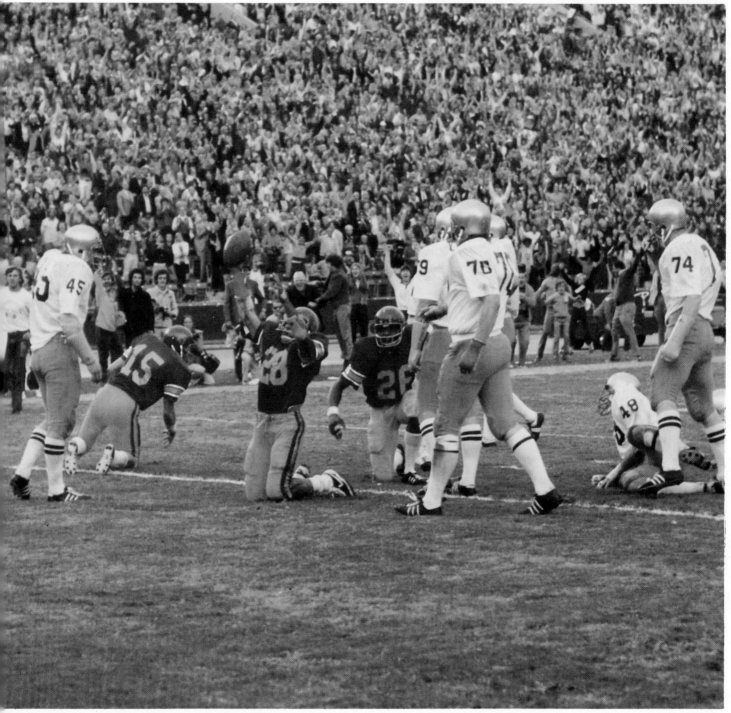

Dave Farmer   Anthony Davis   Shelton Diggs

9

TROJANS

John McKay with 1974 Trojan team during 55-24 victory

"Tommy Trojan"

USC All American Song Girls for 1975-76. Left to right, Kim Chavalas, Karen Waier, Debbie Anderegg, Dolly Zachary, Zivia Wilson, D'Arcy Dietrich

Ara Parseghian with the famous Trojan horse

NOTRE DAME

Nick Eddy

Ken MacAfee

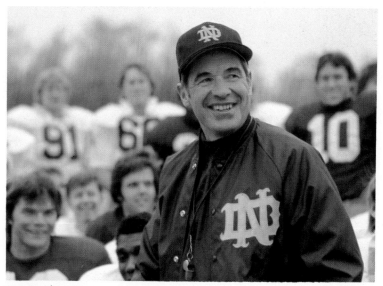

Dan Devine

Ross Browner   Randy Harrison   Luther Bradley

13

"Hi" "I'm Knute" "I lived up here"

FIGHTING IRISH

Coach Dan Devine with team before big game

ACKNOWLEDGEMENTS

Compiling the first comprehensive history of America's oldest intersectional football rivalry — Notre Dame University versus University of Southern California — posed a challenge which could only be met by hundreds of dedicated people.

Realizing it would require another volume to acknowledge everyone who contributed to this historic effort, the Editors, with sincere apologies to many who are being omitted, wish to take this opportunity to publicly express our sincere appreciation to:

Notre Dame University

Carol Lynch — Coach Devine's Administrative Assistant — who made 2,500 miles seem much closer... Herb Juliano, Director of Sports & Games ... D. "Chet" Grant, resident sports historian ... Roger Valdisari, S.I.D. ... Norma Villanucci ... Bruce Harlan, Notre Dame photographer ... Mary Ann Carr ... Joe Doyle, South Bend Tribune.

University of Southern California

Nick M. Pappas, Associate Director of Athletics ... Mary Wilson ... Dr. Richard Perry, S.I.D. ... Russ Ewald ... Jack Neahan ... The Doheny Library ... Lorraine Ullman ... John Reynolds ... Leonard Wines ... Jim Appleton ... Marv Goux.

Other Wonderful Supporters

Jim "Dink" Lenihan ... Ron Parker ... John McPhillips ... Frank Butler ... Gwynne Wilson ... Morley Drury ... Richard Rosenthal ... Sam Pedace ... Joe Fagen, Fagen Graphics ... Don Sanford, Sanford Studios ... Arnold Frankel, for USC color photos ... Dennis Clappier ... Marvin McCorgary ... George Totten ... Paulette Chapman, Taylor Publishing ... James F. Watson, for the 1976 action photos ... Larry Chaffers of Carpenter/Offutt Paper, Inc. ... Chief Samuelson ... and ... many, many more wonderful supporters.

The Editors

Manufactured in the United States of America

First Printing — 1977

ISBN: 0-8467-0361-0
LCCN: 77-9156

Published by Fiske/Milne Publishers
1800 North Highland Ave. Suite 506
Hollywood, Calif. 90028

Distributed by
Two Continents Publishing Group
30 East 42 Street
New York, N.Y. 10017

Published by arrangement with
Chief Samuelson and Associates, Inc.

TABLE OF CONTENTS

INTRODUCTION
By John McKay

When I grew up as a Catholic in West Virginia, I loved Notre Dame and its football team. The Fighting Irish were the first team in any sport I cheered for. I think they've always had that fascination for young Catholic kids, and today I still cheer for them — except when they play USC. My family listened to all the Irish games on the radio. When they lost, it was like a funeral in our house.

Notre Dame has lent a lot of dignity and tradition to college football. The enthusiasm of their student body is tremendous, their fight song is inspiring and I get goose bumps when I go back to South Bend and see the leaves falling and the golden dome shining in the sunlight.

There is no intersectional rivalry that compares with USC-Notre Dame, because it has nationwide interest. It captures the mid-west, the west and the east, and unlike other intersectional series, it has been an annual event since 1926. We've met Notre Dame 14 times since I became Head Coach, and the outcome has either determined or help determine who was National Champion 10 times.

It amuses me that coaches say they like to play Notre Dame, but when it comes time to schedule them, few teams stand in line. Ohio State hasn't taken a chance since 1936. UCLA played the Irish twice in the early 60's and lost twice, and that was the end of the series.

The 1962 game turned out to be our best game of the season, and we won our first National Championship at USC, 25-0 before 82,000 fans in Los Angeles. This still ranks as one of my biggest wins.

But the reality of the 1966 loss was something that I had to live with, and I was determined to learn from it. The next year I took the films of that game out at every opportunity. I watched that 51-0 destruction at least once a week, and sometimes every day. It was the only game I've ever coached that I replayed in my mind long after it was over. I still have that film and once in a while I'll watch it again.

I normally dislike pep talks and rarely give them, but I'll admit that before the 1967 game in South Bend, I was a little emotional and told my players "Not many people can say they've ever played in the USC-Notre Dame game, it will be heard all over the world. No matter where you go the rest of your lives, you will remember you've played in this game. To lose it would be a crime. You're too good. This time you're better than Notre Dame and if you lose, you'll know you lost to an inferior team."

For the first time since 1939, USC was victorious in Notre Dame Stadium. We won 24-7 and I was carried off the field. This ranks as one of my greatest thrills as a coach. The 1972 and 1974 victories in the Coliseum were played by two of my best teams. They showed great character in coming from behind to win.

In 1971 before the game in South Bend, I told my players "We're back here together in the greatest hotbed of football, Notre Dame, and this is the game that typifies college football. This is what it's all about. This is what I've believed in since I was a little kid. And I still believe in it."

Notre Dame-USC is the greatest in college football.

John McKay
Tampa Bay, Florida — 1976

DAN DEVINE
HEAD FOOTBALL COACH
UNIVERSITY OF NOTRE DAME

INTRODUCTION

There is no way that one can recognize the special significance of a Notre Dame-USC game unless you have participated as a Coach or as a player. It is definitely the sporting contest, professional or amateur, of the year.

Prior to coming to Notre Dame, I personally was exposed to many rivalries as a coach; Michigan vs. Michigan State, Arizona State vs. Arizona, Missouri vs. Kansas, Missouri vs. Oklahoma, Green Bay vs. Chicago Bears, Green Bay vs. Minnesota Vikings. These are truly great rivalries and have a tremendous impact on football, college and professional. However, after once participating in the Irish-Trojan contest, everything else becomes rather drab and colorless.

There is an aura of excitement that comes over the campus on the Monday prior to the game that is difficult to put into words. The 1975 contest was emotional because of the embarrassing defeat suffered by the Irish at SC in 1974. I would say that our preparation for the game would have been different had we not graduated most of the players who played in the '74 game.

By mid-week the team and staff draw closer together than at any time during the entire season. The pep rally Friday night is an event one could not imagine, unless you were here on campus that evening. People come hundreds of miles by bus just to be at the pep rally, and get caught up in the tremendous emotional impact that it has on everyone present. The game suddenly becomes a crusade of revenge for the bitter disappointment of the previous year. Players and coaches alike make statements that they would probably not make at any other point in the season. When the team retires for the evening across the lake from the Golden Dome, they do so with a quiet and solemn attitude. The next morning again there is a special solemnity to the pre-game mass, breakfast and team meeting.

When we finally took to the field after our pre-game warmup I felt I was running 3 feet off the ground. The tremendous reception the squad and coaches received, particularly during the introductions, brought forth feelings of exhilaration and determination. The pre-game huddle, closeness of the players all trying to touch one another and the coaches was unbelievable. The Captains met in the middle of the field, and during the coin-toss both teams edged slowly towards the middle of the field so that after the flip the entire middle of the field became engulfed with Notre Dame and Southern Cal players. Had not both teams been so well disciplined some type of disorderly brawl could have erupted even before the kick-off.

When the game starts, the normal ebb and tide strategies prevail. However, there is a certain intensity about the play of both teams, and the conduct of both benches. The conduct is not unsportsmanlike, but it is as every player on both sides of the field is intimately involved in the game. In normal situations, you have some players who let their disappointment in not participating show in their faces. On the players' faces grim determination is outlined, but can only be seen from the sidelines. Noting the disarray of your bench, you glance across the field to see if things are in better order on the other side and the same chaos, anxiety and determination exist. This is truly America's greatest sporting event, exceeding the World Series and the Super Bowl.

I feel that God has blessed my life in many ways, and one of them is giving me the chance to have a part to play in one of my profession's greatest moments.

JOHN ROBINSON
HEAD FOOTBALL COACH
UNIVERSITY OF SOUTHERN CALIFORNIA

My first occasion, as a Trojan, to meet Notre Dame was in the Coliseum in 1972. I was an assistant coach to John McKay.

We were undefeated and had to win that game to clinch the National Championship. Notre Dame had lost only one game up to then. Anthony Davis, along with the entire team, had a great afternoon and we won.

The thing that impressed me most about it was not the win, however, but that the game was in that category of being bigger than any other football game played in the United States. Sure, the people of Texas and Oklahoma feel that as respective opponents, they have the same bigness, and they may. But Notre Dame/USC is one of those elite games that is second to none, with great nationwide interest. The entire coaching staff has that feeling at USC. Coach McKay knew it was special and treated it that way.

1973 was my first trip to South Bend and my first loss as an SC coach. We were the defending national champs and the game meant a great deal. AD had scored 6 TD's the year before and the Irish were particularly focussed, to say the least. It was obviously impressive going back there, all the words other people say, you feel.

Father Hesburg told me in our locker room after the game "I haven't seen this campus as aroused in ten years." Notre Dame played like it. They played an almost perfect game against us, error-free. They did a great job. They had the National Championship that year.

It used to be, at least from what I have heard from their tradition, no matter who you were and came there, you were afraid of Notre Dame. Notre Dame was the team, Notre Dame was the people, and Notre Dame was the spirit, when you came to South Bend. I think when USC comes to South Bend — that whole thing is balanced out. There's a fear of us. When we go back there, we are special to them. My impression is that when SC comes to South Bend, it's different than when anybody else comes there.

As a coach for the Oakland Raiders for one year I experienced a strong rivalry with the Pittsburgh Steelers. But the crowd doesn't bring as much to those games as the crowd brings to the Notre Dame games. To them, there is something special going on down on the field. You feel it in the air before the kickoff, the crowd becomes highly emotional, electricity fills the air, a special feeling and charged atmosphere fills the stadium.

It's such an honor to have either of these jobs, head coach at USC or at Notre Dame, it's an honor to be in the position . . . nothing better can happen to you, than to be involved in this great series. I think there's a chance that the 50th anniversary of the Notre Dame/USC game can be for the National Championship. I certainly hope so.

ARA PARSEGHIAN

When I became coach at Notre Dame in 1964, never in my fondest dreams did I vision that we could be battling for the national championship in the final game of the season. But that was my introduction to Southern California in what is surely the greatest intersectional series in college football.

In previous coaching, I had more or less been involved in conference or regional play. Our Miami (Ohio) teams seldom ventured out of our own geographic area. At Northwestern, only three games a year were against non-conference opponents.

Thus, I had never been involved in a truly national, intersectional series. But what a series this Southern Cal-Notre Dame game turned out to be.

Southern California was just a team at the end of a 10-game schedule in my first year, but I did know that Knute Rockne and Howard Jones started the series almost 40 years earlier and that it had been played every year since with a brief interruption in World War II.

The impact of the game didn't really hit me until that November 28, 1964, when we were 9-0 and the Trojans 6-3. And more than 80,000 fans — our largest crowd of the season — were there.

Painfully, I recall what happened. We led 17-0 at the half, but had shut off two good S.C. chances. And we had two more chances to put it away in the second half, but we failed.

Southern California rallied and then got the ball after a penalty on our punt. They were in our territory and with 1:33 left, Craig Fertig's pass to Rod Sherman — Tony Carey fell down on the play — beat us 20-17.

That set the stage for the rivalry that was to make it the game of the year. We won in 1965 and 1966, Southern Cal with O. J. in 1967 and we tied in 1968 and 1969. That meant after six games we were all even 2-2-2.

The nation loved it. In the 11 years I was involved, almost 800,000 fans watched in person. Six times, the game was on national television. And though Southern Cal ended up winning six times in 11 years, it was just a great series for college football.

In coaching, each person usually has a nemesis, a team that beats him, or makes things tough, year in and year out. Usually, it's a traditional foe, and in my case at Notre Dame, it was surely Southern California.

At Miami, Cincinnati usually gave us trouble. At Northwestern, it was Wisconsin. Those Badgers twice knocked Northwestern out of the Rose Bowl with November victories.

Well, Southern California did that, too. Twice, the victories knocked us out of the national championship. But as I look back, I see that there usually was national significance in the game.

In the 11 years of my association in the series, we won the national title twice, but Southern Cal won it three times. John McKay took his Trojans to seven Rose Bowls in those 11 years. But our Notre Dame teams played in five bowls in the last six years after the school ended its long-time moratorium on post-season play.

And the players, they were really something. Southern Cal had Heisman Trophy winners O. J. and Mike Garrett. We had John Huarte. And there were dozens of others who were just great stars. For those 11 years, we had 34 all-Americans, Southern Cal had 30.

I can talk about Larry Conjar scoring four touchdowns in 1965 when all four Notre Dame backs gained more yardage individually than Garrett. I can tell you about the problems of our great 1966 game when we had to play reserves and defensive players on offense in order to salvage the national championship.

But from the other side of the field, I know that McKay can tell about O. J. and Ron Yary, about Anthony Davis, and his own son, J. K., Sam Cunningham, Sam Dickerson, and dozens of others.

There were great moments. Scott Hempel's field goal hit cross bar and bounced back onto the field in 1969. Eric Penick's 85-yard touchdown run from a two-tight-end formation caught the Trojans by surprise in 1973.

Every game was pretty closely contested, though fans probably remember that big rally by S.C. in 1974. But in the series, we led in nine of the games, and were tied in another. Only in 1972 did the Trojans lead all the way.

As I look back now after having been involved deeply in almost one-fourth of the games in the series, I feel fortunate to have been involved in this rivalry. It was — AND IS — the great series of college football.

EDWARD KRAUSE
DIRECTOR OF ATHLETICS
UNIVERSITY OF NOTRE DAME

The 50th anniversary of the Notre Dame-Southern California football series in 1976 brings to mind a game that was called by most, at the time, the greatest comeback in the history of collegiate football. The 1931 game is still remembered as one of the 10 greatest football games ever played.

Notre Dame had been picked to win the National Championship in 1931. Knute Rockne had won the National title in 1929 and 1930, and by virtue of his also winning it in 1924, the year of the Four Horsemen, had retired the Jack Rissman Trophy, symbolizing the championship.

On March 31, 1931, tragedy struck the country when Knute Rockne was killed in a plane crash. Before his death, Rockne had looked forward to the 1931 season and confided to many of his close friends that this team would go undefeated.

Co-Coaches Heartley "Hunk" Anderson, and Jack Chevigny took the team through the first seven games unbeaten — only a 0-0 tie with powerful Northwestern marred the season. On November 21, 1931, the newly constructed Notre Dame Stadium was filled to capacity for the first time for the visiting Trojans.

The game was billed as the battle for the National Championship and it was all Notre Dame for the first three quarters, with the Irish leading 14-0 going into the fourth quarter.

Suddenly, behind the brilliant quarterbacking of Homer Griffith and Orv Mohler, the Trojans scored twice in the final quarter, but missed the extra point after 1 touchdown, making the score 14-13. With only one minute to play, Coach Howard Jones sent a substitute into the game with a play. Quarterback Orv Mohler wouldn't accept the substitution and chased him off the field. Mohler elected to let John Baker try a field goal from the Notre Dame 23 yard line. Baker kicked the goal and Southern California won the game 16-14.

It was with a great deal of nostalgia and clarity that I remember this great contest because I played, as a "first year man," the majority of the game against such football greats as Aaron Rosenberg, Ernie Smith, Erny Pinckert, John Baker and many others.

It was only fitting that after their victory the Trojans were awarded the Knute Rockne Memorial Trophy, newly established by the University, to symbolize that year's National Championship.

The University of Southern California was the first winner of the Trophy. The Trojans' great play and sportsmanship down through the years only served to prove that they were a worthy first recipient.

It is great victories such as this one, and others by both teams, that have helped this contest become the greatest continuing collegiate football series in America.

JESS HILL

There is no question, in my mind, that the USC-Notre Dame football series is the greatest intersectional rivalry, with image and prestige in the country. The Trojans have been very courageous through the years to continue playing Notre Dame home and home, since 1926. With the exception of 1943, 1944 and 1945, the war years, the contest has proven to be a great, great rivalry and is not only an artistic success, but a financial success as well.

We owe the game to Knute Rockne, the coach of Notre. Dame, Howard Jones, USC's coach, Willis O. Hunter, who was the Director of Athletics at USC, and of course Gwynn Wilson, who at the time was the Graduate Manager. Gwynn was the one who actually contacted Rockne about starting the series.

The Notre Dame series has proven to be very, very outstanding in every respect, because our philosophy has been in scheduling, that we play the best in the country and when you play Notre Dame — you are playing the best. Year after year, year after year they are consistently one of the strong, strong football teams in the country, and I think there's no disgrace in ever losing to Notre Dame, but there is a great deal to be gained by defeating Notre Dame. We have had our problems through the years in defeating them. They are mighty, mighty tough and they have some fine football players back there all the time.

One of the greatest moves that the two institutions ever made was establishing this intersectional rivalry in football — this competition. It's always been very competitive, very tough, and very aggressive. At times we had some minor disagreements, but nothing ever imperiled the continuity of the competition between USC and Notre Dame. I sincerely hope that the USC-Notre Dame series will continue forever, and I think it will.

There are some schools that will play Notre Dame occasionally, and some schools that won't play them at all. The philosophy at USC is, "to be the best you have to play the best." Had we not played Notre Dame through the years, I think USC's win and loss record overall would have been much better.

An experience I'll always remember was in 1929, when we played Notre Dame at Soldier Field in Chicago.

I was a second string fullback behind Jim Musick, who weighed about 215 lbs. I weighed all of 166 lbs., so I was the second string fullback. But I played in that game, and when I ran out onto the field and saw that crowd there was nothing in the annals of sports history that could match it. There were reported to be 123,000 people there. They did establish a paid admission record that day of 112,912 people. At both ends of the field behind the goal line, they had set up extra seats. These seats extended at least 75 yards to the regular seating area, and from end line to end line. The seats were all filled and the place was absolutely packed. Notre Dame beat us that year in a great game 13-12. Howard Jones' inability to make extra points was the downfall.

My relationship with the University of Notre Dame, with Father Theodore Hesburg, Father Edmund Joyce, and Ed Krause has always been on the highest level that it could be. They are wonderful and outstanding people with a deep sense of integrity and a great competitive spirit. It has been a privilege and pleasure for me as a coach and as Director of Athletics to have had the opportunity of meeting the wonderful people from Notre Dame. They are dedicated to excellence. I believe that is the success of any athletic program — dedication to the heritage and tradition of excellence. I think that both USC and Notre Dame epitomize what good athletics are all about. In fact this game, to me, does epitomize what intercollegiate football is and should be all about.

THE GAME IS ON
BY CAMERON APPLEGATE

FOREWORD

Calvin Coolidge was in the White House and you could buy a brand new Ford Roadster for $260 . . . In Chicago, Johnnie Torrio's newly formed syndicate, aided by the strong right arm of a young hoodlum by the name of Al Capone, grossed $70 million from bootleg booze, gambling, and broads. Howard Johnson borrowed $500 and turned a patent medicine store in Wollanston, Massachusetts, into a restaurant, hoping to start a chain. Louis Armstrong switched from the clarinet to trumpet and Tommy Manville switched from his first wife to his second (it took seven more wives and forty-two years to finally wear him out). Miller Huggins suspended Babe Ruth for misconduct, fined him $5,000, and sent him home from St. Louis in the middle of a road trip. Battling Siki, one of the best early black heavyweights, was killed in a barroom brawl in Hell's Kitchen, and Benny Leonard, possibly the greatest lightweight of all time, retired undefeated because his mother asked him to, "before you get hurt." Senator Robert LaFollette died and Robert F. Kennedy was born. A New York bookie, Tim Mara, bought the New York football Giants' franchise for $2,500. In Dayton, Tennessee, William Jennings Bryan and Clarence Darrow locked ideological horns in the celebrated "Monkey Trial" . . . and in Munich, Germany, an obscure paperhanger had the first volume of his memoirs published . . . he called it "Mein Kampf."

Yes, it had been a great year, but the trim, good looking young man racing through Union Station in Los Angeles on that gray autumn day wasn't looking back. Right now he was concentrating on what would have been called then, "a dazzling bit of broken field running" in pursuit of the Sunset Limited. Clutched in one hand was an overnight bag, in the other, two tickets to Lincoln, Nebraska. Following a few paces behind and fading fast, limped a lovely but exhausted girl. At the Pullman steps the young man tossed the bags to the porter, then slid to a stop to wait for the girl. Quickly he grasped the handrail with his left hand and encircling her waist with his right arm, managed to swing them both up to the bottom step as the locomotive gathered speed.

"Some way to treat a bride," she gasped.

It was Monday, November 23, 1925. Gwynn Wilson, the graduate manager of the University of Southern California football team, and his wife, Marion, were on their way to meet the legendary Knute Rockne, head football coach and athletic director of the University of Notre Dame whose Fighting Irish were playing the University of Nebraska that Thursday, Thanksgiving Day.

"What a hell of a day," thought Wilson as he settled in his seat, "but it's finally happened." It had been hectic. At 9:00 o'clock that morning he had been in the office of Harold Stonier, executive secretary of USC, trying once more to sell his idea of a USC-Notre Dame football game. The idea of playing Notre Dame in the Coliseum had been discussed many times at USC, but because of the cost of travel, and uneasiness about the apparent invincibility of Eastern football teams*, Stonier, the No. 2 man to Chancellor von Kleinsmid, had been unenthusiastic about traveling to Indiana. No college football team from the west had ever traveled east of the Rockies to play.

But times were changing and several factors weighed heavily in Wilson's favor that autumn morning.

For one thing, Wilson had two staunch allies in USC head football coach Howard Jones and athletic director Willis O. Hunter. Jones knew that a game with Notre Dame would give USC national recognition, and furthermore, Notre Dame didn't scare him much. When coaching at Iowa in 1921, he had snapped a 20-game Notre Dame winning streak and jokingly agreed to give Rockne, his long time friend, a return match. Jones was ready.

Also, Stonier, an astute business man as well as a dedicated educator, had begun to feel that perhaps the time had come for USC to make a bid for national prominence in football. They were already widely respected in track, having won the IC4A twice during the Twenties, but then students and alumni don't usually storm the stadium with dollar bills clutched in feverish palms to watch a track meet. Stonier knew that. He also knew that USC, a growing school of 2,000 students, needed added revenue to support the increasing costs of a quality athletic program. Football would have to bear more than its share of financial burden. This means a full football stadium every Saturday. And how do you do that? Gwynn Wilson had an idea.

"Hal," he began, "I've been thinking about a USC-Notre Dame game again, and I think I know how we could make it work."

"Go on," said Stonier.

"Well, to begin with, it would be a series. A 'home and home' series, each year we alternate. The first year for example, we would play Notre Dame out here in the Coliseum. The following year we would travel east and play them on their own field, or anywhere that could accommodate the crowd." Wilson grew more enthusiastic. "The next year back in California, and so on. We could offer them a $20,000 guarantee

---

*Notre Dame had just rolled over Stanford in the Rose Bowl that year, 27 to 10.

here if they would match it there, and I'm sure they would."

Stonier listened thoughtfully. "Well, Gwynn," he said after a long pause, "that may be the answer, why don't you go talk to Rockne about it?"

"Well, he's in Lincoln, they're playing Nebraska Thanksgiving Day."

"Catch a train."

"I'll have to make some arrangements," Wilson answered, "and reservations . . ."

"I mean today."

It was what Wilson had hoped to hear, yet he heard it with mixed emotions, after all, he had been married less than a year, and . . .

"I'd really like to go, Hal, but I kind of hate to leave my wife. We've only been married a short time —"

"Today. Take her with you," Stonier interrupted.

Wilson nearly went into shock. It was 1925, before unlimited expense accounts, and wives, even brides, of university employees just didn't make business trips with their husbands. But Stonier said, "Take her with you," and Stonier was boss.

Luckily she went.

Harold Stonier, executive Secretary of USC in 1925

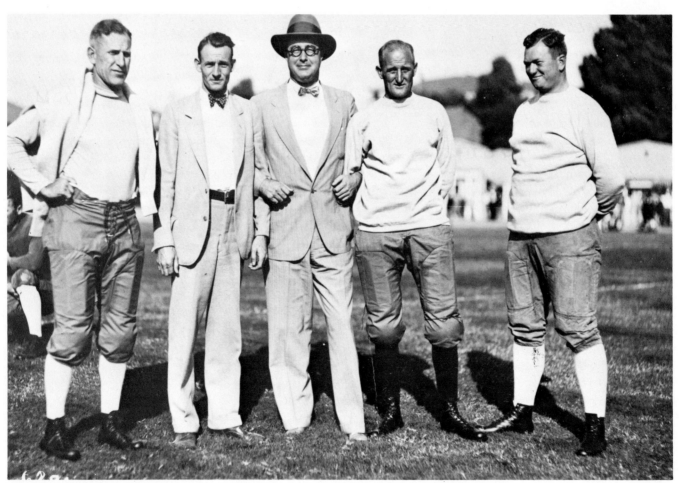

Left to Right, Head Coach, Howard Jones, Gwynn Wilson, George Bovard, Willis O. Hunter and Bill Cole

1925
CHAPTER 1

Elmer "Gloomy Gus" Henderson wasn't the most charming of all men. As a matter of fact there were those who said he had all of the charisma of a dyspeptic dragon, but he was a good football coach. In 6 years at USC, he had posted a 46-7-0 record for a win percentage of .868, and that's much better than just respectable. There was just one soft spot in the record. In those 6 years he had never been able to beat California. Rumor has it that whereas the alumni was more than happy to forgive old Gloomy Gus for his rather melancholy personality, losing 5 out of 5 to their arch rival Cal was unpardonable, and for this inadequacy he was unceremoniously dumped at the end of the 1924 season.

Whatever the reason, the search for a new coach was on. Naturally the name Knute Rockne was the first mentioned. Secretary Stonier had approached him at that time with an offer to become USC's head coach. Rockne had thought kindly of the idea, primarily because his wife, Bonnie, had fallen under the spell of Southern California, and it was said, "What Bonnie wanted from Rock, she usually got."

Father Matthew Walsh, the president of Notre Dame, however, was under the spell of no one but Holy Mother, the Church, and the Notre Dame Alumni. He was not about to release a winning coach. Rockne wired his regrets.

So when the two men met amid the crunch of people in the lobby of the Lincoln Hotel, they were not strangers to each other.

Rockne inquired, "What are you doing here?"

"I'd like to talk to you about a football game," Wilson replied.

"Well, I can't talk to you now, but I'll get you a reservation on the team train back to Chicago, we'll talk about it on the way home," Rockne said. "In the meantime, I'll get you a couple of tickets to this ball game."

Wilson and his wife did attend the game, which Notre Dame lost 17 to nothing in a driving blizzard. Afterwards they boarded the team train to Chicago. Rockne, noted more for his cunning on the gridiron than his attention to social detail, had neglected to inform Wilson that the train was full and that the "reservations" were in the team car. Rockne and Bonnie occupied the compartment in the forward section of the car, Wilson and his wife were given the only remaining space available . . . a single lower berth. Not that it really mattered, no one got much sleep anyway. Team trains then were not that much different than team planes are now, a few penny ante poker games, laughter if you've won, conversation if you've lost . . . most of it right out of the locker room. Marion Wilson probably learned a few new words that night.

The breakfast call came at 7:00 a.m. the next morning. Wilson and his wife were invited to breakfast with Rockne and Bonnie. But try as he might, Wilson's attempts to talk of a football game were avoided by Rockne, who always managed to swing the conversation back to his team . . . their injuries . . . their low morale because of the losses that year to Army and Nebraska. Lunch brought no better results, Rockne continued to shift the talk away from the game idea.

But Wilson was not about to be put off and after lunch he suggested that he and Rockne adjourn alone to the observation car where they would not be disturbed.

There they talked of everything but the game; but after hours of conversation, Rockne could no longer avoid giving his answer.

"Wilson, I'm gonna say no, and I'll tell you why. You know what they're calling my team in South Bend . . . all over the country, as a matter of fact?"

Wilson shook his head.

"Rockne's Ramblers," growled the Rock. "And I don't like it. We're gonna play at home more, I'm pretty sure I can get a game with the Western Conference."

Wilson knew that some of the big mid-western powers would avoid playing Notre Dame, Rockne could rub some people the wrong way, but others of the Western Conference (later known as the Big Ten) would jump at the chance.

So as the train pulled into Inglewood Station just outside Chicago, Wilson began to feel that it had been a wasted trip. The team was to transfer to South Bend, and Wilson and his wife had planned on spending a few days with her relatives before making the return trip to Los Angeles.

"Maybe in a couple years," Rockne said, "but not next year."

The two men said goodbye and Wilson returned to his seat.

Gwynn Wilson was a 26-year old graduate manager, sent to bargain with the greatest football legend of the time. Later a director of the 1932 Olympics, and a founder and ass't general manager of Santa Anita race track until his retirement in 1960, Wilson remembers what happened next this way:

"Marion thought it kind of strange that Knute had turned the proposal down flat, inasmuch as Bonnie had seemed so enthusiastic about coming back to Southern California for a game.

"You see, while Rockne and I were talking in the observation car, Bonnie and Marion were also talking. Marion was a little bit shocked at the way the people in Nebraska had treated the fans and team from Notrè Dame. Of course, in those days we considered visiting teams as guests in southern California, rather than intruders. Why, we even used to have the hotel put little baskets of fresh fruit in their rooms during their stay in Los Angeles.

"Anyway, Marion told me that Bonnie Rockne had liked the idea of coming out to California, and was sure that Knute would too. She suggested that I go back and try again.

"Now there was no way I could go back there and knock on his door and start begging, but as it turned out, I didn't have to.

"From where I was sitting I could see the door to Rockne's compartment. I kept watching it and pretty soon the door opened and Rockne walked out kind of twirling his cigar around between his thumb and forefinger. I had seen him do it often when he was under some kind of tension. He didn't come down the aisle to us immediately. He stopped and talked to some of his players, like maybe he didn't want to seem too anxious. Anyway, he finally sat down opposite me, and with a kind of sheepish grin on his face, he says to me, 'Gwynn, maybe you'd better tell me about that game again.'

"So I did, and he promised to call me the following morning after he had talked to Father Walsh.

"Believe me, by nine o'clock the next morning, my nails were nearly chewed down to the first knuckle. Finally the telephone rang . . . It was Rockne.

" 'Gwynn,' he said, 'the game is on.' "

One week later, Father Matthew Walsh announced that the first game of what was to become the oldest inter-sectional football rivalry in the United States would be played in the Los Angeles Coliseum, December 4, 1926. The second would be played at Soldier Field in Chicago in the autumn of 1927.

So the battle was joined . . . and for the next fifty years two proud universities would enter into yearly combat, neither asking for, nor giving quarter, with the national championship at stake no less than twenty times.

1926
CHAPTER 2

THE GREATEST GAME I EVER SAW
. . . Rockne 1926

In 1926, Rockne's undefeated Irish were rolling down on their second national championship like a runaway train when suddenly the locomotive was derailed, and by *Carnegie Tech*. Thrice beaten *Carnegie Tech*! After crushing every opponent in eight straight games, Notre Dame had expected no more than a tune-up in preparation for USC the following week. Instead, they were soundly trounced in what one sportswriter called, "one of the greatest upsets of all time." Now that may have been somewhat of an overstatement, but you could hardly have convinced Rockne of that, even if you could have found him. He wasn't in Pittsburgh, he was in Chicago watching the Army-Navy game.

The reasons for Rockne's absence were never clear. Only one man knew. That was Rockne — and he wasn't talking. To his eternal credit he assumed all of the blame, even though for a time he was the "laughing stock of college football." Probably he was at Soldier Field to scout Navy which would appear on Notre Dame's schedule for the first time in 1927. At any rate, he placed the team in the able hands of two assistants, "Hunk" Anderson, and Tommy Mills, with instructions to start the second team in order to rest the first team for the long trip and the following week's USC game. The strategy seemed sound, but the shrewd Rockne had been out-Rockned.

"Men," Wally Steffen, the Carnegie Coach had shouted, "Knute Rockne thinks you so poor as football players, he's starting his second team against you, and he's so sure they'll win, he's not even here! He's in Chicago watching Army and Navy play some real football." Obvious as the ploy was, it worked. By the time the Notre Dame first team was sent in, the momentum was all on the side of Carnegie Tech and they won 19-0 going away.

In the meantime, USC was having its own tune-up against Montana, with much better results. Coach Howard Jones flooded the field with reserves and annihilated the Grizzlies 61-0.

Sometime in 1925, an unknown sportswriter with a flair for drama had christened Howard Jones' USC football team, "The Thundering Herd." It was a *nom de guerre* calculated to strike fear and respect in the hearts of opposing teams as well as undying loyalty in the breasts of the student body and alumni, but it was more fiction than fact. "The Thundering Herd"

averaged less than 175 pounds per man and a little over 5 feet 10 inches in height. But what they lacked in size, they made up for in guts. Led by All-American quarterback, Mort Kaer, and SC's first All-American, Brice Taylor at guard, team captain Jeff Cravath at center and tackle Jesse Hibbs, the line, though small, was strong enough to play Jones' style of no-nonsense football. They rarely passed and very seldom tried to fool the opponent with a reverse or trick play.

Since Jones had taken the helm of USC football they had lost only three games. Because of his success, he had been signed to a new three-year contract on November 30, 1926.

The 1926 team was considered by many to be the equal of any of the big Eastern powerhouses and had lost only one game, that to Stanford by one point, 13-12.

Although meeting Notre Dame was a new experience for USC, it was not their first crack at an Eastern team. They were, in fact, undefeated in five inter-sectional games dating back to their 14-3 Rose Bowl victory over Penn State in 1923.

As Gwynn Wilson and Sec'y Stonier had hoped, the game that was to shoot USC into national prominence was by no means ignored on the West Coast. Although the game was scheduled for Saturday, December 4, the headline in the Los Angeles Times on November 17, 1926, read "COLISEUM SOLD OUT FOR NOTRE DAME-USC CLASH."

Rockne, in his usual wily manner, was not about to let his boys forget about the Carnegie Tech defeat, nor would he let them take USC lightly. Instead of bringing his team directly to Los Angeles for practice, he had planned two stops along the way for workouts and would not disembark in Los Angeles until the eve of the game.

From the Los Angeles Times, December 1, Dateline Tucson, Arizona: "Knute Rockne and his Notre Dame football players of assorted nationalities, jokingly referred to as the 'Fighting Irish,' blew into this town this evening on a blast of red hot atmosphere which ought to acclimate them and possibly raise a few blisters. They get their initial work-out tomorrow, December 2, on the University of Arizona gridiron."

While Rockne and his group were tuning up, Jones and his team were not idle. Another quote from the L.A. Times, December 2, 1926: "If Knute Rockne's Notre Dame gridders defeat USC at the Coliseum Saturday afternoon, the South

Notre Dame Coach, Knute Rockne with team in Tuscon, Arizona two days before the first game to be played December 4, 1926

Bend boys will have to step high, wide and handsome. This was proven conclusively last night when Howard Jones sent his Trojans through their last scrimmage of the season for the benefit of a few privileged onlookers. The Cardinal and Gold athletes displayed speed and power in abundance . . . last, but not least by any means, Morley Drury ran signals with the varsity for the first time since injuring his knee in the California game more than a month ago."

Howard Jones, in his normal quiet manner, had little to say before the game, but felt that his team would be ready. Rockne, always the canny strategist, was trying to convince the Trojans in particular and the world in general that the 1926 Irish were a rather scrubby lot. "If we could have ended the season about a week ago, we would have been all right, but the boys are pretty well fagged out now and we're just taking a chance. I don't know how the boys will hold up, but they'll try," said Rockne.

A capacity crowd of 76,000 fans was on hand for the game and tickets normally selling for $3.00 per seat were being scalped at $1.00 a yard line and there were plenty of takers. When the "Thundering Herd" galloped onto the field, a cheer went up that some said could be heard in Santa Monica, 20 miles away. The bookmakers, however, were more impressed with Notre Dame's reputation than home town loyalty. They installed the Irish as a ten point favorite.

In the first quarter neither team was able to advance the ball deep in the other's territory. Notre Dame Quarterback Charles Riley passed for fifteen yards to Dahman. Mort Kaer returned the Notre Dame punt 20 yards and later rolled 17 yards off tackle. The first quarter of the game was scoreless.

Early in the second quarter, Kaer quick-kicked on second down. Notre Dame took over on their own 26-yard line. With Christie Flanagan, team captain, Tom Heardon and Harry O'Boyle now in the game, and Riley still at the controls Notre

All American, Mort Kaer sweeping right end for USC

Dame began to move. The highlight of the drive was a split buck to O'Boyle, who went 27 yards over Hibbs, down to USC's 16 yard line. Kaer who made the saving tackle seemed to be the only Trojan who was not completely fooled. The ball was placed down on the right of the field and Riley, with three blockers leading, raced around left end for the score . . . a 75 yard march.

O'Boyle's point after was partially blocked by Cravath, but the tip gave the ball just the lift it needed to be good. Notre Dame led 7-0.

After the exchange of punts after the kickoff, Kaer made a 30-yard run off left tackle which seemed to bring the USC offense to life.

After Kaer made two yards on a line plunge he passed successfully to Al Behrendt for 38 yards. Notre Dame co-captain Gene Edwards made the saving tackle on his own one. Kaer then went off left tackle for the score completing a 71-yard drive.

Brice Taylor took too much time on the extra point and it was blocked. The first half ended Notre Dame 7, USC 6. There was no score in the third quarter. USC missed an opportunity when left end Morris Badgro caught a 40-yard pass from Kaer, but was ruled offside by Referee Frank Burker and the ball was brought back to USC's 35 yard line. What might have been a USC advantage was nullified by a penalty. A few minutes later Notre Dame's Flanagan intercepted a Kaer pass to end the drive.

In the fourth quarter USC got the break it needed when Al Scheving blocked a Flanagan punt and Cravath recovered on USC's 43-yard line. Don Williams, a 165 pound sub-quarterback, carried the ball eight straight times down to the Notre Dame 5-yard line. On his ninth carry, Williams went in for the score. So punishing were his runs that Flanagan had to be helped from the field. He was replaced by John "Butch" Niemiec.

Morley Drury's extra point attempt hit the left upright and bounced back. No good. USC 12, Notre Dame 7.

O'Boyle returned the kickoff to his 25 yard line and then on first down Riley, with two men leading interference, ran to his right and then suddenly on the dead run rifled a pass to Niemiec for a 28-yard gain. On the next play another pass attempt by Riley was picked off by USC's Manuel Larraneta to end the drive.

The Irish defense held, but so did the Trojans'. Butch Niemiec was forced once more to punt from his own 25 yard line. Howard Elliot received and returned it to Notre Dame's 40 yard line, but lost the ball to Notre Dame on a fumble. With just six minutes to play and the ball on Notre Dame's 42 yard line, the crafty Rockne looked down the bench at a frail looking youngster wearing No. 11. "Get in there, and do your stuff," crackled Rockne.

Into the game went Art Parisien, replacing Riley at quarterback. The crowd was stunned. Chuck Riley was the backbone of the team, and to remove him at this crucial point seemed suicidal on the coach's part. But Rockne was playing his hole card, and it turned out to be an ace.

Little Art Parisien was not over a 148 pounds soaking wet. Six weeks before he had been smothered under an avalanche of Northwestern football beef and carried from the field with what was diagnosed as a bruised heart. Doctors advised Rockne not to let him play and Rockne hadn't planned to. He had brought the boy west only as a gesture of kindness.

Notre Dame had the ball and needed a touchdown. Parisien, a great left-handed passer, could not be left in the game long enough to take a beating. He had to move the team down the field for a score or be removed. On the very first play on the hidden ball trick (in the single wing attack of those days this could also be described as a spinner play), Parisien hit the center for four yards. On the next play he passed to Butch Niemiec for a 35-yard gain and a first down on USC's 20 yard line. O'Boyle went out of bounds to the left without gaining. Diamond then was thrown for a 3 yard loss by Bert Heiser when he attempted to circle left end. Frank Hogan replaced Miller for Notre Dame. John Fredericks then replaced Notre Dame's All-American Bud Boeringer at center.

Notre Dame now had a third down on USC's 23 yard line. Parisien took the ball from center and ran far to his left. The USC defense sensing a run, came up and Parisien fired the ball to Niemiec who was wide open on the five yard line. Niemiec easily ran the ball in for six points.

Cravath blocked Niemiec's try for extra point, but it didn't matter . . . Notre Dame had the game won 13-12, and Parisien had done it. He had taken his team 60 yards in 6 plays. Vince McNally replaced him on the play after the kickoff, then intercepted an SC pass to preserve victory and end the game.

The game was a contrast of teams and style. Notre Dame with a deceptive shift, hid the ball effectively. Their passing and misdirection plays were highlighted by the brilliance of individual performances. On the other hand, USC, with powerful drives over tackle, amassed an almost unbelievable number of men ahead of the ball carrier and rarely varied their attack with a forward pass. They relied instead on their remarkable speed and drive, led by the running of Kaer and Williams. The teams were so equal that first downs were the same, ten apiece. The totals show that yards from scrimmage were Notre Dame 162 and USC 132. However, Notre Dame gained 132 of these yards passing, whereas USC gained only 39.

In the locker room after the game, Jones and Rockne met and shook hands. "Well, we almost did it," said Jones. "Congratulations, Knute."

"Thanks," smiled the Scandinavian coach of the Fighting Irish. "It was the greatest game I ever saw."

USC had lost the game. But they had proved to themselves and the nation that they were capable of playing football with anybody.

Entertaining live that night at Grauman's Chinese Theater in Hollywood, Al Jolson finished his first number, then cocked his head, rolled his eyes and grinned, "Folks, you ain't seen nothing yet."

. . . It seems to apply here.

Morton Kaer was USC's first All American back. "Devil May Kaer, the Red bluff Terror," stood only 5-10, and weighed 174, but during the years from 1923-26, he was USC's most exciting runner. As a junior in 1925, Kaer scored 114 points, which stood as an SC record for 43 years until O. J. Simpson broke it in 1968.

USC Captain Jeff Cravath

Notre Dame fullback, Harry O'Boyle

USC's Don Williams hands off to Mort Kaer

Notre Dame quarterback, Art Parisien

1926

STARTING LINE-UPS

	Trojans		Notre Dame	
30	Badgro	L.E.R.	Maxwell	38
10	Hibbs	L.T.R.	McManmon	64
16	Taylor	L.G.R.	Mayer	58
8	Cravath (Capt.)	C.	Boeringer	31
13	Gorrell	R.G.L.	J. Smith	43
11	Cox	R.T.L.	Miller	44
23	Moser	R.E.L.	Voedisch	37
28	Kaer	Q.B.	Edwards (Capt.)	1
31	Wheeler	L.H.R.	Hearden (Capt.)	9
21	L. Thomas	R.H.L.	Flanagan	33
3	Laraneta	F.B.	O'Boyle	7

SOUTHERN CALIFORNIA

1	Heiser, H.B.	21	L. Thomas, H.B.	
2	Drury, H.B.	22	Beatlie, T.	
3.	Laraneta, F.B.	23	Moser, E.	
4	Thompson, H.B.	24	Morrison, T.	
6	Lee, F.B.	25	Williams, Q.B.	
7	Behrendt, E.	26	McCaslin, E.	
8	Cravath, C.	27	DeGroote, G.	
9	Friend, T.	28	Kaer, Q.B.	
10	Hibbs, T.	29	Baldridge, C.	
11	Cox, T.	20	Badgro, E.	
12	Hershberger, G.	31	Wheeler, H.B.	
13	Gorrell, G.	32	Lavelle, E.	
14	Schaub, G.	33	Scheving	
15	Dorsey, E.	34	Bonham, Q.B.	
16	Taylor, G.	35	Ford, Q.B.	
17	Fox, C.	36	Cruickshank, T.	
18	M. Thomas, F.B.	37	Dihel	
19	White, G.	38	McCabe	
20	Elliott, Q.B.			

NOTRE DAME

1	Edwards, Q.B.	39	Niemic, L.H.	
2	R. Smith, R.G.	40	Ransavage, R.T.	
3	Riley, Q.B.	41	Moore, R.E.	
4	McNally, Q.B.	42	Leppig, R.G.	
5	Roach, L.H.	43	J. Smith, L.G.	
7	O'Boyle, F.B.	44	Miller, L.T.	
8	Collins, F.B.	46	Wallace, R.E.	
9	Hearden, R.H.	50	Kizer, L.G.	
10	Dahman, R.H.	51	Duperier, R.E.	
11	Parisien, Q.B.	53	Coleirch, R.E.	
12	Chevigny, R.H.	58	Mayer, R.B.	
30	Walsh, L.E.	60	Poliski, R.T.	
31	Boeringer, C.	63	McGrath, F.B.	
33	Flanagan, L.H.	64	McManmon, R.T.	
34	Benda, R.E.	65	Marelli, L.G.	
35	Fredericks, C.	68	Duncolovic, R.H.	
36	Wynne, F.B.	70	Moynihan, C.	
37	Voedisch, L.E.	75	Hogan, L.T.	
38	Maxwell, R.E.	82	Stein, L.T.	

OFFICIALS

Referee — Frank Birch
Umpire — Jack McCord
Headlinesman — Jay Wyatt
Field Judge — Arthur Badenoch

1927
CHAPTER 3

"IT LOOKS LIKE I PULLED A BONER"
. . . John Schommer, Game Official . . . 1927

Schommer wasn't the only one that year. On a warm September evening in Chicago's Soldier Field, an aging overweight prizefighter named William Harrison Dempsey, attempted and nearly succeeded in doing something no other heavyweight had done before. He came damned close to regaining the championship title he had lost the year before to "Gentleman Gene" Tunney, ex-Marine and current light-heavyweight champ.

The first battle, held in Philadelphia in a pouring rain just twelve months earlier, had been billed as a contest of "brain against brawn, cunning versus brute strength, the sly fox challenging the ravening wolf," etc., etc., etc. It had a surprise ending. The younger, lighter Tunney, a 4 to 1 underdog, obviously had abandoned his study of Shakespeare for a time to concentrate on ring tactics. He jabbed the thirty-one year old ex-champ silly, made him look clumsy and out of shape (which he was), slashed him at will and easily won the decision. After the fight, Dempsey, though nearly a million dollars richer for the night's work, was disconsolate. "Honey," he said to actress Estelle Taylor, his wife at that time, "I forgot to duck."

For a time the second fight on the 22nd of September of the following year, looked as though it might be a replay of the first. But in the seventh round, after a series of combinations topped off by a couple of short rights, Dempsey landed a looping left that dumped a dazed Gene Tunney on the canvas.

Now Dempsey, whose ring courage and ferocity no one doubted, wasn't called "The Manassa Mauler" for nothing. Once the bell rang he had the disposition of a sex starved cobra and the killer instinct of a cornered tiger.

In this case it may have been his undoing.

Savagery had always been a Dempsey trademark. It had carried him from the brawling copper mines of Colorado, through lumber camps and hobo jungles into professional fighting where his first purse was less than $3.00. That was in 1915. Six years later 91,000 fight fans paid $1,626,580 to watch him annihilate beautiful Georges Carpentier of France. It was the first million dollar gate. In 1923 he floored Luis Angel Firpo, "the Wild Bull of the Pampas" seven times the first round, then had been himself knocked out of the ring and returned to K.O. the giant Argentinian in 57 seconds of the second round.

So the man who stood snarling over the fallen champion was no cream puff. He had been responsible for bringing over $10,000,000 through fight arena gates in twelve years, $4,000,000 of that had been his. He had brought prizefighting from smoky half-filled arenas to the million dollar gate, and he was not about to let Tunney, or anyone else for that matter, get to his feet without taking another shot at him on the way up. Unfortunately for Jack that was a no-no. The rules had been changed the year before. In the precious few seconds it took referee Dave Barry to persuade Dempsey to back off to a neutral corner for the count, Tunney's head cleared and he was on his feet at the count of nine. He prudently concluded discretion to be the better part of valor and stayed away from the taunting ex-champ for the next three rounds and won the decision. Tunney had been on the canvas for at least thirteen seconds, so naturally the fight became known as the battle of the "long count," and Dempsey emerged the hero. He found himself far more popular in defeat than he had ever been in victory. Gene Tunney couldn't have cared less. He didn't want to stay around the Avenue of Cauliflower Ears too long anyway. He had won two of the most famous fist fights of the century, and come out virtually unmarked. The following year Squire Tunney retired to his country estate in Westchester with the Bard of Avon and his socialite bride . . . not too well liked, but young, unscarred, and a millionaire.

104,943 people had paid an unbelievable $2,658,660 to see two men who didn't even dislike each other try to beat one another senseless. From a live box office standpoint in the fight game, it's still a record.

The sports world had barely recovered when two months later Soldier Field was the site of yet another record and another blunder.

On the 26th of November 120,000 people, the largest crowd ever assembled to see a college football game, watched unbeaten USC take the field against once defeated Notre Dame. Five days before, the Trojans had departed from Arcade Station in Los Angeles, the first far western football team to invade the east. The bookies immediately established them as 8-5 underdogs to Notre Dame.

Howard Jones predicted an offensive battle, inasmuch as

Notre Dame's John Frederick and Elmer Wynn brings down Morly Drury after short gain

USC had proven themselves a mighty scoring machine, averaging 44 points a game. Only starting halfback Don Williams had been left at home.

Williams had suffered a broken back in the Trojans' 27-0 pasting of Washington State the week before and would not be up and about for at least six more weeks.

The Irish, however, had not been so lucky. Injured the week before in Notre Dame's thrashing of Duke 32-0 was the great halfback and hero of last year's game, Butch Niemiec. It was predicted by Rockne that he "probably wouldn't get into the game, but would be suited up on the sidelines." Now Coach Rockne, who was the soul of integrity in any endeavor *except* the winning of football games, had been known to use a little mild mis-direction before. Remember, it was Niemiec who had caught a pass from supposedly infirm Art Parisien for the winning TD the year before. So now fans and Trojans alike wondered whether Rockne would try another fast one and insert Niemiec if or when victory was in doubt.

USC's Morley Drury kicked off to John Elder. With the first down on their own 29 yard line, Notre Dame was unable to move and Elder punted on third down. The punt was short and the Trojans took over on Notre Dame's 40 yard line. This was a break for SC and led by All-American Drury they drove to the Notre Dame 8 yard line. The Irish defense stiffened and held. But with fourth and goal from the 8, Drury dropped back to pass and threw a perfect strike to Russ Saunders, who was all alone in the end zone. The point after touchdown was missed when the snap from center was low and Saunders in his haste was not able to put the ball on end and instead laid it on its side. Drury's kick didn't even clear the line of scrimmage.

Drury kicked off to Chris Flannigan who then made 9 yards in two plays. On the next play Ray Dahman was stopped

cold and on fourth and 1 on their own 34 yard line Notre Dame elected to punt. The punt by Dahman was short and went out of bounds on the Trojan 45 yard line.

Referee John Schommer, however, signaled that the Trojans had used their hands illegally on the play and penalized them 15 yards. This gave Notre Dame a new breath of life and a first down on their own 49 yard line.

Again SC held. Dahman punted and Notre Dame captain and All-American guard John Smith downed the ball on the Trojan 6 yard line.

It was now Notre Dame's turn to be stubborn, and stubborn they were. They held. USC All-American tackle Jesse Hibbs punted the ball 63 yards to the Notre Dame 46 yard line.

Suddenly Notre Dame caught fire and with Flanagan and Frank Collins carrying they drove to the USC 27 yard line and a first down. Two plays later, quarterback Charles Riley found Dahman all alone in the USC end zone for an easy six points. Dahman made the extra point just as easily and Notre Dame led 7-6.

The remainder of the first half was played on the ground, neither team getting near the other's goal. At the half — Notre Dame 7, USC 6.

In the third period Dahman punted from behind his own goal line and Drury returned it 20 yards to Notre Dame's 23 yard line. Don Moses carried for one yard. Drury gained nothing at right tackle in two tries. With a fourth down and 9 yards to go, Drury dropped back to pass. His pass was intended for end Lowry McCaslin, who was wide open in the end zone, but Charles Riley was on the job and went high in the air to intercept on his own 3 yard line. He turned upfield and after 2 or 3 steps was tackled by Saunders. Riley, as if hit by a truck, went flying and so did the ball, which bounced crazily through the end zone, chased by Francis Tappaan and McCaslin. McCaslin recovered and the crowd went wild, a safety . . . SC now led 8-7.

The radio announcer, Bob Zuppke, the famous Illinois coach, broadcast the score as such, but while the scoreboard was being changed, . . . ready for the boner?

Referee John Schommer stepped in and signaled an incomplete pass! The USC players led by Drury, McCaslin and Saunders encircled Schommer and protested. The crowd recognized the blunder, and even though heavily pro-Notre Dame, lustily booed the call. The ruling stood.

A minute or two later order was restored and the game continued. Notre Dame, first down on its own 20 yard line.

Neither team was able to move the ball consistently in the remainder of the quarter or in the fourth quarter. What had started out as an offensive show turned into a defensive battle, highlighted by the running of Drury and Flanagan, and a punting duel by Ray Dahman (44.5 yard average) and Jesse Hibbs (49 yard average).

The game ended with Dahman intercepting a Drury pass at the Notre Dame ten yard line. Final score, Notre Dame 7, USC 6.

For the second year in a row the failure to make the extra point when needed had cost USC victory over Notre Dame, but again they had proved they were ready, willing and able to play football with anyone in the country.

But if SC was disappointed in the game, the spectators certainly were not . . . except of course, the 10,000 who were caught in a monumental traffic jam and got to the field ten minutes late . . . they missed the only scoring of the day.

The controversy over the disputed call raged on for days. Nonpartisan coaches and fans who had viewed the game were almost unanimous in their agreement that Southern California should have been awarded a safety on the fumble recovery, but a decision had been made on the field, and it was final.

Even referee Schommer, after looking at the game film which definitely showed Riley in possession of the ball, muttered, "It looks like I pulled a boner."

Morley Drury, "The Noblest Trojan of Them All," combined offensive and defensive power to be named the first back in Grantland Rice's annual All American selection in 1927. A versatile running and passing quarterback, he also captained the 1927 Trojan squad. Drury was known as a highly intelligent and resourceful leader, who was a keen student of the strategy of the game. In 1969, football's Centennial year, Morley Drury was named on the Pac 8's all time 1920-1969 backfield along with Ernie Nevers of Stanford, George Wilson of Washington, and O. J. Simpson of USC . . . pretty distinguished company. He was named to the college football Hall of Fame in 1954.

Notre Dame's great quarterback, Charles Riley

Coach, Notre Dame University
KNUTE K. ROCKNE

UNIVERSITY OF NOTRE DAME — 1927

NAMES AND NUMBERS OF PLAYERS

1	Fred Collins, Full	27	Gus Bondi, Guard	55	Greer, Guard
2	Joe Morrissey, Quarter	28	John Poliskey, Tackle	56	William Dew, Full
3	Jerry Ransavage, Tackle	29	Edmond Collins, End	58	William Cassidy, Guard
4	William Hurley, Half	30	Moon Mullins, Half	59	John McSorley, Half
5	Jack McGrath, Tackle	31	T. F. Kennaley, Quarter	61	John Christiansen, Guard
6	Frank MsCarthy, Center	33	Christie Flannagan, Half	62	Bertram Metzger, Guard
7	Timothy Moynihan, Center	35	R. L. Donahue, Tackle	63	Thomas Kasais, Guard
8	Charles Riley, Quarter	36	William Jones, Guard	64	Thomas Qualters, Full
9	George Murrin, Guard	37	John Doarn, Tackle	65	Edward White, End
10	Chile Walsh, End	38	Herbert Schultz, Tackle	66	John Prendergast, Center
11	John Voedisch, End	40	Jack Cannon, Guard	67	Bernard Hugger, Center
12	John Chevigney, Half	41	Eugene Mahoney, Tackle	68	W. P. Byrne, Full
13	John Law, Guard	42	George Leppig, Guard	69	J. F. Merak, Tackle
14	Joe Benda, End	43	John Smith, Guard (Capt.)	70	T. S. McLaughlin, Tackle
15	Arthur Denchfield, Full	44	Fred Miller, Tackle	71	Robert Brannon, Half
16	James Hurlburt, End	45	John Frederick, Center	72	John Harrington, End
17	John Colerick, End	46	Joseph Nash, Center	73	Sam Richards, Tackle
18	John Niemiec, Half	47	Thomas Murphy, End	74	Chris Wilhemmy, Half
19	Thomas Byrne, End	48	John Vezie, End	75	Louis Norman, Center
20	J. M. Brady, Quarter	49	Elmer Wynne, Full	76	Marion Heffernan, End
21	Albert Gebert, Quarter	50	Joe Locke, Guard	79	Howard Smith, Half
22	Joseph Prelli, Half	52	D. Shay, Full	82	John Redgate, Half
23	Charles McKinney, Quarter	52	James Bray, Half	83	John Winberry, End
24	Edwin Stein, Tackle	53	Raymond Smith, End	84	John Elder, Half
26	Ray Dahman, Half	54	Thomas Noon, Tackle		

UNIVERSITY OF SOUTHERN CALIFORNIA — 1927

NAMES AND NUMBERS OF PLAYERS

1	Rockwell Kemp, Quarter	15	Russell Saunders, Half	28	Clark Galloway, Guard
2	Capt. Morley Drury, Quarter	16	Templeton	29	Beatie
3	Ryan	17	Don Williams, Quarter	30	Charles Boren, End
4	Chambers	18	Max Thomas, Full	31	Porter
6	Don Moses, Full	19	Cecil Hoff, Tackle	32	Leslie Coyle, Half
8	Bob Gowder, Guard	20	Howard Elliott, Quarter	33	John Ward, Tackle
8	Al Scheving, Tackle	21	Lloyd Thomas, Half	34	McCabe
9	Wilcox	22	Herschel Bonham, Full	35	Frank Anthony, Guard
10	Jesse Hibbs, Tackle	23	Jim Moser, Tackle	36	Aleksi
11	Francis Tappaan, End	24	Harry Edelson, Full	37	Kreiger
12	Tony Steponovich, End	25	Nathan Barragar, Center	38	Schaub
13	Dihel	26	Lowery McCaslin, End	39	Fox
14	Lavelle	27	Bert Heiser, Guard	41	Laisne

OFFICIALS

Schommer — Chicago — *Umpire*
Barnell — Chicago — *Referee*
Eckersall — Chicago — *Head Linesman*
Griffith — Iowa — *Field Judge*

1928
CHAPTER 4

"HE JESTS AT SCARS THAT NEVER FELT A WOUND"...WM. SHAKESPEARE
ROMEO AND JULIET...1595
(Scene 2, Line 1)

Of course it was lost love, not lost yardage that the Bard had in mind when he penned those immortal lines. Unless, of course, he had played the game, and that's entirely possible. They had been playing a form of football in the British Isles for some three hundred years at that time and certainly any mention of wounds and scars in connection with football is appropriate . . . ask anyone who has played the game.

For the second year in a row, Howard Jones and his "Thundering Herd" brought an unbeaten record to the game. Despite being held to a scoreless tie by California, the 1928 USC team was probably the best ever. At least until that time. They led the nation in offensive scoring and ranked number two behind Georgia Tech, also unbeaten *and* untied.

The magical passing of All-American Don Williams, the deceptive running of "Racehorse Russ" Saunders and above all the tactical ability of Coach Jones had turned the Trojans into an offensive threat with the ability to score often with lightning-like rapidity and from nearly any position on the field.

The Fighting Irish of Notre Dame on the other hand, were having their problems. They had not lost three games in a single season since Rockne had become coach in 1918. This year they were already over quota. They had lost first to Wisconsin, then to Georgia Tech, and after upsetting powerful Army 12-6, lost once more to Carnegie Tech. It was a disheartened Notre Dame squad that Rockne brought to Los Angeles that year.

The one bright spot in an otherwise gloomy season was the stunning win over heavily favored Army, and they had to field a twelve man team to do that: eleven players and the ghost of George Gipp.

George Gipp never played football against USC, but no book about football, especially Notre Dame football, would be complete without mention of this remarkable athlete. Although he died at the end of the 1920 season, many of his records still stand. His deportment off the field raised an occasional eyebrow, but on the gridiron he was a one-man gang. Earlier in that season Notre Dame had trailed Army at halftime 17-14. Rockne was giving his usual crackling speech, when he looked up and saw Gipp leaning against the door, helmet on the back of his head, taking a long drag on a cigarette.

"As for you, Gipp," he snarled, "I suppose you don't have any interest in this game?"

"Listen, Rock," drawled Gipp, "I've got a five hundred dol-

USC's 1928 National Championship team which was unbeaten, but tied by California 0 to 0

lar bet on this game, and I don't aim to blow it."

Gipp put on a dazzling second half show, and the Irish won 27-17. A few months later he was dead.

He had climbed out of a sickbed to play Northwestern in the final game of the 1920 season. The chill wind from Lake Michigan whistling over the ice-covered field had put him back in bed. This time with pneumonia . . . He never got up.

On the eve of the 1928 Army-Notre Dame game, a sellout as usual, Rockne sat with Grantland Rice, the dean of American Sportswriters.

". . . You recall Gipp," said Rockne, "he died practically in my arms eight years ago next month. He's been gone a long time, but I may have to use him tomorrow."

Rockne continued, not in the machine gun kind of vocal delivery he normally used, but very quietly spoke of Gipp's last hours and his baptism into the Catholic Church . . . "After the little ceremony, I sat with him on his bed . . . Gipp looked up at me and said, 'Rock, I know I'm going . . . but I'd like one last request . . . Sometime when the going isn't so easy, when the odds are against us, ask a Notre Dame team to win one for me — for the Gipper. I don't know where I'll be then, Rock, but I'll know about it, and I'll be happy.' A moment later he was gone.

"Grant, I've asked the boys to pull one out for Gipp. Tomorrow I might have to."

He did and the rest is history.

At the half, with the score tied 0-0, Rockne assembled his discouraged players in the locker room, closed the door, and began to speak, slowly at first as though he were groping for words.

"Boys," he began, "it will be 8 years next month since I visited a mighty sick young man in St. Joseph's Hospital. He was breathing his last few breaths in this world . . ."

Under the Golden Dome they still tell about how Rockne's close friend, Mayor Jimmy Walker of New York, who was in the locker room, began to sob and the two NYPD officers assigned to guard the door bit their lips to hold back the tears. And how an aroused Notre Dame team charged back onto the field with almost religious zeal. It was said that when Jack Chevigny, a gallant little halfback with a big heart, slammed into the end zone for the first Notre Dame score, he held the ball aloft with one hand and shouted, "Here's one of them, Gipper." It was not documented then and would be hard to verify now. Chevigny, who later coached the University of Texas, was killed in the 1945 Marine assault on Iwo Jima.

Notre Dame scored once more and won the game, 12-6.

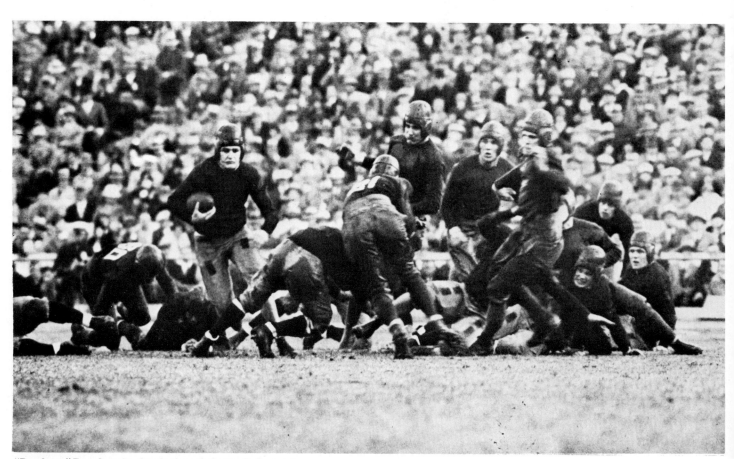

"Racehorse" Russ Saunders breaks through the line for large gain

Somewhere, the Gipper must have been very happy.

Not so, Rockne. He was on the verge of physical collapse from fatigue and ill health. He had tough USC to face with a team still demoralized over their 27-7 loss to Carnegie Tech, and worse yet, the Sage of South Bend was fresh out of miracles.

As there was only one George Gipp, there could be only one "Win one for the Gipper" play, and it had been used.*

Again a full house of 80,000 fans filled the Coliseum on December 1, 1928, under cloudless, warm skies. The field was lightning fast and the men of Troy ran the Irishers right out of the stadium.

As predicted, the passing of Williams to Lowry McCaslin and Harry Edleson, the running of Saunders through holes opened by Hibbs and Francis Tappaan, put the Trojans ahead at halftime 20-0. In the first quarter Notre Dame center Tim Moynihan broke his wrist and was lost for the rest of the game. The big play and the one that sealed the Irishers' doom, was made by USC defensive end Tony Steponovich. In the second quarter "Butch" Niemiec, who had been hurt in the Carnegie Tech game and was being used only to pass the ball, retreated to pass from his own 20 yard line. Steponovich, playing it brilliantly, leaped up and batted the ball down. Before it hit the turf he picked it off his shoelaces and raced 18 yards for the touchdown.

Notre Dame was held scoreless until the third quarter when Jack Chevigny, behind beautiful blocking by sub Frank Leahy and All-American Fred Miller, raced 51 yards up the middle to score. The point after was good. USC 20, Notre Dame 7. The Irish scored once more in the fourth quarter against the USC second team, but it didn't do much good. Earlier in the quarter, the Williams-McCaslin passing combination had clicked again, and the final score was 27-14, USC.

For Notre Dame it had been a disastrous year. Five wins and four losses, and for the only time in Rock's career, one of his teams gave up more points than they scored, 99 to 107.

Rockne gathered his troops and retreated to the friendly bastions of South Bend. There, they licked their wounds and set about plotting next year's revenge, and the Trojan upstarts who dared to challenge the football supremacy of the east, were voted national champions the following week. Georgia Tech finished second and in the Rose Bowl that year they needed all the help they could get to beat California. They got it from Cal's Roy Riegals who ran the ball 80 yards in the wrong direction to give Tech a safety and an 8-7 victory.

Notre Dame's "Butch" Niemiec, Halfback

USC's Captain and All American, Jesse Hibbs holds 1928 National Championship trophy

*It seems somewhat unlikely that Gipp ever made that death-bed speech to Rockne. Some say that a South Bend newspaper reporter was in the room at the time, but there was no documentation of the scene. It is even doubtful that Rockne was with Gipp at the time of his death. More likely Gipp's mother, brother and sister were with him, and that he had been in a coma for three hours prior to his death. That Rockne made the locker room speech, there can be no doubt, there were, of course, many witnesses . . . Among them Frank Leahy, who related it to Wells Twombly in his biography, "Shake Down the Thunder."

49

UNIVERSITY OF NOTRE DAME — 1928

NO.	NAME	POS.	WT.	HT.
	Acers, Julian	Half	170	5'11"
25	Bondi, Gus	Guard	175	5'9"
57	Brady, James	Quarter	140	5'7"
20	Bray, James	Half	166	5'11"
43	Cannon, John	Guard	187	5'11"
24	Carideo, Frank	Quarter	172	5'7"
15	Cassidy, Wm.	Guard	172	5'9"
12	Chevigny, John	Half	168	5'9"
56	Christman, Norbert	Quarter	152	5'7"
27	Collins, Ed	End	169	6'
1	Collins, Fred	Full	170	5'8"
17	Colrick, John	End	175	6'
30	Conley, Thomas	End	170	5'11"
58	Covington, Walter	Full	165	5'11"
31	Dew, Billy	Half	168	5'10"
30	Doarn, John	Tackle	200	5'11"
45	Donoghue, Richard	Tackle	212	6'2"
84	Elder, John	Half	165	5'8"
50	Gebert, Albert	Quarter	160	5'8"
37	Herwit, Norn	Guard	183	5'9"
9	Kassis, Tom	Center	185	5'11"
5	Kerjez, Frank	End	180	5'11"
10	Kenneally, Tom	Quarter	145	5'7"
13	Law, John	Guard	163	5'9"
26	Leahy, Frank	Center	180	5'11"
	Leahy, Bernard	Half	175	5'11"
41	Leppig, George	Guard	180	5'9"
22	Locke, Joe	Guard	165	5'10"
8	McGrath, Jack	Tackle	195	6'
6	Mahoney, Gene	Tackle	189	6'
25	Metzger, Bert	Guard	165	5'9"
44	Miller, Fred	Tackle	190	6'
23	Montroy, Jack	Half	175	5'10"
2	Morrissey, Joe	Quarter	166	5'10"
7	Moynihan, Tim	Center	191	6'1"
21	Mullins, Moon	Half	175	6'
11	Murphy, Tom	End	185	6'1"
60	Nash, Joe	Center	175	5'10"
18	Niemiec, John	Half	170	5'7½"
47	O'Brien, John	End	170	6'2"
74	O'Connor	Full	172	5'10"
	Prendergast, John	Center	165	5'11"
36	Ransavage, Jerry	Tackle	182	5'11"
54	Savoldi, Joe	Full	192	5'11"
40	Shay, Geo.	Full	160	5'9"
	Stephan, Joe	Half	159	6'
32	Twomey, Ted	Tackle	191	6'
3	Vezie, H. M.	End	175	6'
16	Vlk, George	End	170	6'
	Williams, Bo	Full	180	5'10"
14	Yarr, Tom	Center	185	5'10"

UNIVERSITY OF SOUTHERN CALIFORNIA — 1928

NO.	NAME	POS.	WEIGHT	HEIGHT
29	Anthony Frank	Tackle	185	6'1½"
27	Apsit, Marger	Half	171	5'11"
18	Baldridge, Lyle S.	Guard	207	6'
25	Barrager, Nathan	Center	179	6'
36	Bell, Howard	Tackle	185	5'10"
14	Bond, Ward	Tackle	194	6'2½"
22	Bonham, C. Herschel	Full	170	5'9"
32	Boren, Charles	Guard	175	5'10"
5	Brown, Everett W.	Quarter	160	5'9"
4	Chambers, Mahlon	Quarter	152	5'8"
42	Deranian, Vaughan R.	Guard	195	5'10"
43	Durkee, Harvey	End	173	5'10"
30	Decker, George	Tackle	176	6'
24	Edelson, Harry	Half	168	5'8"
2	Duffield, Marshall D.	Quarter	168	5'8"
28	Galloway, Clark	Guard	185	5'11"
7	Gowder, Robert	Guard	190	5'11"
13	Ford, William W.	Full	162	5'11"
10	Hibbs, Jesse J. (Capt.)	Tackle	183	6'
20	Hill, Jesse T.	Full	165	5'9"
33	Hirsch, Willis	Center	200	6'1"
6	Hoff, Cecil W.	Tackle	181	5'11"
8	Kemp, Rockwell	Quarter	147	5'6"
19	Kreiger, Karl W.	End	173	6'1½"
45	Laisne, Eugene L.	Half	175	5'8½"
23	McCabe, Hilton	Center	184	6'
26	McCaslin, Lowry	End	168	5'11"
3	Mortensen, Jesse	Half	180	6'2"
49	Norton, Francis	Half	162	5'10"
50	Philp, Stewart	Half	160	5'8½"
40	Porter, John	Guard	185	5'10"
15	Saunders, Russell	Full	175	5'8½"
38	Schaub, Alvin R.	Half	190	6'3"
1	Seitz, William L.	Tackle	195	6'3"
35	Shaw, Jesse	Tackle	194	6'1"
34	Snider, James	Full	170	5'11"
12	Steponovitch, Tony J.	End	173	5'10"
11	Tappaan, Francis D.	End	170	5'10"
16	Templeton, George B.	Center	170	5'10"
44	Thiede, Clifford	Quarter	170	5'9"
21	Thomas, Lloyd	Half	180	5'10"
31	Truher, James	End	180	6'2"
41	Ward, John	Tackle	190	6'2"
37	Wilcox, Ralph	End	170	5'10"
9	Wilcox, Thomas	Full	180	5'10"
17	Williams, Don	Quarter	158	5'9"
39	Winfield, Irving	Guard	178	5'10"

1929
CHAPTER 5

"BEST DAMN TEAM I EVER HAD"
. . . Rockne 1929

Sportswriters called it the Golden Age of Sports. Westbrook Pegler dubbed it the Era of Wonderful Nonsense; F. Scott Fitzgerald christened it (with bathtub gin) the Jazz Age . . . to most people it was the Roaring Twenties. It had been a decade of excesses and it was drawing to a close, not with a roar, but a cry of panic.

In September of 1929 the New York Stock Exchange hit an all-time high, and a million and a half Americans were "playing the market," most of them on margin. It sounded so easy to become a millionaire. You put up 10% of the face value of the stock in cash, your broker puts up the other 90% then you sit around and wait for the stock to go up (which it would most assuredly do) then sell at a profit, pay your broker, and retire.

Not wishing to be rich was regarded as a sign of laziness or sheer stupidity. Doctors, window washers, charwomen, bankers, shoeshine boys and shopkeepers all played America's favorite new game. Most of them lost.

On "Black Thursday," October 24, 1929, the bubble burst. It seemed no one had confidence in speculation anymore and wanted to sell. Prices plummeted, thirteen million shares were traded, and thousands of new millionaires both real and of the paper variety, were wiped out.

But Wall Street was thousands of miles away. The important thing was to beat Notre Dame into submission for the second year in a row. Coach Jones was sure they could do it, and even the Los Angeles sportswriters made no attempt to hide the fact

Notre Dame's 1929 National Champions

that they were certain USC would repeat as national champs.

After the total destruction of UCLA it looked like a downhill run all the way. Against the first five opponents, USC averaged 44 points a game and allowed only 7, and set a school season scoring mark of 492 points, which still stands. They stumbled, however, against Cal. 15-7. Jones angrily juggled and re-juggled the lineup in hopes of getting it right in time for the November 16th battle with Notre Dame at Soldier Field.

He did and the next week smeared Nevada 66-0. The Trojans were ready for Notre Dame and left Los Angeles on November 11 for Chicago with blood in their eyes. It was, after all, Notre Dame that had replaced them as No. 1 in the nation after the Cal loss, and the Trojans wanted the top spot back. It wouldn't be easy. Knute Rockne's boys were looking for the first undefeated Notre Dame season since the days of the Four Horsemen in 1924, and it looked as if they might find it. So far they were undefeated through six games.

Rockne himself was not having such a good year. Phlebitis had claimed his once swift legs, and he was in a wheelchair most of the time. His doctors had even forbidden him to attend most practices and the team was being handled by assistant coaches Hunk Anderson, Tom Lieb and Jack Chevingy. He had missed the Carnegie Tech game entirely and was not even supposed to listen to the USC game on radio. Rockne was as always tougher to handle than a mule on ice, nothing was going to keep him away from the now famous USC-Notre Dame feud. Even though he was on the sidelines during the game, he was barely visible, and let his coaches call the game . . . to a point.

In the 1927 game in Soldier Field, 120,000 fans showed up for the game, but only an estimated 99,800 actually paid. In the two years since, the stadium had been improved and in the 1928 game every one of the 120,000+ fans paid to get in. USC and Notre Dame had now played before two of the three biggest football crowds in history. The biggest was Notre Dame-Navy, 1929, 122,000, Soldier Field.

USC got off to a fast start and looked far the superior team. The big Trojan line stiffened after the opening kickoff and Notre Dame punted weakly to SC's 48 yard line. Fullback Don Moses led the charge for USC as they drove past mid-field. On third down quarterback Marshall Duffield quick-passed over the middle to Marger Aspit and he raced 25 yards unmolested to score. Duffield missed the extra point. The SC fans were aghast. Not again! they thought.

In the second quarter, USC punted to Notre Dame quarterback Frank Carideo and he returned it to his own 46 yard line.

On first down, halfback John Elder faded back to pass and from his own 35 yard line heaved the ball to Captain Tom Conley who caught the ball on USC's 10 yard line and waltzed in for a touchdown. Elder's pass travelled 55 yards in the air.

USC's Ernie Pinkert, Halfback

With the score now tied 6-6, Carideo missed the extra point.

At halftime with the score still tied, Rockne could no longer endure being a phantom coach. The doors to the Notre Dame dressing room swung open and the coach was wheeled slowly into the room. His doctors said later, "It was touch and go, he should have been in a hospital, not a locker room, . . . if that clot had moved, he would have died right there."

Rockne tried to stand, and couldn't, but he could still speak.

"Boys," he started, his voice only an echo of its usual high pitched whine, "get out there and play them hard the first five minutes. They'll hate it, but play them hard. Remember, I'll be upstairs, but I'll be watching you. Go ahead now and hit 'em hard."

He talked for several more minutes, his voice growing stronger with each word.

"Win, win! WIN!" he shouted, "that's the only reason for playing . . . crack 'em CRACK 'EM!'" . . . his voice lowered, "I'll be watching."

The doors of the dressing room shot open and not a man looked right or left as the fighting Irish took the field. Six minutes later fullback Joe Savoldi plunged over the SC goal line for 6 points. Frank Carideo's extra point attempt was good and Notre Dame led 14-6. The Rockne oratorical magic was still there.

On the ensuing kickoff, Notre Dame kicked deep to USC's 4 yard line. The Irish, charged up now and full of fight charged down the field, only to have Russ Saunders break through and race 96 yards for a TD. For a moment it appeared that the momentum had changed again, but when Don Musick missed the point after touchdown, the game was over.

SC's failure to make the extra point had led to their downfall for the third time against Notre Dame. Final score Notre Dame 13, the University of Southern California, 12.

This time it was Coach Howard Jones' turn to take the loser's long journey home, and puzzle all the way why that point after touchdown seemed so elusive and so costly.

Rockne's phlebitis seemed to improve a bit and his team went on to win the '29 championship. After the last game of the season "Curly" Lambeau, the first Green Bay Packer, asked Rockne,

"What kind of team you got?"

"The best damn team I ever had," said Rockne. "But I can't tell 'em that."

"Why?"

"They might believe me," said the Rock.

Notre Dame's future great coach, tackle Frank Leahy

USC's Jim Musick, Fullback

NOTRE DAME VARSITY ROSTER — 1929

NO.	NAME	POSITION	NO.	NAME	POSITION
1	Donoghue, Bernard	Left Half Back	39	Listzwan, Tom	Full Back
2	Kenneally, Tom	Quarter Back	40	Bondi, Gus	Right Guard
3	Murphy, Emmett	Quarter Back	41	Twomey, Ted	Right Tackle
4	Metzger, Bert	Left Guard	42	Provissiero, Phil	Left Guard
5	Koken, Michael	Left Half Back	43	Host, Paul	Left End
6	Grisanti, Al	Right End	44	Law, John	Right Guard
7	Moynihan, Tim	Center	45	Reiman, Fred	Center
8	O'Brien, Ed	Left Half Back	46	Culver, Al	Right Tackle
9	Christman, N.	Quarter Back	47	O'Brien, John	Left End
10	Gebert, Al	Quarter Back	48	Kosky, Frank	Right End
11	Murphy, Tom	Right End	50	Zoss, Abe	Right Guard
12	Brill, Martin	Right Half Back	51	Wharton, T.	Tackle
13	Cannon, Dan	Right Half Back	52	Seymour, Albert	Guard
14	Bloemer, Bernard	Guard	53	Kremer, Theodore	Full Back
15	McNamara, Regis	Left Tackle	54	Savoldi, Joe	Full Back
16	Vlk, George	Right End	57	Rogers, John	Center
17	Colrick, John	Left End	60	Nash, Joseph	Center
18	Schwartz, Marchmont	Left Half Back	61	Griffin, James	Left End
19	Cannon, John	Left Guard	62	Keeney, Bernard	Quarter Back
20	Howard, Al	Full Back	63	Yarr, Thos.	Center
21	Mullins, Lawrence	Full Back	64	Lyons, James	Right Guard
22	Locke, Joseph	Left Guard		Mahaffey, Thos.	Guard
23	Kaplan, Clarence	Right Half Back	65	Yelland, John	Center
24	Carideo, Frank	Quarter Back	66	McMammon, Art	Right Tackle
25	O'Connor, Paul	Full Back	67	Schwartz, Chas.	Left Tackle
	Piggott, Robert	Full Back	69	Mahoney, Henry	End
26	Shay, George	Full Back	70	Manley, John	Tackle
27	Collins, Ed	Left End	72	Whelan, Vince	Left Guard
28	Massey, Robert	Left Guard	73	Williams, Aubrey	Full Back
29	Cronin, Carl	Right Half Back	75	Donoghue, Richard	Left Tackle
30	Conley, Tom	Left End	76	Brannon, Bob	Left Half Back
31	Kerjes, Frank	Left End	77	Kassis, Tom	Right Guard
32	Leahy, Bernard	Left Half Back	78	Bailie, Roy	Right End
33	Vezie, Manfred	Right End	80	Cavanaugh, Vince	Center
34	Thornton, Joe	Right Tackle	81	Carberry, John	Right End
35	Leahy, Frank	Left Tackle	82	Conway, Pat	Full Back
36	Izo, George	Tackle	83	Carmody, James	Tackle
37	Herwit, Norman	Left Guard	84	Elder, John	Left Half Back
38	Cassidy, William	Left Guard			

UNIVERSITY OF SOUTHERN CALIFORNIA VARSITY ROSTER — 1929

NO.	NAME	POSITION	NO.	NAME	POSITION
1	Seitz, William	Tackle	27	*Aspit, Marger	Half
2	*Duffield, Marshall	Quarter	38	*Galloway, Clark	Guard
3	*Mortensen, Jesse	Half	29	*Anthony Frank	Tackle
4	Chambers, Mahlon	Quarter	30	Baker, John	Guard
5	Brown, Everett	Quarter	31	Truher, James	Tackle
6	Sheffer, Clarence	Full	32	Thiede, Cliff	Quarter
7	*Gowder, Robert	Guard	33	Hall, Robert	Tackle
8	Kemp, Rockwell	Quarter	34	Whittier, Julian	Guard
9	Wilcox, Thomas	Full	35	*Shaw, Jesse	Guard
10	*Hoff, Cecil	Tackle	36	Musick, James	Full
11	*Tappaan, Francis	End	37	Wilcox, Ralph	End
12	*Steponovich, Anthony	End	38	Jurich, Anthony	End
13	Stephens, Barry	Half	39	Winfield, Irving	Guard
14	Bond, Ward	Tackle	40	Hirsch, Willis	Center
15	*Saunders, Russell	Quarter	41	Ward, John	Tackle
16	*Templeton, George	Guard	42	Deranian, Vaughan	Guard
17	Pinckert, Ernest	Half	43	Durkee, Harvey	End
19	Kreiger, Karl	End	44	Arbelbide, Garrett	End
20	Hill, Jesse	Full	45	Mason, Thomas	Tackle
21	*Moses, Don	Full	46	Decker, George	Tackle
22	Shaver, Gaius	Quarter	47	Williamson, Stanley	Center
23	Mallory, Thomas	Half	48	Dye, George	Center
24	*Edelson, Harry	Half	49	Joslin, J. Howard	End
15	*Barragar, Nate (c)	Guard	50	Becker, Henry	Half
26	Hammack, Harold	Half	51	Berry, Clark	Guard

54   (*S. C. Monograms Earned)

1930
CHAPTER 6

"HIS LAST COMMAND . . ."
Grantland Rice . . . 1931

The University of Notre Dame du Lac was founded in 1842 by a French priest, the Very Reverend Edward Sorin, C.S.C. Throughout its long history, the Holy Cross Fathers have guided their University with a just but firm hand and have endowed Notre Dame with rich tradition. Part of that tradition is strict adherence to the rules. There are no exceptions, even for star running backs.

Joe Savoldi knew the rules, and he probably wasn't the first, nor the last, to bend them a little for the sake of love. "Bend a little" is probably too delicate a phrase, in Joe's case it was more like a compound fracture. In 1930 it was forbidden by the University for a student to marry. Joe did, as a freshman. The only thing worse than marrying as a freshman was divorcing as a sophomore. Joe did that too, thus incurring the wrath of the school on the former infraction, and the wrath of the Church and the Holy Cross fathers on the latter.

On November 13, just three weeks before the Irish were to meet USC in Los Angeles, Joe Savoldi, called by most experts the finest running back since George Gipp, was expelled.*

Savoldi's unplanned departure left Rockne with only one quality running back (a Californian at that), Larry "Moon" Mullins, and he was not completely well. He had injured a knee two weeks before in the 14-0 victory over Northwestern, and then against Army, the week before the USC game, had re-injured it. Notre Dame had won 7-6, but it was costly. Mullins could not play.

This prompted the Los Angeles sportswriters who had covered both games to return home glowingly confident of a Trojan victory again that year. Some predicted USC by four touchdowns.

When apprised of what the sportswriters had said, Rockne stated, "I'm afraid we're going to take an awful beating from Southern California, but I'm willing to bet we won't be defeated by any four touchdowns as some of the Los Angeles writers seem to feel. I do think though, we'll be lucky to hold SC to a two touchdown victory."

It seemed logical. The Trojans, led once more by talented quarterback Marshall Duffield, and bolstered by brilliant performances from All American Gar Arbelbide at end and halfbacks Gus Shaver and Orv. Mohler , had flattened everyone they met that season with the exception of Washington State, who squeaked by with a one point win, 7-6. USC had scored 382 points against their opponents' 39, an average game score of 42 to 4 for the season! There was no way they could lose. It was generally conceded that the Notre Dame line simply could not absorb the punishment that the larger, heavier USC team would be able to dish out.

Joe Savoldi, Notre Dame's great running back was expelled from school

*Years later, after a successful wrestling career, Savoldi completed his education in his middle years and became a high school science teacher.

Rockne, whose defeatist attitude was so uncharacteristic that someone should have been suspicious, philosophized, "We are sorta like John Paul Jones*, only different in one respect. We haven't given up the ship yet, but we sure have the lifeboats ready."

Now we see Rockne at his wily best.

It's a long train ride from South Bend, Indiana, to Los Angeles, California, and it was Rockne's custom to make several stops along the way to let the team loosen up and blow off a little steam. The last and most important stop before the Coliseum was Tucson. There the Irish held their last practice sessions, which also helped them become accustomed to the heat of California's autumn.

Some 5,000 spectators watched those sessions that year, among them the Los Angeles sportswriters who always made that trip before the game to cover the drills and interview the Notre Dame players. This year they were particularly interested in scouting Rockne's replacement for the physically ailing Moon Mullins, and the morally stained Joe Savoldi.

What they saw didn't impress them much. A medium sized fullback wearing number 31 on his jersey was running short bucks into the line without much enthusiasm or success.

According to the roster, Number 31 was third string fullback, Dan Hanley. Hanley was big, strong and willing, but lacked experience and speed.

Bucky O'Connor, on the other hand, was a medium-sized speedster who loved to run wide. Guess who was wearing number 31 that day in Tucson . . . Obvious, perhaps, but one Los Angeles reporter was deceived enough to interview him and file the story, never suspecting he was talking to O'Connor, not Hanley. That, of course, is exactly what Rockne wanted . . . So much in fact he had stayed up half the night coaching Bucky in the fine art of side stepping direct questions.

The University of Southern California, lulled into a false sense of security, *actually invited Rockne to address their team at a pre-game banquet!* This is a little like asking the Boston strangler for a neck massage. Rockne graciously accepted.

The coach of the Fighting Irish of Notre Dame stood before the assembled USC team and pled for mercy. He explained his team's weaknesses and elaborated on their injuries, all the while praising the SC team as one of the finest he had ever seen.

"When that game is over tomorrow," he said, ". . . and I know you'll do everything you can to hold down the score . . . I'd like to ask you fine young men of Troy to come over and congratulate my boys on a fine game. It will mean so much to them to have a firm handshake and a kind word from a team like yours . . . Thank you, and when we meet again next year, I hope the odds are a little kinder toward Notre Dame. Bless you and good fortune."

And they believed him. According to Frank Leahy, who sat down front at the banquet, the USC team walked out infused with the spirit of American sportsmanship, vowing to do the only decent thing and not mutilate Notre Dame too badly. "Rock," said Leahy, "could turn an entire enemy camp into a group of contrite children." USC had plenty to be contrite about the next day.

"BUCKY" O'CONNOR

Flashy Notre Dame half brought to earth after tearing off a little yardage.
—"Times" Photo by Fred Coffey.

Notre Dame's "Bucky" O'Connor, Halfback

Before a crowd of 98,000 the Irish of Notre Dame methodically dissected the best football team USC had fielded in years. Their line outrushed the Trojan forwards, their backs outran the Trojan backs, and the SC tacklers fell before the Notre Dame blockers like petals in a chill winter wind. The Trojan secondary seemed to spend the entire day in a state of confusion.

Notre Dame elected to receive. They moved the ball to USC's 20 yard line, but failed on a fourth down pass play and turned the ball over to the Trojans who promptly fumbled on the first play. Notre Dame halfback Marchy Schwartz passed to quarterback Frank Carideo in the end zone for 6. Carideo converted . . . the score, 7-0. After the kickoff and an exchange of punts, Notre Dame's other halfback, Marty Brill, pitched to Bucky O'Connor, who sliced around right end for 80 yards and a touchdown. Carideo missed the extra point. In

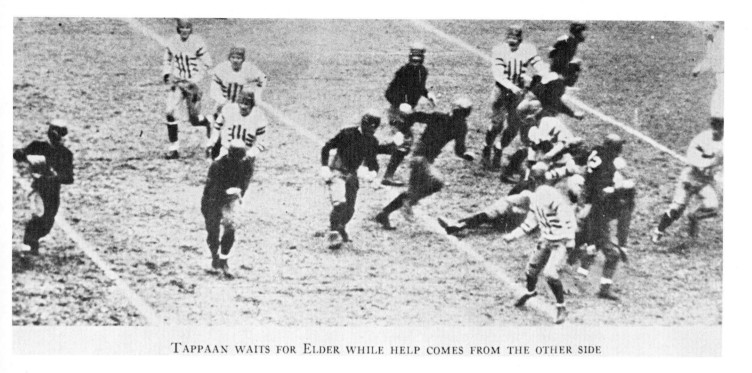

TAPPAAN WAITS FOR ELDER WHILE HELP COMES FROM THE OTHER SIDE

the second quarter Hanley caught a touchdown pass from tackle Nick Likats, but it was called back. Notre Dame was offside . . . Southern Cal was in shock. The half ended, Notre Dame 13, USC 0.

In the third quarter, Schwartz again passed to O'Connor for a touchdown, leading the reporters to suspect that perhaps he wasn't Hanley after all. Notre Dame 20, USC 0.

Mercifully, Rockne had flooded the field with substitutes, but it didn't matter much. The Irish continued to hammer away. Likats charged in the end zone once more to make the final score 27-0.

It had been a game of outstanding individual performances, Frank Carideo, All American quarterback, Bucky O'Connor, who filled in so ably for the ailing Moon Mullins, "Pee Wee guard" Pete Metzger, who successfully held off future All American Johnny Baker who outweighed him by 35 pounds . . . Perhaps the most brilliant play of the game was not performed on the gridiron that day, but in a banquet hall the night before. It was one of Rockne's best, and one of his last.

It was the 19th consecutive victory without a defeat or a tie for Notre Dame. They finished the season 10-0-0, and won the national championship for an unprecedented third time in a row and gained permanent possession of the Rissman trophy.

The team was welcomed back in South Bend by thousands of students, alumni, and friends . . . Rockne was hailed as the greatest coach of all time. It was predicted that the 1931 team under his leadership would be invincible. It was not to be.

Knute Kenneth Rockne had barked his last command.

Frank Carideo Notre Dame's All American Quarterback

ROCKNE

What possibly can be written about Knute Rockne that has not already been written, re-written, read and re-read? What anecdote has not been told and re-told. And how many myths created . . .

Two generations of football players and fans have fed upon Rockne stories written by Grantland Rice, Arch Ward, Red Smith, and Rex Beach. Paul Gallico, Ring Lardner, Westbrook Pegler and Henry McLemore knew him and quoted him often. He was covered by Heywood Broun, Damon Runyon, and Braven Dyer . . . a veritable sportswriter's Hall of Fame.

From 1919 when he had his first undefeated season, until 1931 when he took off on that ill-fated flight to California, it's a pretty sure bet that nearly every word he uttered in public was quoted, re-quoted and frequently misquoted. In the Golden Age of sports, he was "good copy!" . . . A Johnson of the gridiron with a hundred Boswells.

But these are facts. He was not a large man . . . 5'8", and when he played end for Notre Dame he weighed around 145. He was not a handsome man, he was nearly bald and had a nose that looked as if someone had been cracking walnuts on it (a foul tip caused that, not a blocked punt). Westbrook Pegler once said he had a face like a battered oil can. "An old punched-up prelim fighter." Rock never forgave him.

He had button-bright blue eyes that twinkled constantly and a high pitched voice that was seldom stilled. That voice . . . according to those who have heard him speak had all the mellifluous quality of a pneumatic hammer. But when Rockne talked, everybody listened.

Knute Rockne had something that set him apart from other men. He did not come to greatness as a football coach because he was the only one around. It was an era of giants . . . Pop Warner, Fielding Yost, Fritz Crisler, Bob Zuppke and Amos Alonzo Stagg . . . fast company on any track. Yet he stood out among them not just because of his football genius, but because he had that rare gift of being able to inspire men. Call him an orator or an actor, a salesman or psychologist, he was all of those things and more. He had focus, dedication, devotion and he had devoted most of his life to the systematic study and teaching of the game . . . A man of deep charm and amazing personality.

Such was the power of his leadership that when, because of his recurring phlebitis he was unable to accompany his team to Annapolis for the 1929 Navy game, he was able to inspire his men in typical Rockne fashion from a thousand miles away. At 9 o'clock the morning of the game, he sent a wire to Tom Lieb, the acting coach who was having breakfast with the team at the Gibson Island Country Club where they were quartered. He was instructed to have the squad lined up outside a designated telephone booth at ten o'clock.

At the appointed time the telephone rang, and one by one every member stepped to the phone to listen to the coach. What he said to each man is not known, but Frank Leahy, a tackle on that '29 squad later related that most of the boys left the booth in tears. Of course, Frank Leahy had been known to weep at a sad weather report, but George Maypole, a member of the Notre Dame Board of Governors, was also there and reported that, "A sudden change of attitude was immediately discernible."

Of course, they stormed on the field that afternoon and rolled over Navy 14-7. The Rockne magic worked even by long distance telephone from half a continent away.

Coach Knute Rockne did with college football what Champion Jack Dempsey did with professional prizefighting. Dempsey took boxing up from smoky fifty dollar club matches to the million dollar gate. Rockne made a million dollar business out of a college game that used to be watched by a handful of students and a few alumni on a Saturday afternoon in autumn. The last trip Rockne made to USC in 1930, it took 21 extra cars on the team train to accommodate, in Grantland Rice's words, "friends of Rockne."

From 1918, when Rockne first became head coach, until 1927, Notre Dame doubled its enrollment . . . and its funds. Like it or not, the Holy Cross fathers would have to admit that for the three decades from 1921 until 1951, the University of Notre Dame du Lac was better known for its football prowess than for its academic achievement. The story is told that during World War II a Japanese unit tried to sing the Notre Dame Victory March as they attacked, seeking to demoralize the American defenders . . . they thought it was the national anthem. It could have happened — it has been translated into at least a dozen languages.

The facts and fantasy surrounding Notre Dame football and the men who play it are created every autumn and are easily and constantly confused. Myths and legends wash over each other and obscure the truth, and the mists of time fog the memory.

Hollywood doesn't help . . . in one Rockne picture they portrayed the Notre Dame shift being conceived by the Coach as he watched chorus girls in a New York theatre hop from right to left to a dance routine.

". . . A crazy lie . . ." growled Father Frank Cavanaugh.

Father Frank should know. He was a classmate of George

Gipp, he was in the chapel when Rockne converted from Lutheranism to Catholicism, and when Frank Leahy was a sophomore tackle, Father Frank was proctor of his dormitory. Later he was the head of the arts and science department of the university. He has kept records on the coaching careers of both Rockne and Leahy.

"Then there was the scene where they had George Gipp being discovered by Rockne while he played inter-hall football. They had him kicking a (stray) ball back to Rock and then had Rock begging to come out for the team . . . That was fiction too," says Father Frank.

Not so, according to another Notre Dame historian and Rockne biographer, Tim Cohane, former sports editor of Look.

"The Gipp story has stood the test of time and the attempts by the smart-pants school of mod sportswriters to debunk it."

Father Cavanaugh . . . mod . . . smart-pants?

Wells Twombly, sports columnist for the San Francisco Examiner: "There is some question whether Gipp actually said on his deathbed, 'Sometime, Rock, when the team is up against it . . .'"

Tim Cohane: "And Gipp, dying . . . for sure said to Rockne before he passed out, 'Someday when the going is tough, ask the boys to win one for the Gipper.'"

"Years later," writes Cohane, "when debunkers tried to attack it (the story) Frank Wallace tracked down the roots." Wallace claims that an old priest who was in the hospital room at the time had confirmed Gipp's request.

"It seems unlikely," writes Twombly. "It has been suggested that a South Bend newspaperman was in the room with him at the time. Certainly, he would have reported it. It's entirely possible that the last three hours of his life were spent in a coma."

The old priest alluded to by Wallace was more than likely Father Pat Haggerty, who converted Gipp on his deathbed. But if he was indeed there, he never confirmed or denied the story publicly.

Another seam in the cloak of legend.

But these are facts. Knute Kenneth Rockne was born in Voss, Norway in 1888, and was brought to Chicago five years later with his mother and three sisters by his father Lars, a carriage maker, who had come to America to enter his carriage in World's Fair competition.

Knute (pronounced Ca-nute) was a high school dropout, but later changed his mind so drastically that he labored five years as a postal clerk to save $1,000 to go to the University of Illinois. After he had enrolled at Illinois, he heard from two friends that Notre Dame was considerably less expensive, and would probably take pity on a poor Christian youth who thirsted for an education. The fact that he was a Lutheran and was lacking a high school diploma bothered Rockne not a bit.

He talked the good Fathers into a high school equivalency exam, which he passed with a 92.5 grade and matriculated in 1910, a 22 year old freshman. For the next four years he was a busy young man.

Science was his major, chemistry and football were his favorite subjects, and he was good in all three. Scholastically he carried a 90+ average and in his spare time he edited the *Dome*, waited on tables, played the flute, and even found time to try a little semi-pro boxing with Gus Dorais as cornerman. He was much better at football.

As captain of the 1913 Notre Dame team, he, along with Dorais and Joe Pliska was credited with integrating the forward pass with a running attack by fullback Ray Eichenlaub so skillfully that they surprised heavily favored Army 35-13. It was the first time the two teams had met.

It was Jesse Harper's first year as coach, and he was undefeated. It was Rockne's third year on an undefeated team, and he played well enough that season to be named third string All American end by Walter Camp.

After graduating *magna cum laude,* he spent the next four years as assistant chemistry professor and assistant football coach . . . and waiting. In 1918 the wait ended. Jesse Harper retained his title as Athletic Director, but turned the coaching reins over to his assistant. At the age of 30, Knute Rockne became head football coach of the University of Notre Dame. His first season he lost one game. He didn't lose another until 1921. By the end of the 1927 season his record stood at 80 wins, 8 losses and 5 ties. But by the sixth game of the 1928 season, the Irish were 3 and 2, and it was obvious that this was not going to be another overwhelming Rockne team. After they barely won a squeaker from Pitt, 9-0, it is said that Rockne decided to call on a higher power for a little help, or a new play or something. He went to the church on campus and knelt at the altar. There was only one votive candle burning.

"What's that for?" he whispered to the priest.

"It's for the football team," murmured the good father, "I lit it myself."

Rockne had become a convert in 1925, but he was still able to temper his Roman Catholicism with Scandinavian realism.

"Don't be so cheap with the wax," he growled.

At the end of the 1930 season his record was 120 wins, 12 losses, 5 ties for a .989 average. In eleven years he had become a legend. But the legend had feet of clay. That was a great part of his charm. He had his share of vanity, he was known to lose his temper on occasion; he could be suspicious and secretive, and he was not averse to stretching the truth once in a while so long as it didn't hurt anyone seriously . . . and might win a football game. And he was a lousy businessman. He was a sucker for any kind of deal that looked as if it might make money, and a soft touch for anyone who said he needed some. On $11,000 a year with 5 kids he could hardly break even.

Once, while Rockne was in New York on a speaking engagement, Columbia University announced it had signed him to a five year contract at $30,000 a year with an option for five additional years at $35,000. It was true. There was no doubt but that it was Rockne's signature on the contract.

"Why didn't you tell us you were unhappy here?" asked Father Matthew Walsh, Notre Dame president at that time.

"Father, I was emotionally and physically exhausted when I signed that contract," said Rockne. "Help me get out of it."

"I'll do what I can," said Father Walsh, and he did.

The lure of money couldn't hold a candle to the siren call of Notre Dame. Our Lady had won again.

For Rockne, 1931 promised to be one of the best years ever. A few weeks in Florida during the winter seemed to have eased the chronic phlebitis, and he returned to South Bend in the early spring feeling better than he had for years. Even his financial future looked optimistic. Since 1927 he had been involved in advertising campaigns for Studebaker of South Bend. Now they had offered him $10,000 to do six lectures on salesmanship . . . they were even thinking of naming a car after him, and it was rumored that he might take over the presidency of Studebaker Motor Car Company.

A motion picture producer in Hollywood had offered him the part of a coach (specially written for Rockne) in the movie version of the stage hit, *Good News,* and the job of technical director on a series of football shorts. They asked him to come to California to discuss it . . . they also mentioned $50,000.

Rockne took a train to Kansas City and there, on March 31st, boarded a Fokker Tri-motor bound for Los Angeles. It never got there. A few miles southwest of Bazaar, Kansas, later on that clear Tuesday morning, a farmer out inspecting his fields, heard an explosion in the sky. Shielding his eyes, he looked upward in time to see pieces of an airplane, followed by a trail of black smoke plummet to the ground. The debris was scattered over acres of winter wheat and it was the next day before the flight or the passengers were identified.

The flight was Trans-continental and Western Airway, a Fokker Tri-motor . . . destination Los Angeles. Rockne and seven others were aboard. It was just a few weeks after his 43rd birthday.

They buried Knute Kenneth Rockne, the man, on the afternoon of April 5th, 1931. Six members of his last team were pall bearers and the cathedral bells of Notre Dame tolled the Victory March in funeral cadence.

But Knute Rockne, the legend, will live as long as football is played at Notre Dame . . . or anywhere.

IRISH ROSTER — 1930

NO.	NAME	POS.	WT.		NO.	NAME	POS.	WT.
1	Jaskwhich, Chas.	Q.	164		38	Harris, James	L.G.	185
2	Vejar, Laurie	Q.	168		40	Terlaak, Robert	R.G.	180
3	Murphy, Emmett	Q.	154		42	Cavanaugh, Vincent	C.	175
4	Metzger, Bert	R.G.	155		44	Kosky, Edwin	L.E.	182
9	Cronin, Carl	Q.	155		46	Goldstein, Sam	L.T.	178
10	Sheeketski, Joe	R.H.	165		47	O'Brien, John	L.E.	185
11	Host, Paul	L.E	173		48	Lukats, Nicholas	L.T.	178
12	Brill, Marty	R.H.	190		50	Tobin, John	R.H.	180
13	Connolly, John	L.H.	160		52	Kerjes, Frank	R.G.	192
14	Mahoney, Dick	R.E.	175		53	Pierce, William	L.G.	185
16	Vlk, George	R.E.	175		61	Coughlan, Tom	L.G	180
17	Bailie, Roy	L.E.	173		62	Massey, Robert	L.G.	170
18	Schwartz, Marchmont	L.H.	170		64	Rogers, John	C.	170
20	Howard, Al	F.B.	170		65	Bassett, Charles	R.T.	180
21	Mullins, Larry	F.B.	175		66	Kurth, Joseph	R.T.	197
22	Koken, Mike	L.H.	162		68	Agnew, Edward	C.	178
23	Kaplan, Clarence	R.H.	156		69	Kassis, Tom	R.G.	185
24	Carideo, Frank	Q.	175		70	Butler, Frank	C	202
25	O'Conner, Paul	R.H.	180		74	Hoffman, Frank	R.T.	198
27	Bice, Leonard	L.E.	172		76	Yarr, Tom	C.	195
30	Conley, Tom (Capt.)	R.E.	175		78	Carmody, James	R.T.	200
31	Hanley, Daniel	F.B.	195		80	McManmon, Art	R.T.	202
32	Greeney, Norman	L.G.	185		81	Culver, Alvin	L.T.	212
33	Leahy, Bernard	L.H.	175		82	Donaghue, Richard	R.T.	215
36	McNamara, Regis	L.T	192					

TROJAN ROSTER — 1930

NO.	NAME	POS.	WT.		NO.	NAME	POS.	WT.
27	**Apsit, Marger	L.H.	180		56	Kennedy, John G.	R.G.	185
44	*Arbelbide, Garret W.	R.E.	183		23	Mallory, Thomas O.	L.H.	180
28	Armistead, William D.	R.T.	198		20	Maloney, Alpert L.	Q.	153
30	*Baker, John W.	L.G.	180		59	Matson, Floyd A.	R.E.	180
61	Barry, Nelson W.	Q.	167		24	Mohler, Orville E.	Q.	163
19	Beatty, Blanchard	Q.	158		36	*Musick, James A.	F.	195
12	Biggs, W. Henry	R.E.	170		30	Norene, George W.	C.	175
16	Black, Rupert	R.G.	185		69	Norris, Neil	R.E.	180
14	Bond, Ward E.	R.T.	195		70	Owens, James C.	Q.	165
60	Brown, Everett W.	F.	165		17	*Pinckert, Erny	R.H.	189
29	Brown, Raymond C.	R.T.	196		32	Plaehn, Alfred G.	L.T.	196
21	Clarke, Eugene C.	R.E.	185		57	Ramey, Theron A.	R.G.	185
46	Decker, George W.	R.E.	178		54	Ritchey, Wm. Bert	F.	180
42	Deranian, Vaughn R.	R.G.	190		22	*Shaver, Gaius	F.	180
2	**Duffield, Marshall D.	Q.	175		35	**Shaw, Jess M.	R.G.	198
64	Fraga, John	L.H.	170		48	Smith, Ernest F.	R.F.	199
31	Gentry, Byron B.	L.G.	180		40	Sparling, Ray C.	L.E.	175
33	*Hall, Robert H.	L.T.	211		13	Stephens, Barry B.	R.H.	160
26	Hammack, Harold E.	R.H.	180		15	Thompson, Roderick A.	L.F.	198
43	Hawkins, William J.	C.	185		45	Tipton, Howard D.	R.H.	185
53	Hooper, Wesley W.	L.H.	175		34	Whittier, Julian C.	C.	214
55	Jensen, Robert C.	L.G.	175		37	**Wilcox, Ralph O.	L.E.	175
49	Joslin, Howard	R.E.	176		47	*Williamson, Stanley	C.	196
					39	Winfield, J. Irving	L.G.	202

1931
CHAPTER 7

". . . THE BIGGEST UPSET SINCE MRS. O'LEARY'S COW KICKED OVER THAT LANTERN . . ."
Trojan El Rodeo . . . 1931

It would be hard to blame that unknown Trojan sportswriter for such a mild overstatement. It had been a long dry spell. Since the USC-Notre Dame series had started in 1926, the Irish had won four out of five games. Understandably the 1931 Trojans came to Notre Dame's new stadium with blood in their eyes, and revenge in their hearts. But they had more than that going for them.

The men of Troy brought with them a great defense, a better offense, and a strong determination to recapture the national championship that had eluded them for the last two seasons, thanks to Knute Rockne and the Fighting Irish.

USC had been taken by surprise in their opener. Overconfidence and little St. Mary's had beaten them 13-7, but it must have taught them something. The next game, they blanked Oregon State 30-0. Washington State managed only 6 points to 38 for USC. The next four opponents didn't fare nearly so well. They scored not a single point against the Thundering Herd's 147.

Coach Jones had drilled the troops behind closed gates for ten days and with the help of a bye, the Trojans were well rested, 100% fit, and ready for a fight. And a fight it would be.

Heartly "Hunk" Anderson, the new Notre Dame head coach, was not without experience. He was able and so far had proved himself to be a worthy successor to the late Rockne. His 1931 team had established itself as number 1 in the nation, and had only one blot on its escutcheon, a 0-0 tie with Northwestern, the second game of the season.

The Irish defense was certainly just as awesome as the Trojans', having yielded only 12 points all year. Their offense was led by three All-Americans, halfback Marchie Schwartz, tackle Joe Kerth, and captain Tom Yarr, who played center.

For the first time, three Los Angeles radio stations broadcast the game. Since not everyone owned a radio in those days, many public parks set up bleachers accommodating four to five thousand "spectators." An estimated 10,000,000 football fans from coast to coast heard that game . . . until then, the largest listening audience in broadcast history. And what a game they heard!

Tad Jones, Howard's little brother, and a successful coach in his own right (Yale 1920-27) until his retirement, predicted in his nationally syndicated column that the Irish would win by two touchdowns, and win their third national championship in a row.

Mercifully, there is no record of what Howard probably said to brother Tad.

Joe Kurth, Notre Dame's All American Tackle

John and Ken Baker—USC

Tom Yarr, Notre Dame Captain and All American

After the kickoff, the Trojans drove to the one yard line, only to lose the ball on fullback Jim "Sweet" Musick's fumble. It was then Notre Dame's turn to be the bully on the block. Spearheaded by Schwartz and Steve Banas, the Irish drove from their own 45 to score the first touchdown. Charlie Jaskwhich made the extra point good. At the half, Notre Dame 7, USC 0.

In the third quarter, the Irish continued their winning ways. Schwartz punched over from his ten yard line, Jaskwhich again scored the point after, and the score was 14-0.

Then something happened, what it was no one seemed to know. Perhaps it was the Notre Dame pile-up on Jim Musick that forced him from the game with a broken nose that inflamed the USC team. Or maybe it was the inspiration that Orv Mohler brought into the game with him when he substituted for Musick. Whatever it was, it started to work for the Trojans. Mohler replaced Shaver as quarterback, and Gus took Musick's spot at fullback (can you see that happening in 1976?). It proved to be a winning combination. With Shaver and Mohler alternately cracking the Notre Dame line for

steady gains, and a slashing reverse run by Ray Sparling around the left halfback position, the Trojans pushed the ball to the Irish one yard line. Gus Shaver drove over for the touchdown and . . . Johnny Baker's kick for the extra point was blocked.

Notre Dame was forced to punt after failing to make a first down after the kickoff. Once more the Trojans drove deep into Irish territory. Mohler flipped a perfect lateral to Shaver, who ran it into the end zone. This time Johnny Baker didn't miss. Score, Notre Dame 14, USC 13.

The capacity crowd of 50,000 was on its feet now. With less than four minutes to play, Coach Jones must have felt the spectre of missed kicks and one point losses sitting on his shoulder.

When the Trojans took possession again there were less than three minutes to play. Gus Shaver threw a fifty-yard pass, the longest of his career, and Sparling made a spectacular catch. Shaver again, this time to Bob Hall on a misdirection play to the 17. A 5-yard penalty against Notre Dame moved the ball to the 12-yard line, but then Notre Dame's powerful

1931 Notre Dame and USC All Americans

line hurled Sparling back to the 15 . . . Gordon Clark fumbled Mohler's pass . . . Time was running out for SC, and that spectre on Howard Jones' shoulder grew heavier. He then sent Homer Griffith into the game with a play, but Mohler, a very clever quarterback, knew exactly what to do. He waved Griffith off the field, and with less than sixty seconds, and Notre Dame expecting a pass on third down, he called a place kick. Big Johnny Baker dropped back to the 23 yard line. Captain Stan Williamson snapped the ball, Mohler held . . . the kick was good.

The Trojans had done the almost unbelievable feat of spotting powerful Notre Dame, who had won twenty-five consecutive games, 14 points going into the final period, and then scoring 16 points in the last fifteen minutes to win. It was only the second time in twenty-seven years that the Fighting Irish of Notre Dame had been humbled on their own playing field.

With the 16-14 victory over the Irish came the Dickinson, and ironically the Knute Rockne Memorial Trophy, symbolic of the national championship. It had begun to appear that whoever wins the Trojan-Irish war falls heir to that honor.

At the presentation ceremony of the Rockne Trophy in the Trojan dressing room immediately after the game, Jones, even more silent than usual amid the tumult, accepted the award, then suddenly leaned toward Jack Rissman, donor of the trophy bearing his name, and shouted above the din, "Jack do you know where Rockne's buried?"

"I'll take you there," replied Rissman.

An hour later Howard Jones and the entire Thundering Herd stood bare-headed in Highland Cemetery at the grave of their bitterest adversary on the field, their most respected opponent . . . a beloved enemy. In the chill November evening they paid silent tribute to the fallen warrior.

From the Trojan Annual, El Rodeo . . . "The greatest football game of the year . . . the biggest upset since Mrs. O'Leary's cow kicked over that lantern in Chicago, way back in the last century . . . the most thrilling contest that any football fan has ever seen . . . a contest which had radio listeners pie-eyed, limp yet hysterical when it was all over . . . that was the Trojan-Notre Dame game . . ."

1931 UNIVERSITY OF NOTRE DAME VARSITY FOOTBALL ROSTER

NO.	NAME	POSITION
1	Jaskwhich, Charles	Q.B.
2	Millheam, Duke	R.H.
3	Murphy, Emmett	Q.B.
4	Foley, Joe	Q.B.
5	Vejar, Laurie	Q.B.
6	Rohrs, George	R.E.
7	Mahoney, Dick	R.E.
8	McGuff, Al	Q.B.
9	Christman, Norb	Q.B.
10	Sheeketski, Joe	R.H.
11	Host, Paul	L.E.
12	Brancheau, Ray	R.H.
13	Connelly, John	L.H.
14	Franklin, Randolph	R.E.
15	Canale, Frank	L.E.
16	Mahaffey, Tom	L.G.
17	LaBorne, Frank	L.H.
18	Schwartz, Marchmont	L.H.
20	Bice, Leonard	L.E.
21	Burke, Vince	Q.B.
22	Koken, Mike	L.H.
23	Krusiec, E. F.	F.B.
24	Boland, Raymond	Q.B.
25	Bolger, Charles	L.E.
26	Cronin, Carl	R.H.
29	Hagen, Lowell	F.B.
20	Melinkovich, George	F.B.
32	Greeney, Norman	L.G.
33	Leahy, Bernie	R.H.
34	Leonard, James	F.B.
35	Captor, Albert	F.B.
36	McNamara, Regis	R.T.
38	Harriss, James	L.G.
40	Rouland, Ray	R.E.
41	Schumacher, Al	L.H.
42	Cavanaugh, Vincent	R.G.
43	Beirne, Roger	L.E.
44	Kosky, Edwin	L.E.
45	Witucki, Bernard	C.
47	Alexander, Benjamin	C.
48	Lukats, Nick	F.B.
49	Barstow, Fred	R.T.
50	Tobin, John	R.H.
51	Gorman, Tom	C.
52	Leding, Mike	L.T.
53	Pierce, Bill	R.G.
54	Grundeman, Reuben	F.B.
56	Zoss, Oscar	C.
57	DeVore, Hugh	R.E.
58	Kreuz, Paul	R.G.
59	Whelan, Vincent	C.
60	Banas, Steve	F.B.
61	Jehle, Frank	L.T.
62	Acers, Julian	L.H.
63	Halpin, Robert	C.
64	Rogers, John	C.
65	Flynn, Jack	R.T.
66	Kurth, Joe	R.T.
67	Gildea, Hubert	L.E.
68	Pivarnik, Joe	L.G.
69	Krause, Ed.	L.T.
70	Cousino, Bernard	R.T.
72	Wunsch, Harry	L.G.
73	Schrenker, Paul	L.G.
74	Hoffman, Frank Nordy	R.T.
75	Kozak, George	R.T.
76	Yarr, Tom (Capt.)	C.
77	Vyzral, Edward	R.T.
78	Carmody, James	R.T.
79	Mariani, H.	L.T.
81	Culver, Alvin	L.T.

1931 UNIVERSITY OF SOUTHERN CALIFORNIA VARSITY FOOTBALL ROSTER

NO.	NAME	POSITION
12	Griffith, Homer O.	Fullback
13	Stephens, Barry B.	Right Half
14	Rosenberg, Aaron	Left Tackle
15	Thompson, Roderick A.	Left Tackle
16	Black, Rupert	Right Guard
17	Pinckert, Ernie	Right Half
19	Beatty, Blanchard	Quarterback
20	Durkee, Harvey	End
21	Clarke, Eugene C.	Right End
22	Shaver, Gaius R.	Quarterback
23	Mallory, Thomas O.	Left Half
24	Mohler, Orville E.	Quarterback
25	Erskine, Robert A.	Right Half
26	Hammack, Harold E.	Right Half
27	Palmer, Ford I.	Left End
28	Biggs, Henry	Left End
29	Brown, Raymond C.	Right Tackle
30	Baker, John W.	Left Guard
31	Gentry, Byron B.	Left Guard
32	Plaehn, Alfred G.	Left Tackle
33	Hall, Robert H.	Right Guard
34	Stevens, Lawrence C.	Right Guard
35	Youel, Curtis L.	Center
36	Musick, James A.	Fullback
37	Bescos, Julius A.	Right End
38	Jurich, Anthony F.	Right End
40	Sparling, Ray C.	Left End
41	Clark, Gordon G.	Left Half
42	Dye, John T.	Right Guard
43	Hawkins, William J.	Center
44	Arbelbide, Garrett W.	Right End
45	Tipton, Howard D.	Left Half
46	Williamson, Frank E.	Left Guard
47	Williamson, Stanley (c)	Center
48	Smith, Ernest F.	Right Tackle
49	Joslin, Howard	Fullback
51	Ridings, David E.	Right Guard
53	McNeish, Robert C.	Left Half
54	Sherman, Thomas H.	Fullback
55	Edwards, Joseph	Left End
57	Brouse, Willard R.	Quarterback
60	Barber, Richard	Fullback
61	Fay, Kenneth J.	Right Half
65	Walker, Charles	Half Back
70	Owens, James C.	Quarterback

1932
CHAPTER 8

YOU GOTTA HIT HARD TO KNOCK A GUY'S PANTS OFF
. . . Bob Ray 1932

"Hunk" Anderson was a fierce competitor. And tough. Rockne considered him his all-time guard in '19, '20, and '21, when he was named All American. At 170 pounds, he was as tough as an old cavalry boot. They said the only man who ever matched him on the line was Iowa's Hall of Fame tackle, Duke Slater, and he weighed 220. Nor was Anderson's willingness to do battle necessarily confined to the gridiron. Grantland Rice said of him, "pound for pound, the roughest human being, when aroused, I've ever known." And Coach Anderson was aroused. He had joined Rockne's coaching staff in 1923, and was not accustomed to losing. But in 1932, neither was Howard Jones.

The Trojan horse had galloped roughshod over every opponent they had faced thus far. Undefeated in eight games, they had allowed only 13 points. Six of the eight teams they had played were held scoreless.

The Irish of Notre Dame had nothing to be ashamed of, for that matter. They had won seven out of eight, losing only to Pitt. 12-0, and had rolled up 255 offensive points against only 18 scored against them.

But when the two titans clashed on December 10, at the Coliseum, before 100,000 football fanatics, it was all one way.

The Trojans outfought, outplayed, outgained, and outscored the Irish every step of the way. They succeeded in demoralizing the Notre Dame backfield, one of the best in the country, they ripped the line with short but consistent gains and as a result of a Homer Griffith to Bob McNeish pass the Trojans went into the locker room at halftime ahead   to 0.

Climaxing a powerful 26-yard drive, USC's quarterback Griffith slashed through the Notre Dame line for a second touchdown. Expert punting kept the Irish buried deep in their own territory, and paved the way for SC's 3rd Nat'l Championship.

The Trojans, it should be mentioned, had an invisible ally aboard the Notre Dame team train from South Bend. It is called influenza, and it can do more to wipe out a team than eleven Bronko Nagurskis.

The Irish looked good on the stats (they outgained the Trojans 218 yards to 110½), but the 13-0 score was a little embarrassing.

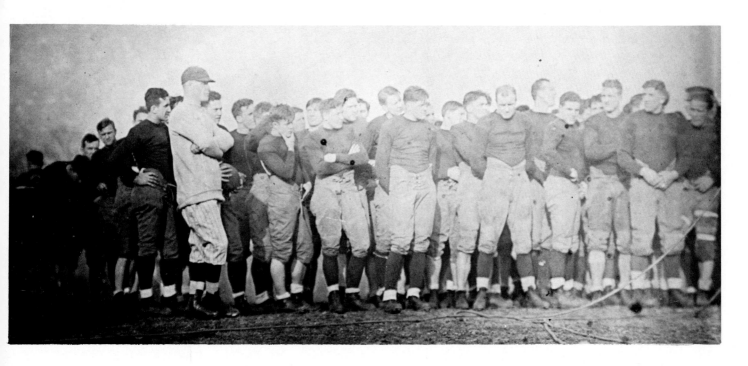

1932 USC backfield, left to right, Cal Clemens, Gordon Clark, Dick Barber and Orv Mohler

Nor was the embarrassment confined to the score. Left end Ray Sparling, playing one of the best games of his career, tackled Notre Dame halfback Nick Likats so hard that Nick finished the play with his pants at half mast. Wrote L.A. Times sport columnist, Bob Ray, the next day, ". . . The tackle didn't look much different than any of the others . . . but you gotta hit hard to knock a guy's pants off."

Notre Dame's Nick Lukats lost pants in '32 game

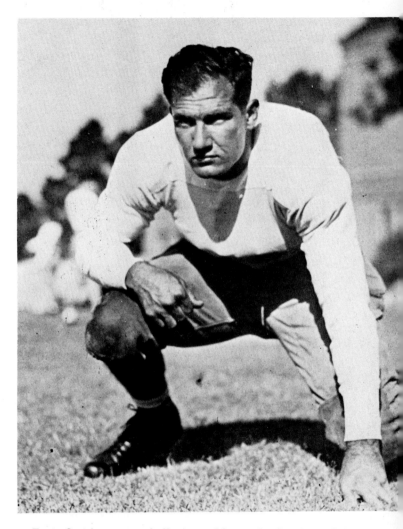

Ernie Smith was one hell of a tackle on the Southern California elevens of 1930, '31 and '32 that won 28 of 31 games, including Rose Bowl victories over Tulane and Pittsburgh. The 1930 and '31 Trojans averaged 37 points per game. Coach Howard Jones called the 6 foot 2½, 212-pound All American "the best tackle I have ever seen." With Smith, Orv Mohler, Gus Shaver, Ernie Pinckert, Johnny Baker and Bob Hall leading the way, Southern Cal ran up a string of 20 straight wins in 1931-32. Not even Notre Dame could stop them, losing 16-14 and 13-0. In 1935 he joined the Detroit Lions and played pro ball until 1937. Ernie Smith keeps his hand in football today as a member of the Tournament of Roses Committee. He is also a successful insurance executive.

NOTRE DAME ROSTER — 1932

NO.	NAME	POSITION	WT.
47	Alexander, Benjamin	Center	181
60	Banas, Stephen P.	Full	185
49	Barstow, Fred A.	Left Tackle	200
12	Brancheau, Raymond	Right Half	185
21	Burke, James V.	Quarter	145
19	Canale, Frank S.	Left End	190
14	Carideo, Angelo, Jr.	Quarter	165
56	Costello, Albert T.	Right Half	185
57	DeVore, Hugh J.	Right End	181
65	Flynn, John J.	Right Guard	190
51	Gorman, Thos. A.	Center	190
32	Greeney, Norman J.	Left Guard	190
38	Harris, James M.	Left Guard	188
11	Host, Paul A. (Capt.)	Right End	175
1	Jaskwhich, Charles J.	Quarter	164
22	Koken, Michael R.	Left Half	168
44	Kosky, Edwin S.	Left End	185
66	Kurth, Joseph J.	Right Tackle	204
69	Krause, Edward W.	Left Tackle	220
52	Leding, Michael J.	Left Tackle	180
34	Leonard, James R.	Full	190
48	Lukats, Nicholas P.	Left Half	185
30	Melinkovich, George J.	Full	180
3	Murphy, Emmett F.	Quarter	160
9	McGuff, Albert L.	Left Half	171
82	Pfefferle, Richard J.	Left Tackle	196
53	Pierce, William C.	Right Guard	180
68	Pivarnik, Joseph J.	Right Guard	195
20	Rascher, Norbert H.	Right End	188
76	Robinson, John J.	Center	200
81	Roach, Thomas G.	Right Tackle	205
71	Schiralli, Rocco V.	Left Guard	175
10	Sheeketski, Joseph L.	Right Half	170
33	Tobin, John E.	Right Half	178
26	Vairo, Dominic M.	Left End	192
5	Vejar, Laurie	Quarter	150
84	Wunsch, Harry F.	Right Guard	212

SOUTHERN CALIFORNIA ROSTER — 1932

NO.	NAME	POSITION	WT.
60	Barber, Dick	Full	185
56	Bardin, Oliver	Right Guard	196
39	Beard, Francis	Full	190
37	Bescos, Julius	End	170
28	Biggs, Henry	End	176
16	Bright, Kenneth	Center	185
29	Brown, Raymond (C)	Left Tackle	202
21	Browning, Ward	Right End	190
41	Clark, Gordon	Left Half	175
18	Clemens, Cal	Right Half	185
57	Coughlin, Alvie	Right Tackle	190
58	Dunning, Corwin	Center	186
42	Dye, John	Right Guard	200
25	Erskine, Bob	Right Tackle	210
61	Fay, Kenneth	Right Half	180
31	Gentry, Byron	Center	185
63	Getz, Robert	Full	187
12	Griffith, Homer	Quarter	185
65	Harlan, Dave	Right Tackle	225
33	Harper, Hueston	Right Guard	210
15	Jorgensen, Ellwood	Center	217
55	Lady, George	Left Tackle	220
49	Love, Robert	End	180
44	McGinley, Francis	Left Guard	195
53	McNeish, Robert	Left Half	178
62	Matthews, Garland	Quarter	170
24	Mohler, Orville	Quarter	174
36	Morrison, Robert	Full	185
52	Norris, Neil	End	190
50	Packard, Dave	Right Tackle	205
27	Palmer, Fred	Right End	190
32	Plaehn, Al	Left Tackle	195
19	Reboin, Al	Quarter	170
51	Ridings, Eugene	Full	190
14	Rosenberg, Aaron	Left Guard	208
43	Seixas, John	Left End	175
26	Shannon, Kenneth	Half	179
48	Smith, Ernie	Right Tackle	212
47	Smith, Stanley	Left Guard	182
40	Sparling, Ray	Left End	180
34	Stevens, Lawrence	Right Guard	201
45	Tipton, Howard	Left Guard	185
13	Warburton, Irvine	Quarter	154
46	Williamson, Frank	Left Guard	192
59	Wilkins, Morton	Right Tackle	200
23	Wotkyns, Haskel	Quarter	167
35	Youel, Curtis	Center	191
	Ostling, Gerald	Tackle	190
	Bateman, Paul	Half	185

1933
CHAPTER 9

"DON'T TAKE YOUR HANDS OFF COTTON WARBURTON UNTIL THE REFEREE'S WHISTLE STOPS THE PLAY"
. . . Hunk Anderson, Notre Dame Coach, 1933

In 1933, Adolph Hitler was sworn in as chancellor of the Third Reich, and shortly thereafter in one of the first radio speeches ever beamed to the German people, he sold them on the idea that, "Private enterprise cannot be maintained in the age of democracy . . ." Then promptly and secretly set fire to the Reichstag to prove it. Any semblance of German democracy died in the ashes. The I. G. Farben and Krupp families were delighted and pledged Adolph their undying support. A dim-witted German communist was blamed for the fire and oddly enough, nearly everyone who knew anything about the fire died mysteriously (and conveniently) within a month. The flames from the burning Reichstag spread and engulfed most of Europe for the next twelve years.

In the United States, Franklin Delano Roosevelt, who had survived an assassination attempt earlier that year while president-elect, was serving his first term in the White House . . . and the New Deal had been dealt. It was a year of initials, the AAA, CCC, NRA, CWA, and the PWA, all organized by the government as a kind of alphabetical counterattack aimed to free the U.S. from the relentless grip of the depression.

That year, 6,000,000 piglets were slaughtered and buried, and thousands of acres of standing grain crops were burned in a vain attempt to bolster plummeting farm prices . . . yet in a land of such plenty, there were hungry children.

At no time in our history had the American Dream come so close to becoming a nightmare.

Nearly every day you could read about the exploits of a pair of small-time brigands named Bonnie and Clyde, or the daring of the Dillinger gang (in October of that year they robbed the police arsenal in Peru, Indiana, of enough weapons to start a small war, which they did), or of the cunning of that monument to maternal tenderness, Ma Barker, and her four charming sons.

But the human being is one of nature's toughest and most resilient creatures. Especially the American human being. Give him a little diversionary escape, and he can adapt to almost any situation. Even in a world of chaos, diversion abounded.

You could enter a dance marathon . . .

Or you could go to the movies. Bank Night was a good time to go, it cost only two bits and you might win a couple of hundred dollars or a set of dishes. Up on the screen (a) Gary Cooper, (b) William Boyd, (c) Richard Barthelmess, check one of the above, with the remnants of the Lafayette Escadrille would be attempting to adjust to civilian life by flying the mail through hurricanes. If you tired of "sheer murder sending mere boys up in crates like those," you could watch *Little Women*, or *Gold Diggers of 1933*, or King Kong carry Fay Wray through, or Mae West stalk Cary Grant through the bedroom, grunting her immortal invitation to, "Come up and see me sometime."

Or you could go to a football game.

"Hunk" Anderson in his last year as coach for Notre Dame

On November 25, 1933, 25,037 football fanatics jammed the gates at Notre Dame stadium and plunked down $73,000 to watch USC become the first team since 1908* to defeat the Irish in three consecutive meets. Obviously, not everyone was broke during the depression.

Led by All Americans Aaron Rosenberg at guard, and Cotton Warburton, the diminutive but explosive quarterback, the men of Troy again bearded the lion in his den, or the leprechaun in his own shamrock field, 19-0.

The first quarter could hardly be classified as a thriller. It developed into a kind of kicking duel with neither team making any serious penetration. The Irish showed surprising defensive strength, however, until Cotton Warburton came in in the second quarter. After that they needed more than strength. They needed a net. Or a shotgun. Birdshot would have done; Cotton weighed 147 and towered 5'6½", but he was speedy as a roadrunner and slippery as an eel. The Irish barely laid a hand on him all day.

As a result of the powerful passing and running attack the Trojans mounted in the second quarter, the outcome of the game was never in doubt. With Rosenberg opening gaping holes in the Irish line for fullback Haskell Wotkyns and Warburton, the Trojans moved out for a sustained 61-yard march to the Irish end zone. It was climaxed by Cotton's 35-yard run through a broken field, and capped by his three short plunges, the last from the three for the score. Larry Stevens made the point after good, and the Trojans led 7-0.

In the third quarter USC took to the air, with Bob McNeish hitting his receivers with deadly accuracy. The last one of the period was a short flat-zone pass to Homer Griffith who danced over standing up. Stevens fumbled the pass from center and was tackled attempting to run the ball in for the extra point.

Shortly before the final gun, Notre Dame made one more attempt to get back in the ball game. Andy Pilney, the Irish halfback, tried a long touchdown pass to Johnny Young, the other halfback, but Trojan halfback Cal Clemens intercepted and set up Warburton's final scoring play of the game. From the 29-yard line Cotton picked up 8, Julie Bescos lost 2 . . . Cliff Propst gained 9. Warburton then sliced to the 1-foot line and on the next play carried it over. Final score, 19-0, USC.

Before the game Hunk Anderson had instructed the Notre Dame team, "Don't take your hands off Warburton until the referee's whistle stops the play."

Even though the Trojans' 13-7 defeat by Stanford had cost them a shot at the Rose Bowl and their third national championship, the victory over Notre Dame was no less important. The series was now tied 4 and 4. True, it was not one of Notre Dame's strongest teams, but then as now, when the Fighting Irish meet the men of Troy, the gridiron becomes a battlefield with every inch bitterly contested.

Jesse C. Harper, athletic director of Notre Dame, and his counterpart from USC, Willis O. Hunter, announced after the game that series would be carried on through 1937, thus putting to rest rumors that the Trojans were planning to drop Notre Dame in favor of another Midwest opponent. The series would continue, but Coach Anderson wouldn't be around to see it.

No university in the world is more win oriented than the University of Notre Dame. They simply do not expect to lose, and they don't put up with it for long. That year they lost five, won three, and tied one, the first losing season since 1887. It was Hunk Anderson's worst year . . . and his last.

*Michigan seemed to have the early Notre Dame teams jinxed. From 1887 to 1908 the Wolverines defeated the Irish every time they met, a total of nine times! Once in 1888 on two consecutive days.

Irvine "Cotton" Warburton, USC All American

Wayne Millner, Notre Dame's first year end in 1933

OFFICIAL 1933 UNIVERSITY OF SOUTHERN CALIFORNIA FOOTBALL ROSTER

NO.	NAME	POSITION	AGE	WT.	HT.	NO.	NAME		AGE	WT.	HT.
12	Griffith, Homer	Q.B.	21	185	5'11"	36	Matthews, Robert	R.E.	20	173	6'1"
13	Warburton, Irvine	Q.B.	21	147	5'6½"	37	Bescos, Julius	L.E.	21	173	6'2"
14	Rosenberg, Aaron	L.G.	21	200	6'	38	Fuhrer, Bob	L.E.	21	183	6'2"
15	Hall, King	R.G.	21	215	6'	39	Beard, Francis	F.B.	23	185	5'9"
16	Bright, Kenneth	L.T.	21	201	6'	40	Larrabee, Duane	L.E.	18	177	6'
						41	Clark, Gordon	L.H.	23	178	5'10"
18	Clemons, Cal	R.H.	19	190	5'11"	42	Dye, John	C.	24	196	5'10"
19	Reboin, Al	L.H.	22	174	5'8"	43	Seixas, John	R.E.	23	172	5'9"
20	Cameron, Rod	F.B.	19	170	6'	44	McGinley, Francis	L.G.	21	196	5'11½"
21	Browning, Ward	L.E.	21	196	6'1"	45	Tatsch, Herbert	L.T.	21	205	6'2½"
23	Wotkyns, Haskell	F.B.	20	180	5'9"	46	Williamson, Frank	L.G.	21	190	5'11"
24	Howard, William	Q.B.	20	172	5'10"	47	Propst, Clifford	F.B.	20	190	5'11"
						53	McNeish, Robert	L.H.	21	185	5'10"
25	Erskine, Robert	L.T.	20	216	6'1½"	55	Lady, George	R.T.	21	220	6'3"
26	Shannon, Kenneth	R.H.	21	197	5'10"	56	Bardin, Oliver	R.T.	21	200	5'10"
27	Palmer, Ford (C)	R.E.	22	199	6'	57	Coughlin, Alvie	R.T.	21	214	6'2"
						59	Poulson, Alfred	C.	22	240	6'1½"
29	Hoy, Val	L.G.	18	182	5'9"	60	Burchard, Gerard	L.H.	21	185	5'10"
32	Dittberner, Art	C.	20	216	6'	61	Fay, Kenneth	R.H.	23	180	5'9"
33	Harper, Hueston	R.T.	23	215	6'1"	62	Matthews, Garland	Q.B.	22	172	5'10½"
						66	Ostling, Gerald	L.T.	21	195	6'
34	Stevens, Lawrence	R.G.	21	200	6'2"						
35	Youel, Curtis	C.	22	200	6'	67	Hurst, Joe	R.E.	19	190	6'

OFFICIAL 1933 UNIVERSITY OF NOTRE DAME FOOTBALL ROSTER

NO.	NAME	POSITION				NO.	NAME				
1	McFadden, Daniel T.	Q.B.	20	170	5'10"	42	Becker, Harry P.	R.T.	22	188	6'1"
2	Church, August J.	C.	19	160	5'7"	43	Fulnecky, Karl D.	R.G.	20	196	6'
3	Moriarty, George J.	Q.B.	20	150	5'8"	44	Peters, Martin J.	R.E.	20	187	6'2"
5	Harper, Mell C.	Q.B.	19	170	5'10"	45	Bonar, Reyman E.	Q.B.	21	170	5'8"
7	Beach, Joseph D.	R.H.	20	172	5'10"	46	Allen, Donald L.	R.E.	18	186	6'2"
9	Fromhart, Wallace L.	Q.B.	20	178	5'11"	47	Young, John R.	R.H.	21	177	6'1"
10	Alworth, Sam R.	Q.B.	20	172	5'11"	48	**Lukats, Nicholas P.	L.H.	22	185	6'
11	Layden, Francis L.	R.H.	20	179	6'1"	49	Scafati, Orlando M.	R.E.	20	194	6'1"
12	**Brancheau, Raymond J.	R.H.	23	190	5'11"	50	Miller, Stephen C.	F.B.	18	180	6'
13	Davis, Irwin V.	R.E.	19	177	5'11"	51	**Gorman, Thomas A.	C.	23	190	6'1"
17	*LaBorne, Frank H.	L.H.	23	165	5'11"	53	Thernes, Matthew J.	L.E.	19	189	6'1"
19	Canale, Frank S.	L.E.	22	190	6'	54	Carideo, Fred J., Jr.	F.B.	22	180	5'10"
20	*Rascher, Norbert H.	R.E.	22	184	6'1"	56	*Costello, Albert T.	R.H.	22	180	5'9"
21	Shamla, Richard J.	R.G.	20	188	5'10"	57	**Devore, Hugh J.	R.E.	22	179	6'
22	Ream, William E.	R.E.	20	190	6'2"	60	**Banas, Stephen P.	F.B.	23	185	5'11"
24	Caldwell, Edwin G.	Q.B.	22	163	5'9"	61	Solari, Fred C.	C.	20	198	6'2"
25	Weidner, Fred W.	R.G.	21	170	5'9"	63	Shakespeare, William V.	L.H.	20	179	5'11"
26	*Vairo, Dominic M.	L.E.	19	188	6'	68	**Pivarnik, Joseph J.	R.G.	21	195	5'9"
27	Smith, William R.	R.G.	20	173	5'10"	69	**Krause, Edward W.	L.T.	20	217	6'3"
28	Martin, James R.	R.G.	20	176	5'11"	71	*Schiralli, Rocco V.	L.G.	21	172	5'10"
29	Hagan, Lowell L.	F.B.	21	180	6'	73	Schrenker, Paul E.	R.G.	21	183	5'11"
31	*Hanley, Daniel J.	F.B.	22	188	6'2"	75	Dunn, Thomas J.	C.	19	201	6'2"
32	Pilney, Andy E.	L.H.	20	170	5'11"	76	Cronin, Arthur D., Jr.	R.T.	19	211	6'
33	*Tobin, John E.	R.H.	22	177	5'8"	77	Kopczak, Frank G.	R.T.	19	207	6'
34	**Leonard, James R.	L.G.	22	187	6'	78	Stilley, Kenneth L.	L.T.	20	210	6'1"
35	Gaul, Frank J.	Q.B.	19	167	5'10"	79	Sullivan, Joseph G.	R.T.	20	195	6'
36	McMahon, Joseph P.	L.G.	18	178	5'11"	80	Elser, Donald L.	F.B.	20	215	6'3"
37	Esser, Carl F.	L.T.	20	190	6'2"	81	*Roach, Thomas G.	R.T.	23	198	6'1"
38	Millner, Wayne V.	L.E.	21	189	6'1"	82	Katz, Arthur S. J.	L.T.	20	241	5'9"
39	Mazziotti, Anthony J.	Q.B.	19	190	5'7"	83	Michuta, John F.	R.T.	20	207	6'1"
40	Dunn, Edward R.	C.	19	190	5'11"	84	**Wunsch, Harry F.	L.G.	22	197	5'11"
41	Pojman, Henry F.	C.	19	188	6'						

1934
CHAPTER 10
. . . PLAY YOUR BEST TEN PLAYERS, AND YOUR BROTHER
Tom Layden . . . 1934

To the great surprise of almost no one, Notre Dame had a new coach in 1934. He was Elmer Layden, former Notre Dame fullback and one of the famous Four Horsemen in 1922, '23 and '24.

After graduation, Layden accepted a coaching position at Columbia College in Dubuque, Iowa. His success there caught the eye of the Holy Ghost fathers of Duquesne University in Pennsylvania, which was struggling along with a win percentage of less than 400%. From 1927 until 1933 Coach Layden raised that percentage to over 700%. In December of 1933, he left Duquesne to become athletic director and head football coach of the University of Notre Dame.

His first year as coach of the Irish was solid, but not sensational. At the time of the 1934 meeting with USC, Notre Dame stood 5-3-0. After losing their opener to Texas 6-7, they won the next three in a row, only to be stopped by Pittsburgh 19-0, and the following week by Navy 10-6. Elmer Layden wanted to win this game badly, and so did his team . . . The reasons were obvious.

The intersectional rivalry now stood at four games each. So this was a rubber game. Also, three Trojan wins in a row was irritating beyond belief to the proud Irish. Rumor has it that Michigan was taken off the Notre Dame schedule in 1910 for committing such mayhem.

Coach Layden did have a few things going for him on this ninth meeting, however. The Irish were coming off a two-game winning streak, and two of his most important players, All-American center Jack Robinson, and big George Melinkovich, who had been injured most of the season, returned to the line-up. Moreover, his two excellent halfbacks, Bill Shakespeare and Mike Layden* were both having a good year.

On the other hand, Howard Jones had very little going for him. He had won four, lost five, and had one tie . . . his two first string ends, Ward Browning and Leavitt Thurlow had broken legs, and nobody on the team was having a very good year.

With a loss to Notre Dame his record would be the worst of his career. "I don't know what we can do against Notre Dame," said the coach. "Some of the boys played very badly last Saturday. Those who look good on defense, look terrible on offense and vice versa. It is too late to do much changing, and even if I could, I don't know exactly what it would be."

Coach Jones probably worked harder that year than in any other season at Southern California. But in return his results had been the worst he had ever known. His team had shown very little offense, and almost no defense, and had been crushed by Stanford (VOW?) 16-0 in mid season. One game later they could score only two points against California. USC had been able to beat only one quality team . . . Oregon 33-0, and they were not quite certain how they did that.

Now the Trojans were facing what was considered to be the fastest team they had seen all year. Though Notre Dame's line was outweighed by eight pounds per man, they had the bigger team overall with an average weight of 191 pounds to USC's 188.

Mike Layden, younger brother of head coach Elmer Layden

*The coach's little brother. Actually at 6'1" and 178 pounds, he was the coach's bigger little brother.

Probably because of the poor record posted by Southern California and the so-so performance of Notre Dame, national . . . even local enthusiasm was lukewarm and the attendance reflected the lack of interest. Only 45,000 shivering fans braved the chill of the Coliseum on that December 8th, the smallest crowd in the nine year history of the series.

Led by William Valentine Shakespeare, who naturally could not escape being dubbed "The Bard of Football,"* and Mike Layden, Notre Dame trimmed the Trojans 14-0.

USC did get off to an impressive start, though, stopping Notre Dame's first offensive drive and capturing the ball on a fumble. They marched down to within field goal distance, but Cal Clements failed on an attempted placement, and that ended that.

After several punt exchanges had left the ball mid-field in possession of the Irish, Shakespeare fired a mighty pass from his own 40 yard line to Layden, who had streaked through the Trojans' secondary. Mike fielded the ball with little difficulty and rambled over the goal line with ease. The conversion by Wally Fromhart made it 7-0.

Again in the second period the Irish found themselves in their own territory on the 49 . . . three plays later it was on the 32. This time it was Wayne Millner who slipped behind the Trojan pass defenders. Shakespeare again unleashed one of his bombs, but this one was batted away by Cotton Warbur-

ton who had the play beautifully covered. Millner, however, in one of those impossible efforts, made a diving, stretching catch before the ball grounded on the two yard line. Once more Layden plunged into the end zone, and once more Wally Fromhart converted. Final score . . . 14-0.

Not content with scoring both touchdowns against the Trojans, big little brother Mike stopped the only scoring threat USC was able to put together. In the   quarter, after Warren Hull recovered a fumble, Warburton and Haskell Wotkyns moved it to the one yard line. On what looked like a sure scoring play, Wotkyns charged squarely into the line, met Layden, and dropped like a felled ox on the *one inch line!*

The 14-0 score doesn't really give an accurate picture of the quality of the game. USC had nothing to be ashamed of. The middle of the Irish line took a terrific pounding from Wotkyns, and Cotton Warburton, even though double covered, managed a 29-yard punt return and played a savage defensive game all afternoon. Warren Hull was a workhorse at tackle, alongside of him at right guard, Joe Preininger subbing for injured Bob Sanders, performed nobly . . . as did Gil Kuhn, Cal Clemens, and three graduating seniors, Captain Julius Becos, Herb Tatsch, and Hueston Harper. The entire Trojan line played excellent football, but Notre Dame was just too much for them on that day.

Captain Dominic Vairo and Wayne Millner played bril-

USC's "Cotton" Warburton is stopped by Don Elsner

*Even though he had nearly flunked English that year.

liantly on the wings for the Irish . . . USC could gain no ground on end runs. Joe Sullivan, who was playing his last game*, was a standout at tackle . . . and who knows what the Irish might have done had not George Melinkovich been forced to sit out most of the game. But then if big George had been well, Mike Layden probably would not have played, and for USC he was one Layden too many.

Coach Elmer's father, who used to drop in on Notre Dame practice sessions from time to time, was always free with his advice. One of his best tips was, "Elmer, if you want a winning team, play your best ten players . . . and your brother."

The last few games before the SC-Notre Dame clash Coach Jones, out of desperation, had experimented with inserting more sophomores and juniors in the lineup, and with some success. That must have worried Layden a little. At any rate, he decided to launch a little propaganda campaign.

"We'll be lucky to stay in that football game," he cried. Even the press bought the story. When the team train stopped in Tucson for its last pre-game drill, the Los Angeles Times headlined, "The Cripples Arrive in Tucson."

"You boys sure have that right," wailed Layden. "Even our train is limping."

Rockne would have been proud.

USC's "Cotton" Warburton and Dave Davis

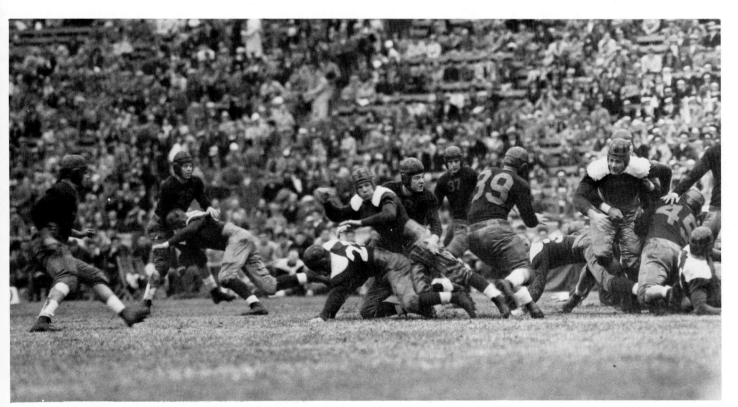

No gain for Notre Dame's Andy Pilney

*Sullivan was named captain of the 1935 team, but died of pneumonia before the season started. He was 19.

UNIVERSITY OF NOTRE DAME — 1934

NO.	NAME	POSITION	WEIGHT	HEIGHT		NO.	NAME			
10	Alworth, Samuel	Quarter	175	5'11"		50	Miller, Steve	Full	180	6'
42	Becker, Harry	Tackle	188	6'1"		38	Millner, Wayne	End	185	6'
1	Bonar, Reyman	Quarter	170	5'8"		3	Moriarty, George	Quarter	150	5'8"
8	Bruno, William	Quarter	175	5'8"		68	Mundee, Fred	Center	190	6'1"
2	Caldwell, George	Quarter	165	5'9"		58	Peters, Martin	End	187	6'2"
15	Canale, Fran	End	190	6'		70	Pfefferle, Richard	Tackle	195	6'2"
54	Carideo, Fred	Full	187	5'10"		32	Pilney, Andy	Half	170	5'10"
18	Church, August	Guard	159	5'7"		51	Pojman, Henry	Center	192	6'
56	Costello, Albert	Half	185	5'10"		76	Robinson, John	Center	200	6'3"
74	Cronin, Arthur	Tackle	201	6'		71	Schiralli, Rocco	Guard	170	5'9"
81	Danbom, Laurence	Full	188	6'		45	Schrenker, Paul	Guard	190	5'11"
29	Davis, Irwin	End	175	5'11"		63	Shakespeare, William	Half	180	5'11"
80	Elser, Don	Full	215	6'2"		21	Shamla, Richard	Guard	183	5'10"
9	Fromhart, Wallace	Quarter	180	5'10"		27	Smith, William	Guard	170	5'10"
5	Gaul, Francis	Quarter	170	5'10"		61	Solari, Fred	Center	205	6'2"
31	Hanley, Daniel	Half	188	6'2"		69	Steinkemper, William	Tackle	215	6'1"
67	Kopczak, Frank	Tackle	196	6'		78	Stilley, Kenneth	Tackle	209	6'1"
72	Lauter, John	Guard	190	6'1"		79	Sullivan, Joseph	Tackle	210	6'
11	Layden, Francis	Half	178	6'1"		53	Thernes, Matthew	End	190	6'1"
64	Martin, James	Guard	188	5'11"		52	Vairo; Dominic (Capt.)	End	196	6'2"
33	Mazziotti, Anthony	Half	190	5'8"		25	Weidner, Fred	Guard	170	5'9"
30	Melinkovich, George	Half	180	6'		12	Wilke, Robert	Half	170	6'
83	Michuta, John	Tackle	207	6'1"		19	Wojcihovski, Victor	Half	182	6'

UNIV. OF SOUTHERN CALIF. — 1934

NO.	NAME	POSITION	WEIGHT	HEIGHT		NO.	NAME			
39	Beard, Francis	L. Guard	185	5'9"		59	Kuhn, Gilbert	Center	190	6'
70	Beatty, Homer	R. Half	184	6'1"		55	Lady, George	R. Guard	222	6'3"
71	Belko, Max	L. Half	192	5'11"		58	Lynch, Ford	Full	175	5'10"
37	Bescos, Julius (c)	L. End	175	6'2"		44	McGinley, Francis	L. Guard	196	5'11½"
49	Bishop, Eames	L. Half	180	5'11"		53	McNeish, George	Center	204	6'3"
61	Brown, George	L. Guard	185	5'11"		62	Matthews, Garland	Quarter	172	5'10½"
21	Browning, Ward	R. End	196	6'1"		36	Matthews, Robert	R. End	173	6'1"
60	Burchard, Gerard	R. Half	197	5'10"		66	Ostling, Gerald	R. End	195	6'
76	Busby, Marvin	R. End	201	6'3"		75	Powers, Russell	L. Guard	187	5'11"
20	Cameron, Rod	Quarter	170	6'		51	Preininger, Joseph	R. Guard	196	6'
18	Clemons, Cal	R. Half	192	5'11"		47	Propst, Clifford	Full	183	5'11"
57	Coughlin, Alvin	R. End	214	6'2"		19	Reboin, Alvin	L. Half	175	5'8"
27	Davis, David	Quarter	166	5'8"		12	Rogers, Hugh	Center	200	5'10"
72	DeHetre, John	Center	185	5'10"		64	Rorison, James	R. Tackle	215	6'3½"
32	Dittberner, Arthur	R. Guard	216	6'		25	Sanders, Robert	R. Guard	190	5'11"
50	Dunaway, Warren	End	175	5'11"		42	Smith, Bob	Full	195	6'
38	Fuhrer, Robert	L. End	180	6'2"		46	Sutherland, James	L. Half	169	5'10"
41	Gill, Bill	L. End	172	6'2"		45	Tatsch, Herbert	L. Tackle	205	6'2½"
15	Hall, King	Center	215	6'		68	Thurlow, Leavitt	L. End	187	6'
33	Harper, Hueston	R. Tackle	215	6'1"		13	Wharburton, Irvine	Quarter	148	5'6½"
24	Howard, William	Quarter	172	5'10"		54	Webb, James	R. Half	178	5'10"
67	Hull, Warren	L. Tackle	224	6'4"		73	Wilensky, Joe	L. Guard	190	5'8"
35	Jorgenson, Ellwood	Center	224	6'		65	Williams, Marshall	Tackle	195	6'
26	Kidder, Allan	L. Half	170	5'11"		29	Wing, Paul	R. Half	184	5'10"
16	Kovac, Peter	R. Guard	205	5'11"		23	Wotkyns, Haskell	Full	175	5'9"

1935
CHAPTER 11

". . . CAUSES MORE TORTURE THAN ANY OTHER GAME EXCEPT RUSSIAN ROULETTE"
. . . Anon. 1935

1935 was a lousy year for almost everybody. The country was still wallowing in the depths of the depression. The Democrats were still blaming the Republicans for the economic collapse of the United States and the Republicans were still accusing the Democrats of weakening the moral fibre of America by organizing the WPA*. Franklin D. Roosevelt asked Congress to enact the Social Security Law and the conservatives were outraged, claiming it would undermine the great American virtues of independence and self-reliance. Senator Harry Moore of New Jersey was of the opinion that it would, "Take all the romance out of life." (Of course, he was under 65, and still working.) Southerners were worried that it might threaten a system that provided them with cheap, almost slave labor in the cotton and sugar fields. And the followers of Dr. Francis Townsend, a retired Long Beach physician who became the self-appointed guardian of the aged, were upset because the Social Security Law provided much less than the $200.00 a month they thought was necessary.

1935 was also a lousy year for Coach Howard Jones and the Trojans of Southern California. After an opening win against Montana 9-0 and followed by a 19-0 victory over the College of the Pacific, they had gone winless in four consecutive games. Stanford shut them out 3-0, Illinois shut them out 19-0, California crushed them 21-7, and they lost to Oregon State 13-7. Not very impressive. They did, however, manage a 20-0 win over Washington State the week before the Notre Dame game, so riding the crest of a one game winning streak, the Trojans invaded South Bend to do battle with one of Coach Elmer Layden's best teams.

Notre Dame had also won its opener, but it was able to sustain a winning season. After they downed Kansas 28-7, they pulled off what many sportswriters called the comeback win of the decade, when they scored two touchdowns in the last two minutes to upset a powerful Ohio State team, 18-13. The Irish had logged one loss, to Northwestern 14-7, and one tie, Army 6-6.

When the two teams met in Notre Dame stadium on November 23rd things seemed to be looking up for the Trojans . . . at least for a time. After only a few minutes of play, Irish fullback Don Elser fumbled and Trojan fullback Cliff Propst

William Shakespeare led Irish to victory in 1935 with his passing

recovered. Three quick plays later, quarterback Dave Davis drove over from the 6-yard line to score. The point after attempt was blocked . . . the Trojans led 6-0. Toward the end of the first period, halfback Owen Hansen recovered an Irish fumble on the Notre Dame 18, but two plays later Propst fumbled and right end Martin Peters fell on the ball for the Irish. Again in the second quarter, a fumble ruined a Trojan chance to score. After SC guard Ed Shuey blocked Bob Wilke's punt, Max Belko recovered for the Trojans, but Davis fumbled on the next play and lost the ball to Notre Dame.

At this point both coaches were probably wondering why some enterprising student of the game hadn't invented a football with a fold-out handle.

The half ended with USC holding on to a tenuous 6-0 lead.

The Notre Dame offensive machine meshed into gear early in the third period. Wally Fromhart, the 22-year-old Irish quarterback who was playing his last game, played it brilliantly. He wiped out the slim Trojan lead almost singlehandedly, first with a leaping catch of Bill Shakespeare's 40 yard pass to score 6, then moments later, fired a 53-yard pass to big Wayne Miller in the end zone for a second touchdown. He also made both conversions.

The Trojans, however, were not quite ready to roll over and play dead. A perfect pass from quarterback Glenn Thompson on the Irish 27 to right end Chuck Williams on the 3, set the stage for USC's last tally of the day. Three plays later, Thompson plunged over . . . Homer Beatty converted and the score was 14-13, Notre Dame.

No one could ever accuse the 1935 Trojans of being quitters. They were still fighting to stay in the ball game when up jumped the devil one more time in the form of Wally Fromhart. Obviously he didn't want the Trojans to forget his last game. He intercepted a Thompson pass on his own 10-yard line and raced 82 yards to the 8-yard line of Southern California. That just about iced the game. On the next play Bill Shakespeare raced around his own left end and crossed the goal line standing up. The final score, Notre Dame 20, USC 13.

So far it had been Howard Jones' most disastrous year at USC with 3 wins and 5 losses. At this point, Howard probably agreed with the coach who once observed, "This game of football causes more torture than any other game except Russian Roulette."

So what do you do when it becomes apparent that you're going to have a cataclysmic season? Well, if you're smart and have time, schedule a couple of teams you have a pretty good chance to beat. So USC, now with 3 wins and 7 losses, loaded the Thundering Herd on the good ship Malolo and took off for Hawaii. Good thinking.

They beat the University of Hawaii 38-6, and Kamehameha 33-7, and ended the season winning 5 and losing 7.

Mike Layden, Notre Dame back, breaks for 5 yard gain in second quarter of 1935 game.

Notre Dame's Andy Pilney is caught from behind

Nick Pappas, now an associate athletic director at USC was a 19 year old, 166 pound quarterback on his first trip to South Bend

OFFICIAL 1935 UNIVERSITY OF NOTRE DAME FOOTBALL ROSTER

NO.	NAME	POSITION						
1	Puplis, Andrew J.	Q.B.	29	Clifford, Jeremiah J.	L.E.	57	Levicki, John J.	R.
2	McKenna, James A.	Q.B.	30	Kovalcik, George J.	L.H.	58	**Peters, Martin J.	R.
3	Moriarty, George J.	Q.B.	31	Darcy, John F.	L.H.	59	Connor, Joseph G.	R.
4	Megin, Bernard E.	Q.B.	32	**Pilney, Andy J.	L.H.	60	Winsouer, Paul V.	C.
5	**Gaul, Francis J.	Q.B.	33	**Mazziotti, Anthony J.	R.H.	61	*Solari, Fred C.	C.
6	Gleason, Joseph T.	Q.B.	34	Zenner, Elmer John	R.G.	62	Marshall, Walter Michael	R.
7	O'Reilly, Charles W.	Q.B.	35	McCarthy, Wm. P.	R.E.	63	**Shakespeare, Wm. V.	L.
8	Bruno, Wm. B.	Q.B.	36	McMahon, Joseph P.	L.G.	64	Martin, James R.	L.
9	*Fromhart, Wallace L.	Q.B.	37	Jackowski, Ralph George	R.H.	65	Kelly, John G.	R.
11	*Layden, Francis L.	R.H.	38	**Millner, Wayne Vernal	L.E.	66	Murphy, John P.	R.
12	Wilke, Robert E.	L.H.	39	McCarthy, Jack G.	L.H.	67	Kopczak, Frank Gregory	R.
14	Marr, John H.	R.E.	40	Dunn, Edward R.	C.	68	Mundee, Fred W.	C.
15	Crotty, Irwin P.	R.H.	41	McCarty, Patrick F.	C.	69	*Steinkemper, Wm. J.	L.
16	Zwers, Joseph B.	R.E.	42	*Becker, Harry P.	R.G.	70	**Pfefferle, Richard J.	L.
17	Schloemer, Bertrand A.	L.E.	43	DiMatteo, Jos. A.	F.B.	71	Race, Adrian J.	R.
18	*Church, August J.	L.G.	44	Van Wagner, Gerard J.	L.H.	72	*Lautar, John P.	L.
19	Wojcihovski, Victor J.	R.H.	45	Emanuel, Dennis G.	L.T.	73	Ruetz, Joseph Hubert	L.
20	McCormick, Nevin F.	R.H.	47	Sweeney, Charles A.	R.E.	74	Cronin, Arthur D., Jr.	R.
21	Psik, Paul R.	R.G.	48	O'Neill, Jos. I., Jr.	L.E.	75	Fogel, John N.	C.
22	Borowski, Chas. C.	L.H.	49	Schilling, Jos. V.	R.T.	78	*Stilley, Kenneth Leonard	L.T.
23	McGrath, Robert A.	F.B.	50	*Miller, Stephen C.	F.B.	79	Schwartz, Wm. S.	R.
24	Hickey, Louis J.	L.E.	51	*Pojman, Henry F.	C.	80	**Elser, Donald L.	F.
25	Chanowicz, Stanley J.	R.T.	52	Skoglund, Leonard Howard	L.E.	81	Danbom, Laurence E.	F.
26	Hack, James Gorman	L.G.	53	*Thernes, Matthew J.	L.T.	82	Belden, Wm. H.	R.
27	Elliott, Francis J.	R.E.	54	**Carideo, Fred J., Jr.	F.B.	83	**Michuta, John Francis	R.
28	Arboit, Ennio B.	R.H.	55	Snell, Edward W.	L.H.	84	Foster, Harvey G.	L.
			56	Kuharich, Jos. L.	R.G.			

OFFICIAL 1935 UNIVERSITY OF SOUTHERN CALIFORNIA FOOTBALL ROSTER

NO.	NAME	POSITION						
12	Shuey, Edward	L.G.	38	Bettinger, George	R.E.	61	Brown, George E.	R.
15	Hall, King	L.G.	39	Pappas, Nick M.	Q.B.	62	Hibbs, Gene	L.
16	Rose, Mason	F.B.	44	Roberts, Gene	R.T.			
18	Keller, Theron	F.B.	45	Henderson, James	R.E.	64	*Rorison, James A.	L.
20	Cameron, Roderick	Q.B.	46	Sutherland, James	L.H.	65	Lund, Robert	L.
21	Hansen, Owen	L.H.	47	**Propst, Clifford M.	F.B.			
			49	Clark, Jack	R.H.	66	Ostoich, Yube	R.
24	**Howard, William N.	F.B.	50	Gaisford, William	L.E.	67	*Hull, W. Bruce	R.
			51	Preininger, Joseph	L.G.	68	Thurlow, Leavitt	L.
25	*Sanders, Robert H.	L.G.	52	Radovich, William	C.	70	Beatty, Homer	R.
26	*Kidder, Allen	L.H.	53	McNeish, George	C.	71	*Belko, Max	L.
27	*Davis, David R.	Q.B.	54	Busby, Marvin	R.T.	72	DeHetre, John P.	C.
29	Wing, Paul	F.B.	55	Kimmerle, Howard	L.E.	73	Wilensky, Joseph	R.
31	Brosseau, Raphael	R.G.	56	Jesse, John	L.H.	76	MacMoore, Robert	R.
32	**Dittberner, Arthur	R.T.	57	Langley, Laurence	R.H.	77	Reed, Robert	C.
33	Williams, Charles	R.E.				78	Rodeen, Donald	L.
35	**Jorgensen, Ellwood	C.	58	Lynch, Ford F.	F.B.	80	Gill, William J.	L.
36	Brown, Ray	L.T.	59	*Kuhn, Gilbert	C.	81	Troxel, William	Q
37	Thompson, Glenn	Q.B.	60	Burchard, Gerard	L.H.			

1936
CHAPTER 12

"WE WERE LUCKY, VERY LUCKY"
. . . Howard Jones, 1936

By the tenth anniversary of the Notre Dame-Southern California football rivalry, several things regarding the series had become abundantly clear. One was that it had indeed become a rivalry in every sense of the word. Regardless of the kind of season either team had, they always seemed to be "up" for each other. Every contest was hard fought with no quarter asked, or given. There had been very few mis-matches, as evidenced by the series standing in 1936 . . . Notre Dame 6 games, USC 4.

Another thing about which Gwynn Wilson and the far-sighted Harold Stonier had been correct was the interest generated by the series. So far, 576,000 football fans had paid over $2,600,000 to see both teams in action, and SC was now recognized as a football power to reckon with.

This year, however, Coach Howard Jones was still having his troubles. He and his team hoped and expected to regain their national prestige after a two year slump. Especially after crushing their first three opponents, including a strong Illinois team 24-6, and playing Washington State to a tie. They then beat Stanford 14-7 and the future looked bright for the Thundering Herd. But the stampede slowed to a walk and was finally stopped by California, then Washington and the Bruins of UCLA held them to a tie.

Now the Fighting Irish of Notre Dame were coming to town favored by 20 points. They had lost only two, one to number one ranked Pittsburgh . . . the other to a very tough Navy team. No one gave the Trojans much of a chance against the stronger Notre Dame. There were 30,000 empty seats in the Los Angeles Coliseum that mild December day, but the 70,000 who were there saw a game they'll never forget. The battle was one of those thrillers for which the Notre Dame-Southern California game has since become famous.

As predicted, Notre Dame attacked like Genghis Khan and the Golden Horde. The Irish took the opening kickoff and needed only 11 plays to reach the USC three yard line. Quarterback Andy Puplis gave to halfback Bob Wilke, who had been responsible for 71 yards of the 87 yard drive (with some help from the other halfback Nevin McCormick who caught his 40-yard pass on 3rd and 4). Wilke started right, then cut swiftly left and dove over center for the first score. The conversion attempt by Puplis was blocked by Jim Henderson of SC and Notre Dame led 6-0.

In the second quarter, Notre Dame substituted an entire new team and within minutes they were knocking at the gates of Troy. With Joe Ruetz at quarter and Vic Wojchihovski, Jack McCarthy and Steve Miller in the backfield, the Irish pounded to the Trojan 15, where Captain Gil Kuhn of USC bobbed up to intercept a McCarthy pass and run it back to the 25-yard line of Southern California. Then on second down, Ambrose Schindler tore through center for 11 yards, twisting and fighting off Notre Dame tacklers. After three Irishmen finally nailed him, Schindler heard Dick Berryman out and to the left yelling for a lateral. Someway Schindler got rid of the ball, either by throwing it or fumbling it . . . at any rate, as it bounced crazily over the turf, Berryman managed to scoop it up and without losing stride managed to race 65 yards downfield with nearly half the Notre Dame team in futile pursuit. The rest of the Irish apparently thought the play had stopped when Schindler was caught, and gave up the chase. Some of the fans thought it was a forward rather than a lateral pass, but the officials judged it a lateral or a fumble . . . a moot point, and there was no dispute on the play. Henderson missed the extra point and the score was tied 6-6.

"When I was trapped," Schindler said later, "I heard Berryman yelling at me to lateral the ball to him. Just as I was about to toss it, a Notre Dame player grabbed my arm as I kind of shoved the ball. It took one bounce and Dick got it and ran for the touchdown."

So the officials were correct in either sense . . . it was what you might call a "fumblateral."

Late in the second quarter Notre Dame once again began to flex their muscles and bullied USC all over the field. Coach Layden had his first team on the field and was determined to score another touchdown before halftime. On first down from the 9 yard line, Wilke fired a pass intended for Puplis. It never reached him. USC defender Bud Langley ambled up from behind the goal line and picked off the pass at the 4 yard line. With an open field ahead of him, Langley, not the fastest halfback on the team, started plodding toward the Notre Dame goal line. At mid-field he seemed to be jogging in place, when out of nowhere streaked Notre Dame fullback Larry Danbom, gaining ground with every step. There was no way Bud could escape.

But help sometimes comes at the most unexpected times

Grenville Landsdell, USC Quarterback is stopped for no gain

1937
CHAPTER 13
". . . GOLDBERG OF NOTRE DAME"
. . . Unknown Motion Picture Producer . . . 1935

Even though Coach Elmer Layden was hampered by new and stricter recruitment rules and eligibility requirements, it was quickly noted that he had brought back to Notre Dame football the dash, verve and elan that had made them champions. The famed "Fighting Irish" spirit, which had somewhat disintegrated since Rockne's death, had returned.

This year they were having another good season . . . not great, but good. It might have been much better. If Notre Dame had been successful in recruiting Marshall ("Biggie") Goldberg, and had been able to put down a last ditch uprising by Carnegie Tech, they probably would have been ranked close to the top. Marshall Goldberg did come to Notre Dame, but as a star halfback for Pitt in 1937, when he ran rampant over the Irish . . . leading his team to a 21-6 victory. Then Carnegie Tech upset Notre Dame so they were meeting USC in their own stadium ranked number 9 in the nation with a 5-2-1 record.

The hapless Trojans, and hapless they were indeed, arrived in South Bend, 20 point underdogs.

Coach Jones, operating under personal, as well as professional strain, just couldn't get lucky. Although he seemed to be working harder than ever, he couldn't turn SC's football fortunes around. He juggled the players and the plays. He tried fielding varsity veterans, then tried starting sophomores. Nothing worked.

To make matters worse, Jones appeared in half empty Notre Dame stadium to do battle minus four starters: quarterbacks Ambrose Schindler and Nick Pappas, halfback Mickey Anderson, and tackle Phil Gaspar. Due probably to USC's dismal record and the depression economy, only 28,920 showed up for the game . . . the lowest attendance in the fifty year history of the USC-Notre Dame series.

But football coaches are like gamblers . . . they never give up. Howard Jones and the Thundering Herd were determined to end the season on a winning note by first beating Notre Dame, then their crosstown rivals, UCLA. For a time it looked as though they might get past Notre Dame. They completely dominated the first two quarters and went to the locker room ahead 6-0 at the half.

One of the main reasons was Grenville Lansdell who started at quarterback for injured Schindler. He turned out to be one of Howard Jones' few pleasant surprises that season. During the first half he did just about everything . . . passing, punting, running and driving the SC offensive down to the Notre Dame 9 early in the second quarter. On second down fullback Bill Sangster gained two. Goal to go on the 7 yard line. Lansdell then passed to Gene Hibbs on the left flank. Hibbs took it on the one yard line and danced easily into the end zone for a touchdown. Bob Hoffman missed the extra point, but the Trojans led 6-0.

At halftime the University of Notre Dame staged a ceremony celebrating their fifty years of football. Some of the enthusiasm of the crowd must have filtered into the locker room, because a fired up Irish team took the field in the second half and scored in both final stanzas.

Late in the third period, the Irish managed to spring little Andy Puplis into the open and the fleet signal caller raced 58 yards for the tying touchdown. The extra point was missed, but the teams were now tied 6-6, and the Irishmen were staging a never-say-die comeback.

During the closing period both SC and Notre Dame had scoring chances. It was still anybody's game in what was beginning to resemble a pier nine brawl with time outs.

It took Mario George Tonelli of the Irish to provide the spark which broke the tie and again send the Notre Dame rooters home from an SC game happy. After halting a Trojan drive on their own 20, the Irish called on fullback Tonelli. He was up to the challenge. He dove through the SC line at left tackle, cut back to his right and took off for what looked like a sure touchdown run through the secondary while the surprised defenders stood and watched. Varsity sprinter Mario George was leaving them for dead. Then out of nowhere shot Trojan halfback Owen Hansen . . . *varsity shot putter Owen Hansen!* Hansen hurled himself at Tonelli's flying feet in one last burst of energy and brought him down on the USC 13 yard line. But Tonelli's spectacular run had so fired up the Irish line that on the next play they opened a hole over left tackle for him and he had little trouble driving in from the 8 yard line . . . the extra point was good and that's the way it ended.

For the Los Angeles Times, sportswriter Braven Dyer wrote his lead. "Fighting like wildcats in one of the fiercest struggles this colorful rivalry has ever produced, the Trojans were beaten here this afternoon, 13-6 . . . it was a savage battle . . ."

The Trojan team naturally was disappointed. They were well aware of some of Jones' personal problems and as team captain Charles Williams said after the game, "We dedicated the game to Coach Jones . . . we fought our hearts out to win that one for him."

USC managed to beat UCLA 19-13 in their last game of the season, ending up with a mediocre record of 4-4-2. Notre Dame *wound up 6-2-1, and Pitt with Marshall Goldberg was named the mythical national champions of 1937. The story went around that Notre Dame lost out on Goldberg because students at that time were expected to attend morning Mass in the campus chapel, and Marshall, who was Jewish, didn't care much for the idea. The real reason probably was that because of Father O'Hara's strict rules on recruiting, no representative of Notre Dame ever called on Goldberg. Prospects were expected to present themselves at the South Bend campus. Goldberg, who lived in Elkins, West Virginia, declined. Anyhow, the real loser was undoubtedly the movie-going public. A motion picture producer who was also a rabid Fighting Irish fan had promised that if Goldberg would matriculate at Notre Dame, he would produce a picture starring the great halfback. When Marshall decided to go to Pitt, the American movie fan was forever robbed of seeing this epic already entitled, Goldberg of Notre Dame.*

Mario Tonelli, Notre Dame fullback breaks loose for long gain

Gene Hibbs scores 6 points for Troy

USC's Grenny Landsdell is stopped after breaking into the clear

Notre Dame's starting eleven for 1937

OFFICIAL 1937 NOTRE DAME FOOTBALL ROSTER

NO.	NAME	POSITION		NO.	NAME	POSITION		NO.	NAME	POSITION
1	*Puplis, Andrew J.	Q.B.		30	*Kovalcik, George J.	R.H.		57	Arboit, Peter S.	L.E.
2	Crowe, Emmett H.	Q.B.		31	Kennedy, Maurice J.	L.H.		58	Tonelli, Mario G.	F.B.
3	Hofer, Willard C.	Q.B.		32	Stevenson, Harry, Jr.	L.H.		59	McGoldrick, James J.	L.G.
4	Kelleher, John C.	Q.B.		33	Thesing, Joseph R.	F.B.		60	Adamonis, Stanley C.	C.
7	*O'Reilly, Charles Wm.	Q.B.		34	Mandjiak, Michael	R.H.		61	Mulcahey, James L.	R.G.
8	Sitko, Steve Joseph	Q.B.		35	Brennan, Thomas J.	L.E.		62	*Marshall, Walter M.	R.G.
9	Archer, Clyde W.	Q.B.		36	Karr, James J.	L.G.		63	Saffa, Farris P.	L.H.
10	Fitzgerald, Raymond C.	R.G.		37	Fox, Harry F.	R.G.		64	Albert, Francis J., Jr.	R.T.
11	**Gleason, Joseph T.	R.H.		38	O'Loughlin, William A.	L.E.		65	Kelly, John G.	R.E.
12	Sheridan, Benjamin M.	L.H.		39	*McCarthy, Jack G.	L.H.		66	*Murphy, John P.	R.E.
13	Sullivan, John E.	L.H.		40	Burnell, Herman J.	L.H.		67	Brew, Francis J.	L.T.
14	Borer, Harold W.	R.H.		41	*McCarty, Patrick F.	C.		68	McIntyre, John A.	C.
15	McMahon, John E.	L.H.		42	Kerr, William H.	L.E.		69	**Ruetz, Joseph H.	L.G.
16	**Zwers, Joseph B. (C)	R.E.		43	Sullivan, Robert E.	R.E.		70	Harvey, Thaddeus H.	L.T.
17	Bossu, August F.	L.G.		44	Morrison, Paul E.	R.H.		71	Race, Adrian J.	R.G.
18	Kelly, John F.	R.E.		45	Emanuel, Dennis G.	L.T.		72	McDonaough, Joseph J.	R.T.
19	Tuck, Frank S.	L.H.		46	Lynn, Bradley N.	R.H.		73	*Beinor, Joseph E.	L.T.
20	*McCormick, Nevin F.	R.H.		47	*Sweeney, Charles A.	R.E.		74	O'Neill, Robert F.	L.T.
21	Finneran, John C.	C.		48	Sullivan, Daniel F.	R.H.		75	Fogel, John N.	C.
22	Borowski, Charles C.	L.H.		49	Gottsacker, Harold A.	F.B.		76	Ely, Eugene J.	L.T.
23	Zontini, Louis R.	L.H.		50	Riffle, Charles F.	F.B.		78	*Kell, Paul E.	R.T.
24	Biagi, Frank W.	L.E.		51	Longhi, Edward J.	C.		79	Binkowski, Benedict F.	F.B.
25	Brown, Earl M., Jr.	L.E.		52	*Skoglund, Leonard H.	L.E.		80	*Simonich, Edward F.	F.B.
26	Corgan, Michael H.	R.H.		53	Broscoe, Edward M.	R.E.		81	Mooney, Alan B.	F.B.
27	Zuendel, Joseph C.	L.G.		54	Hollendoner, Francis J.	R.T.		82	Shellogg, Frederick R.	L.T.
28	Arboit, Ennio B.	R.H.		55	DeFranco, Joseph F.	L.G.		83	*Shellogg, Alec R.	R.T.
29	Clifford, Jeremiah J.	L.E.		56	**Kuharich, Joseph L.	R.G.		84	Foster, Harvey G.	L.G.

OFFICIAL 1937 SOUTHERN CALIFORNIA FOOTBALL ROSTER

NO.	NAME	POSITION		NO.	NAME	POSITION		NO.	NAME	POSITION
15	*Berryman, Dick	Fullback		37	Coleman, William	Left End		57	Utman, Leon	Left Guard
16	Atanasoff, Alex	Center		38	Harmon, Bill	Right Guard		58	Sasaki, Henry	Quarterback
19	Day, Oliver	Fullback		39	*Pappas, Nick	Quarterback		60	*Russell, Lyman	Right Halfback
21	**Hansen, Owen	Left Halfback		40	Nave, Doyle	Quarterback		62	**Hibbs, Gene	Left End
23	Galvin, Glen	Left Halfback		41	*Peccianti, Angelo	Fullback		68	Thomassin, John	Left Guard
24	*Schindler, Ambrose	Quarterback		42	*Tonelli, Amerigo	Center		64	Carpenter, Kenneth	Left Tackle
25	Anderson, William	Right Halfback		43	Stevenson, Ed	Left Halfback		66	*Wehba, Ray	Left Guard
27	Sangster, William	Fullback		44	Gaspar, Phillip	Right Tackle		67	Moore, Casey	Left Tackle
28	*George, Ray	Right Tackle		45	Hoffman, Robert	Left Halfback		68	Stoecker, Howard	Left Tackle
29	Keller, Don	Fullback		47	*McNeil, Don	Left Tackle		70	Smith, Harry	Right Guard
31	**Brosseau, Raphael	Left Guard		49	Engle, Roy	Fullback		71	Shell, Joseph	Right Halfback
32	*Jones, James	Quarterback		50	Fisk, William	Left End		72	DeHetre, John	Center
33	**Williams, Charles (C)	Right End		52	*Radovich, William	Right Guard		73	Winslow, Robert	Right End
34	*Halvorsen, Ray	Left Guard		53	Slatter, James	Right End		75	*Norton, Miles	Right Guard
35	Morgan, Boyd	Right Halfback		54	Noor, Dennis	Left End		77	Reed, Robert	Center
36	Stanley, Ralph	Right End		56	Jesse, John	Left Halfback		78	Landsdell, Grenville	Quarterback
								79	Fisher, Robert	Right Tackle

1938
CHAPTER 14
"THE FOUR HORSEMEN, FAMINE, PESTILENCE, DEATH AND BUTTERFINGERS"
. . . Peter Arno, 1967

Alabama beat them 19-7 in the opening game and Washington upset them 7-6, but the Trojan football team was coming back. After four losing seasons in a row, Coach Jones had brought his team to what was considered by all to be the best since the National Champs of 1931.

The week before meeting Notre Dame in Los Angeles, the Trojans had defeated UCLA 42-7 and clinched their first Rose Bowl bid in six seasons. They were to meet undefeated, untied Duke.

But before they saw Duke, the Trojans had to meet another undefeated, untied team.

Notre Dame.

Coach Layden had brought the Irish the number 1 ranking in the country for the first time since the days of Knute Rockne.

Notre Dame had so dominated their opponents that only Northwestern had gotten close. The Irish had pulled out a 9-7 victory. Every other team had fallen, and fallen hard; Kansas 52-0, Army 19-7, Navy 15-0, and the school's 300th victory, Minnesota 19-0. Defense was the Irish game. They had allowed only 39 points to eight opponents.

Despite his team's great record, Layden was concerned by his lack of backfield speed. His anxiety increased when star halfback Ben Sheridan was injured in the team's stopover at Tucson, Arizona, and went from starter to doubtful.

More than 104,000 people, a Coliseum record, showed up on a mild sunny day to watch the two teams battle for what could possibly mean a National Championship for the winner.

Layden's fears about the slowness of his backfield were further augmented when in the first quarter starting fullback Joe

USC's Oliver Day breaks through Notre Dame line for good gain

Thesing had to leave the game with an injured ankle. Ben Sheridan was next. Try as he might, the left halfback could not last out the first quarter and had to be removed. Notre Dame, playing with only two starting backs, never got inside the Trojan 15 yard line.

Statistically, the first quarter was played on even terms, but late in the second quarter things started to pop when the Irish took possession of the ball after SC had missed a 25 yard field goal.

What happened next is not clear. On the fourth down with 22 to go, and less than a minute to play in the half, someone on the Notre Dame team decided to gamble. Bob Saggau, a former Iowa high school star and a great halfback, dropped back to punt. Instead of kicking, however, he ran with the ball and nearly broke away for a first down . . . perhaps even a touchdown. But he didn't get away and the Trojans gained possession of the ball.

Braven Dyer, reporting for the Los Angeles Times, wrote, "The Irish took the ball and were guilty of a boner seldom seen in high school competition . . . Steve Sitko sent Bobby Saggau around left end, naturally he didn't make it . . . it was dumb strategy and Elmer Layden fairly jumped out of his boots on the sidelines."

Sportswriter Paul Lowry: ". . . an error in judgment . . . a mental lapse on quarterback Steve Sitko's part in failing to kick on fourth down." And then Charles Curtis, writing

"There was a question fired at Layden about the fourth down play . . . 'A Notre Dame quarterback is always right,' he answered, and that is that."

Thirty years later in his book, *It was a Different Game*, Layden recalls, "We had the ball with fourth down and six yards to go on our own 40 yard line . . . unfortunately the gamble didn't work . . . Steve Sitko, our quarterback, was criticized later for calling such a daring play. But Steve was not to blame at all. The play had been sent in from the bench. It didn't work. Nothing worked that day."

At any rate the Trojans had possession of the ball on the Irish 39 yard line. SC quarterback Ollie Day then entered the game and promptly went over left tackle for nine yards and immediately called time out. Then with only five seconds remaining to play, Day faded back and threw a 48 yard pass to Antelope Al Krueger for a touchdown. The extra point was missed, but USC led 6-0. The SC fans, thirsty for victory after a four year dry spell, went wild.

The Irish were not the only casualties of those cliff hanging heroics. The unfortunate Trojan, whoever he was, who had spent hours planning that portion of the half-time activity which involves the flashing of colorful cards in the SC cheering section, very likely suffered a nervous breakdown. The Trojan rooters got so carried away, they threw nearly every

card in the air. At halftime the only thing they could do with their hands was sit on them. It's doubtful that any SC fan cared much about that . . . the important thing was — they were ahead of Notre Dame!

The third period found Southern California doing nothing but protecting their 6 point lead. Notre Dame tried every trick in the book, but could not move the ball against the Trojans.

Five plays into the fourth quarter, USC got their second break when Milt Piepul fumbled going through the line and Jimmy Jones recovered on the Irish 35 yard line. The passing of Micky Anderson and the running of Jack Banta drove USC to Notre Dame's 3 yard line, where Anderson slashed through left tackle into the end zone for the score. This time Gaspar's extra point was good. The score was 13-0, and that's the way it ended.

Mario Tonelli, Notre Dame Fullback, a game breaker

It was a stunned and disappointed Notre Dame team that was kept in the locker room for 30 minutes after the game, while Coach Elmer Layden made the rounds, speaking words of condolence and congratulations to each of his boys. "We have no excuses," Layden said later. "Our boys didn't play their best game by a long shot, but we lost to a fine team. The Trojan line was hitting very hard," added Layden. "Gosh, they were big and tough," muttered Ed Beinor, Notre Dame's All American tackle. Everyone on the Notre Dame squad agreed.

Tony Tonelli, the pudgy Trojan guard (no relation to Mario, the Irish hero of 1937), best expressed the sentiments of his team. "Listen, give the Headman credit for this one. He gave us everything he had in practice and I guess the scoreboard proves that it was plenty good enough."

Outstanding players are hard to select in a game where every participant contributed to strong team effort, but the consensus was that Al Krueger and Bob Winslow, hard hitting ends, had rendered the Irish offense helpless on the wings. Bob Hoffman for steady back-up of the line, and hard blocking . . . Banta for his line smashing and quarterback Mickey Anderson for running, passing and all around generalship.

SC was matched by the Irish in individual ability, but on this day the Trojans seemed to function more efficiently as a team than did Notre Dame. Sitko and Piepul, Earl Brown and Johnny O'Brien — Beinor and Saggau all played excellent football. But on December 3rd of 1938 they were no match for the Trojans. "What a line," exclaimed Coach Paul Schissler, formerly of Oregon State. "It's superb. That's Howard Jones' best Trojan team and I'll bet Elmer Layden will agree with me." Elmer Layden did.

Years later, Layden chuckled over a cartoon by Peter Arno which appeared in the fall of 1967. It showed four football players galloping down the field with one allowing a pass to slip between his hands. On the sidelines a morose coach was saying, "There they go, The Four Horsemen — Famine, Pestilence, Death . . . and Butterfingers." Layden was fond of wondering aloud which of the four Harry Stuhldreher, the quarterback of the famous foursome, would have called "Butterfingers."

Well it certainly would not have been Elmer Layden. He may have bobbled the ball a bit during the USC game, but he didn't fumble. Despite that loss, Notre Dame with an 8-1-0 record was given the top national ranking the following week. Duke was number two, and in fourth place the University of Southern California, which defeated Duke in the Rose Bowl 7-3.

1938 Notre Dame Captain, Jim McGoldrick with Head Coach Elmer Layden

USC's Boyd Morgan attempts to sweep Irish end

NOTRE DAME ROSTER — 1938

NO.	NAME	POS.	WT.		NO.	NAME	POS.	WT.
64	Albert, Francis	L.G.	210		45	Leonard, Robert	F.	190
56	Bechtold, Joseph	R.T.	207		51	Longhi, Edward	C.	195
73	Beinor, Joseph	L.T.	207		11	Marquardt, Clarence	R.H.	173
24	Biagi, Frank	L.E.	180		72	McDonough, Joseph	R.T.	177
79	Binkowski, Benedict	F.	187		63	McGannon, William	L.H.	170
17	Bossu, August	R.G.	188		58	McGoldrick, James (C)	L.G.	175
35	Brennan, Thomas	R.E.	187		68	McIntyre, John	C.	186
67	Brew, Francis	L.T.	205		81	Mooney, Alan	C.	190
53	Broscoe, Edward	R.E.	185		44	Morrison, Paul	R.H.	185
25	Brown, Earl	L.E.	178		47	O'Brien, John	R.E.	188
40	Burnell, Herman	R.H.	180		1	O'Meara, Walter	Q.	165
26	Corgan, Michael	R.H.	185		71	Peipul, Milton	F.	207
2	Crowe, Emmett	Q	170		69	Rassas, George	L.E.	196
55	DeFranco, Joseph	L.G.	175		50	Riffle, Charles	R.G.	205
21	Finneran, Jack	C.	190		34	Saggau, Robert	L.H.	185
84	Gallagher, Thomas	L.T	204		12	Sheridan, Benjamin	L.H.	171
49	Gottsacker, Harold	F.	195		80	Simonich, Edward	F.	205
66	Gubanich, John	R.G.	170		8	Sitko, Steven	Q.	183
70	Harvey, Thaddeus	R.T.	215		32	Stevenson, Harry	L.H.	190
3	Hofer, Willard	Q.	190		13	Sullivan, John	L.H.	180
54	Hollendoner, Francis	L.T	208		43	Sullivan, Robert	R.G.	197
78	Kell, Paul	R.T.	209		33	Thesing, Joseph	F	190
18	Kelly, John	R.E.	186		58	Tonelli, Mario	F.	188
57	Kelly, Peter	L.G.	188		16	Tuck, Frank	L.H.	175
42	Kerr, William	L.E	190		23	Zontini, Louis	R.H.	175

SOUTHERN CALIFORNIA ROSTER — 1938

NO.	NAME	POS.	WT.		NO.	NAME	POS.	WT.
25	Anderson, William C.	Q.	176		35	Morgan, Boyd	R.H.	189
16	Atanasoff, Alex	C.	188		46	Morrill, Charles	L.G.	185
33	Banta, Jack	F.	185		40	Nave, Doyle	Q.	178
51	Beeson, Robert	L.H.	185		54	Noor, Dennis	R.E.	195
61	Benson, Carl	R.T.	200		74	Norman, Charles	L.H.	190
15	Berryman, Richard	R.H.	189		41	Peccianti, Angelo	F.	180
37	Coleman, William	L.E.	189		21	Peoples, Robert	F.	180
19	Day, Oliver	Q.	166		39	Phillips, Floyd	L.G.	175
80	Dempsey, Ed	C.	190		55	Robertson, Robert	R.H.	185
59	Doyle, Don	L.T.	205		58	Roquet, Russell	L.T.	200
72	Elberg, Alton	L.T.	196		60	Russell, Lyman	L.H.	206
49	Engle, Roy	F.	174		27	Sangster, William	F.	168
79	Fisher, Robert	R.T.	205		71	Shell, Joseph	R.H.	196
50	Fisk, William	L.E.	178		53	Slatter, James	R.H.	194
23	Galvin, Glen	L.E.	173		70	Smith, Harry	L.G.	217
44	Gaspar, Phil	R.T.	217		65	Snyder, Ed	L.E.	170
28	George, Ray	R.T.	204		12	Sohn, Ben	R.G.	234
34	Halvorsen, Ray	R.T.	211		36	Stanley, Ralph	R.E.	190
67	Harmon, Bill	C.	190		43	Stevenson, Ed	L.H.	183
45	Hoffman, Robert	L.H.	196		68	Stoecker, Howard	L.T.	212
56	Jesse, John	L.H.	184		38	Stonebraker, John	R.E.	216
32	Jones, James	R.H.	175		75	Swirles, Frank	Q.	165
29	Keller, Don	Q	172		63	Thomassin, John	L.T.	200
52	Klenk, Quentin	R.T.	208		42	Tonelli, Amerigo	R.G.	222
62	Krueger, Al	L.E.	178		57	Utman, Leon	R.G.	194
78	Lansdell, Grenville	Q	178		66	Wehba, Ray	L.E.	186
47	McNeil, Don (Capt.)	C.	205		73	Winslow, Robert	R.E.	188
64	Mena, Salvador	R.E.	195					

1939
CHAPTER 15
"ELMER . . . HISTORY WILL PROVE YOU GREAT"
. . . Joe Petritz, 1939

Elmer Layden was an unusual man. Not only was he an exceptionally good coach . . . he was, in the judgment of his contemporaries, a schedule maker beyond belief. But on November 25 of 1939, Coach Layden was no doubt wishing he could do something about rescheduling a game that had been agreed on some 14 years earlier. He knew he was in for a battle. Not that a fight scared Elmer Layden or any man on the Notre Dame team, but he did fear that the Trojan offensive power would be too much for the Irish line. He had just cause for concern.

The men of Troy were enjoying their best season since 1932, coming to South Bend undefeated with one tie. The record of the Fighting Irish wasn't really all that shabby . . . they were coming to the battlefield with a 7-1 season going for them. Their only loss, a one point upset by Iowa 7-6. But USC's 13-0 victory of 1938 was still fresh in their minds.

Said Coach Layden ". . . This team (USC) potentially has the most versatile offense of any eleven in the country."

Said Coach Jones, ". . . The cold and snow will make our job just that more difficult."

The following afternoon before 56,000 cold damp fans in Notre Dame stadium, the favored Trojans wasted no time in attempting to establish territorial rights. As far as they were concerned, the entire playing field rightfully belonged to the University of Southern California. They refused to relinquish an inch.

Powered by All American guard Harry Smith, Phil Gaspar (healthy for this meeting), and 224 pound Ben Sohn, the Trojans stopped the Irish offense dead in its tracks. Three plays after they had received the opening kickoff, they were minus five yards and had to give up the football to SC who promptly marched from their own 33 to the Notre Dame 2 in 10 plays.

Grenny Lansdell bucked it over from the 2 yard line. Bob Robertson missed the extra point. 6-0, U.S.C.

The Irish defense tightened somewhat and they were able to hold their own until late in the second period. Then USC moved to a first down at the Notre Dame 2 yard line, but left end Bud Kerr prevented a USC touchdown with a crushing tackle on Doyle Nave, who fumbled into the end zone. Harry Stevenson recovered for the Irish. The half ended, USC 6, Notre Dame 0.

Doyle Nave, USC's star in the Rose Bowl

The score remained 6-0 until early in the fourth quarter when Bob Sheridan passed over the middle to Captain John Kelly and gave the Irish a first down on SC's 10 yard line, and in two plays Milt Piepul drove the ball in for the score. Piepul was a bit anxious on the extra point and missed it wide to the right.

The Trojans got hot again after that and began slashing the middle of the Irish line like eleven Jack the Rippers. Starting from Notre Dame's 42 yard line, with Lansdell carrying the ball seven out of the eight times it took to score, SC drove once more into the end zone. Bob Jones made the extra point and SC led 13-6.

Jones' kickoff went out of bounds and the Irish took possession on their 35 yard line. USC was penalized 5 yards for offsides, and then Sheridan suddenly broke into the clear and dashed 60 yards for a touchdown. Notre Dame's conversion attempt by John Kelleher was no good.

But with the Irish now mounting an offensive, the Trojans got serious again and put the game out of sight when Amby Schindler broke through tackle and went 45 yards to a touchdown.

With little more than a minute to play the score was SC 20, Notre Dame 12. And that's what it was at the final gun. In the locker room after the game, Coaches Jones and Layden had nothing but praise for each other's team.

"Notre Dame displayed the strongest attack we've met all year," smiled Jones. "I was glad when it was over."

"So was I," also smiled Layden, but through gritted teeth. "USC was the best team we've met all year."

If Coach Layden had lasted a few more years at Notre Dame, he would have had the last laugh. Eleven years passed before USC whipped the Irish again. And on their home ground . . . well let's just say that the Trojan horse made the trip to South Bend regularly for 28 years before they launched another successful assault on the walls of Notre Dame. That was in 1967 . . . but that's another story.

In the years 1934 through 1940 when Layden served as Notre Dame head football coach and athletic director, he became famous in coaching circles for his ability to make profitable football dates with the schools of the Western Conference (now the Big Ten). During those six years he restored Iowa and Purdue to the Notre Dame schedule, arranged games with Ohio State, Minnesota and Illinois for the first time and as his biggest coup, talked Fielding Yost, athletic director of Michigan, into a home and home series.

Joe Petritz, Notre Dame sports information director in 1939, told him, "Elmer, as an athletic director . . . history will prove you great."

Notre Dame Captain, Benny Sheridan with Head Coach Elmer Layden

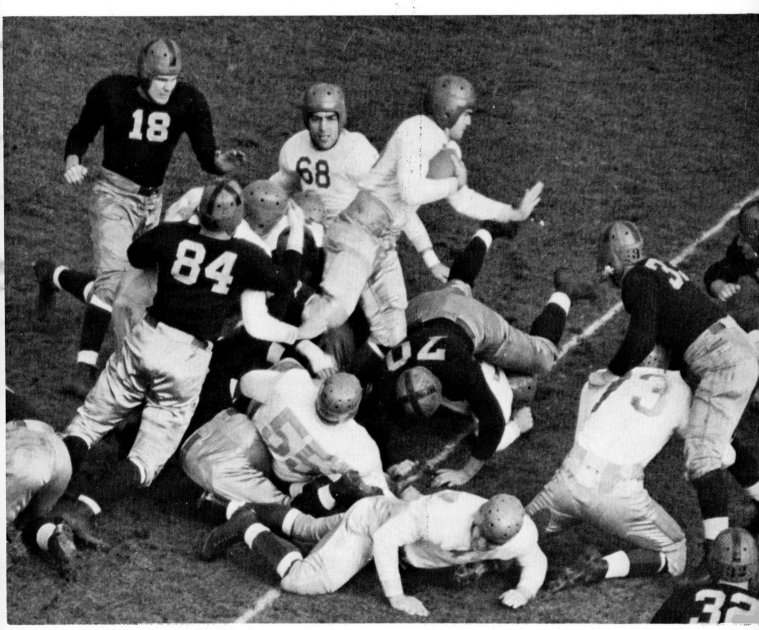

USC's Grenny Landsdell hits the Notre Dame line

OFFICIAL 1939 NOTRE DAME FOOTBALL ROSTER

NO.	NAME	POSITION
1	O'Meara, Walter C.	Q.B.
2	Hayes, Clarence W.	Q.B.
3	Hargrave, Robert W.	Q.B.
4	Kelleher, John C.	Q.B.
7	Koch, Robert J.	Q.B.
8	*Sitko, Steven J.	Q.B.
11	Rockne, Knute K., Jr.	R.H.
12	*Sheridan, Benjamin Mason	L.H.
13	Stelmaszek, Edward T.	L.G.
14	Schmid, Charles W.	R.T.
15	Juzwik, Steven R.	R.H.
16	Bagarus, Stephen, Jr.	R.H.
17	Laiber, Joseph	R.G.
18	*Kelly, John F. (Capt.)	R.E.
20	Marko, Peter J.	L.H.
21	Finneran, John C.	C.
23	**Zontini, Louis R.	R.H.
24	Biagi, Frank W.	L.E.
25	Petschel, Howard K.	R.E.
26	Corgan, Michael H.	R.H.
27	Kristoff, Walter W.	R.H.
28	Chlebeck, Andrew J.	F.B.
29	Kovatch, John G., Jr.	R.E.
30	McCabe, George J., Jr.	L.H.
31	Leonard, Robert J.	F.B.
32	**Stevenson, Harry, Jr.	L.H.
33	**Thesing, Joseph R.	F.B.
34	*Saggau, Robert J.	L.H.
36	Maloney, John M.	C.
37	Lee, Albert B.	F.B.
38	Bairley, Roy J.	R.T.
39	Barber, Robert A.	R.E.
40	Hogan, Donald J.	L.H.
41	Rively, Clair M.	L.T.
42	*Kerr, William H.	L.E.
43	Sullivan, Robert E.	R.G.
44	Crimmins, Bernard A.	R.H.
45	O'Reilly, Martin G.	C.
46	Ames, Richard F.	R.G.
47	*O'Brien, John D.	R.E.
48	Sheridan, Philip F.	L.E.
49	Maddock, Robert C.	R.G.
50	Riffle, Charles F.	R.G.
51	Osterman, Robert T.	C.
52	Pepelnjak, Nicholas F.	L.H.
53	Prokop, Joseph M.	R.H.
54	Robinson, Angus	L.T.
55	*DeFranco, Joseph F.	L.G.
56	*Ebli, Raymond H.	L.E.
57	Kelly, Peter M.	L.G.
58	Arboit, Peter S.	L.E.
59	Bereolos, Hercules	L.G.
61	Korth, Howard J.	R.G.
63	McGannon, William V.	L.H.
64	Albert, Francis J.	L.T.
65	Schrenker, Henry P.	L.G.
66	*Gubanich, John A.	R.G.
67	Ford, James B.	C.
68	*McIntyre, John A., Jr.	C.
69	Rassas, George J.	L.E.
70	*Harvey, Thaddeus H.	R.T.
71	*Piepul, Milton J.	F.B.
72	Ostroski, Edward A.	R.G.
73	Brutz, James Charles	L.T.
74	O'Neill, Robert Francis	R.T.
75	Lillis, Paul B.	R.T.
76	Larkin, Edward J.	R.E.
78	Brosey, Henry C.	R.T.
79	Sullivan, Edward J.	L.G.
80	McNeill, Charles E.	F.B.
81	*Mooney, Alan B.	C.
83	Papa, Joseph J.	L.T.
84	*Gallagher, Thomas C.	L.T.

OFFICIAL 1939 SOUTHERN CALIFORNIA FOOTBALL ROSTER

NO.	NAME	POSITION
12	Yank, Lou	Right Guard
14	*Berryman, Richard	Fullback
16	Atanasoff, Alex	Center
18	Bowman, Jerry	Quarterback
19	Bundy, William	Left Halfback
20	*Duboski, Phil	Left Halfback
21	*Peoples, Robert	Fullback
23	Galvin, Glen	Left End
24	**Schindler, Ambrose	Quarterback
27	**Sangster, William	Fullback
28	Robertson, Robert	Right Halfback
29	*Peccianti, Angelo	Fullback
31	Berryman, Robert	Quarterback
32	Jones, Robert	Right End
33	*Banta, John	Fullback
35	Kalinich, Peter	Right Guard
38	*Stonebraker, John	Right End
39	*Phillips, Floyd	Left Guard
40	*Nave, Doyle	Quarterback
42	deLauer, Robert	Right Tackle
44	**Gaspar, Phil	Right Tackle
45	**Hoffman, Robert	Left Halfback
46	Morrill, Charles	Center
49	*Engle, Roy	Right Halfback
50	**Fisk, William	Left End
53	Slatter, James	Right Halfback
55	*Sohn, Ben	Right Guard
56	Green, Max	Right Halfback
57	Utman, Leon	Center
58	Roquet, Russel	Left Tackle
61	Benson, Carl	Right Guard
62	*Krueger, Al	Left End
63	**Thomassin, John	Left Tackle
64	Mena, Salvadore	Right End
65	Cardona, Robert	Center
67	Moore, James	L.T.-Left Guard
68	**Stoecker, Howard	Left Tackle
70	**Smith, Harry	Left Guard
71	**Shell, Joseph (Capt.)	Left Halfback
73	*Winslow, Robert	Right End
78	**Lansdell, Grenville	Quarterback
80	*Dempsey, Ed	Center

*Indicates Major Monograms.

1940
CHAPTER 16
". . . DON'T STAY FOR THE SECOND HALF . . . IT'S A DUD."
. . . Anon. 1940

Coach Howard Jones of the University of Southern California and Coach Elmer Layden of Notre Dame had many things in common. Observing them on their respective benches as they coached their teams, you might have thought them carved out of the same chunk of granite. Both had volatile tempers which they controlled with difficulty but admirable success. Both were conservative, dedicated students *and* teachers of the game, and on the 7th of December, 1940, both were coaching their last football game.

They, of course, didn't know that . . . neither did the 75,000 fans who swarmed into the Los Angeles Memorial Coliseum that afternoon to watch the fifteenth meeting of the Head Man's Thundering Herd and the Fighting Irish of Notre Dame.

The series now stood Notre Dame 7, USC 6 . . . one tie. The Trojans had won the last two, but were coming into this meeting with a season record which was, to put it mildly, lousy. Three wins, three losses, and two ties. Notre Dame's record was somewhat better. They had won the first six games of the season before crumbling before Iowa 7-0 and Northwestern 20-0. 6 and 2 is not all that bad, anywhere except Notre Dame. The alumni was not happy . . . but more of that later.

In 1933, you'll remember, the noble Trojans received a little assistance from an unexpected source, *Hemophilus Influenza.*

As if to prove the balance of nature, and the fact that the God of Methodists and Catholics plays no favorite, one-half of the USC team fell victim to the same bug seven years later. While the healthy members of the Trojan team stood around the practice field waiting for enough players to scrimmage with, the balance of the team studied their offensive moves with penciled diagrams on the bed linens of the Good Samaritan Hospital. The Irish, a meager 3-2 favorite, stopped for their customary hard workout in Tucson, and then again in Pomona for a light workout the day before the game. The next afternoon, they wasted no time.

Within the first five minutes, team captain Milt Piepul, the big Irish fullback kicked a twenty-five yard line field goal to send Notre Dame ahead.

Piepul's field goal came on the tenth play after the opening kickoff after USC quarterback Bob Robertson's quick kick

squirted out of bounds on the SC 48 yard line. The Irish went to work immediately.

Steve Juzwick, the Notre Dame right halfback skirted right end for 19 yards on the first play. Then with the help of Piepul and left half Bob Saggau, Steve managed to move the ball to the Trojan 17. That was the end of the line. The Irish went into place kick formation, and with Bob Hargrave holding, Big Milt had no trouble splitting the uprights.

The Trojans retaliated with rapid and deadly efficiency. Robertson fielded Piepul's kickoff and charged up the field for a 32 yard gain. On the next play, he fed the ball to Jack Banta on a reverse and the right halfback swept right end for 11 yards to the Irish 47.

Then the Trojans attacked the weak left side of the Notre Dame line. SC right guard Ben Sohn and right tackle Bob De Lauer ripped a hole over left guard for speedy fullback, Bobby Peoples, who knew exactly what to do with it. He slammed into the Notre Dame secondary where Hargrave, Piepul and Saggau waited as a three man welcoming committee. Bounding Bob didn't even pause to say hello. He slanted right and sidestepped all three. Only Juzwik and right end John O'Brien had a chance at him now. Juzwik managed to give him a shove, but he regained his balance and eluded O'Brien's desperate stab at the goal line. It was a beautiful 46 yard touchdown run and he did it alone . . . not a single blocker in front. It was also Southern California's only score of the day. The extra point attempt was missed.

The Trojans continued their rampage for the remainder of the quarter, opening huge holes in the Notre Dame line. Robertson made it to the Irish 19 yard line once before being tackled from behind. On another play, Robertson passed to Bob Peoples who made a dazzling catch on his knees at the Notre Dame 7. The opportunity to score was lost, however, when Jack Banta was thrown for a four yard loss on a reverse play that hadn't worked all afternoon.

The quarter ended USC 6, Notre Dame 3.

Now USC's invisible opponent began to play a major part. In order to rest his flu-bitten first string, Coach Jones sent in the second team early in the second quarter. Bill Bundy, SC's best blocking back had played only a few minutes before taking himself out of the game, and the rest of the regulars were

Bernie Crimmins, Notre Dame Fullback

so exhausted they could barely stand. The substitution proved costly.

Said Coach Jones after the game, "I didn't think the Irish subs would drive 85 yards in 11 plays on us." But they did.

SC substitute quarterback Bob Berryman fumbled the pass from center on the first play of the second quarter, preventing De Lauer from attempting a field goal. The Irish recovered on their 13 yard line and cut and slashed the Trojan line to ribbons. Milt Piepul, who had begun to look like a one man gang, climaxed the 85 yard march with a 3 yard plunge into the end zone, then kicked the extra point to make the score 10-6. That was all the scoring for the day, and the game was only 17 minutes old.

Jones rushed his regulars back on the firing line, but it was too late. True, they had had a few minutes rest, but it had also cooled them off. They were never able to get going again, except for a brief threat late in the fourth quarter, but that died aborning due to penalties and fumbles.

After the first half, the most inspired assault probably came at the end of the game, and that one was verbal and from none other than the winning coach, Elmer Layden. For a while he

USC's Bob Robertson attempts to crack Irish line

100

took on all comers.

With only seconds to play USC's Berryman had tried a long desperation pass to right end Joe Davis. Milt Piepul's substitute halfback, Bernie Crimmins, leaped high in the air to break it up. To Coach Layden it looked like a good play, to the field judge it looked like interference. The ruling gave USC a first down on the Notre Dame 20 . . . and Layden high blood pressure on the Notre Dame bench. The Trojans had time for only two plays, both of them incomplete passes.

At the final gun Layden stormed onto the field, his temper completely out of control, and verbally flayed all the officials, then seeing Jones approaching to give him the customary congratulations, met him with an icy stare and as they shook hands Layden growled, "Howard I've seen home town decisions before, but not like this." Jones beat a hasty retreat, but Elmer wasn't through yet. At the end of the ramp leading to the Notre Dame locker room, he ran into Willis Hunter, athletic director and Chancellor von Kleinschmid of USC. They did not escape his wrath.

Still boiling, Layden stormed into the Notre Dame dressing room. "Bernie," he said to Crimmins, later head coach at Indiana, "did you push that SC guy?"

Crimmins summoned all his courage. "Yes coach, I did."

"Oh boy," muttered a thoroughly cooled Layden.

He then went to the official's dressing room to apologize. From there to USC's dressing room to shake Howard Jones' hand more warmly, and for the last time. Next season Layden would be the first commissioner of the National Football League, and coach Howard Jones would be dead.

Witnesses say that Layden was so determined to apologize to Chancellor von Kleinschmid that he perched on the hood of the von Kleinschmid's car in the parking lot to wait for him.

Another witness also relates that on the way back to the locker room from the parking lot, Layden collided with a straggling SC fan who obviously had been warding off the late afternoon chill with a little anti-freeze of the 100 proof variety.

"Well," said Layden, picking up the fan's bedraggled SC pennant from the sidewalk and handing it to him, "how did you like the game?"

"First part's O.K.," said the Californian, "but don't stay for the second half . . . it's a dud."

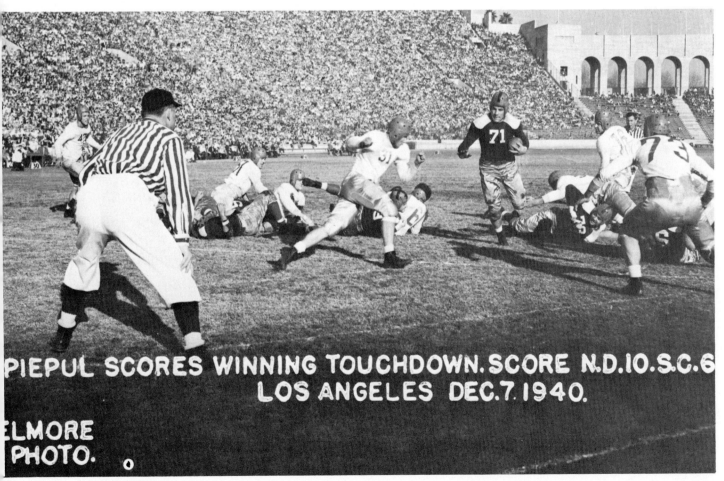

PIEPUL SCORES WINNING TOUCHDOWN. SCORE N.D.10.S.C.6
LOS ANGELES DEC.7.1940.

ELMORE PHOTO.

Notre Dame's star back, Milt Piepul

SOUTHERN CALIFORNIA ROSTER — 1940

NO.	NAME	POSITION	AGE	WEIGHT
25	**Anderson, Mickey	Q.	22	175
33	**Banta, Jack	R.H.	21	187
57	Batinski, Louis	L.H.	20	190
51	Beeson, Robert	L.H.	22	191
43	Belloni, Jack	F.	19	187
34	Bennett, Frank	R.T.	22	202
61	*Benson, Carl	R.G.-L.T.	22	202
31	Berryman, Bob	Q.	22	191
73	Bledsoe, Willmar	R.H.	19	186
15	Bleeker, Melvin	F.	19	187
18	Bowman, Jerry	Q.	20	174
19	Bundy, Bill	L.H.	20	192
65	Caronda, Robert	R.G.	22	204
49	Culler, William	C.	18	204
24	Danehe, Richard	R.T.	19	217
36	Davis, Joe	R.E.	20	195
23	Davis, William	Q.	20	160
42	*de Lauer, Robert	R.T.	19	222
80	**Dempsey, Ed	C.	23	201
59	Doyle, Don	R.G.	23	230
20	*Duboski, Phil	L.H.	22	196
56	Green, Max	R.H.	20	186
63	Haskell, David	R.E.	20	183
47	Hindley, Lewis	L.E.	19	182
32	Jones, Bob	R.E.	21	198
52	Klenk, Quentin	R.T.	21	208
62	**Krueger, Al	L.E.	21	183
27	Maley, Duane	L.G.	18	190
16	McGarvin, Tom	L.E.	23	188
64	Mena, Salvador	R.E.	22	190
46	*Morrill, Charles	C.	20	184
72	Musick, Bill	F.	20	198
40	Nash, Russert	L.E.	19	170
29	Nelson, Robert	R.H.	19	180
45	Norris, Ash	L.T.	19	223
21	**Peoples, Bob	F.	22	190
38	**Phillips, Floyd	L.G.	22	190
67	Pranevicius, John	L.G.	20	183
28	*Robertson, Bob	Q.	22	189
58	Roquet, Russel	L.T.	23	211
44	Sargent, Hugh	R.G.	21	208
79	Seixas, William	L.G.	18	185
55	**Sohn, Ben	R.G.	20	226
75	Swirles, Frank	Q.	21	166
38	Thomas, Ronald	L.G.	18	208
35	Verry, Norman	R.G.	19	239
68	Willer, Donald	L.T.	19	195
41	Williams, Hal	L.E.	21	187
78	Woods, Ray	Q.	20	174
54	Woods, Roy	R.G.	20	203

NOTRE DAME ROSTER — 1940

NO.	NAME	POSITION	AGE	WEIGHT
16	*Bagarus, Stephen	R.H.	21	160
59	Bereolos, Hercules	R.G.	21	193
68	Brock, Thomas	C.	21	188
73	*Brutz, James	L.T.	21	209
43	Creevy	R.H.	20	182
44	*Crimmins, Bernard	F.	21	185
42	Dove, Robert	L.E.	19	188
26	Earley, William	R.H.	19	171
56	Ebli, Raymond	L.E.	21	205
23	Evans, Frederick	L.H.	19	174
84	**Gallagher, Thomas	L.T.	23	208
9	Girolami, Anthony	Q	19	193
66	**Gubanich, John	R.G.	21	161
3	*Hargrave, Robert	Q.	20	172
2	Hayes, John	Q.	22	164
40	Hogan, Donald	L.H.	20	189
15	Juzwik, Steven	R.H.	22	185
57	*Kelly, Peter	L.G.	22	184
61	Korth, Howard	R.G.	21	179
29	Kovatch, John	R.E.	20	177
17	Laiber, Joseph	R.G.	20	172
37	Lee, Albert	F.	22	180
31	Leonard, Robert	F.	23	197
75	*Lillis, Paul	R.T.	19	210
49	Maddock, Robert	L.G.	20	204
63	McGannon, William	L.H.	21	172
81	McHale, John	C.	19	201
18	Murphy, George	R.E.	20	170
64	Neff, Robert	R.T.	20	236
47	**O'Brien, John	R.E.	22	187
33	O'Brien, Richard	R.E.	19	175
45	O'Reilly, Martin	C.	20	179
51	Osterman, Robert	C.	21	202
5	Patten	Q	20	169
54	Peterson	R.T.	19	214
71	**Piepul, Milt (C)	F.	22	206
69	Rassas, George	L.E.	24	182
70	Rymkus, Louis	L.T.	21	223
34	**Saggau, Robert	L.H.	20	189
48	Sheridan, Philip	L.E.	23	180
79	Sullivan, Edward	L.G.	20	188
72	Sullivan, Lawrence	L.T.	21	219
74	Ziemba, Walter	R.T.	21	225

1941
CHAPTER 17

". . . FRANK LEAHY . . . A CHIP OFF THE OLD ROCK"
J. Ray Hunt . . . 1941

Great football talent can be born almost anywhere, but the University of Notre Dame seems to have all the essential elements necessary for the nurture and maturation of living legends. Most of whom become legendary in their own time. First there was Jess Harper, then Gus Dorais and Knute Rockne. Goerge Gipp, and the Four Horsemen.

In 1941 Francis William Leahy took a giant step toward joining that select group . . . in his first year as the head football coach of Notre Dame he was undefeated. The Irish had their first perfect season since Rockne's last in 1930.

Upon closer scrutiny, it may be inaccurate to stamp a 1941 date on the birth of a legend. Who can compute without error the gestation period of genius. And those who worked with him closest, his players, his assistants, his friends, even his enemies . . . and he had more than a few . . . agree that Coach Frank Leahy was an absolute genius on the football field. The incubation could have begun in Winner, South Dakota, when 12-year-old Frank borrowed his older brother Gene's monogram sweater so he could look like a *real* football player in scrub games. It might have started when Earl Walsh, a teammate of George Gipp's at Notre Dame, now coaching Winner High School, decided to use him at tailback, or when brother Gene enrolled him at Notre Dame and turned him over to his old friend and former coach at Greighton College, Tommy Mills, who was Rockne's freshman coach.

More than likely, it happened the moment Leahy presented himself to Rockne at the University of Notre Dame and immediately and permanently fell under the spell of both.

"Coach Rockne," said Leahy, "I'm from South Dakota."

"Oh yes! It's Leahy, of course. Heard a lot about you from Earl Walsh . . . hear you play football pretty well. You're a fine looking boy. Just fine." Rockne paused, sensing a loneliness in the boy, spoke softly.

"Feel scared as hell, don't you Frank . . . You'll get over that lost feeling in a couple of days, I did. If you need to talk to me in the meantime, I'll be around. I'm not one of those coaches who hides in the office."

From that day on until the day of his death, Frank Leahy was consecrated to Rockne and his memory and to the University of Notre Dame. Regardless of what happened, his devotion never wavered or faltered, or strayed. To Frank Leahy being head coach of the University of Notre Dame was next to being

anointed . . . trusted to continue the search for the Holy Grail . . . bearer of the Cross and the honor of Our Lady.

Leahy had played tackle on Rockne's championship team in 1929 but in a practice drill just before the SMU game which started Notre Dame's 1930 season, he tore the cartilage in his knee so badly that he knew immediately that he would never play football again. The physical pain Leahy could handle, but the soul shattering knowledge that he had played his last game for Notre Dame, and the fact that he had convinced himself that no college would be interested in hiring a coach who didn't play his senior year, was destroying him. But as it turned out fate had merely stepped in to nudge the legend along a bit. Rockne, impressed with young Leahy's singular dedication to the game and capacity for hard work, made him

Notre Dame's new head coach, Frank Leahy with Captain Paul Lillis

USC's Bob Jones has extra point blocked in the first half by John Kovatch

a sort of unofficial assistant coach. For the remainder of the season he sat at the right hand of the Master.

After graduation he became assistant to his old friend Tommy Mills at Georgetown, then to Michigan State as Jim Crowley's line coach. When Crowley moved on to Fordham, Leahy went along and there carved the famous Seven Blocks of Granite. Six years later, in 1939, he took his first head coaching job at Boston College. After a short but successful tenure there (winning 9 and losing 1 his first and only season) he was offered the head coaching position at Notre Dame. Because of an Alma Mater clause in his contract, he was able to accept, much to the anger of the Boston College alumni and the chagrin of the 1941 Notre Dame opponents.

The Fighting Irish rolled over Arizona 38-7 in the opener, then crushed Indiana, Georgia Tech., Carnegie Tech., and absolutely humiliated Illinois 49-14. The Irish juggernaut slowed only temporarily . . . a scoreless tie with Army . . . but then picked up speed once more and rolled through the gates of Notre Dame stadium to meet SC undefeated in eight games.

Sam Barry, who became USC's interim coach after the death of Howard Jones, probably wished he were somewhere else that November afternoon. Somewhere comparatively warm and friendly, like a French Penal colony.

Justin M. (Sam) Barry was the Headman's top assistant and friend. He was also the Trojans' basketball and baseball coach, and a good one. Jones had brought him to SC from Iowa where he also had been an assistant coach. Sam had stepped in just a few weeks before practice had begun for the 1941 season. The Trojan record was atrocious. They had been out of the gate six times and in the money only twice. Barry couldn't be held entirely to blame, Jones didn't leave him much. Remember, 1940 was his poorest year.

Coach Leahy, with the caution and pessimism which would become his trademark at Notre Dame, refused to take the Trojans lightly. He had played tackle against them in 1929 and assisted Rockne in 1930. He was well aware of the intensity with which USC played this game. Frank Leahy was much too smart a football coach to risk being bitten by an underdog.

"The fact that this team has won only two games in six outings means nothing at all. Remember that 1931 game here — we lost 16-14 after we had the game won. We want no repetition of that one. Also bear in mind that injuries early in the season were the main cause for the Trojans' poor record to date. Southern California has proved on more than one occasion that it can pull itself together for one great game. You can expect that Saturday's game will be that one. Don't let that fact escape your memory."

As a coach, Leahy left nothing to chance. He proved it in his next eleven years as coach of the Fighting Irish.

Notre Dame received the opening kickoff and unable to gain after three plays, called on Frederick Evans to punt, but Ralph Heywood broke through to block the kick and the ball bounded out of bounds on Notre Dame's 33 yard line. Getting a first down on Notre Dame's 20, Bobby Robertson passed on 4th down to Heywood who caught the ball in the end zone for the first 6 points. Walt Ziemba, the Irish center, blocked the extra point attempt.

Early in the second quarter with SC backed up on their own 2 yard line, Heywood got off a poor kick that went to his own 33 yard line. On first down, Steve Juzwik, running from the "T" formation, took a reverse to his right and ran the ball down to the Trojans' 7 yard line. Twice Evans hit the line for no gain, and then Leahy sent in Bob Hargreave at quarterback. Fullback Evans circled to his left side and went in standing up. Juzwik kicked the goal and Notre Dame led 7-6. On the next

Steve Juzwik scores for Notre Dame from the six yard line

series, after Robertson fumbled on his own 46 yard line, behind the passing of Angelo Bertelli and the running of Juzwik, Notre Dame drove the ball down to score again. Juzwik took over, but missed the conversion.

With less than six minutes remaining in the half, it was now USC's turn to throw the ball. Bob Musick completed his first to Doug Esick for a first down on the Irish 46 yard line. Musick then ran the ball to the 44 yard line. With second down and 8, Musick threw again to Esick on the Notre Dame 5 yard line. After one play gained nothing, Musick on a reverse lateral pitched out to Bill Bledsoe who leaped high in the air and into the end zone. This time it was John Kovatch's turn to block the SC try for an extra point. The half ended Notre Dame 13, Southern California 12.

Notre Dame bounced back in the 3rd quarter with vengeance. Bertelli continued his aerial attack. He completed three in a row, one to Bob Dove and two to Harry Wright. With a second down on SC's 17 yard line, Bertelli threw in the flat to Evans who took the ball on the 12 and evaded three Trojan tacklers as he ran into the corner of the end zone for the score. Juzwik kicked the goal and the count was 20-12.

USC got one more tally late in the 4th quarter, when Bob Robertson went eight yards off left tackle. SC now having learned their lesson about trying to kick extra points against Notre Dame, tried to pass the ball. But it was incomplete out

of Esick's reach. The final count was Notre Dame 20, USC 18. The Shades of SC's inability to make the extra point had once again returned to haunt SC and cost them victory against Notre Dame. "If only I could have kicked each point after touchdown," sadly lamented Trojan Bob Jones.

Sam Barry said after the game, "It was the greatest show of passing talent I've ever seen from anyone," referring to Angelo Bertelli's 13 out of 21 pass completions.

Coach Leahy should have been quietly congratulating himself on his foresight. Never a man to gamble if he had a choice, Leahy had ensured the likelihood of his first year success at Notre Dame by making sure that a number of good young football prospects he had thoughtfully loaned to several New England prep schools, but earmarked for Boston College in the fall, went with him to Notre Dame. Estimates of the number varied from 7 to 27. Apparently there were about twelve. But the important thing was . . . one of them was Angelo Bertelli.

War clouds were beginning to gather over the blue Pacific. Two weeks later, on December 7, the Japanese bombed Pearl Harbor. But on the 23rd of November, the day after the game, there was more newspaper coverage of Notre Dame and her 32 year old coach, than of the approaching storm . . . at least in South Bend. Chicago wasn't far behind. In the *Times*, columnist J. Ray Hunt started a series on Leahy.

"They said there would never be another Rockne," he wrote. "But when Leahy's victories marched through Arizona, Indiana, Georgia Tech, Carnegie Tech and Illinois, they began to change their tune . . . Our search for another Rockne is ended, we've got his prize pupil . . . A young man has come along to replace the Old Master. There is a new Rockne."

He entitled his series, "The story of Frank Leahy, a chip off the old Rock."

Sam Barry led the Thundering Herd back to Southern California, their heads bloody, but unbowed. A few weeks later he was called into the Navy. He was probably hoping for a nice quiet combat zone where all he had to worry about were Kamikaze pilots or U-boats, instead of the Fighting Irish of Notre Dame.

Frank Leahy, to no one's surprise, was named coach of the year. He read his press clippings for a time, then pushed them aside, and sat musing. ". . . a new Rockne . . . the Rockne touch . . ." His eyes narrowed, his jaw set, and within a month he committed a sacrilege.

He announced that he was doing away with "the Notre Dame system," a brain child of Rockne's, and heaven forbid . . . going to the T-formation!

The new coach was not "another Rockne, a new Rockne" . . . He was Francis William Leahy, and he was very much his own man.

OFFICIAL 1941 NOTRE DAME FOOTBALL ROSTER

NO.	NAME	POSITION		NO.	NAME	POSITION
1	Earley, William J.	R.H.		47	McBride, Robert J.	L.G.
2	Creevy, Thomas E.	Q.B.		48	Bertelli, Angelo B.	L.H.
3	**Hargrave, Robert W.	Q.B.		49	*Maddock, Robert C.	L.G.
4	**Wright, Harry C.	Q.B.		40	Walsh, Robert M.	R.G.
5	Patten, Paul E.	Q.B.		51	Bolger, Matthew J.	L.E.
9	Girolami, Anthony G.	Q.B.		52	Filley, Patrick J.	L.G.
15	*Juzwik, Steve R.	R.H.		53	Prokop, Joseph M.	F.B.
17	*Laiber, Joseph J.	R.G.		54	Ellefsen, Charles R.	R.E.
18	Murphy, George E.	R.E.		55	Ashbaugh, Russell G.	Q.B.
20	Kudlacz, Stanley A.	C.		56	*Ebli, Raymond H.	L.T.
21	Lanahan, John F.	C.		57	McLaughlin, David T.	R.G.
23	*Evans, Frederick O., Jr.	F.B.		58	Miller, Thomas S.	R.H.
28	Riordan, Wilbur E.	R.G.		59	*Bereolos, Hercules	L.T.
29	*Kovatch, John G.	R.E.		60	Webb, Robert B.	L.G.
30	Chlebeck, Andrew J.	F.B.		64	*Neff, Robert H.	L.T.
31	Tessaro, Edward A.	R.H.		66	Smyth, William K.	L.E.
32	Warner, John A., Jr.	L.H.		67	Hines, Michael L.	R.T.
33	O'Brien, Richard C.	R.E.		68.	Brock, Thomas J.	C.
35	McGinnis, John J.	R.E.		70	Rymkus, Louis	R.T.
36	Peasenelli, John J.	R.H.		72	Sullivan, Lawrence P.	R.T.
37	Miller, Creighton E.	F.B.		73	**Brutz, James C.	L.T.
40	Hogan, Donald J.	L.H.		74	*Ziemba, Walter J.	C.
42	*Dove, Robert L.	L.E.		75	**Lillis, Capt. Paul B.	R.T.
43	Creevy, Richard C.	L.H.		79	Sullivan, Edward J.	L.G.
44	**Crimmins, Bernard A.	R.G.		80	McNeill, Edward C.	F.B.
45	*O'Reilly, Martin G.	C.		82	Postupack, Joseph V.	F.B.
46	Barry, Norman J.	R.E.				

1941 SO. CALIFORNIA FOOTBALL ROSTER

NO.	NAME	POSITION		NO.	NAME	POSITION
12	*Bledsoe, William	R.H.		62	Noble, William	C.
15	*Bleeker, Melchor	L.H.		65	Seixas, William	L.G.
18	Elliot, Ian	R.H.		67	Pranevicius, John	L.G.
19	Bledsoe, Leonard	R.H.		69	*Thomas, Ronald	L.G.
25	*Bundy, William	L.H.		71	Crowther, James	R.T.
29	Crittenden, Muir	L.H.		72	Verry, Norman	R.G.
32	Manning, Richard	F.B.		73	Aguirre, John	L.T.
33	Musick, William	F.B.		74	Hodges, Bryce	R.T.
40	**Anderson, Michael	Q.B.		75	McCall, Frederick	L.T.
43	Taylor, Paul	Q.B.		77	*Willer, Donald	L.T.
44	**Robertson, Robert	Q.B.		78	**deLauer, Robert (Captain)	R.T.
45	Musick, Robert	F.B.		79	Fuhrman, Seymour	L.T.
46	Browning, Richard	Q.B.		80	*Davis, Joseph	R.E.
49	*Woods, Raymond	Q.B.		82	**Jones, Robert	R.E.
50	Bianchi, Stephen	C.		83	Essick, Douglas	L.E.
51	Green, Maximillian	C.		85	Nash, Russell	L.E.
55	Danehe, Richard	C.		86	MacPhail, Peter	R.E.
58	Maley, Duane	C.		87	Heywood, Ralph	L.E.
60	Chantiles, Thomas	R.G.		88	Schildmeyer, Robert	L.E.
61	Sargent, Hugh	R.G.		89	*Hindley, Louis	L.E.

1942
CHAPTER 18

"YOU MAY HAVE BEEN THE BEST COACH IN THE COUNTRY LAST YEAR MR. LEAHY, BUT . . ."
Jerald Herndon, Class of '21 . . . 1942

On November 18, 1942, the siege of Stalingrad was 95 days old and Josef Stalin sent his defending troops a directive which could not be misunderstood. "There is only one road out of Stalingrad, and that road is forward. Stalingrad will be saved by you, or wiped out with you." British forces under Field Marshall Bernard Montgomery had captured El Alamein and the Axis strength in Africa had been broken. In the South Pacific the four month old battle for Guadalcanal raged on and did so for two more months before a combined force of U.S. Marines and Army pushed the stubborn Japanese into the sea.

In the Los Angeles Coliseum that day another battle took place. It was infinitely less important and no intelligent comparison could be made to the gut chilling danger faced by any fighting man in the early years of World War II. But yet to the twenty-two determined young men who faced each other on the football field that afternoon, it was a kind of a war. And it was important to them. On second thought, it might be unwise to underrate the significance of contact sport played in the spirit of fierce competition. Remember the Duke of Wellington's observation that "The Battle of Waterloo was won on the playing fields of Eton."

Both teams had been hit hard by the draft, and further decimated by the large numbers of eligible athletes who had flocked to the recruiting offices rather than to football tryouts, so theoretically they should have been about even. They were not. Notre Dame came into the conflict 6-2-1, USC a very mediocre 3-3-1. Strangely enough, in light of the disparity of record, the betting odds were nearly even. Probably because of an upsurge in local enthusiasm for the new coach of the Trojans, Jeff Cravath, who at center, captained the Thundering Herd in their first game against Notre Dame in 1926. Paul Zimmerman, Los Angeles Times sportswriter, was so confident in his optimism that he predicted in print on the morning of the game, "We step boldly forward and pick Southern California by a 27 to 20 score." Paul should have stepped timidly backward and remained silent. SC lost 13-0.

The entire blame could certainly not be laid at the feet of the new coach of the SC Trojans. Newell Jefferson Cravath was very possibly one of the best centers in the west during his playing seasons in 1924-1926. He was a good coach. He was

also unlucky. On that November day the two major contributions to his misfortunes were Angelo Bertelli and the T-formation.

The story goes that when Coach Leahy decided to install the T formation in order to take advantage of the speed, shiftiness and durability of halfback Dippy Evans and Bertelli's brilliant passing, Leahy called Angelo into his office to explain. He concluded the explanation with, "This is it, Angelo, football's future."

"I handle the football on every play, right?" asked Bertelli.

"Very true, Angelo. On every play."

"How many new plays do I have to memorize next month?"

"About 80 or 100," replied Leahy, but you'll do splendidly, lad. Splendidly."

He did. His first touchdown pass to Creighton Miller* was good for 48 yards. In the second quarter, he threw his second touchdown pass of the day from the Trojan 12 yard line to Bob Livingston, who faked defensive back Bob Musick out and rambled the needed ten yards for the 6 point tally. John Creevy made the extra point, and the score was 13-0 and remained that until the end of the game.

But just because the scoring stopped, doesn't mean the action did. Bill Seixas of Southern California, and Bob McBride of Notre Dame, had a disagreement at mid-field. It would have seemed to be a mis-match. Seixas giving away five inches and 15 pounds. The winner of the bout is not recorded. Two plays later, Irish tackle Jim White was really overmatched. He had the temerity to take on the referee. He lost and sat out the rest of the game.

Deep in the fourth period, Irish halfback Dick Creevy fumbled and SC guard Harry Adelman recovered on the 27 to give Troy its last chance. Halfback Paul Taylor passed to Bill Bledsoe on the 20, Jim Hardy ran over left guard to the 15 and a first down. Taylor then threw a pass intended for Hardy, but guess who got there first. Angelo Bertelli.

Apparently heeding the old Chinese proverb that "where there is no witness, there is no crime," the officials had lost complete control of the game. Players were clipping, gouging, and kneeing at will. For most of the afternoon the officials had, in a rather shy and retiring manner, suggested such con-

---

*Nephew of Don Miller, one of the 4 Horsemen.

duct was unbecoming to young gentlemen and had given warnings instead of penalties. Their eyesight had sharpened somewhat by the fourth quarter, however. When they detected Notre Dame's George Tobin and Southern Cal's Hubie Kerns slugging it out on the field, they suspected that there might be a difference of opinion serious enough to eject both players, which they did.

Tension had built up to pressure cooker level by the end of the game, and when the final gun fired, the valve blew. Both teams and a part of the crowd of 95,000 converged on the field to continue the brawl. It was ten minutes before order was restored and Jeff Cravath and Frank Leahy walked off the field arm in arm.

What they said to each other is anyone's guess. They were both intelligent men with adequate eyesight. Publicly, Jeff Cravath said, "We were beaten by a good team." But in an unguarded moment he was heard to say, "If I have to win that way, I never want to win."

Leahy was silent, as were his players who had been ejected from the game.

Cravath admonished his team, "Remember, keep your mouths shut."

The consensus was that the Irish had the edge. They had been able to score more infractions with 11 (observed) to 6 for SC, and lost three players to SC's two.

Joe Savoldi, who you will remember deserted football for wrestling back in 1930 after his matrimonial adventures, cancelled a lucrative engagement in the ring to watch his alma mater whip Troy. He probably saw better fights on the gridiron that afternoon than he would have in the prize wrestling ring anyway.

The Trojans played three more games, but their win loss percentage didn't change. They ended the season 5-5-1.

With the win over Troy, Leahy and the Irish posted a 7-2-2. Not bad for a second year coach, but then you can't please everybody.

Jerald Herndon, a disgruntled alumnus of the class of '21, wrote in part, "You may have been the best coach in the country last year Mr. Leahy, but junking the classic Notre Dame box formation for the questionable T formation is, in my humble estimation, a stupid move . . . This is a foolhardy experiment. Going to the T after an undefeated season makes as much sense as breaking up a full house to draw for four of a kind. Stand pat, Coach, and play the cards you have! . . ."

"You couldn't believe the nonsensical stories that were making the rounds." Said Leahy in his biography, Shake Down the Thunder, "They said that when word got out that I was switching to the T-formation, a huge crack appeared in the marble bust of Rockne that was sitting on a pedestal in the field house. They said it had to be rushed out for emergency repairs before anyone saw it . . . Unbelievable, but true. Some also said that pieces of the Golden Dome slipped loose and showered down on the students. These stories were designed to show that Our Lady was displeased with Frank Leahy."

If so, She sure didn't stay that way for long. Over the next nine seasons Leahy coached (time called in '44 and '45 for Navy duty) he went undefeated in five of them.

Fortunately for Jeff Cravath and the Trojans, they didn't have to look at Frank Leahy or the Fighting Irish for the next three years. The series was suspended from 1943 to 1946.

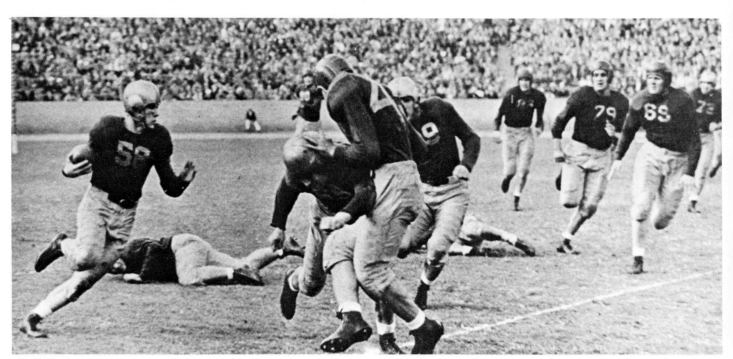

Tom Miller tries to sweep right of Trojan line

Robert Livingstone, star Notre Dame halfback

Creighton Miller, spark plug of Notre Dame's 1942 Victory

ANGELO BERTELLI

Angelo Bertelli, Notre Dame, 1941-42-43, an All-American quarterback and Heisman Trophy winner in 1943, and winner of the Walter Camp Trophy the same year. Frank Leahy, Grantland Rice and George Trevor all called him "the Best Passer in Football." As leader of Notre Dame's finest elevens, Bertelli was able to play in only six games in 1943, before being called to the Marines, yet his passing record (26 completions of 35 attempts for 11 touchdowns and a .743 percentage) earned him all the top honors. He served in the Marines for three years, rose to the rank of Captain.

Upon his discharge in 1946, he joined the Los Angeles Dons of the AAFC, then in 1947 and '48, he played with the Chicago Rockets also of the AAFC. In 1972 he was elected to the College Football Hall of Fame.

NOTRE DAME ROSTER — 1942

NO.	NAME	POS.	AGE	WT.
1	*Earley, William	R.H.	21	173
2	Creevy, Thomas	Q.B.	20	185
3	*Wright, Harry	R.G.	22	190
9	Creevey, John	Q.B.	19	205
15	O'Connor, William	R.G.	19	185
17	Tobin, George	R.G.	21	191
18	*Murphy, Capt. George	R.E.	21	170
21	Lanahan, John	C.	21	188
23	**Evans, Frederick	L.H.	21	175
25	Piccone, Cammille	L.H.	20	186
29	Cusick, Francis	L.E.	20	180
30	Limont, Joseph	R.E.	19	190
33	Krupa, Edward	R.H.	20	182
37	*Miller, Creighton	R.H.	20	188
40	Livingstone, Robert	L.H.	20	175
42	**Dove, Robert	L.G.	21	195
43	Creevy, Richard	L.H.	21	182
44	Coleman, Herbert	C.	19	195
45	Szymanski, Francis	R.T.	19	205
47	*McBride, Robert	L.G.	20	198
48	*Bertelli, Angelo	Q.B.	21	171
49	Meter, Bernard	L.G.	18	190
51	Dwyer, Eugene	R.E.	20	190
52	Filley, Patrick	L.G.	20	178
53	Cowhig, Gerard	F.B.	21	205
54	Huber, William	R.E.	19	197
55	Ashbaugh, Russell	R.H.	21	178
58	Miller, Thomas	L.H.	21	183
64	*Neff, Robert	R.T.	22	215
65	Mello, James	F.B.	21	188
68	*Brock, Thomas	C.	22	195
69	Clatt, Corwin	F.B.	18	198
70	*Rymkus, Louis	L.T.	22	218
71	White, James	L.T.	21	210
72	Sullivan, Lawrence	R.T.	22	205
73	Brutz, Martin	L.G.	19	190
74	**Ziemba, Walter	C.	23	225
75	Higgins, Luke	R.T.	21	210
76	Czarobski, Sigismunt	R.T.	20	205
80	Adams, John	L.T.	20	225
82	Yonakor, John	L.E.	21	222

TROJAN ROSTER — 1942

NO.	NAME	POS.	WT.	HT.
88	Adelman, Harry	L.G.	188	6'
50	*Bianchi, Steve	C.	190	5'11"
12	**Bledsoe, Bill	Q.	184	6'1½"
15	**Bleeker, Mel	Q.	185	5'10"
33	Callanan, Howard	R.H.	157	6'
60	Clark, Don	L.G.	192	5'10"
80	**Davis, Joe	R.E.	200	6'1"
83	*Essick, Doug	L.E.	196	6'3"
27	Evans, John	L.H.	182	5'8½"
79	Fuhrman, Seymour	L.T.	205	6'
21	Hardy, Jim	L.H.	176	5'11"
87	*Heywood, Ralph	L.E.	192	6'2"
81	Jacobsmeyer, Walt	R.E.	160	5'10"
24	Jamison, Dick	L.T.	190	6'1"
49	Kerns, Hubie	F.	173	5'11½"
44	Kroll, Darrell	F.-R.H.	180	6'½"
68	Littlejohn, LeRoy	C.	206	6'1"
86	MacPhail, Pete	R.E.	190	6'
32	*Manning, Dick	R.H.	190	5'9"
75	*McCall, Fred	L.T.	200	6'3"
28	McCardle, Mickey	L.H.	165	5'11"
45	*Musick, Bob	F.-Q.	190	5'11"
62	Noble, Bill	R.T.	203	5'10½"
52	Pappas, Tom	R.T.	186	6'1"
19	Parsons, Earle	L.H.	183	6'½"
29	Porter, Vincent	R.H.	169	5'11"
65	Seixas, Bill	R.G.	185	5'7"
43	*Taylor, Paul	R.H.-F.	190	6'1½"
69	**Thomas, Ron	R.G.	200	5'11"
72	*Verry, Norm	R.T.	233	6'1"
55	Wolf, Joe	C.	203	6'2"

1946
CHAPTER 19

"WHO THE HELL IS THIS COY McGEE YOU STUCK IN MY LINE-UP?"
. . . Frank Leahy, 1946

By 1946, hostilities had ceased over much of the world. But in 1946 hostilities were about to break out again against two old foes. The University of Southern California and the University of Notre Dame.

The war had made many changes in the game of football. The platoon system was born, and struggled through a shaky post-natal period until 1953, at which time it expired. But not for long. In 1954 it was re-born and managed this time to survive adolescence and come to maturity in 1965. Players returning from the service were older, bigger, and wiser.

In 1946, Southern California brought to Notre Dame 54 football players whose average weight was 197 pounds, whose height averaged 6'1", and who ranged in age from 19 to 27.

They were met by 73 Fighting Irishmen who averaged 197 pounds, 6 ft. 1 inch, and 22 years of age . . . and who were unbeaten.

It was the twentieth anniversary of the first meeting of the two, and the Trojans had not fared too well. The series stood at ten wins for the Irish, six for USC, and one tie. And it didn't appear that things were going to improve much for the Californians for some time to come. Notre Dame was loaded. The '46 team was considered by most superior to Rockne's undefeated champions of 1930.

Nevertheless, the Trojans, who had dedicated this game to Howard Jones, were, as always, determined to win. They were 5 and 3 for the season, but hope, however frail, is fond . . . and they hoped to win this for the Headman.

The Irish, of course, had something else in mind, and did what nearly everyone expected them to do. They defeated Southern California in what would appear to be a very convincing but rather routine way, 26-6. The wide margin of the Irish victory in no way reflects the bitter struggle that took place that November afternoon.

The dramatics started early. Coy McGee, a fourth string halfback who wasn't even on the starting roster for Notre Dame, ran the SC opening kickoff back 80 yards for a touchdown, but the play was called back. That seemed to instill a little caution in both teams, consequently the balance of the first half was spent probing and feinting like two fighters who had a healthy respect for the other's ability to counter punch.

The punch, counterpunch, came in the second quarter when a Notre Dame drive was halted on the Trojan 17 because of Johnny Lujack's fumble. USC's Newell Oestreich sent a towering quick kick 83 yards into the Irish end zone. Good kick . . . too good. When the ball edged in a few inches past the goal line, of course, it gave the home team the ball on their

Bob Livingstone rolls right for Notre Dame

own 20. One running play later little Coy McGee*, the Texas cyclone, stampeded for home like a horny heifer. 77 yards unmolested for the first Irish tally of the day. The point after was missed, but it didn't take them long to make up for that. After forcing SC to kick, Notre Dame took over on their own 30. They were unstoppable. Sub quarterback, George Ratterman, directed a 70 yard assault highlighted by a 22 yard pass to end Leon Hart for six, and capped by Fred Early's one point conversion. Score at the half, Notre Dame 13, Southern Cal 0.

The Trojans came out fighting for the second half. Hitting hard, John Ferraro, Jim Callanan, and Walt McCormick stopped the Irish and Bob Musick recovered McGee's fumble on the Notre Dame 45. With George Murphy running the club, the Trojans passed and ran for a first down on the 10. Milford Dreblow smashed left tackle for four yards, and Musick picked up another at center. Murphy then fired a perfect strike to Johnny Naumu, but Irish halfback Terry Brennan interfered and knocked him down. The penalty against the Irish moved the ball to the one yard line. Naumu again, first for one foot, and then on the next play he went over for the fourth touchdown scored against the Irish this season. He missed the conversion, but the Irish lead was cut to 13-6. The period ended a minute later. At this point some Trojan rooters (those with memories long enough) had begun to wonder if they might be witnessing a re-play of the 1931 SC-Irish game, when USC won 16-14 in the last quarter. Whatever hopes those fond memories kindled were quickly extinguished by Coy McGee. After a 60 yard march in seven plays, Cyclone Coy pumped over the line for another tally. The point after was missed, but minutes later Oestreich's punt was caught at mid field by Russ Ashbaugh, another Irish quarterback (they had seven suited up) who moved it to the Trojan 25. Floyd Simmons ran it to the 13 and Gerry Cowhig ploughed through right tackle then cut back quickly and went over standing up. Fred Early converted for the final point.

USC's Don Garlin picks up 8 yards

*At 5'10" and 160, Coy McGee might never have been called *little* at Notre Dame before 1946. But with a line that averaged 6'1", 210, and the backfield 6' and 180, that year he was "little" Coy McGee.

112

22-6. The Irish had done it again. But it hadn't been all that easy. It could have gone either way several times. In the waning minutes of the third quarter, when the Trojans were fired up as a result of their first score, they had Johnny Lujack trapped on his own 16 yard line. At least they thought they had.

On third down and 6 to go, Johnny dropped back to pass. The Trojan line rushed him. Finding all his receivers covered, he elected to run and slithered and slipped to the Irish 37 before they got him. Two plays later the Irish scored. If Johnny had been sacked and forced a fourth down punt, the Trojans might have . . . but who knows?

Shortly before the end of the game, Bob Musick picked off a Notre Dame pass and ran to the one foot line. The Trojans swore it was a touchdown, but the referee said his knee hit the ground on the one foot line . . . but who knows? One thing was certain. Notre Dame, under Frank Leahy, played hard football . . . the mid-west variety with blockers using both hands and forearms much more freely than Pacific coast teams. It wasn't until 1949 and '50 that rules clarifying use of arms in offensive and defensive blocking were adopted.

Coy McGee carried the ball only six times that afternoon, but gained 146 yards. According to the Los Angeles Times' Braven Dyer, "far and away the best performance of the game."

Coach Frank Leahy wasn't there to see it. He had a severe cold and on the order of his doctor had stayed home. Moose Krause, former All American football *and* basketball player for Notre Dame, now one of Coach Leahy's assistants, guided the team that day. Leahy, always the perfectionist, called the dressing room minutes before the game and dictated a starting lineup just in case Moose forgot. Moose didn't forget, but he committed a sacrilege. He substituted McGee for one of the starting halfbacks. After the game he called Coach Leahy.

"I figured he'd be happy because we looked so good." Krause remembers. "I was actually looking for a word of praise for myself."

Instead, Leahy's first words were, "Who in the hell is this Coy McGee you stuck in my lineup?"

Notre Dame's decisive victory over Southern California bumped Army out of the top spot in the final Associated Press Poll of the year. Army's weak showing against Navy while the Irish were mastering the men of Troy, dropped them to the number two spot. It was the first time since the beginning of the 1944 season that Army had not topped the weekly poll. Now the Irish were judged the best college team of 1946, as they would be in 1947, 1948, and 1949 . . . The best four years in the football history of Notre Dame. 36 wins, 2 ties and no losses.

Yes, Johnny had come marching home again, and the years of steady careful recruiting were beginning to pay off.

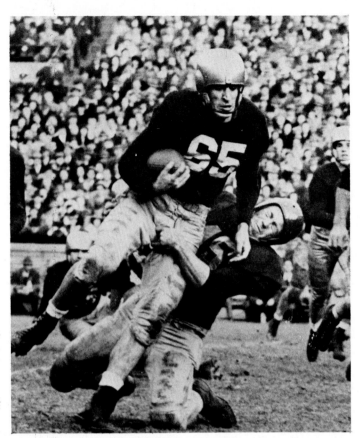
Jim Mello is hit by Bob Musick of Troy

George Ratterman, played behind Johnny Lujack at Notre Dame, and Otto Graham in professional football

OFFICIAL 1946 SO. CALIFORNIA FOOTBALL ROSTER

NO.	NAME	POSITION
12	*Murphy, George	Quarterback
15	Riggs, Leo	Quarterback
16	Betz, Bill	Quarterback
18	*Lillywhite, Verl	Quarterback
21	Webb, Bob	Left End
23	Naumu, Johnny	Left Halfback
25	Ragan, Terry	Left Halfback
27	*Doll, Don	Left Halfback
28	*McCardle, Mickey	Quarterback
29	*Garlin, Don	Left Halfback
31	Battle, Art	Right Halfback
32	*Dreblow, Milford	Right Halfback
33	*Gray, Gordon	Right Halfback
37	*Porter, Vincent	Fullback
38	Kerns, Hubie	Right Halfback
40	Oestreich, Nowell	Fullback
42	Conforti, Dan	Center
43	*Whitehead, Duane	Fullback
44	*Kirby, Jack	Left Halfback
45	*Musick, Bobby	Fullback
47	Rossetto, John	Fullback
49	Linehan, Tony	Left End
50	Juhnke, Martin	Center
52	*Antles, Russ	Center
54	Gibson, Bill	Left End
55	*McCormick, Walt	Center
56	Tolman, Ernie	Right End

NO.	NAME	POSITION
57	Pourchot, Ray	Left End
58	Schutte, George	Right Tackle
59	Romer, Al	Left Tackle
60	*Clark, Don	Right Guard
61	Jansen, Jim	Right Guard
62	Semeniuk, Walt	Right Guard
63	Cave, Reese	Right End
64	*Garzoni, Mike	Right Guard
65	Stall, Joe	L. Tackle-L. Guard
66	Bastian, Bob	Left Guard
68	Pierson, Mel	Left Guard
69	Snyder, James	Left Guard
71	*Ferraro, John	Left Tackle
72	*Aguirre, John	Right Tackle
74	Hendren, Bob	Right Tackle
75	*Musick, Jackie	Left Guard
77	Perrin, Jay	Left Tackle
78	*Romer, Marshall	Right Tackle
80	*McKinney, Harry	Right End
81	*Hardy, Don	Left End
82	Cleary, Paul	Right End
83	*Essick, Doug (Capt.)	Right End
84	Snyder, Frank	Right End
85	*Rae, John	Left Guard
86	Wright, Dudley	Right End
88	*Callanan, Jim	Right End
89	*Salata, Paul	Left End

OFFICIAL 1946 NOTRE DAME FOOTBALL ROSTER

NO.	NAME	POSITION
1	*Earley, Fred	Right Halfback
3	Brown, Roger	Quarterback
6	Heywood, William	Quarterback
7	Begley, Gerald	Quarterback
8	Tripucka, Frank	Quarterback
9	*Ratterman, George	Quarterback
10	*Creevey, John	Fullback
11	*Brennan, James	Right Halfback
12	*Ashbaugh, Russell	Quarterback
14	Sitko, Emil	Right Halfback
15	*Agnone, John	Left Halfback
16	*Skoglund, Robert	Left End
17	*Tobin, George	Guard
18	*Flanagan, James	Right End
19	McGee, Coy	Left Halfback
20	Smith, William L.	Left Halfback
21	Statuto, Arthur	Center
22	McNichols, Austin	Center
24	Coutre, Lawrence	Right Halfback
25	*O'Connor, William (Zeke)	Left End
26	McGehee, Ralph	Right Tackle
27	Espenan, Ray	Left End
28	*O'Connor, William (Bucky)	Left Guard
29	Dougherty, James	Center

NO.	NAME	POSITION
30	*Gompers, William	Right Halfback
31	*McGurk, James	Fullback
32	*Lujack, John	Quarterback
33	Kosikowski, Frank	Right End
34	*Limont, Paul	Left End
35	Zalejski, Ernest	Left Halfback
36	Frampton, John	Left Guard
37	*Brennan, Terence	Left Halfback
38	Martin, James	Left End
40	*Livingstone, Robert	Left Halfback
41	Connor, Charles	Left Guard
42	*Rovai, Fred	Right Guard
43	*Potter, Thomas	Left Guard
44	LeCluyse, Leonard	Fullback
45	Michaels, William	End
46	*Walsh, William	Center
47	*McBride, Robert	Right Guard
49	*Meter, Bernard	Right Guard
50	Walsh, Robert	Left End
51	*Scott, Vincent	Left Guard
53	*Cowhig, Gerald	Left Halfback
54	*Sullivan, George	Right Tackle
55	Swistowicz, Michael	Right Halfback
56	*Zilly, John	Right End

NO.	NAME	POSITION
57	*Slovak, Emil	Right Halfback
58	*Wendell, Martin	Center
59	Zmijewski, Al	Right Tackle
60	Strohmeyer, George	Center
61	*Russell, Wilmer	Left Tackle
62	Simmons, Floyd	Right Halfback
63	Budynkiewicz, Ted	Tackle
64	*Urban, Gasper	Right Tackle
65	*Mello, James	Fullback
66	Vangen, Willard	Center
67	*Panelli, John	Fullback
68	*Fallon, John	Right Tackle
69	*Clatt, Corwin	Fullback
70	*Schuster, Kenneth	Left Tackle
71	*Higgins, Luke	Right Guard
72	*Fischer, William	Left Guard
73	Brutz, Martin	Right Guard
74	*Signaigo, Joseph	Left Guard
75	*Mastrangelo, John	Right Guard
76	*Czarobski, Zygmont	Right Tackle
80	Cifelli, August	Left Tackle
81	Connor, George	Left Tackle
82	Hart, Leon	Right End
83	Wightkin, William	Right End

114

1947
CHAPTER 20

. . .SHAKE DOWN THE THUNDER
. . .Notre Dame Victory March . . .1900(?)

The 1947 Notre Dame football team may have been the best college team fielded anywhere, any time. Certainly in the considerate opinion of knowledgeable critics of the game, the Irish teams from 1946 to 1950 had only two serious rivals, Army and Michigan. The strength and depth of the 1947 team was awesome. There were those who declared that the Irish of that year compared favorably with any professional team. Their attack was swift, paralyzing and absolutely implacable. And what was even more frightening was the fact that the first team was only a little better than the second, the second only a little better than the third, the third just slightly better than the fourth, and so on. And they brought a squad of 66 with them to the Los Angeles Coliseum. Probably the 5th stringers on the roster would have made the first string on any PCC team.

When the University of Notre Dame and the University of Southern California took the field on December 6, before a crowd of 104,953 football fanatics, both teams were undefeated. The similarity ended there.

It's quite possible that the Trojans had read the advance notices on the numbing Irish attack and got a little nervous. Press releases like those can turn even the strongest stomachs to aspic and agile fingers to stone . . . and that's what happened. On the second play of the game, Verl Lillywhite fumbled and Irish Captain George Conner recovered. From the Trojan 33 yard line they powered their way to the 12 for a first down, but the men of Troy got over their shock and held at the 7. Coach Leahy's ace place kicker, Fred Early, came in and booted from the 13 on an extremely difficult angle. It was fast, it was neat, and it was good.

Within a couple of plays the Irish were back on the offensive and mounted an 88 yard attack which they completed in 17 plays. Johnny Lujack completely confused the Trojan defenders with the variety of his attack. First calling on Livingstone to run, then passing to John Pannelli, then on Sitko to carry and passing to Livingstone and handing off to Panelli, two more passes to Panelli and a give to Sitko for a one yard touchdown run. The point after of course, was good. Fred Early couldn't have missed that day if he had been wearing his grandfather's eyeglasses and his grandmother's hobble skirt.

The Trojans were dazzled, but not dead . . . yet.

They managed to piece a drive together from the Irish 40 when SC quarterback Jimmy Powers intercepted a Lujack pass. Then on the offensive, he mixed passes with running plays to advance the ball to the 8 yard line of Notre Dame. Halfback Jack Kirby flew around right end and dove into the end zone for a touchdown. Place kicker Tom Walker made the extra point good and the score was 10-7, and the momentum was on the side of USC. Before the end of the half, they had another chance to score when All American end Paul Cleary eluded the Notre Dame safety man and was wide open for a touchdown pass from Powers, if he could have stretched just a few more inches, they might have gone into the locker room at halftime ahead. But the pass flew just beyond his fingertips, and the half was over.

The second half was different. The fighting Irish set about with machine-like precision to dismantle the Trojan defense and they did. On the first offensive play, Sitko, aided by beautiful interference, galloped 76 yards to score. Lujack got even for Powers' interception of his pass in the second quarter. He intercepted Powers' pass in the third and ran it from his 10 yard line upfield to the 47 before being dropped. Lujack didn't throw a pass in the last half . . . he didn't have to. His ground game was going just great. That Notre Dame line was opening holes that a wagon train could have lumbered through. And they did it for Sitko, Panelli and Coy McGee in the third quarter and Terry Brennan's sub, halfback Bob Livingstone in the fourth.

Livingstone's spectacular run was set up early in the fourth quarter when the Trojans were gasping their last desperate breath. Cleary had recovered a fumble for SC at midfield, and John Rosetto hammered his way through the Irish reserves to the 34. Dean Dill completed a short pass to Stan Cramer for four yards, then Dill with two carries made the first down on the 24. Mickey McArdle and Dill tried valiantly for another first down, but nothing worked and the Irish took over on their own 8. Rather, Bob Livingstone took over, and ran 98 yards for another Irish touchdown. (Poor Bob was supposedly suffering from bad feet as a result of Army duty.) The straw that broke the camel's back came moments later when SC's Wilbur Robertson shoveled a desperation lateral to . . . Alfred Zmijewski, a fourth or fifth string Irish tackle, who just happened to be there. No one was more surprised than Alfred, but he was one of Coach Leahy's lads, and as such had been so thoroughly drilled that reflex action took over. He grabbed the toss and puffed 72 yards for another touchdown which Notre Dame needed like a moose needs a hatrack. Faultless Fred Early converted and the score was 38-7, and the game, mercifully, was over.

It had been some years since USC had been called the Thundering Herd. Probably because it had been some years since they had thundered. It was too bad, because in 1947 they had at least rumbled a little. In any other season eight straight wins would have been impressive. In the early postwar years it's doubtful that ten King Kongs and a Mighty Joe Young would have startled Notre Dame. So once more the Fighting Irish had shaken the thunder down from the sky. They had shaken more than that. They shook the Trojans so badly that 3 weeks later they lost 49-0 to Michigan in the Rose Bowl.

Notre Dame — unbeaten, untied and virtually unchallenged, was once more selected as the outstanding football team of the year . . . winning the honor for the second straight year in the weekly poll conducted by the Associated Press. Johnny Lujack, George Connor, Bill Fischer, Ziggy Czarobski, and Leon Hart were named All American.

It was a very good year.
For the Irish, that is.

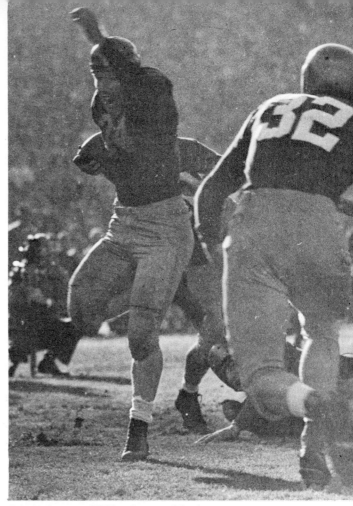

Jack Kirby scores USC's only score of the day

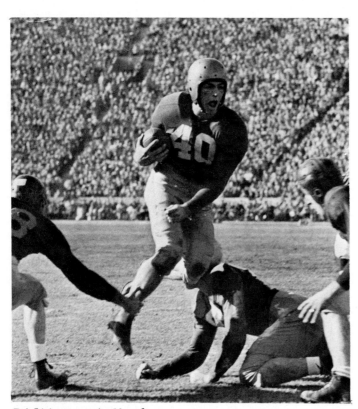

Bob Livingstone gains 10 yards

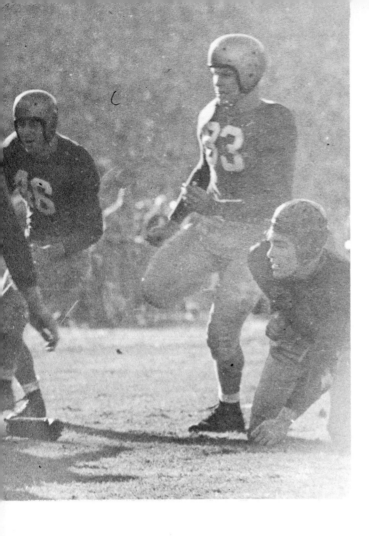

JOHN LUJACK

GEORGE CONNOR

George Connor, a tackle on the first All Century Team, was a big, fast, mobile lineman who played on Frank Leahy's great 1946-1947 teams and opened gaps for such ball-carriers as Johnny Lujack and Terry Brennan. On defense, he was a crushing tackler. Once, before an important Army game, he told the Irish, "The sons of slum and gravy are coming to the campus of beans and sausage." Whatever that meant. Coach Leahy said of him: "He had the agility to sort out the ball-carrier and the toughness to break up the power play. He was indestructible." Notre Dame placed only one man on the All Century Team . . . George Connor. If big George is, therefore, the best Notre Dame player ever fielded, then he must be just about the best who ever played. In 1948 he joined his Notre Dame teammate Johnny Lujack and the Chicago Bears. He played until 1955. He entered the College Football Hall of Fame in 1969.

John Lujack, an All-American quarterback at Notre Dame in 1946 and '47, was the last of the truly magnificent triple-threat tailbacks. Following the East-West Game at San Francisco on January 1, 1948, East Coach Bernie Bierman said: "You don't have to worry about a team with Lujack in charge. Just turn the reins over to him and relax." Coach George Halas, who had him on the Chicago Bears, later added, "Completely stripped of all his amazing football skills, Lujack is still indispensable for one thing — his poise." In three years at Notre Dame with every opponent primed for the Irish, the 6-feet, 180 pound Lujack, calm, deliberate, unhurried and unruffled, was in emergency or crisis the personification of poise. "He threw a pass like a frozen rope and blocked like a whipsaw." As an unknown sophomore, subbing for the great Angelo Bertelli, in the 1943 Army game, Lujack took charge right from the kickoff and engineered a 26-9 victory with all the poise and finesse of a seasoned pro. A strong field commander, when he gave orders others listened. Three years later in the historic deadlock with a powerful Army eleven, Lujack downed mighty Doc Blanchard single-handedly in the open field which had never been done before, to prevent a touchdown. Johnny Lujack, injured, played the full 60 minutes of that bruising game. He was that kind of man. He played from 1948 to '51 with the Chicago Bears. In 1960 he was elected to the College Football Hall of Fame.

UNIVERSITY OF SOUTHERN CALIFORNIA — 1947 ROSTER

NO.	NAME	POS.	WT.	NO.	NAME	POS.	WT.	NO.	NAME	POS.	WT.
66	*Bastian, Bob	R.G.	205	12	**Murphy, George	R.E.	210	80	Fletcher, Oliver	F.	195
61	Bayless, Bill	R.T.	220	40	*Oestreich, Newell	R.H.	185	38	Futrell, Lou	R.T.	300
54	Beck, Gene	C.	180	77	Perrin, Jay	L.H.	180	29	**Garlin, Don	L.T.	210
39	Beck, Harry	R.H.	185	25	Plyley, Earl	R.H.	190	33	***Gray, Gordon	Q.	175
41	Betz, Bill	F.	190	15	Powers, Jim	R.G.	195	57	Hachten, Boyd	L.G.	205
73	Bird, Jim	R.T.	220	65	**Rea, John	L.E.	205	43	Hatfield, Harold	Q.	170
45	Burke, Don	F.	225	16	Robertson, Wilbur	R.T.	225	74	*Henndren, Bob	F.	205
51	Busch, Ernie	C.	195	47	*Rossetto, John	L.H.	185	24	Kirby, Jack	R.H.	180
21	Cantor, Al	L.H.	170	32	Roundy, Jay	F.	185	42	Kordich, John	L.E.	190
60	**Clark, Don	L.G.	195	89	*Salata, Paul	F.	175	18	**Lillywhite, Verl	R.T.	210
82	*Cleary, Paul	R.E.	195	78	*Schutte, George	L.E.	200	86	*Linehan, Tony	R.G.	205
61	Colley, Tom	R.G.	200	69	Snyder, Jim	L.E.	200	83	*Lloyd, Dave	R.E.	200
34	Craig, Rod	L.H.	175	84	Stillwell, Bob	L.G.	200	67	Lowell, Russ	L.T.	210
81	Cramer, Stan	L.E.	190	79	Swope, Jesse	F.	195	44	Martin, Bill	L.H.	180
36	*Curry, Edsel	R.H.	190	3	**Tannehill, Ted	R.G.	200	75	**McCall, Fred	L.E.	205
50	*Davis, George	C.	195	88	Tolman, Ernie	L.H.	170	28	***McCardle, Mickey	R.T.	215
63	Dickson, Charles	R.G.	195	37	Vukovich, Mel	C.	200	55	**McCormick, Walt	P.-K.†	185
19	Dill, Dean	Q.	195	1	Walker, Tom	R.E.	190	58	Meyer, William	R.T.	220
27	**Doll, Don	R.H.	185	72	White, Keith	L.G.	200	64	Monson, James	R.E.	190
71	***Ferraro, John	L.T.	240	59	*Willumson, Don	Q.	190				

UNIVERSITY OF NOTRE DAME — 1947 ROSTER

NO.	NAME	POS.	WT.	NO.	NAME	POS.	WT.
12	Ashbaugh, Russell	Q.B.	175	44	Leonard, William	E.	190
7	Begley, Gerald	Q.B.	170	16	Lesko, Alex	E.	180
11	Brennan, James	R.H.	160	40	Livingstone, Robert	L.H.	168
37	Brennan, Terence	L.H.	173	32	Lujack, John	Q.B.	180
3	Brown, Roger	Q.B.	180	38	Martin, James	L.E.	203
63	Budynkiewicz, Theo.	R.T.	205	65	McCarty, Thomas	F.B.	185
56	Burnett, Albert	E.	195	19	McGee, Coy	L.H.	165
51	Carter, Donald	C.	200	26	McGehee, Ralph	L.T.	211
84	Ciechanowicz, Emil	T.	230	45	Michaels, William	E.	190
80	Cifelli, August	T.	225	25	O'Connor, William	E.	200
69	Clatt, Corwin	F.B.	200	39	Oracko, Steve	G.	193
81	Connor, Geo. (Capt.)	L.T.	220	67	Panelli, John	F.B.	190
41	Connor, John	G.	185	61	Russell, Wilmer	T.	200
17	Couch, Leo	G.	200	34	Saggau, Thomas	H.B.	170
24	Coutre, Lawrence	H.B.	170	73	Saul, Frank	G.	200
76	Czarobski, Ziggy	R.T.	213	70	Schuster, Kenneth	T.	210
29	Dailer, James	G.	180	74	Signaigo, Joseph	R.G.	205
1	Earley, Fred	H.B.	170	62	Simmons, Floyd	F.B.	195
27	Espenan, Raymond	E.	189	14	Sitko, Emil	R.H.	175
31	Fallon, Joseph	G.	190	20	Smith, Lancaster	L.H.	165
72	Fischer, William	L.G.	230	28	Spaniel, Frank	H.B.	180
36	Frampton, John	G.	190	21	Statuto, Arthur	C.	200
22	Gay, William	H.B.	180	60	Strohmeyer, George	C.	195
30	Gompers, William	R.H.	175	54	Sullivan, George	R.T.	206
52	Grothaus, Walter	C.	197	55	Swistowicz, Michael	H.B.-F.	175
82	Hart, Leon	R.E.	216	8	Tripucka, Frank	Q.B.	178
47	Helwig, John	T.	198	64	Urban, Gasper	T.-G.	200
53	Helwig, Joseph	G.	200	46	Walsh, William	C.	205
49	Hudak, Edward	T.	200	42	Waybright, Douglas	E.	180
18	Johnson, Frank	E.	185	58	Wendell, Martin	L.G.	198
33	Kosikowski, Frank	R.E.	202	83	Wightkin, William	R.E.	205
57	Lally, Robert	G.	185	71	Wilke, Clifford	H.B.	190
43	LeCluyse, Leonard	F.B.	188	59	Zmijewski, Alfred	T.	200

1948
CHAPTER 21

"THANK YOU, SIR, THAT'S ENOUGH"
. . . Bill Gay to Referee 1948

The twentieth meeting of these two honored foes took place once again in the Los Angeles Coliseum. The reason for two consecutive games on the west coast was that both participants were desirous of returning the series to its original pre-war schedule, odd years at South Bend, even years at Los Angeles.

Next year the teams would play at Notre Dame. After that? . . . well rumor had it that USC would not renew. And who could blame them, after all. Bravery is one thing, but masochism is another. The series now stood at 12-6-1. The Trojans hadn't won since 1939, and no one gave them much of a chance this year. Or next year for that matter. Football talent seemed to pour onto the campus of Notre Dame like lemmings marching to the sea. They came from every high school, every prep school, the Army, the Navy and the Marine Corps. And Coach Leahy knew what to do with them.

Because of the war, Johnny Lujack, George Connor, and Ziggy Czarobski, could have played another year by merely stretching out their scholastic programs. Instead they decided to graduate. Leahy didn't try to dissuade them, he didn't really need them. So off went Lujack and Connor to join the Chicago Bears and Ziggy went.

Poor Coach Leahy was left with only Leon Hart and Bill Fischer, both All Americans, Emil (Red) Sitko, Bill Walsh, John Papelli, Coy McGee, and a young man named Terry Brennan . . . waiting in the wings were men like Bill Gay, Ernie Zalejski, and Johnny Mazur. No, Notre Dame was not bereft of football talent. Not yet.

Jeff Cravath's Trojans were coming into the game with a so-so record of 6 wins and 3 losses. He had no individual stars of the magnitude of Notre Dame's Hart or Fischer or Sitko, but he did have a crew of good solid performers, led by a passing quarterback of great ability, Jimmy Powers, who directed the Trojans to their only tally against Notre Dame the year before.

Leahy, of course, was bringing to town another undefeated team. They were 9-0 for the season, and 26-0-1 since 1946. The only smudge on the purity of their record was a scoreless tie with Army in November of 1946. The current win streak stood at 21 straight.

The crowd of 100,571 who came to the Coliseum that December day, must have felt a little like the spectators who used to jam the original Coliseum centuries ago in Rome, when a game between the Christians and lions was scheduled.

They knew who the winner would be, but they wanted to be in on the kill.

This time they were fooled . . . the Christians damn near ate the lions.

The three touchdown underdogs outcharged, outfought, and nearly outscored the South Bend Supermen.

The resolve of the Trojan team was immediately apparent when on the opening kickoff, half of the SC squad hit Terry Brennan so hard he fumbled. And that was the first of many. Throughout the contest SC's savage tackling caused seven fumbles which resulted in six Trojan recoveries. During the first half USC's expert punting kept the Irish deep in their own territory, but in the closing minutes of the second quarter Leon Hart took a short pass from Irish quarterback Frank Tri-

Notre Dame halfback, Bill Gay

Trojan halfback, Jack Kirby breaks open around left end

pucka on the Trojan 40 and was immediately hit by Trojan halfback Jay Roundy. Now Roundy weighed only 180 to Hart's estimated 245, so you can guess how that encounter came out. Hart spun, went to the turf with one hand, but caught his balance and took off. He was hit three more times, but tackling Leon Hart was a little like trying to bulldog a full grown Brahma bull. He scored. The point after was good and the Irish led 7-0. A couple of plays later Frank Tripucka, who was rated by many to be Lujack's equal at ball handling, though not on defense, was severely injured and had to be carried from the field. The Trojans had fought like demons and held the greatest football machine in the United States to just one touchdown in the first half.

Nor were they out of miracles. In the third quarter, they ran the opening kickoff and hammered their way to the Irish 23 yard line before losing the ball on downs. But once more they fought the invaders to a standstill. SC's Jack Kirby (remember him? He scored SC's only tally in the 1947 game) intercepted one of Bob Williams' passes and returned it to the Notre Dame 42, beginning USC's first touchdown drive. Dean Dill was sacked when he faded back to pass and lost 5 yards, but on the next play Kirby made the second of three spectacular catches he contributed that afternoon and ran the ball to the 18. He then picked up three more yards just as the gun sounded ending the quarter.

The first play of the final period Dill sent his receivers out and dropped back to pass. Seeing them all covered, he raced up the middle for a first down on the 6. Art Battle and Bill Martin took turns battling (if you'll pardon the expression) to the 1 yard line. The Trojan line then opened a hole at left tackle, and Martin waltzed in standing up. Dill's extra point attempt was good, and the score was 7-7. A brand new ball game.

With time rapidly running out, Kirby fielded Bob Williams' punt and again ran it to the Notre Dame 42. The next play he punched 16 yards for a first down. The march was on. Battle made a yard, then Dill hit Ernie Tolman with a pass for another first down on the 18. Dill ran for another first down when he found his receivers covered . . . Martin broke through a big hole at tackle, to the 6, and a first down. Battle slammed to the 4, and Martin drove over left tackle for the touchdown. Only two Trojans had ever scored two touchdowns against Notre Dame in one game. Gus Shaver in 1931, and Cotton Warburton in 1933. Dill's extra point was again good and the score was 14-7, *Southern California!*

The scoreboard clock showed 2 minutes 30 seconds to play.

Cardiac time at the Coliseum. USC fans were either babbling hysterically, or staring at each other in utter disbelief. Could it be possible that the lowly Trojans might slay the Irish dragon? It could not. Notre Dame halfback Bill Gay saw to that.

Charlie Peterson kicked off and Gay made an easy catch,

cut to his right, picked up speed and blockers and ran unimpeded to the 13 yard line. Williams gained 5 over center. On the next play, realizing that the clock was catching up with him, he took to the air. He missed Gay in the end zone on his first attempt, but came right back with the same play. This time the pass looked long, but Gay kept running. Gene Beck, the Trojan defender, closed in. Gay got to the end zone, but Beck got to Gay before Gay got to the pass.

"I stumbled," said Beck.

"Pass interference," said Field Judge Orian Landreth, and placed the ball on the 2 yard line.

"I'm anxious to see the movies," said Jeff Cravath.

It's dangerous to allow any opposing football team to get to your 2 yard line with less than a minute to play. In the case of the 1948 Irish it was suicide. "Six Yard" Sitko rammed right guard for 6 and steady Steve Oracko tied the score with a perfect conversion.

There were 34 seconds left . . . The Irish tried an onside kick and recovered, but time had run out. Nobody won.

The Trojans probably should have been happy with a tie after facing such overwhelming odds, but after coming so close to winning, a moral victory soured into moral defeat.

Nor were the Fighting Irish of Notre Dame much happier. Their string of 28 games without defeat was still intact, but it was sorely bent. So confident were they, that in the closing minutes of the game, as USC lined up to kick to Notre Dame after their touchdown drive, Billy Gay calmly walked over to the referee and asked: "Mr. Referee, how much time is left?"

"Two minutes and 35 seconds," the referee replied.

"Thank you sir, that's enough," said Gay, and ran that kickoff back 86 yards to set up the tying touchdown.

"*Without a doubt,*" *intoned Coach Leahy after the game, "this is one of the best teams we met all year. Sterling coaching by Mr. Cravath and fine team play made possible your impressive showing today, but the spirit of all of you contributed to this fine performance this afternoon.*"

It sounded like a benediction, but the rumors had already started to surface regarding both coaches. USC was unhappy with Jeff Cravath for not winning enough games, and a part of the Notre Dame academic community was disturbed because Frank Leahy was winning too many!

It seems that about the only person involved with the 1948 game in the Coliseum who was relly happy was City Council President Harold Henry. He had succeeded the previous year in pushing through legislation making it illegal to drink in the Coliseum during football games. It was a success. Last year they had toted away a full truckload of empty whiskey bottles after the game. This year, he proudly reported to the Los Angeles Times, it was only half a truckload.

Frank Tripuka was considered Lujacks equal in ball handling for Notre Dame

Emil Sitko scored the equalizing touchdown for Notre Dame with 32 seconds to go

SOUTHERN CALIFORNIA — 1948

NO.	NAME	POS.	WT.
46	Anderson, Harry	F.	185
72	Ashcraft, Walt	R.T.	230
55	Barnes, Mercer	C.	205
66	**Bastian, Bob	L.G.	205
31	*Battle, Art	R.H.	170
20	Beaman, George	L.H.	170
65	Beck, Gene	C.	180
41	*Betz, Bill	F.	190
73	*Bird, Jim	L.T.	220
45	Burke, Don	F.	225
21	Cantor, Al	L.H.	170
63	Christoffersen, L.	R.G.	220
62	Colley, Tom	R.G.	200
81	*Cramer, Stan	L.E.	190
50	**Davis, George	C.	195
69	D'Ambrosi, Jasper	L.G.	210
19	*Dill, Dean	Q.	190
27	***Doll, Don	L.H.	185
68	Downs, Bob	R.G.	205
61	Mendenhall, Bob	L.G.	200
64	Monson, James	R.G.	200
12	***Murphy, George	Q.	190
58	Nix, Jack	R.E.	190
77	Peters, Volney	L.T.	215
59	Peterson, Charles	R.T.	215
15	*Powers, Jim	Q.	175
33	Pucci, Ralph	R.H.	180
16	Robertson, Wilbur	Q.	170
25	Rogers, Don	L.H.	175
32	*Roundy, Jay	R.H.	180
78	**Schutte, George	R.T.	210
37	*Scott, Joe	L.H.	160
84	*Stillwell, Bob	R.E.	200
79	*Swope, Jess	R.T.-L.T.	210
88	*Tolman, Ernie	L.E.	205
49	Vukovich, Mel	L.T.	215
89	*Willumson, Don	R.E.	190
80	Fletcher, Oliver	R.E.	2
38	Futrell, Lou	R.H.	1
29	***Garlin, Don	L.H.	1
57	Hachten, Boyd	C.	1
52	Hamilton, Tom	C.	2
85	Hatfield, Harold	L.E.	2
74	**Hendren, Bob	R.T.	2
54	Henke, Ed	R.T.	2
56	Jessup, Bill	R.E.	1
24	*Kirby, Jack	L.H.	1
36	Kordich, John	R.H.	1
86	**Linehan, Tony	L.E.	2
83	**Lloyd, Dave	L.E.	2
67	*Lowell, Russ	L.G.	1
40	Mann, John	F.	1
75	Mantel, Lee	L.T.	2
44	Martin, Bill	F	1
51	McGee, Bob	L.T.	2
60	McMurtry, Paul	R.G.	2

NOTRE DAME — 1948

NO.	NAME	POS.	WT.
7	Begley, Gerald	Q.	175
37	***Brennan, Terence	L.H.	170
63	*Budynkiewicz, Ted	R.T.	205
54	Cantwell, Philip	E.	194
4	Carter, Thomas	Q.	173
80	*Cifelli, August	L.T.	219
51	Cottor, Richard	F.	185
24	*Coutre, Lawrence	R.H.	170
29	*Dailer, James	G.	185
27	*Espenan, Raymond	L.E.	188
68	**Fallon, John	R.T.	194
72	***Fischer, William (Capt.)	L.G.	226
41	*Flynn, William	E.	190
36	*Frampton, John	L.G.	190
73	Gaul, Francis	R.T.	210
22	Gay, William	H.B.	170
60	Groom, Jerome	C.	210
52	**Grothaus, Walter	C.	192
82	**Hart, Leon	R.E.	223
47	Helwig, John	G.	190
61	Higgins, William	G.	175
49	Hudak, Edward	T.	200
18	Johnson, Frank	G.	190
57	*Lally, Robert	R.G.	185
30	Landry, John	L.H.	180
16	Lesko, Alexander	L.E.	18
70	Mahoney, James	T.	19
38	**Martin, James	L.E.	20
19	**McGee, Coy	L.H.	15
26	**McGehee, Ralph	R.T.	20
40	McKillip, Leo	R.H.	17
39	*Oracko, Stephen	L.G.	19
67	***Panelli, John	F.	18
34	Saggau, Thomas	H.	17
14	**Sitko, Emil	R.H.	18
15	Smith, Eugene	R.H.	17
20	*Smith, Lancaster	L.H.	15
28	Spaniel, Frank	R.H.	18
55	**Swistowciz, Michael	F.	19
8	**Tripucka, Frank	Q.	17
48	Wallner, Frederick	F.	19
46	***Walsh, William	C.	20
42	**Waybright, Douglas	L.E.	18
58	***Wendell, Martin	R.G.	19
83	*Wightkin, William	R.E.	19
9	Williams, Robert	Q.	18
56	Yanoschik, Philip	C.	19
12	*Zalejski, Ernest	L.H.	18
59	Zmijewski, Alfred	R.T.	20

1949
CHAPTER 22

"MR. LEAHY WILL BE OUR COACH FOR AT LEAST ANOTHER YEAR"
. . . Moose Krause, Athletic Director, Notre Dame, 1949

Somewhere in the middle or late 1930's, Robert L. Ripley, in his syndicated cartoon panel, "Believe It or Not," astounded the American newspaper-reading public by announcing that if the Chinese were to start marching past a given point four abreast, the procession would never end. The obvious explanation being, of course, that there were so many of them being produced that the line could go on forever.

In the late 1940's the opponents of Notre Dame must have felt that someone, somewhere, had set up a starting point and was trying the experiment with Irish football players.

It started in 1945 when thousands of fine young football prospects who had graduated from high school as rawboned, callow kids in 1942, returned from the battlefields of Europe and the South Pacific as men in 1945. It created something unprecedented in college recruiting . . . an almost bottomless well of football talent. The main thing was to get to the pump before the well ran dry. And no one could ever accuse Frank Leahy of being slow when it came to recruiting. (Remember how the Boston College prospects suddenly appeared at Notre Dame for Leahy's first season?)

Lt. Francis W. Leahy was discharged on November 15, 1945, after a year and a half with the Submarine Command in the South Pacific in charge of athletic programs. Armed with Irish wit and charm, an impressive record, and messianic zeal, he appeared at the well and began to pump.

For the next four years Notre Dame was so rich in gifted players, that the question was not so much which eleven men do we field today, but rather *how many* can we play today. In 1947, 39 Irishmen saw action against Army, including some freshman 5th stringers. They still won 27-7. Every varsity player had so many replacements available that no one dreamed of relaxing.

Leahy was accused of running up scores to look good in the national polls. He swore that was untrue, and it makes sense. How can you drill into a team the importance of winning for six days, then on the seventh tell them to take it easy because your team is ahead by a big margin.

"It was my policy," Leahy said later to his biographer, Wells Twombly, "to put my best team on the field and wait for them to do their duty . . . Should they perform expertly and should the opposition appear feeble, then the honorable thing to do was place my next best players on the field. If they

should be as adept as the first line, then it was incumbent on me to go to my next best grouping, to give them all the chance to play for the honor of Our Lady. It was not my fault if the fourth string continued to score touchdowns after that."

Despite such restraint, Notre Dame swarmed on their own field November 6 with a 4 year record of 1183 points scored against opponents, compared to 235 given up. An average of 32-6 per game. A win today would give them a record of 37 games without defeat. There was very little chance they would lose.

The heart of Notre Dame's T, Quarterback Bob Williams and Center Walt Grothaus

Leon Hart, Notre Dame's right end, at 6' 4" 245 lbs., All American, 4 year starter and Heisman Trophy Winner

Their intended victim, the University of Southern California, brought with them to South Bend a record of 5 wins, 2 losses and 1 tie. And a lot of courage. With only a fair line, a backfield riddled with injuries and playing on an alien and enemy field in sub-freezing temperatures against an undefeated team, most of whom were graduating seniors ready to lay down their lives for the honor of Our Lady in their last game . . . it took a lot of courage just to show up.

By the end of the first quarter they probably wished they hadn't.

The first ten minutes of the first period was evenly played, then with the ball on the Trojan 40, SC in possession, quarterback Jim Powers decided to gamble on fourth down and 2. He was criticized by sportswriters the following day for taking the chance. If it had worked, he would have been Saturday's hero. But it didn't work. He threw a perfect pass to Bob Stillwell on the right flank, but Bob couldn't hang on. If the gamble had paid off, SC would have had a first down on about the 44. As it was, it was Notre Dame's ball on the 40.

On third and 10, Bob Williams fired a 40 yard pass to Leon Hart for the first score. Steve Oracko made the conversion . . . 7-0, Notre Dame. Before the Trojans had a chance to catch their breath, Jim Martin had returned an SC punt to the Trojan 34. Powers passed on first down to Pat Duff. It was a little high, but it worked out all right for the Irish. Pat leaped high in the air and tipped it right into the hands of his teammate, halfback John Petitbon who raced down the sidelines for 43 yards and the touchdown. SC's Bill Jessup blocked the extra point. At the end of the first quarter, 13-0.

Just before the end of the second period, Notre Dame's third All American, Emil Sitko, made it 19-0 when he slashed from 5 yards out.

The second half didn't get any better for the Trojans. As if they didn't have enough trouble with the weather, fumbleitis, and Emil Sitko (graduated now from Six-Yard-Sitko to Eight Yard Emil), Leahy pulled Leon Hart into the backfield as a fullback. Hart on the line was dangerous. Hart in the backfield was calamitous . . . he wasn't the Four Horsemen, he was the whole cavalry. Although he played in the backfield that day, he became the only lineman in history to win the Heisman trophy.

The second half grew even more dismal for the men of Troy. They battled hard, of course, but were no match for the Irish defense. They were never able to penetrate past the 18 yard line of Notre Dame. The Irish on the other hand, seemed to have little difficulty in scoring in the second half. Frank Spaniel, a substitute halfback, scored 6 with a 13 yard run. Oracko missed the point after, and Notre Dame led 25-0.

The fifth and final touchdown came as a climax to a 54 yard march with Bill Barrett, another Irish halfback (they had ten) first catching a 31 yard pass, then cracking over center for the final tally. This time the conversion was good, the Irish had won their 10th in a row, 32-0, and played their 37th consecutive game without defeat.

The number of rumors continued to increase in direct proportion to the length of the winning streak. Now it was said that Lou Perini, the owner of the Boston Brave baseball team would be awarded a professional football franchise if he could sign Leahy to a contract.

For several years just before or just after the USC game, it was popular to predict that Coach Leahy would replace Jeff Cravath. Just the year before, a sportswriter had facetiously asked Cravath during an interview, "Is it true you're going to replace Frank Leahy at Notre Dame in 1949?" Jeff chuckled.

One such rumor was confirmed by Leahy many years later. A former SC football player who had become successful in the motion picture business, was willing to come up with $50,000 and a retirement home in Palm Springs if Leahy would come to Southern California.

According to the Los Angeles Times, the Coach himself told two friends after the 1949 game that he wouldn't be coaching at Notre Dame much longer.

When informed of this, Moose Krause, Notre Dame athletic director stated: "Mr. Leahy will be our coach for at least another year."

There were more indications of things to come. Notre Dame had had another victorious year, but they were losing ten regulars and an equal number of reserves. The Trojans, on the other hand, were losing only four of their eleven starters.

Orv Mohler, USC All American—1930

But the University of Southern California had suffered a much more tragic loss than the graduation of a few football players. Col. Orv Mohler, All American quarterback in 1930 and one of the all-time Trojan greats, the architect and hero, along with Johnny Baker of the 1931 16-14 upset of Notre Dame, was killed the day before the game. The B-25 he was piloting developed engine trouble during a routine flight. As the bomber lost altitude, he ordered his co-pilot and a third crewman to bail out. They did, and he rode it to the ground. The big plane slammed into a hill near Montgomery, Alabama. He was 40 years old.

SOUTHERN CALIFORNIA ROSTER — 1949

NO.	NAME	POS.	WT.
12	Robertson, Wilbur	Q.B.	170
15	Powers, Jim	Q.B.	175
16	Gifford, Frank	Q.B.	190
18	Brame, John	Q.B.	190
19	Schneider, Dean	Q.B.	190
21	Cantor, Al	L.H.	180
23	Fouch, Johnny	L.H.	187
25	Rogers, Don	L.H.-R.H.	175
26	Moloney, Jerry	L.H.	180
27	Bowers, Bill	L.H.	180
29	Williams, Johnny	L.H.	175
31	Battle, Art	R.H.	170
32	Roundy, Jay	L.H.-R.H.	180
33	Pucci, Ralph	F.B.	180
34	Craig, Rod	R.H.	180
35	Buckberg, Bob	R.H.	180
36	Duff, Pat	R.H.	180
37	Scott, Joe	R.H.	160
38	Williams, Jim	R.H.	180
41	Stillwell, Don	R.E.	180
42	Sevier, Ron	R.G.	220
43	Trent, Goodwin	L.G.	195
44	Martin, Bill	F.B.	200
45	Burke, Don	F.B.	230
46	Anderson, Harry	R.H.	185
47	Vukovich, Ned	F.B.	206
49	Cziguth, Joe	R.T.	227
50	Davis, George	C.	195
51	McGee, Bob	L.T.	230
52	Brown, John	R.T.	210
53	Conforti, Dan	C.	200
54	Borg, Rinaldo	L.E.	200
55	Barnes, Mercer	C.	205
56	Gobel, John	R.E.	200
57	Hachten, Boyd	C.	195
58	Goller, Winston	R.E.	190
59	Peterson, Chuck	L.T.	215
60	McMurtry, Paul	R.G.	225
61	Boies, Herb	L.G.	205
62	Colley, Tom	L.G.	200
63	Sanbrano, Al	R.G.	206
64	Monson, Jim	R.G.	200
65	Beck, Gene	C.	180
66	Moore, Jim	L.G.	220
67	Hayes, Norm	R.G.	215
68	Downs, Bob	R.G.	205
69	D'Ambrosi, Jaspar	L.T.	210
72	Ashcraft, Walt	R.T.	240
73	Bird, Jim	R.T.	230
74	Conde, John	L.T.	215
75	Heidenthal, Ed	R.T.	215
77	Peters, Volney	L.T.	216
78	Crosbie, Bob	R.T.	215
79	Swope, Jess	L.G.	225
80	Jessup, Bill	R.E.	175
81	Cramer, Stan	L.E.	190
83	Nix, Jack	R.E.	190
84	Stillwell, Bob	R.E.	200
85	Hatfield, Harold	L.E.	205
86	Linehan, Tony	L.G.	200
88	Baldock, Alvin	L.E.	195
89	Zimmerman, Don	L.E.	180

NOTRE DAME ROSTER — 1949

NO.	NAME	POS.	AGE	HT.	WT.
1	Mazur, John E.	Q.B.	19	6'1"	185
3	Whiteside, William A.	Q.B.	20	5'10"	172
4	Carter, Thomas L.	Q.B.	22	5'11"	173
6	Dickson, George C.	Q.B.	26	5'11"	170
7	Begley, Gerald C.	Q.B.	21	6'1"	175
9	Williams, Robert A.	Q.B.	19	6'1"	180
12	Zalejski, Ernest R.	F.B.	23	5'11"	185
14	Sitko, Emil M.	R.H.-F.B.	25	5'8"	180
15	Smith, Eugene F.	H.B.	19	5'9"	170
19	Dailer, James H.	G.	22	5'9"	185
21	Connor, John F.	E.	21	6'0"	190
22	Gay, William T.	L.H.	21	5'10"	168
23	Petitbon, John E.	H.B.	18	5'11"	180
24	Coutre, Lawrence E.	H.B.	21	5'9"	170
26	Bush, John L.	F.B.	19	6'0"	185
27	Hovey, William A.	H.B.	22	5'10"	175
28	Spaniel, Francis J.	H.B.	20	5'10"	184
30	Landry, John W.	F.B.	23	6'1"	180
31	O'Neil, John D.	F.B.	20	6'	185
37	Barrett, William C.	H.B.	19	5'8"	179
38	Martin, James E. (Co-Capt.)	L.T.	25	6'2"	204
39	Kiousis, Martin J.	G.	19	5'11"	190
40	McKillip, Loe	H.B.	20	5'10"	175
41	Caprara, Joseph A.	F.B.	19	6'	198
44	Swistowicz, Michael P.	F.B.	22	5'11"	195
47	Gander, Fidel J.	F.B.	19	6'1"	190
48	Cotter, Richard A.	H.B.	20	6'1"	178
49	Helwig, John F.	G.	21	6'2"	194
50	Groom, Jerome P.	C.	20	6'3"	210
51	Boji, Byron Bela	C.	19	5'11"	186
52	Grothaus, Walter J.	C.	23	6'2"	192
53	Banicki, Frederick	T.	18	5'10"	190
54	Bartlett, James J.	C.	20	6'3"	196
55	Hamby, James H.	C.	18	6'1"	195
56	Yanoschik, Phillip	C.	24	6'	195
57	Feigl, Charles	C.	20	6'1"	185
60	Lally, Robert J.	G.	20	6'	185
61	Johnson, Frank A.	G.	22	6'	195
62	Oracko, Stephen F.	G.	22	6'	185
63	Wallner, Frederick W.	G.	21	6'2"	208
64	Burns, Paul Eugene	G.	20	6'2"	205
65	Modak, Daniel	G.	22	6'1"	197
66	Perry, Arthur R.	G.	19	5'11"	198
67	Johnston, Frank A.	G.	20	5'8"	184
68	Higgins, William P.	G.	22	5'11"	180
69	Zambroski, Anthony J.	G.	19	5'11"	196
70	Mahoney, James E.	T.	22	6'1"	204
71	Cifelli, August B.	T.	24	6'4"	230
72	Hudak, Edward J.	T.	21	6'2"	200
73	Nusskern, John	T.	24	6'2"	215
74	McGehee, Ralph W.	T.	21	6'1"	202
75	Toneff, Robert	T.	19	6'1"	232
76	Zancha, John D.	T.	19	5'10"	195
77	Daut, John Donald	T.	18	6'1"	205
78	Zmijewski, Alfred A.	T.	21	6'1"	200
79	Huber, Thomas E.	T.	20	6'2"	195
80	Waybright, Douglas G.	E.	22	6'1"	186
81	Flynn, William J.	E.	22	6'2"	197
82	Hart, Leon J. (Co-Capt.)	R.E.	20	6'4"	245
83	Wightkin, William J.	E.	22	6'2"	204
84	Espenan, Ray	E.	22	6'2"	188
85	Mutscheller, James F.	E.	19	6'1"	194
86	Jonardi, Raymond C.	E.	19	6'2"	188
87	Ostrowski, Chester C.	E.	19	6'1"	196
88	Dolmetsch, Robert E.	E.	19	6'2"	195
89	Koch, David A.	E.	19	6'2"	190
90	Kapish, Robert J.	E.	19	6'0"	187

1950
CHAPTER 23
"WHAT DID YOU DO DURING THE WAR, BUDDY?"
. . . Jeff Cravath, 1950

If you like surprises, you would have loved the 1950 football season. Unless, of course, you were a Notre Dame fan. Among the first titans to topple that season were the Fighting Irish. Purdue saw to it that they never reached game number 40 without defeat by posting a 24-14 victory over Leahy's legions. From there it was all downhill . . . they finished the season 4-4-1.

Mighty Army was sunk by Navy. Ohio State and Southern Methodist started the seasons like twin tornadoes on a collision course. When they met, it was S.M.U. that breezed away a winner, 32-27. They were unbeatable until they tangled with the Longhorns of Texas, who tamed the tornado 23-20, only to lose to the Tennessee Volunteers in the Cotton Bowl. Tennessee got to the Cotton Bowl by beating Southeast Conference champions, the Kentucky Wildcats, who went on to stop Alabama's long winning streak, 13-7 in the Sugar Bowl. On the Pacific coast everybody's pre-season pick, Stanford finished fourth, but PPC champion California fell before Michigan 14-6 in the Rose Bowl. Sound confusing? It was.

The only unbeaten team that emerged unscathed on New Year's Day was Princeton, and that was probably because it was against their policy to engage in post season play. They stayed home and watched; television was very big that year.

As a matter of fact, TV was so popular that season, it was blamed for the lack of attendance at the Coliseum, but that was not the only reason . . . the lacklustre records of both teams must have had something to do with the fact that only 70,000 fans, the smallest crowd to see a home game since 1934, were willing to pay to see USC with 1 win, 5 losses, and 1 tie, clash with Notre Dame, 4-3-1.

For mighty Notre Dame such a season performance was humiliating, but still it was good enough to establish them as ten point favorites over the faltering Trojans.

But something happened to the pussycats who had rolled over the week before and allowed themselves to be stroked to a 39-0 defeat by the Bruins of UCLA. They attacked the Irish like a pride of famished lions. Before this day was over, nine Notre Dame players were injured and taken out of the game. Three on stretchers. Trojan end Bill Jessup hit John Petitbon so hard on the USC goal line, that John was out to lunch for fifteen minutes. Pat Cannamela nailed Irish quarterback Bob Williams with a head-on tackle that sent Bob to Good Samaritan Hospital until the bells stopped ringing. It was clean football, but it was rough.

The first quarter was tense, fierce, and scoreless. The Trojans fumbled twice and blew a chance to score, but they never stopped trying.

In the closing seconds of the first quarter, a clipping penalty put SC back on their 6 yard line. A towering punt by Jessup to Bill Gay moved the ball to the Irish 46 just as the gun signaled the end of the period.

It took only 14 plays for skipper Bob Williams to navigate the 54 yards needed for the first Irish score. He did an excellent job of mixing passing and running plays. On fourth and 11 he lofted a beautiful pass to Petitbon. SC center Lou Welch was there also and tackled the Irish halfback on the one yard line. Petitbon nearly scored on that play, but he didn't remember it. As he fell forward toward the goal line, he met Jessup head on and spent the rest of the day dozing. Williams ran it in from the 1, Vince Meschievitz converted. 7-0 Notre Dame.

There were less than ten minutes in the quarter, but the Trojans needed less than 30 seconds to tie the score. Meschievitz kicked off to Jim Sears, who tucked the ball under his arm on the 6 yard line and set sail. He cut to his left and picked up two crushing blocks from John Conde and Al Carmichael . . . a few yards downfield Sol Naumu took out the last defender and nobody got close after that. (The last man to so humiliate Notre Dame by returning a kickoff all the way for a touchdown was another Trojan, Racehorse Russ Saunders in 1929 . . . he ran one back for 95 yards, but the Trojans lost 13-12.) Frank Gifford converted and the score was 7-7.

In the second half both teams played a strong defensive game. The Irish found themselves in a hole when after an exchange of punts, Jessup booted a 52 yard punt to the Irish 20. They couldn't get started. Winston Gollar and Volney Peters hit Billy Barrett* so hard, that he was carried off the field. On fourth from the 20, Bob Williams dropped back to punt. Through the Irish defense tore co-captain Paul McMurty, a 31 year old guard from Rio Hondo, Texas (no, that's not a typo, a 31 year old guard from Rio Hondo, Texas) and blocked the kick. The ball bounced around crazily in the end zone, Peters got his hands on it, but couldn't control it or gain possession before it rolled out of bounds. Nevertheless it was a two point safety, and those two points loomed larger and

*At 5'8" and 180 Barrett was somewhat overmatched. Winston Gollar was 6'2" and 200 lbs., Peters 6'4", 220 . . . ouch!

larger as the last 25 minutes of the game ticked off.

Wilbur Robertson, the Trojan quarterback, elected to play his cards close to his vest for the rest of the game, and it paid off. For the first time in eleven years the Trojans had whipped the fighting Irish. It's not what you could call a sound thrashing, 9 to 7, but it's a win.

Jeff Cravath was the man of the hour. Fans who the week before were shouting for his head, now milled about the dressing room doors waiting for a glimpse of their hero. Players who threatened to desert the squad after the UCLA game, carried the coach across the field on their shoulders. But through the tumult and the shouting echoed a whispered question: "Will this win save Coach Jeff Cravath his job?"

It didn't.

Los Angeles columnist Braven Dyer (check on this) wrote after Cravath was fired: "Jeff Cravath is a war casualty. Yes the war is now past by five years, but it was five years ago that Jeff Cravath lost control of his squad and he has never completely regained the reins . . . They were not putting out."

"I know it," Cravath answered. "But look, a lot of these kids have just returned from service. They aren't taking this game of football very seriously. And how can I bark at a boy who's had two years in the Pacific or fifty missions over Germany? If I do, one of them is liable to say, 'What did you do during the war buddy?' ".

There were no such chinks in Frank Leahy's armor, after all, hadn't he spent a year and a half in the South Pacific on Midway, Guam, and Saipan (after they were safe . . . no one wanted to lose a celebrity officer) talking to submarine sailors about football?

It wouldn't have made any difference anyway; Leahy was made of sterner stuff. Can you imagine someone walking up to the Coach and asking, "What did you do in the war, buddy?"

Jim Sears of USC runs kick off back 94 yards for touchdown

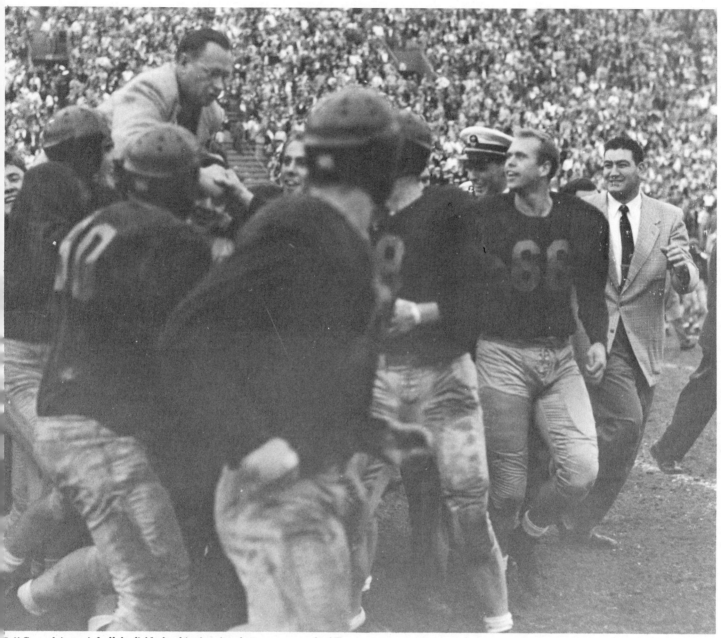

Jeff Cravath is carried off the field after his victorious last game as coach of Troy

JEFF CRAVATH

If "Gloomy Gus" Henderson was the most pessimistic of Trojan coaches, and Howard Jones the most colorless, and if it is necessary to label coaches, then tag Jeff Cravath the unluckiest.

Newell Jefferson Cravath was very possibly the best center to play for SC until Stan Williams made All American in 1931. After his playing days were over in 1926, Cravath assisted Howard Jones for a couple of years, then took a head coaching job at Denver University. A few years later he returned to California to coach junior college, but when Howard Jones asked him to come back to USC as line coach, he quickly accepted.

Then when the Headman died in 1941, Cravath left to coach San Francisco University with some success, and probably would have stayed. However, Sam Barry had recommended him as a possible replacement in 1942, when Sam went to the Navy. So San Francisco released him and Cravath returned to his Alma Mater as head coach number 13. That number should have told him something. He was about as lucky as a love sick gelding. Jeff Cravath was so unlucky that he ran into accidents that had started out to happen to somebody else.

To begin with, he coached in the worst of all possible times. The war years. Even so, he won a lot of games . . . but the wrong ones. He also lost a lot of games . . . and they were the wrong ones too.

His first team finished 5-5-1, better than Sam Barry's record the season before, but Cravath had to take credit for the first loss ever to UCLA . . . that loss sent the Bruins to their first Rose Bowl and the SC alumni to the nearest bar.

He got even with UCLA the following year, and held the Bruins at bay for the next three years. From 1943 through '45 he built up a 5-0-1 record against the cross-town rivals. But in 1946 the Bruins did it to him again and went to the Rose Bowl.

Mr. Lucky had a hard act to follow. Howard Jones had never lost a Rose Bowl game. In 1943 and 1944, it looked as though Jeff would carry on that winning tradition. First by beating Washington 29-0, then Tennessee 25-0 the following year. But hapless Coach Cravath was destined to score yet another first. In 1945 he became the first Trojan coach to lose in the Rose Bowl. Two years later he became the first Trojan coach to lose two in the Rose Bowl. That year he was sure he had it made when he beat UCLA 6-0 and got the Rose Bowl bid. He had an undefeated season going for him until he met Notre Dame, the last regular game of the year. You remember what happened next — the Irish took care of that unblemished record 38-7 and so demoralized the Trojans that they bowed to Michigan 49-0 in the Rose Bowl, thus dimming the glory of

their 32-0 triumph over Ohio State and the 39-14 victory over California earlier that season.

The strange thing is that in his nine year coaching career at USC, Cravath held the edge on UCLA 8-3-1, on Cal 5-3-1, and on Stanford 3-2-1. But he couldn't beat them at the right time. He had six shots at Notre Dame, but the best he could do until his last year was that 14-14 tie that snapped a 21 game winning for the Irish.

By 1949 the muted rumble of disaffection was building to a roar. Cravath's team was beaten by Cal 16-10, Stanford 34-13, and Notre Dame 32-0. The season record wasn't all that bad 5-3-1. But again he had lost to the wrong teams, at the wrong time.

The following year he would have needed a miracle to keep his job . . . no, more than a miracle. He beat Notre Dame 9-7 the last game of the season . . . *that* was a miracle, and it didn't help. The season opened with a loss to Iowa followed by a tie with Washington State, a loss to California, and a 39-0 humiliation by UCLA. The alumni was not happy. Now the autumn of uncertainty slipped into the winter of their discontent. Gone was the memory of seven winning seasons. Gone was the glory of the undefeated 1944 season with the 28-21 upset of powerful San Diego, the 28-20 win over heavily favored Stanford, of the broken Notre Dame win streak and the final victory over the Irish.

The same fans who cheered those wins and the same teams who carried him from the fields of victory now stood over him in his defeat like an angry mou waiting to pluck the flesh from the bones of a fallen tyrant.

But that's football.

Jeff Cravath's contract had two more years to run when he was asked to resign. He expected it.

"He was too sensitive," wrote one columnist.

"He was too nice a guy," said one of his players.

He should have listened to Leo Durocher. Baseball isn't the only game where nice guys finish last.

Cravath's luck remained consistent to the last. He retired to a dream far away from the roar of the crowd . . . a farm in the Imperial Valley that he worked with a close and long time friend. As he was driving his battered old pickup into town one morning, Lady Luck played one final lousy trick on Jeff Cravath. The driver of a   either failed to see or ignored a stop sign and plowed broadside into the truck. Jeff took the full impact on the driver's side. He was knocked through the door on the other side and died there in the dusty road while they waited for an ambulance.

SOUTHERN CALIFORNIA — 1950

NO.	PLAYER	POS.	WGT.	NO.		POS.	WGT.
88	*Baldock, Al	E.	200	61	McClelland, Brennan	G.	220
55	*Barnes, Mercer	C.	205	51	McGee, Bob	T.	225
69	Barry, Al	G.	210	60	**McMurtry, Paul	G.	225
52	*Beck, Gene	C.	185	26	Moloney, Jerry	H.	180
27	Bowers, Bill	H.	180	25	Naumu, Sol	F.	180
38	Bozanic, George	Q.	190	77	**Peters, Volney	T.	220
42	Cannamela, Pat	G.	205	81	Petty, Dick	E.	180
21	Carmichael, Al	H.	195	78	Peviani, Bob	T.	210
67	Casten, A.	T.	215	33	**Pucci, Ralph	F.	175
20	Colgrove, Neil	Q	165	12	*Robertson, Wilbur	Q.	170
74	*Conde, John	T.	210	53	Sampson, Ben	C.	200
31	Cutri, Cosimo	H.	175	63	Sanbrano, Al	G.	210
49	Cziguth, Joe	T.	225	91	*Schneider, Dean	Q.	190
15	Demirjian, Ed	Q.	170	37	*Scott, Joe	H.	160
68	*Downs, Bob	G.	210	32	Sears, Jim	H.	170
36	*Duff, Clint (Pat)	H.	180	41	Souers, Glenn	F.	180
23	*Fouch, John	H.	187	84	Stillwell, Don	E.	180
35	Genther, Dick	F.	190	75	Van Doren, Bob	T.	215
16	*Gifford, Frank	Q.	190	50	Welsh, Lou	C.	195
83	Goller, Winston	E.	200	66	Wiker, Bruce	G.	215
85	**Hatfield, Harold	E.	202	73	Willhoite, Elmer	G.	215
86	Hattig, Bill	E.	175	29	*Williams, John	H.	175
65	Heydenreich, John	G.	210	89	*Zimmerman, Dan	E.	180
80	**Jessup, Bill	E.	185				

NOTRE DAME — 1950

NO.	NAME	POS.	WGT.	NO.		POS.	WGT.
52	Alessandrini, James	C.	198	86	Jonardi, Raymond	E.	188
79	Bardash, Virgil	T.	210	28	Johnson, Murray	H.	195
37	*Barrett, William	H.	180	67	Johnston, Frank	G.	184
54	*Bartlett, James	C.	202	84	Kapish, Robert	E.	187
82	Benson, Robert	E.	195	80	Kelly, Robert	E.	200
60	*Boji, Byron	G.	205	91	Koch, David	E.	190
25	Buczkiewicz, Edward	H.	182	30	**Landry, John	F.	180
64	*Burns, Paul	G.	208	12	Marchand, Gerald	F.	175
26	Bush, John	H.	190	1	*Mazur, John	Q.	190
49	Caprara, Joseph	F.	192	40	*McKillip, Le.	H.	175
65	Carter, Daniel	G.	200	81	Meschievitz, Vincent	E.	215
4	Carter, Thomas	H.	173	70	Modak, Daniel	T.	205
48	**Cotter, Richard	H.	180	78	Murphy, Thomas	T.	210
43	David, Joseph	H.	175	85	*Mutscheller, James	E.	194
88	Dolmetsch, Robert	E.	195	87	*Ostrowski, Chester	E.	196
71	Dunlay, James	T.	205	24	Paolone, Ralph	H.	195
83	Emerick, Louis	E.	210	66	*Perry, Arthur	G.	198
69	Epstein, Frank	G.	205	23	*Petitbon, John	H.	190
57	Feigl, Charles	C.	200	62	Seaman, Thomas	G.	200
32	Flood, David	H.	185	15	Smith, Eugene	H.	170
51	Flynn, David	C.	195	61	Stroud, Clarke	G.	200
74	***Flynn, William	T.	197	75	*Toneff, Robert	T.	240
90	French, William	E.	195	63	**Wallner, Frederick	G.	202
47	*Gander, Fidel	F.	190	77	Weithman, James	T.	195
5	Gaudreau, William	Q.	178	17	Whelan, John	H.	180
22	**Gay, William	H.	175	3	Whiteside, William	Q.	172
50	**Groom, Jerome (C)	C.	215	9	**Williams, Robert	Q.	185
55	*Hamby, James	C.	200	6	Wise, John	Q.	185
89	*Helwig, John	E.	194	72	Zambroski, Anthony	G.	196
68	Higgins, William	G.	180	76	Zancha, John	T.	195
27	Hovey, William	H.	175				

1951
CHAPTER 24

"WHEN I SAW HIM COMING, I NEVER KNEW WHETHER TO SAY HELLO OR GENUFLECT"
. . . Joe Doyle, 1951

For Frank Leahy and the Fighting Irish the nightmare of 1950 was over. It had been the closest thing to a losing season in 17 years. Hunk Anderson's 1933 3-5-1 debacle was worse, but before that you had to go all the way back to the turn of the century to find a more disastrous season. In 1887 Notre Dame played one game . . . and lost. To Michigan, 8-0.

But in 1951 the future looked brighter. Recruitment regulations had relaxed somewhat, and even though Leahy was not, as he stated some years later, altogether pleased with some of the methods used to induce talented players to huddle under the Golden Dome, he learned to make "necessary compromises . . . in the pursuit of excellence."

Just what those inducements were was never made clear by the coach. One can only guess. One thing is amply clear, however. There was a limit to how far Frank Leahy would compromise even in search of his holy grail . . .

In August of that year the football brotherhood was rocked by the revelation of a cribbing scandal at West Point. Twelve of the Academy's most gifted players were dismissed. Many of them were Catholic, and Notre Dame certainly could have used them. Yet when Joseph P. Kennedy called Leahy and offered to send them to Notre Dame, he declined.

The word "send" when used by the patriarch of the Catholic Kennedy clan, clearly implied persuasion and probable financial assistance. Leahy politely thanked him and said no. It's possible of course, that the Coach's reasons for demurring may not have been completely altruistic. Relations between Notre Dame and Army had been strained for some years and Leahy had fond hopes of easing that tension. Obviously re-suiting Cadets in Notre Dame uniforms, shouting *about face,* and sending them against their former comrades-in-arms, would be like inviting twelve illegitimate sons to a family reunion, to challenge the rightful heirs for a piece of mom's apple pie. Hardly a way to ameliorate an already delicate situation.

The stress probably started the first time the two met in 1913 when Rockne, Dorais, Eichenlaub, et al surprised the hell out of favored Army and beat them 35-13. Over the next 34 years (time out in 1918; the Army was otherwise occupied), the strain tightened with each Irish win. It snapped in 1947 after 26 wins for Notre Dame, 6 for the Cadets and 3 ties

. . . the United States Military Academy took the University of Notre Dame off its schedule. Small wonder. By that time even the Army mascot was exhibiting symptoms of hypertension.

Col. Earl (Red) Blaik, the Army coach and Frank Leahy had several things in common. They had both become head coach of their respective schools at the same time . . . 1941. They were both good coaches, and both men of towering egos and both poor losers. "There's a difference between a good sport and a good loser," was one of Blaik's favorite sayings.

It was, to use a cliche, a case of the irresistible force meeting an immovable object. Except in this instance Notre Dame proved to be generally irresistible, and West Point quite movable . . . at least where the Irish were concerned. Since their upset win in 1931, the Cadets had been able to whip Notre Dame only twice, 1944 and '45. They tied the Irish in 1946, and lost to them in 1947. Red Blaik had had enough. In 1951 Leahy wanted to renew the traditional gridiron hostilities because of rumored accusations that he was destroying Notre Dame's schedule.* The Coach had fences to mend, therefore Joe Kennedy's generosity went unaccepted.

The University of Southern California's 1950 season was no less a nightmare, but they had an additional problem. They needed a coach. Time was running out, and after six weeks of frantic search, no one could agree. Willis O. Hunter, SC's athletic director and the faculty favored Ray Elliott from the University of Illinois. They even had him flown out from Champagne-Urbana for a conference. He flew back unsigned. That was just as well with a large group of the alumni who preferred Paul Brown of the Cleveland Browns. The old grads had a signed petition showing a strong preference for Brown, and suggesting that the board of trustees offer him enough money to make the job attractive. Brown must not have thought too much of the offer, whatever it was . . . there is no record of any comment by him.

So USC President Fred Fagg, Jr. did the logical thing. He named the Trojan track coach as head football coach. His name was Jesse T. Hill, and he admitted later that he took the job when the University couldn't seem to find anyone else.

The last time USC had made a panic decision like that was

---

*The Army-Notre Dame rivalry did not resume until 1957. The Irish squeaked by that year 23-21. The following year Army retaliated 14-2. The two did not meet again until the evening of Oct. 9, 1965. The Cadets lost that night, and have yet, 11 years and 5 games later, to beat the Fighting Irish. The record now stands 33-7-3. Maybe Blaik was right.

in 1941 when Howard Jones' unexpected death left the Trojans without a coach. Sam Barry got the call then and the memory of his calamitous 2-6-1 season had not dimmed.

If the alumni had any trepidity concerning the naming of Jesse Hill, they could have saved themselves the agitation. His credentials were solid. As an all-around athlete he had few equals in the history of Southern California sports. As a track man, his 25⅞ long jump won the 1929 IC4-A title. As a running back, he led the PCC 8 the same year with an average of 8.2 yards per carry. From his graduation in 1930 until 1938, he played professional baseball with the Yankees, the Senators and the Athletics, among others. He doubled between first base and the outfield and ended his playing career with a lifetime batting average of .306.

In 1946 he returned to USC as freshman football coach. In 1948 he succeeded Dean Cromwell as track coach and the following two years produced national championship track teams. He may have been a dark horse in the Trojan Coach sweepstakes, but he was a good bet. He was a winner. In six years his teams won 45, lost 17, tied 1, and went to the Rose Bowl twice.

After the dismal 2-5-2 season the year before, no one expected miracles from Hill, but he damned near pulled one off anyway.

California was unbeaten in 38 straight regular season games going all the way back to 1947 when USC rolled over them 39-14. When the Bears and Trojans met in Berkeley on October 20th, they were both undefeated, but Cal ranked #1 in the nation, and SC was generally ignored. But they had a secret weapon, Frank Gifford. He had plenty of help from Pat Cannamela, and together they ran the favored Golden Bears right off the field, 21-14. For thrills it was compared to the last minute upset of Notre Dame in 1931.

Going into the eighth game of the season with Stanford, the Trojans were still undefeated, but the Indians got to them 27-20, then UCLA added to their embarrassment by administering a 21-7 beating. (Still not as bad as the 39-0 shellacking the Trojans had taken from the Bruins the year before.)

So on a rainy December 1st, two recuperating cripples met in the Los Angeles Coliseum. Frank Leahy's Fighting Irish with a 6-2-1 record* took the field, they found themselves in an unaccustomed position . . . underdogs! The Trojans with a 7-2-0 were slightly favored.

The game started out rough, and never got any gentler. The first quarter was scoreless unless you were keeping count of after-whistle blocks and knees to nose shots. In the second quarter Notre Dame guard Tom Seaman and Trojan tackle Bob Van Doren decided to make each other honest. Instead of punching in the pile-up, they stood toe to toe and slugged it out for nearly a half a minute. The officials declared it a draw and sent them both to the showers. You had to give Seaman

*They had celebrated their 400th win just two weeks before, when they defeated North Carolina 12-7.

USC's Pat Cannamela, Full back, was the inside threat while Frank Gifford took the outside

credit for guts, 5-11 and 198 going against Van Doren's 215 pounds distributed over 6-3.

Interspersed with the gouging and elbowing, some football was being played. It took the Trojans only two minutes of the second half to get on the scoreboard. SC halfback Frank Gifford passed from his own 38 to co-captain Dean Schneider who made a sensational catch for a first down on the Irish 44, before the first quarter ended, Gifford, Harold Han, and Bob Buckley had moved the ball to the Irish 23. On the fourth play of the second quarter, Gifford ran 8 yards around left end with Pat Duff blocking and drew first blood. The usually accurate Gifford blew the conversion, but the Trojans led 6-0.

Notre Dame retaliated almost immediately. Johnny Mazur, playing his last game for the Irish, left the field when the Trojans kicked off, and an 18 year old freshman quarterback trotted on in his place and started to dissect the Trojans with cold precision. His name was Ralph Guglielmi and he went right to work. His first pitch from the Irish 23 gained 13 yards, and a first down on the 39. His second hit Petitbon for 10, the next dropped softly into the hands of Chet Ostrowski for 35 yards and a first down on the Trojan 15. About that time the SC defense had figured out that young Ralph's aerial attack was going to kill them, so they made the necessary adjustments. So did he. He switched to a ground attack with Johnny Lattner carrying and evened the score 6-6. Bob Joseph missed the extra point and both teams went into the locker room at half

Notre Dame Captain and All American, Jim Mutcheller

Frank Gifford, USC All American

time, dead even.

In the third period the intrepid men of Troy got lucky and took advantage of it. Guglielmi made one of his very few mistakes that day and threw a wobbly pass that was batted around and finally settled in the arms of SC halfback Dick Nunis who moved it to the Irish 34 before he was nailed. Dean Schneider hit Jim Sears with a flank pass on the left which he carried to the five, and then over on the next play. Faultless Frank missed the conversion again, however, so the count was 12-6 . . . for a short time.

Near the end of the quarter Guglielmi mounted a ground attack in which he alternated hand-offs to Johnny Lattner and Neal Worden that split the SC defensive line wide open. In a matter of minutes they covered the 73 yards needed and tied the score again. Once more Joseph missed the conversion so the tally remained at 12-12.

Then somebody goofed. The Trojans with the aid of some fine passing by Schnelder and inspired running by Johnny Williams, and Leon Sellers and two good receptions by Sears, found themselves on the Irish 8. First down and goal to go. It looked like a sure touchdown for USC. Whose idea it was to try a touchdown pass to 5-6 Cosimo Cutri in the end zone, with 6 foot 190 pound Irish Dan Shannon in the way, no one knows . . . but it doesn't matter. It didn't work. The Trojans lost the ball and the combination of Guglielmi, Lattner, Worden and Petitbon was just too much for the men of Troy to handle. It

didn't take long for the Irish to score another 6. This time Joseph didn't miss and nailed the coffin shut while the corpse of Tommy Trojan still quivered inside. 19-12.

There were still six minutes to play, but big Bob Toneff, senior Irish guard, wouldn't let the Trojans have any fun. It was his last game and he wanted to be sure the Trojans remembered him. They did. His 6-2, 230 pounds made a lasting impression.

"This group of lads," said Coach Leahy later in the dressing room, "most of them very young and inexperienced, bowed to nobody in eagerness to learn, hard work, spirit and courage."

Frank Leahy could make a simple post game locker room statement sound like a prince of the Holy Roman Empire thanking his crusaders for vanquishing an army of Saracens.

"When I used to cover Notre Dame and he was head coach," confessed Joe Doyle, "I always had a problem. I didn't know whether to say hello or genuflect."

Coach Leahy was just a little short of ecstatic, and he had a right to be. After all, Guglielmi and most of the Irish wrecking crew would return next year, and he had once more managed to prove that to the valiant heart nothing is impossible. The Phoenix had arisen from the ashes. He didn't even mind when his team dragged him fully clothed into the showers with them during the post game hysteria. It had never happened before, and it had dampened his dignity . . . but it was sort of nice . . . kind of like being baptized all over again.

Note: All Americans that year, Frank Gifford, Pat Cannemela, USC; Bob Toneff, Tackle, ND; Mention . . . Jim Mutscheller, ND

way they were expected to. Early in the first period, Jim Sears ran a Lattner punt back to the Irish 44, Leon Sellers got a first down on the 31, but someone on the Trojan line was offside and the penalty wiped out the gain so the drive petered out. That seemed to set a pattern for SC's play the rest of the day. The Trojans got another chance a few plays later when Notre Dame was again forced to punt. This time Johnny Lattner made one of his very few mistakes and the ball rolled dead on the Irish 41 — but another offside penalty put them in a fourth down situation with 3 yards to go. Jim Sears elected to try for it, but slipped and gave up the ball to Notre Dame on their 33.

A short time later, with the ball once again in the hands of the Trojans (to use the phrase loosely), Sellers fumbled and Lattner recovered on SC's 45. Walter Ashcraft stopped Lattner on the 26, one of the few times anyone had his way with Johnny that day, but then Ashcraft was big enough to have his way with an M-60 tank . . . if he could catch one.

In the second quarter the momentum seemed to have shifted to Notre Dame. They played it smart and with the help of Lattner's talented toe, kept the Trojans deep in their own territory. The defensive play of Shannon and Captain Jack Alessandrini kept the SC running game bottled up, but the real villain of the piece as far as the Trojans were concerned, was the ubiquitous John Lattner in the secondary.

"Lattner is a real defensive tiger," said SC end Tom Nickoloff after the game. "Every time I ran a pass pattern in his zone, he was on me like a leech. I just couldn't shake him." His punting must have unnerved the Trojans too. His average for the season was only 36 yards, but he could surely kick where the receivers weren't.

Apparently the Trojans had not yet learned that long shot gambling was not going to pay off on this particular day. They tried one more 4th down run . . . with the same measure of success. The Irish took over on their own 40 yard line, but granted the men of Troy a reprieve. Leahy's lads had to punt again and Al Carmichael ran it out of bounds on the SC 40 but someone was offside again, so Lattner re-kicked. This time Sears fielded the ball on the 25 and took off, but the cheers of the Trojan rooters were choked off before they were heard. After a couple of steps, Jim pitched a lateral off to his right intended for Al Carmichael. It was a good play . . . it had worked the week before against UCLA when Al had shoveled the ball to Jim. There was one difference, however. In the Bruin game, Jim was there to receive. In the Notre Dame game, apparently Al didn't know Jim was going to return the compliment, and wasn't there to accept it. He was nowhere near. But Irish guard Menil Mavraides was, and grounded the ball on the Trojan 19.

Lattner moved it to the 9. The Irish came out of the huddle

Joe Heap, Notre Dame All American, picks up 10 yards

Ralph Guglielmi—Notre Dame Quarterback and All American

and went into the T-formation . . . it was third and 3. But instead of snapping the ball, the Irish shifted from the T to the single wing and half the Trojan line jumped offside. Frank Leahy called it, "the Notre Dame Trick Shift." Nearly everyone else called it the "Sucker Shift." Call it what you will, it worked. It was now first and 4 . . . four plays later Lattner slammed over for the first score of the game. It was six minutes and 25 seconds into the second quarter. Bob Arrix missed the conversion . . . 6-0 Notre Dame. The half ended without any serious threat from the University of Southern California. Not so as far as Notre Dame was concerned. They nearly scored again in the closing minutes of the second quarter, but Ralph Guglielmi overthrew Lattner who had outrun all the SC defenders and was in the clear on the Trojan 15.

It was not too late for the Trojans to pull this one out if they could change their ways . . . but they couldn't. Carmichael slipped and fell on the five yard line with the kickoff, and another offside penalty forced Des Koch to punt from the end zone and Lattner brought it back to the 46 yard line of Troy. The Irish worked to within field goal distance. This time Bob Joseph set up the ball properly on the 17 yard line and Arrix didn't miss. 9-0 Notre Dame with 9 minutes and 45 seconds left in the third quarter.

The Hillmen, as they had come to be called, still had plenty of time to overcome a nine point deficit . . . or so they thought. They tried, oh, how they tried. Jim Sears intercepted a pass on the Irish 22 and the Trojan rooters came back to life, but only momentarily. Allessandrini tore through the SC line and dumped Aramis Dandoy for a loss and the Trojans had to settle for a field goal attempt from the 35. It was too far for Koch. The ball bounced out of bounds on the 4 yard line.

Lady Luck hadn't completely deserted the Trojans; she was just playing coy. In the last quarter SC was forced to punt again but retained the ball because Notre Dame roughed the kicker. From the 23 Sears faded and threw a 50 yard pass to Jim Hayes who made a spectacular catch, but couldn't stay on his feet and fell on the 28 yard line of Notre Dame. If he had stayed on his feet it's quite likely he would have scored. Jim's inability to stay on his feet must have annoyed the Lady, because now she turned her face away from the men of Troy. With time running out, Jim Sears signalled for a fair catch of a Lattner punt. Al Carmichael had other things in mind. He swooped in like a hungry falcon and gobbled the ball up on the first bounce and flew to the one yard line. Naturally it was called back because of a clipping penalty. Sellers carried seven of the next nine plays . . . he was the only one who could stay on his feet. At least it took an Irish defender to bowl him over. SC players had been hitting the turf all afternoon without so much as an angry hand being laid upon them. SC couldn't even make a first down from the Irish 3 in the last series of the game. That's the way it ended. Notre Dame 9, USC 0.

There was some criticism of Notre Dame's use of the "sucker shift."

"It was standard procedure and USC was aware of it," said Frank Leahy. "The original genius at the sucker shift was Fritz Crisler. He invented it. No one could have been more surprised than I when they suddenly made a big noise about it."

Said Jesse Hill, "I thought it was definitely uncalled for. It was a definite attempt to draw the defense offside. They used it only when they were inside the 10 yard line."

"That shift is an evasion of the spirit of the rule."

". . . Southern California, a team that was most bold about remaining on our schedule," mused Leahy later. ". . . A heroic contest. The young men of Troy were undefeated, untied and already champions of their conference. lhey had scored in every game they played, but we shut them out 9-0. What a fine opponent SC was. On the occasions when we beat them, their band gallantly saluted us with Notre Dame Victory March, a most wonderful gesture . . . one that never failed to bring tears to my eyes."

The same thing probably would have brought tears to the eyes of Jesse T. Hill as well, had it not been for a strong streak of sanity that runs through his family. Notre Dame remained an anathema. The Irish once more destroyed the dreams of an unbeaten, untied season for Southern California. It would have been their first since 1932 . . . it was now 14 years since the Men of Troy had successfully invaded South Bend.

There was some consolation. The Trojan victory over UCLA had put USC in the Rose Bowl for the 11th time and they beat Wisconsin 7-0 . . . the first time a Pacific Coast Conference team had defeated a Big Ten team since the 1947 agreement between the two conferences.

And it came just 23 years after Jesse Hill's first Rose Bowl appearance as a fullback on Howard Jones' Thundering Herd that stampeded over Pitt 47-14.

Art Hunter, Notre Dame All American tackle

UNIVERSITY OF SO. CALIFORNIA SQUAD — 1952

NO.	NAME	POS.	WT.		NO.	NAME	POS.	WT.		NO.	NAME	POS.	WT.
2	Contratto, James	H.B.	176		42	Smith, James	F.B.	172		65	Abajian, Al	G.	175
5	Demirjian, Ed*	H.B.	176		43	Koch, Des*	F.B.	204		66	Peviani, Robert**	G.	212
16	Hooks, Roger*	Q.B.	200		44	Sellers, Leon*	F.B.	190		67	Scheliga, Jack	G.	198
18	Bukich, Rudy*	H.B.	196		46	Han, Harold*	F.B.	187		68	Pavich, Frank	T.-G.	224
20	Goux, Marv	Q.B.	179		47	Kirkland, Al	H.B.	181		69	Ison, Olin	E.-G.	179
21	Carmichael, Al**	H.B.	185		49	Fouch, Ed	T.	228		72	Weeks, Charles*	T.	221
23	Hawthorne, Addison	F.B.	190		50	Welsh, Lou** (Co-Capt.)	C.	193		73	Willhoite, Elmer**	G.	201
25	Welch, Harry*	H.B.	172		51	Meyer, Bernie	T.	205		74	DaRe, Mario	T.-E.	212
26	Nunis, Richard*	H.B.	180		52	Riddle, William*	Q.B.	200		75	Van Doren, Robert** (Co-Capt.)	T.	211
27	Dandoy, Aramis	H.B.	178		53	Sampson, Ben	C.	192		77	Ashcraft, Walter*	T.	235
29	Clayton, Frank	H.B.	184		54	Petty, Richard	C.	199		78	Thomspon, Kenneth*	T.	218
31	Tsagalakis, Sam	H.B.	170		55	Heydenreich, John	T.	211		79	Barry, Al.	G.-T.	220
32	Sears, James**	H.B.	164		56	Timberlake, George	C.	197		80	Nickoloff, Thomas*	E.	217
34	Calabria, Ron	H.B.	177		57	Greenwood, Charles	E.	202		81	Weber, Thomas	E.-T.	209
35	Exley, Landon	H.B.	176		58	Hooks, Robert*	E.	202		83	Ketels, Henry	E.	193
36	Crow, Lindon	H.B.	189		59	Ferguson, Richard	E.	194		84	Stilwell, Donald*	E.	185
37	Psaltis, James*	F.B.	189		60	Ane, Charles*	T.-Q.B.	256		85	Hayes, James	E.	191
38	Bozanic, George*	Q.B.-H.B.	205		61	Gelder, Marv	G.	192		86	Hattig, William**	E.	168
39	Strickland, William	H.B.	189		62	Cox, Robert*	G.	190		88	Miller, Ron*	E.	196
40	Skrjloff, Ron	F.B.	216		63	Artenian, Mickey	G.	185		89	Barnes, Jack	E.	177
41	Bianchi, Monte	F.B.	194		64	Pucci, Ed*	G.	211					

UNIVERSITY OF NOTRE DAME SQUAD — 1952

NO.	NAME	POS.	HT.	WT.		NO.	NAME	POS.	HT.	WT.
2	Carey, Thomas F.* '55	Q.B.	5'10"	175		53	Schrader, James L.* '54	C.	6'2"	206
3	Guglielmi, Ralph V.* '55	Q.B.	6'	180		54	Nowack, Arthur C. '54	C.	6'1"	208
4	Bucci, Donald '55	Q.B.	6'	180		56	Cook, Edward J. '55	C.	6'1"	210
6	Martin, Robert L. '54	Q.B.	6'2"	185		60	Varrichione, Frank* '55	T.-G.	6'	207
7	Buczkiewicz, Edward '53	Q.B.	6'	177		62	Seaman, Thomas J.* '53	G.	5'11"	198
8	Bigelow, James '55	Q.B.	5'11"	170		63	Frasor, Richard '55	G.-C.	5'11"	190
9	Galvin, Patrick J. '55	Q.B.	6'	185		65	Lee, Jack* '55	G.	5'11"	190
10	Paterra, Francis F.* '54	H.B.	5'11"	190		66	Robst, Paul K. '54	G.	5'11"	195
14	Lattner, John J.* '54	H.B.	6'1"	190		67	Palumbo, Samuel* '55	G.	6'	195
15	Callaghan, Leo P. '55	H.B.	6'1"	185		68	Alessandrini, Jack* (C) '53	G.	5'11"	197
16	Morrissey, Rockne J. '54	H.B.	5'9"	165		69	Bardash, Virgil* '53	G.-T.	6'	206
17	Whelan, Jack D.* '53	H.B.	5'11"	180		71	Taylor, Robert H. '55	T.	6'2"	200
18	Reynolds, Paul R.* '55	H.B.	6'	180		73	Bush, Joseph R.* '54	T.	6'3"	206
19	Getschow, Lee E. '53	H.B.	6'	175		74	Ready, Robert* '55	T.	6'3"	208
20	Carrabine, Eugene* '55	H.B.	6'1"	178		75	Pasquesi, Anthony L. '55	T.	6'4"	212
24	Joseph, Robert '54	H.B.	5'9"	165		76	Poehler, Fred* '54	T.	6'4"	210
28	Sarna, Edward '54	H.B.	5'11"	175		78	Murphy, Thomas F.** '53	T.	6'1"	210
29	Galardo, Armando '54	H.B.	5'10"	170		79	Weithman, James C. † '53	T.	6'	190
30	McHugh, Thomas L. '54	F.B.	6'1"	190		80	Hunter, Arthur* '54	E.	6'3"	221
32	Flood, David** '53	H.B.	5'10"	185		81	Kohanowich, Albert '53	E.	6'1"	189
33	Shannon, Daniel J.* '55	F.B.	6'	190		82	O'Neil, Robert* '53	E.	6'2"	195
42	Heap, Joseph L.* '55	H.B.	5'11"	175		83	Penza, Donald* '54	E.	6'1"	200
45	Rigali, Robert J. '54	H.B.	5'8"	172		85	Mavraides, Menil* '54	G.	6'1"	205
48	Worden, Neil J.* '54	F.B.	5'11"	185		86	Mangialardi, Fred* '54	E.	6'1"	195
49	Stephens, Jack '55	H.B.	6'2"	190		88	Cabral, Walter K.* '55	E.	6'3"	205
52	Szymanski, Richard* '55	C.	6'2"	210		90	Matz, Paul A. '55	E.	6'1"	191

1953

CHAPTER 26

"BETTER ME THAN JOHNNY LATTNER, HUH FRANK?"
. . . Floss Leahy, 1953

Jesse Hill seemed to be doing all right in his third year as Trojan coach. At least there was no audible grumbling from the alumni . . . not yet. So far, Notre Dame was the only traditional rival his teams hadn't humbled, and they weren't likely to accomplish that this year either. Stanford and UCLA had avenged last year's losses, and with a 13-13 tie with Washington, the Trojans limped on the field against one of the mightiest Notre Dame teams in history with a 6-2-1 record, 13½ point underdogs, and a roster of walking wounded that looked like the casualty list from the Battle of Bastogne.

Veteran guards Ed Pucci and George Timberlake were infirm; Al Baldock, the 6-3 200 pound end was ailing, and both first string tackles Ed Fouch and Mario Da Re were sidelined. Center Dick Petty and Co-Captain Tom Nickoloff at right end were the only healthy Trojans on the line. Coach Hill had just two healthy regulars on the line. The rest were subs. In the backfield, Aramis Dandoy had played only half of the last five games. Quarterback and co-captain George Bozanic and regular fullback Harold Han were doubtful starters. The Trojans were barely alive . . . but as Cicero said back in the first century B.C. "While the sick man has life, there is hope."

In 1953 the substitution rules were changed again to allow players to enter the game only once a quarter, thus slowing down the trend toward specialization made possible by the two platoon system. The change didn't matter much to Coach Hill, he had barely enough healthy bodies to make up one platoon, let alone two.

The Notre Dame team was in great physical shape. Much better than their coach. He was so ill that his doctor had forbade him to make the trip to Los Angeles. Assistant Joe McArdle was in charge along with Bill Early. Other members of the Irish brain trust were Bob McBride and Johnny Lujack.

Leahy had collapsed during the Georgia Tech game in October with what was thought to be a heart attack, and given the last rites of the Catholic Church at halftime. In the third quarter, the Irish stormed on the field to "Win this one for the Coach" and broke a 7-7 tie to bury undefeated Georgia Tech 27-14.

But they didn't bury Frank Leahy . . . not for a long time. What had been hurriedly diagnosed as cardiac arrest turned out to be acute pancreatitis, brought on by overwork, faulty diet and tension.*

Johnny Lattner, Notre Dame Heisman Trophy winner

"Coaching burns out a man's insides," Leahy once said.

He shouldn't have been suffering any anxiety that beautiful November afternoon. The team he fielded that day could have gone intact into the NFL. One writer was of the opinion that if the entire first team had been named All American there would have been little argument. The consensus was that the 1953 backfield of Guglielmi, Worden, Heap, and Lattner was every bit the equal and in some ways superior to the Four Horsemen or the powerhouse backfield of 1930.

It was far from a rout . . . until the third quarter.

The Trojans took the opening kickoff and drove 62 yards to

The Coach was tough, he survived six more administrations of the rites in the next twenty years.

Notre Dame's Fred Mangialandi puts shoulder to Des Koch

the Notre Dame 15 before they were halted. Irish lightning struck a few plays later. It was fourth and one to go on the Notre Dame 40 . . . SC in possession. Aramis Dandoy punted a low fast one right into the arms of Joe Heap who was already in forward motion on the 7 yard line. He didn't stop or even slow down for the next 93 yards. Guglielmi missed the conversion and the score was 6-0, ten minutes into the first quarter . . . SC rooters were stunned, but not ready to start writing the obituaries. They started sharpening their pencils, however, when on the next Notre Dame series the Irish methodically chewed their way 61 yards in 9 plays, qnly one play a pass. Braven Dyer of the Los Angeles Times noted that the Irish line ripped holes in the Trolan line that, "the whole Notre Dame band could have marched through, had they been there." Lattner capped the drive with a nine yard run around his own left end for his first of four touchdowns that day. Guglielmi added one more point and the score was 13-0 as the quarter ended.

Des Koch, playing his last game for USC, returned Don Schaefer's punt 43 yards early in the second quarter, and with the assistance of Leon Sellers and Lindon Crow, moved the ball from the Irish 31 to the 5 yard line. Substitute quarterback Landon Exley pitched off to big Des on the next play, and he slid into the end zone just inches from the sideline. Sam

Tsagalakis made the point after good. Score now 13-7, and things looked brighter for SC . . . but not for long. The fact that the Southern California cripples would dare to score must have stung the pride of the Irish. It took them only four plays after the kickoff to roll the necessary 68 yards to score. Neil Worden did most of the damage with a 55 yard run right up the middle. Leon Clarke brought him down on the 2, but in that particular case he needn't have bothered. Worden scored on the next play and Guglielmi pumped another one over and now the score was 20-7.

It didn't take long after the start of the third quarter for Johnny Lattner to remind SC he was still in the game. He and Guglielmi combined their kicking, passing and running talent to bump up the score to 27-7.

But the Trojans just wouldn't lie down and play dead. Jim Contratto came in at quarterback and guided the men of Troy 64 yards in six plays, with some excellent passing. Aramis Dandoy covered the last 12 yards for the touchdown. A successful conversion made it 27-14 halfway into the third period.

Worden and Lattner answered right back . . . with John going over from the 1 to score his third for the day. Guglielmi converted. 34-14.

The last Notre Dame touchdown of the period was some-

Neil Worden rips off long gainer, led by Don Penza

what in the nature of a gift. A couple of busted plays placed the Trojans on their own 4 yard line. What happened next shouldn't happen to any 20 year old college halfback. A lot of them probably had nightmares about it that year, but to Aramis Dandoy it was no dream. He was trapped deep in his own end zone with a ton of Irishmen bearing down on him. A sight like that could make a guy as nervous as a long-tailed cat in a room full of rocking chairs. Aramis did the only logical thing . . . he got rid of the ball. Unfortunately the only target around was Jim Contratto on his left, and he was even deeper in the end zone than Dandoy. Aramis tossed it, Jim missed it, and Pat Bisceglia recovered it for another Irish touchdown.

The Irish were still not through. There was another long run in Johnny Lattner. In the final quarter, the Trojans fumbled on the Irish 35, Notre Dame recovered, and four plays later Lattner rambled home for his fourth and final touchdown. Mercifully the gun sounded less than two minutes later and put an end to the carnage.

All 98,000 fans sat stunned in the stands, the Notre Dame partisans by the joy of victory and the size of the score, and the Trojan rooters by shock, and the size of the score. At that time it was the worst drubbing they had ever received from Notre Dame. Only one other team had ever run up more points

against an SC team, that was Michigan in the 1947 Rose Bowl . . . 49-0. No one player had ever run four touchdowns against them either . . . but all these happened the same afternoon, November 23, 1953.

The dean of Los Angeles sportswriters predicted gloomily, "The win left the all time count of this SC-ND series 16-7-2, in favor of the Irish. It is doubtful if anybody who sat in on yesterday's track meet will live long enough to see it evened up."

Another Times writer decided to smile through his tears and try to get even in print.

"The Fighting Irish — and Italians, Germans, French, Hungarians and Czechs, Bohemians, Poles, and Croats . . . could do no wrong yesterday."

"The Faintin' Irish or the Fightin' Irish . . ." he wrote. "They know how to do both and when." He referred to the case of fragile Frank Varrichione, a 6 foot 207 pound tackle who was overcome during the Notre Dame-Iowa game the week before.

Going into the Iowa game, Notre Dame was undefeated. Coach Leahy naturally was willing to do anything short of assault with a deadly weapon to keep it that way. Minutes before the end of the first half, Iowa was ahead 7-0. Notre Dame had the ball on the Hawkeye 12, but had no timeouts left. Varrichione knew what to do (it has been hinted darkly that his act had been in rehearsal for some weeks). On the way back to the huddle he let out a blood-curdling shriek, clutched his back as though someone had hit him across the kidneys with a bicycle chain, and dropped to the ground. Nobody really bought the act but the officials had no choice . . . time out. Frank was helped off the field gasping for breath. On the next play Guglielmi cooly passed to end Dan Shannon in the end zone, and the Irish, Verrichione included, trotted into the locker room at halftime tied 7-7.* The Irish salvaged their undefeated record with a 14-14 tie.

Jack Geyer, the columnist, suspected a repeat performance in the SC game but with a larger cast. "Just before the first half ended, Notre Dame's Ray Lemek intercepted Dandoy's pass and returned it 58 yards to SC's 42," he wrote. ". . . Since only 10 seconds were left, the Irish began to drop like flies in order to stop the clock . . . four of them were stretched out . . . but two looked around and then got up . . . it looked like the end of a wake."

"Because of the 82° temperature, Notre Dame's team wore light Jerseys. They came apart rather easily, and many time-outs were taken to replace them with new ones," he groused. "In fact, there haven't been so many torn jerseys since the first time somebody put barbed wire around a dairy farm."

Jesse Hill might have answered in the same spirit . . . "That's no bull, he uddered."

The stats were incredible. Notre Dame made 17 first downs . . . but then so did SC. Total yardage from running and passing favored Notre Dame only 367 to 255. SC completed 16 passes to three for the Irish . . . but after all's said and done, it's the score that counts.

Johnny Lattner was named All American that year for the second time, and won the Heisman trophy. Neil Worden was his equal when it came to gaining ground. But Lattner's all around ability and leadership was of inestimable value to Notre Dame . . . something Florence Leahy, the coach's wife knew very well. The story has it that earlier that year as she was chasing one of the eight young Leahys to administer a little parental discipline, she fell on the stairs. She called the Coach.

"Frank," she said, "I'm sorry to call you off the practice field, but I'm in the hospital . . . I broke my left leg." Shocked silence.

"Frank?" she continued.

"Yes, Floss . . . Yes!"

"Better me than Johnny Lattner, huh?"

Trojan coach Jesse Hill might have preferred it the other way around, but had far too much class to say so. He said all the things a gracious coach is supposed to say in defeat. He praised the winning opponent, and he praised the valiant effort of his own team. For him there would be another season.

For coach Frank Leahy, it was his sixth undefeated season at Notre Dame . . . and his last.

Ron Miller, USC left end

Joe Heap led Notre Dame to one sided victory in 1953

Neil Worden, Notre Dame halfback

FRANK LEAHY

"Notre Dame had him long enough . . . now he belongs to me."

Florence Leahy 1973

Francis William Leahy walked and worked and existed on this planet for another twenty years, but one wonders if he really lived.

He was a football coach, coaching football was his life, and after eleven years at Notre Dame where you've won 87 games, lost only 11 and had but nine ties, where do you go? When you've recorded a win percentage of .888, second only to Rockne's .897 in the modern history of Notre Dame football, where do you go? What do you do when you're a living legend at forty-five and have no team to coach. And he was a coach. And, after posting six unbeaten seasons, winning four national championships in seven years, putting together a 39 game winning streak, coaching four Heisman Trophy winners . . . where do you go. For Frank Leahy, nowhere. For him there was no place to coach but Notre Dame. Frank Leahy without Notre Dame was like a sailor without a star. "It's a terrible thing," he once said in his fading years, "to be the ex-head coach of Notre Dame."

He was a coach cast in the traditional mold of what a coach ought to be. Perhaps it is more accurate to say — in the classic fictional image of a coach in the Frank Merriwell or Horatio Alger, Jr., series. He never used a word of profanity in front of his "lads" and during his coaching days took only an occasional drink . . . but never in front of his lads. He was a molder of character, a builder of men. He demanded total dedication to the game, to Our Lady and to winning. He gave the same devotion he expected. He would have died for any or all three . . . He probably did. He exacted absolute loyalty to himself and the team, and he returned it. There was no statute of limitations. Once you were one of Coach Leahy's lads, you had made a contract for life. Oral, but binding.

Years after his coaching days were over, one of his lads, a rookie with the Los Angeles Rams, was given a membership to the Los Angeles Athletic Club. For reasons unknown, even to the rookie himself, he rifled the locker room one afternoon and lifted several wallets. He was apprehended and taken to jail. He used his one telephone call not to contact a lawyer, but to call Frank Leahy.

The coach immediately flew to Los Angeles, contacted a judge he knew who put him in touch with a lawyer. He then met with the club members . . . then got them all together, lawyer, judge and jury, as it were, and managed to get the charges dropped. He gave the rookie a private locker room speech for an hour, then boarded a plane for home.

At the age most men retire, Frank Leahy was dead, burned hollow by seasons of anxiety, pressure, assumed responsibility and disappointment. For him the tragic part of life's drama came after the stadiums had emptied and the echoes of the cheers had died away and he stood alone and did not know it. Over the years the storybook Irish Catholic family had become strangers, for while Leahy the coach was winning at Notre Dame, Leahy the father was losing the home game.

In the latter years, as though doing penance, he maintained an exhausting schedule . . . television appearances, lecture tours speaking out against sin and the evils of communism. Yet he was haunted by the fear that no one understood what he was trying to do for Holy Mother the Church and Our Country.

But hope is a better teammate than fear, and although the body was broken and ravaged by leukemia, arthritis, diabetes, and a failing heart — nearly all the ills that human flesh is heir to, the coach lost neither hope, nor the desire to fight, nor the will to win.

And while he was preaching the virtues of honesty and continence, warning young men about the danger of the occasion of sin and young women about the perils of unwed motherhood, his wife was drowning in a sea of alcohol and his son Jerry became involved in a bizarre plot to smuggle hashish from Amsterdam to the United States in, of all things, cuckoo clocks! It was an unsuccessful venture. The only thing it netted Jerry was a three-year term in prison.

Perhaps he came by that business acumen naturally. Father Frank had been involved in oil, real estate, franchises, all of which had cost him dearly . . . because of an innate and unshakeable honesty.

He was a paradox, an enigma. He could be hard as quartz, or cry at something no more tragic than a detergent commercial. Some said he was as dull as dishwater, others said he had a dry quiet wit that was not always understood. Johnny Lujack tells the following story: During the Notre Dame-Army game of 1946, which ended in a scoreless tie, Irish halfback Bob Livingston missed a tackle. Lujack, always a fierce competitor, screamed at him, "Bob, you dumb son-of-a-bitch!"

Leahy went into shock. When he recovered he began to scream. Lujack says he could feel the heat of the coach's wrath play up and down his spine like a blowtorch.

"Another profane outburst like that, Jonathon Lujack, and you will be asked to disassociate yourself from our fine Catholic University!" he roared. Then his voice dropped and assumed an almost pleading tone. "Oooooh Jonathon, Jonathon, you might well remember when I recruited you I promised your parents you would have a fine Catholic upbringing."

Lujack pulled the hood of his parka up over his head and regarded the turf directly in front of his toes. On the very next play Livingston did the very same thing. Lujack bit his lip, and Leahy looked like a man about to go into cardiac arrest. He took a gulp of air, turned to the bench and announced, "Gentlemen, I fear that Jonathon Lujack is right about Robert Livingston."*

"He was an uncooperative son-of-a-bitch," says one old time Chicago sportswriter, "he was great to the press only after he left Notre Dame."

"He was a giant . . . an absolute giant," said Al Davis, the managing general partner of the Oakland Raiders at the time of Leahy's death. "He was a hell of a kind man, too."

"I loved my Uncle Frank. He was a great man. He was a mean son-of-a-bitch, but a wonderful man," said his nephew Jack. "He had this thing about being called coach. I called him Uncle Coach . . . I never knew a man as brilliant as he was."

As he lay dying in Good Samaritan Hospital in Portland, Oregon, on June 20, 1973, Floss confided to an Episcopal priest, "I met Frank some thirty-eight years ago and I was so in love with him . . . but do you know . . . after all we've been through, I still don't know if he loves me. And he may be up there dying. Can you imagine that?"

More of life's ironies, an Irish Catholic Knight of Malta being attended to during his final hours by a priest of the Church of England because a Catholic priest could not be found.

During the night there was a crisis, and Father Rees, the Episcopal priest, located Father James Larkin, a Catholic friend who gave the coach the last rites for the sixth and final time. As with most strong-willed, courageous men, the heart simply refused to give up. Between four o'clock in the morning and eleven o'clock, his heart stopped beating five times.

At 12:51 p.m., on Thursday, June 21, Francis William Leahy's search for the Holy Grail ended. He had walked the extra mile and fought the good fight, and had never let the lance of Don Quixote drop from his hand . . . they carried him from the field of battle on his shield.

Now once more he was a hero, and there was talk of having the coach buried at Notre Dame . . . the Golden Dome casts a long shadow, and Our Lady is jealous of her sons.

When she heard, Floss Leahy set her chin, her eyes sparkling through the mist of tears and said, "He'll be buried here, here where I can visit his grave. Notre Dame had him long enough . . . Now he belongs to me."

*Wells Twombly reported the incident in "Shake Down the Thunder."

Notre Dame's Frank Leahy

NOTRE DAME ROSTER — 1953

NO.	NAME	POS.	HGT.	WGT.
62	Bisceglia, Pat	L.G.	5'10"	190
4	Bucci, Don	Q.B.	6'	180
73	**Bush, Joe	L.T.	6'3"	204
88	*Cabal, Walt	R.E.	6'3"	205
2	**Caey, Tom	Q.B.	5'10"	175
56	Cook, Ed	R.G.	6'1"	210
82	Edmonds, Wayne	R.T.	6'	195
32	Fitzgeald, Dick	L.H.	5'11"	190
63	Fasor, Dick	C.	5'11"	190
34	Gaffney, John	F.B.	6'1"	185
81	George, Don	R.E.	6'4"	205
3	**Guglielmi, Ralph	Q.B.	6'	180
42	**Heap, Joe	L.H.	5'11"	180
49	Hendricks, Dick	L.H.	6'1"	180
80	*Hunter, Art	R.T.	6'3"	228
89	Kapish, Gene	L.E.	6'1"	193
40	Keller, Dick	R.H.	6'	175
79	Lasch, Bob	L.T.	6'3"	212
14	**Lattner, Johnny	R.H.	6'1"	190
65	**Lee, Jack	R.G.	5'11"	190
72	Lemek, Ray	L.G.	6'1"	207
86	**Mangialardi, Fred	R.E.	6'1"	195
70	Martel, Gene	R.T.	6'3"	211
			6'2"	185

NO.	NAME	POS.	HGT.	WGT.
6	Martin, Bob	Q.B.	6'1"	191
90	*Matz, Paul	L.E.	6'1"	205
85	**Mavraides, Menil	R.G.	6'1"	195
30	*McHugh, Tom	F.B.	5'11"	205
51	Mense, John	C.	6'2"	204
77	Nicula, George	R.G.	6'1"	208
54	Nowack, Art	C.	6'	203
67	**Palumbo, Sam	L.T.	6'4"	212
75	Pasquesi, Tony	R.T.	6'1"	200
83	**Penza, Don	R.E.	5'10"	185
37	Raich, Nick	F.B.	6'3"	212
74	**Ready, Bob	L.G.	5'8"	172
45	Rigali, Bob	R.H.	5'11"	185
9	Schaefer, Don	Q.B.	6'2"	215
53	**Schrader, Jim	C.	6'	190
33	**Shannon, Dan	L.E.	6'2"	215
52	*Szymanski, Dick	C.	6'2"	206
71	Taylor, Bob	L.G.	6'2"	208
69	Trozzo, Bill	T.	6'	207
60	Varrichione, Frank	L.T.	6'1"	195
41	Washington, Dick	R.H.	5'11"	185
38	Wilson, George	F.B.	5'11"	185
48	**Worden, Neil	R.B.		

SOUTHERN CALIFORNIA ROSTER — 1953

NAME			
*Artenian, Mickey			
**Baldock, Al			
Bordier, Bing			
**Bozanic, George			
Brown, Ron			
**Buckley, Bob			
Champlin, Pete			
Clarke, Leon			
*Clayton, Frank			
Contratto, Jim			
*Crow, Lindon			
*Dandoy, Aramis			
*Da Re, Mario			
De Martini, Ed			
Duvall, Gordon			
Exley, Landon			
Fannin, Warren			
Ferrante, Orlando			
*Fouch, Ed			
Galli, George			
Greenwood, Chuck			
Griffith, Chuck			

NAME	POS.	HGT.	WGT.
**Han, Harold	F.B.	5'9"	186
*Hawthorne, Addison	F.B.	5'9"	193
*Hayes, Jim	R.E.	6'4"	195
Hooks, Roger	Q.B.	6'1½"	212
Hubby, Lindsy	R.E.	6'1½"	201
Kaplan, Frank	C.	6'	194
**Koch, Des	L.H.	6'	208
Miller, John	R.T.	6'1½"	191
**Miller, Ron	L.E.	6'4"	205
**Nickoloff, Tom	R.E.	6'3½"	219
*Pavich, Frank	L.T.	6'	213
*Petty, Dick	C.	6'½"	196
**Pucci, Ed	L.G.	6'	216
Rappa, Tony	L.G.	5'10"	185
**Riddle, Bill	Q.B.	6'	201
Salio, Don	L.G.	5'11"	184
Sampson, Vern	C.	6'	206
**Sellers, Leon	F.B.	6'	190
Spector, Irwin	R.G.	5'9½"	194
**Thompson, Ken	R.T.	6'2"	216
*Timberlake, George	R.G.	6'2"	212
*Tsagalakis, Sam	P.K.	5'7½"	165
*Weber, Tom	L.T.	6'2"	206

CHAPTER 27

"ALL AMERICAN!. . . THEY SHOULD HAVE GIVEN THAT BOY AN ACADEMY AWARD"
. . . Iowa fan, 1954

In 1947 Terry Brennan was a thoughtful young student in Father Theodore Hesburgh's philosophy class at Notre Dame. He was also a speedy halfback on Coach Frank Leahy's championship football team.

In 1954 Terry Brennan was a thoughtful young football coach at Notre Dame. At the tender age of twenty-five he had inherited one of the nation's most powerful collegiate football machines, and so far had everyone convinced he knew what to do with it.

Other than a shocking 14-27 upset by Purdue, the Irish juggernaut rolled on unimpeded much as it had done under Coach Leahy. At the time of the 26th meeting of these two intersectional rivals, the Irish record for the season stood at 7 wins and one loss.

On paper, Jess Hill's record at SC looked nearly as good. Other than a 20-7 swamping by Texas Christian, the Trojan horse had galloped along with considerable ease . . . until he stumbled and fell before UCLA 34-0. Their season record, 8 and 2.

The difference, of course, was in the quality of the competition, or so thought the professional oddsmakers who established the Irish 14 point favorites.

So on the afternoon of November 28 in a bone-chilling autumn rain they met again in South Bend and after the first 54 minutes of the game, the Notre Dame fans were rubbing their eyes in disbelief, and the bookmakers were checking airline schedules for midnight flights to Mexico.

The score was 17-14 Southern California, the Irish had the ball 3rd and three on their own 28 and there were less than six minutes to play. Time for Trojan rooters to start folding up blankets, pack the thermos bottles away and get out of those wet clothes and into a dry martini to celebrate an upset victory, right?

Wrong.

With five minutes and fifty-seven seconds to play, Ralph Guglielmi, back to plague the Trojans for the fourth consecutive year, faded back to his left and flipped a little screen pass to Jim Morse who gobbled it up and raced 72 yards for a touchdown. Then to add insult to injury, the Irish graciously accepted the gift of a two point safety in the waning moments of the game to make the final score Notre Dame 23, SC 17.*

The Trojans lost the game, but certainly had no reason to consider themselves losers. They had led through three quar-

ters, and played the vaunted Notre Dame offense to a standstill. The force and speed of their attack had kept the Irish off balance most of the afternoon. The 1954 Trojan team was the first Southern California team since 1946 to score on the Fighting Irish of Notre Dame.

Wilfrid Smith of the Chicago Tribute wrote: "The Trojans earned respect by the power and skill of attack. There were no better players than Marvin Goux, center who recovered three Irish fumbles . . . Ed Fouch, right tackle, was a pillar on the right. Jim Contratto who completed five consecutive passes . . . ranks as one of the game's best generals."

USC's Head Coach Jess Hill with Notre Dame's Head Coach Terry Brennan

Nevertheless, Notre Dame won.

The Trojans had wasted no time getting started. Marvin Goux made the first of his three fumble recoveries only minutes after the opening kickoff when the Irish bobbled the ball on their own 14 yard line. Fullback Gordon Duvall and halfback Ron Calabria hit the line for nine yards, then Aramis Dandoy made it to the 2½ yard line for a first down and on the next play went over right tackle to score. The referee disagreed, but it didn't matter, Contratto sneaked it over from a few inches out on the next play anyway. This time the referee concurred. Sad Sam Tsagalakis converted and the Trojans led 7-0 after only five minutes and 15 seconds of play.

The Irish came roaring back as everyone expected them to do and drove to the Trojan 28, but Duvall and guard George Galli stifled Guglielmi's air attack and smothered the Irish threat.

Early in the second quarter Goux recovered his second fumble and Jim Contratto's punt backed the Irish up to their own 20. The Trojans continued their powerful defensive game and manhandled Guglielmi so roughly that he nearly lost the ball on several occasions. As it was, he wound up clear back on the four yard line, 4th down and 26 to go.

Joe Heap managed to elude Mario Da Rae long enough to punt from the end zone and Ernie Merk brought the ball back to the Irish 20.

But then the Irish got tough. Dandoy could gain only two yards, then had a problem holding on to Contratto's pass on the five, so Tsagalakis attempted a field goal, but it was wide to the left . . . Notre Dame took over and promptly marched 80 yards for the tying touchdown. The drive was highlighted by Joe Heap's 39 yard run through right tackle to the Trojan 30, then Morse raced 13 yards around left end and worked the ball down to the four on a series of T option plays. The Trojans pushed Notre Dame back to the 14, but after a time out the Irish came back with a spectacular bit of razzle-dazzle to score. Quarterback Tom Carey lateraled to Heap, Heap passed to Jim Morse who went over standing up. The point after was good. The score was tied 7-7.

The Trojans threatened once more before the end of the half when Frank Hall intercepted a Guglielmi pass on the Irish 35, but time ran out.

The Trojans started the third quarter looking like anything but 14 point underdogs. Indeed, they hadn't looked like underdogs all day. Dandoy drove from SC's 47 to the Notre Dame 13 behind brilliant blocking by Leon Clarke. Aramis slipped while making a cut to the left to avoid Guglielmi, the last Irish defender who could have stopped him. He didn't fall, but the misstep slowed him enough to allow Guglielmi to catch up and bring him down. On fourth down, Tsagalakis came in and booted a field goal from the 24. After four minutes and 25 seconds of the second half, the score was 10-7.

Aramis Dandoy picks up long yardage on Irish

No one ever expects a Notre Dame team to roll over and give up in the fourth quarter just because they're a few points behind. That's because they never have. And they surely didn't that afternoon. After the Trojans were forced to punt, the Irish marched 106 yards in 33 plays and 10 minutes. From their own 14, they needed only 86 yards for the touchdown, but they were penalized 20 yards during the assault on the walls of Troy. Don Schaefer went the final two yards over right guard for the 6, then made the point after to bring the score to 14-10. For the first time in the game, the Irish led.

Now it was time for the Trojans to stand up and be counted, and they did just that. Somebody had neglected to tell them they didn't have a chance against mighty Notre Dame. They didn't know when they were whipped.

But they knew how to fight, and fight they did. Jim Contratto came in to replace injured Frank Hall, and went right to work. He completed five straight passes to move SC from their 28 to the Notre Dame goal line . . . the last a beautifully arched lob to 6'6" Chuck Griffith who stepped into the end zone. Co-captain Ed Fouch made the conversion good and the Trojans led 17-14 with ten and a half minutes remaining in the game.

The later it got, the better things looked for USC. Heap fumbled, and Orlando Ferrante recovered for Troy. The game was all but iced. After three plays, the Trojans hadn't gained an inch, so Contratto punted. It rolled out of bounds on the Notre Dame 21. Jim Heap picked up three, Schaefer got four. It was third and three on the Irish 28 and . . . well, you know the rest. The walls of Troy, like those of Jericho, came a-tumbling down.

"Fainting" Frank Varrichione—Notre Dame's All American tackle

The Trojans boarded the team plane to head for Southern California and prepare for Ohio State in the Rose Bowl. The Irish had a date in Texas with SMU. They took care of that nicely with a 26-14 win and returned to South Bend with a 9-1-0 record and settled back to receive their accustomed accolades. Joe Heap was named academic All American for the third time, Dan Shannon received All American mention, Ralph Guglielmi was on everybody's All American, and Frank Verrichione was named All American by UP and INS. When appraised of this, one Iowa alumni, recalling Fainting Frank's stellar performance in the 1953 Iowa-ND tie, bellowed, "All American! They should have given that boy an Academy Award."

Frank Verrichione was a good enough football player not to have to rely on his histrionic ability anyway, and it's a good thing. In 1954 two new rules were passed . . . the so-called sucker shift was declared illegal, as was feigning injuries for the sake of gaining time.

Leo Fischer, sports editor of the Chicago American, predicted that after the tussle Notre Dame had with Southern Cal, Ohio State . . . "would have no picnic when it meets those same Trojans in the Rose Bowl."

Well it was no picnic, but the Buckeyes won 20-7.

USC lone score was an 87 yd. punt return by Aramis Dandoy — still a Rose Bowl record.

Jim Contratto sneaks in for Troys first TD

*Marv Goux, now an assistant coach at USC, was called by Jesse Hill, "Pound for pound, the best football player I ever coached at Southern Cal." He had played all but two minutes of the game that day, and in the course of recovering fumbles, centering, blocking, and being slammed on the frozen turf a dozen times, was a little rocky when he bent over to snap the ball. Looking at the world upside down through your legs as centers used to do is bad enough when you're well. If you've had your bell rung as many times as Marv had that day, it's downright bewildering. He was seeing double and passed to the wrong image. Even today he says he sometimes dreams about that bad pass from center.

151

UNIVERSITY OF NOTRE DAME 1954 VARSITY ALPHABETICAL ROSTER

NO.	NAME AND POSITION	WT.	HT.
71	Beams, Byron, T.	218	6'4"
8	Bigelow, James, Q.B.	170	5'11"
79	Bihn, Joseph, T.	208	6'2"
62	Bisceglia, Pat, G.*	192	5'10"
48	Bosse, Joseph, T.	200	6'2"
88	Cabral, Walter, E.**	215	6'3"
15	Callaghan, Leo, H.B.	175	6'1"
2	Carey, Thomas, Q.B.***	180	5'10"
53	Carrabine, Luke, C.	190	6'1"
6	Cooke, Larry, Q.B.	180	6'0"
56	Cook, Edward, G.	217	6'1"
55	Coyne, Bob, C.	200	6'1"
64	Cunningham, Tom, G.	195	6'0"
47	Davin, Dave, E.	190	6'4"
87	Dumas, Jack, E.	185	6'3"
82	Edmonds, Wayne, T.*	207	6'0"
32	Fitzgerald, Dick, H.B.*	190	5'11"
63	Frasor, Dick, C.-G.	185	5'11"
34	Gaffney, John, F.B.	190	6'1"
81	George, Donald, E.*	202	6'4"
21	Gerami, Gerald, H.B.	170	5'9"
35	Gormley, Jim, H.B.	185	5'10"
76	Groble, George, T.	208	6'2"
3	Guglielmi, Ralph, Q.B.***	190	6'0"
42	Heap, Joseph, H.B.***	180	5'11"
49	Hendricks, Richard, H.B.	180	6'1"
5	Hornung, Paul, Q.B.	190	6'2"
24	Hughes, Thomas, F.B.	180	6'0"
89	Kapish, Eugene, E.	187	6'1"
78	Kegaly, John, G.	210	6'3"
40	Keller, Richard, H.B.*	160	6'0"
58	King, Jack, G.	195	5'10"
91	Lasch, Robert, T.	225	6'3"
65	Lee, Jack, G.***	195	5'11"
72	Lemek, Ray, G.*	205	6'1"
85	Loncaric, Louis, C.	187	6'3"
43	Markowski, Joseph, F.B.	185	6'0"
70	Martell, Eugene, T.	224	6'3"
90	Matz, Paul (Co-Capt.), E.**	190	6'1"
11	McDonnell, John, H.B.	165	5'11"
61	McMullan, John, G.	203	5'10"
51	Mense, James, C.	206	5'11"
19	Milota, James, H.B.	170	5'11"
73	Mondron, Robert, T.	202	6'3"
17	Morse, James, H.B.	175	5'11"
80	Munro, James, E.	193	6'0"
39	Murphy, Ed., G.	200	6'2"
68	Nakfoor, Patrick, E.	225	6'4"
77	Nicula, George, T.	210	6'2"
50	Noznesky, Pete. E.	175	6'0"
67	Palumbo, Samuel, T.***	212	6'1"
75	Pasquesi, Anthony, T.	220	6'4"
41	Pinn, Frank, F.B.	185	5'10"
37	Raich, Nicholas, F.B.	188	5'10"
74	Ready, Robert, T.**	220	6'3"
59	Regan, Michael, E.	212	6'2"
18	Reynolds, Paul, H.B.**	182	6'0"
16	Rigali, William, H.B.	175	5'10"
83	Scannell, Robert, E.	190	6'0"
9	Schaefer, Donald, F.B.*	187	5'11"
86	Schramm, Paul, E.	198	6'2"
33	Shannon, Dan (C-C), E.**	198	6'0"
12	Sipes, Sherrill, H.B.	185	6'0"
69	Stanitzek, Frank, G.	205	5'10"
22	Studer, Dean, H.B.	180	5'11"
52	Szymanski, Richard, C.***	215	6'2"
60	Varrichione, Frank, T.***	225	6'0"
28	Williams, Donald, F.B.	180	5'10"
38	Wilson, George, F.B.	190	5'11"
20	Witucki, Jack, F.B.	182	6'1"
84	Zajeski, Benedict, G.	205	6'3"
66	Zervas, Thomas, G.	205	6'1"

UNIVERSITY OF SOUTHERN CALIFORNIA FOOTBALL SQUAD — 1954

NO.	NAME AND POSITION	WT.	HT.
72	Al Adams, T.	231	6'3"
26	Jon Arnett, H.B.	178	5'11"
54	Roger Belnap, C.	197	5'11"
79	George Belotti, T.	231	6'4"
86	Bing Bordier, E.	195	6'0"
39	Ron Brown, H.B.	175	5'11"
34	Ron Calabria, H.B.	178	5'9"
81	Leon Clarke, E.*	213	6'4"
29	Frank Clayton, H.B.**	180	6'0"
12	Jim Contratto, Q.B.*	183	5'9"
36	Lindon Crow (Co-Capt.), H.B.**	186	6'1"
27	Aramis Dandoy, H.B.**	180	5'11"
74	Mario DaRe, T.**	214	6'2"
21	Jim Decker, F.B.*	180	5'10"
40	Gordon Duvall, F.B.*	187	5'11"
56	Dirk Eldredge, C.	180	6'1"
63	Dick Enright, G.	208	6'2"
61	Orlando Ferrante, G.*	198	5'10"
70	Ron Fletcher, T.	217	6'2"
77	Ed Fouch (Co-Capt.), T.**	234	6'3"
52	Marv Goux, C.*	185	5'10"
60	George Galli, G.*	199	5'10"
87	Chuck Green, E.	189	6'0"
89	Chuck Greenwood, E.*	195	6'1"
80	Chuck Griffith, E.	239	6'6"
18	Frank Hall, Q.B.	184	6'0"
83	Emilio Hilario, E.	194	6'1"
16	Roger Hooks, Q.B.	207	6'1"
67	Bob Isaacson, G.	199	6'1"
15	Ellsworth, Kissinger, Q.B.	178	5'10"
44	Wayne Kurlak, F.B.	190	5'11"
82	Chuck Leimbach, E.	188	6'4"
85	Don McFarland, E.	203	6'2"
37	Ernie Merk, H.B.	188	5'9"
64	John Miller, G.*	194	6'1"
75	Frank Pavich, T.**	224	6'0"
84	Chuck Perpich, E.	181	6'2"
25	Fred Pierce, H.B.	173	5'11"
53	Vern Sampson, C.*	209	6'0"
78	Roy Smith, T.	215	6'4"
65	Irwin Spector, G.*	193	5'9"
41	Joe Tisdale, F.B.	191	6'0"
62	Paul Torena, G.	193	5'11"
31	Sam Tsagalakis, P.K.**	165	5'7"
71	Dick Westphal, T.	201	6'1"
68	Laird Willott, G.	200	6'0"

1955
CHAPTER 28

". . . GENTLEMEN, PLEASE DON'T FORGET YOUR POWDER PUFFS . . ."

Jess Hill, 1955

So far Terry Brennan had proved to be as able a coach as he had been a player. In his second season as head coach of the Fighting Irish he brought an 8-1-0 record to the Coliseum for the 27th meeting of these two old foes. The intersectional rivalry now stood at 17-7-2 in favor of Notre Dame, and SC rooters and alumni took little solace in the fact that seven of those losing games had been decided by less than 7 points . . . five of them by 2 points or less.

Nor was the Hillmen's 1955 record a source of much comfort. After an impressive 50-12 win over Washington State, and then trampling Oregon and Texas, the Trojans fell before Washington 0-7, but recovered to win over Wisconsin and California. The alumni, while perhaps not rapturous, were at least placated. But then came losses to Minnesota, Stanford, and USC's cross-town rival, UCLA* and rumors of a coaching change, never far below the surface, began bubbling up again.

Jesse Hill had yet to beat Notre Dame. Of course he should not have been judged too harshly for that; outside of Jeff Cravath's 1950 upset, no Trojan combination had been able to demolish the Irish since Howard Jones and the last of the "Thundering Herds" in 1939.

But hope is ever livelier than despair, so the gallant Trojans once more took the field 7-point underdogs against fifth ranked Notre Dame, whose only loss had been to Michigan State, rated #2 in the nation. However, the 94,892 fans who jammed the Coliseum that cloudy November 26th were in for a surprise. For the Trojan boosters, a pleasant one. For Notre Dame . . . well, a stunning one to say the least.

The Trojan horse came roaring out of the starting gate and scored 21 points in the first 18 minutes, more than the favored Irish tallied in the entire game.

The first time SC got their hands on the ball they scored. With Junior quarterback Ellsworth Kissinger* directing, the Trojans took the opening kickoff 68 yards in eleven plays. The big play of the sequence was a 20 yard pass reception by C. R. Roberts who moved the ball to the Notre Dame 43. Three plays later, unable to move the ball past the 39, Kissinger decided to gamble. On fourth down with six yards to go, he showed disrespect bordering on contempt for the Irish defense

and dropped back to pass. The gamble paid off, so he became a hero. Don Hickman caught the toss on the 21 for a first down. Jon Arnett, C. R. Roberts, and Kissinger worked the ball to the one yard line and "Kissy"* went over on a quarterback sneak and made the conversion . . . USC 7, Notre Dame 0.

The Irish were not impressed . . . yet. They answered with an almost identical march. Sixty-seven yards in eleven plays (not counting a 15-yard penalty for holding). They even showed the same cavalier attitude toward SC's defense that the Trojans had shown for theirs. On his own 40 yard line, fourth

Troy's Aramis Dandoy

153

Paul Hornung lets fly with a long bomb

down and three to go, All American quarterback Paul Hornung, instead of punting, called a running play. Halfback Dean Struder made the first down with plenty to spare. Flushed with success and operating on the premise that success begets success, Hornung tried another running play a little later on third down from the SC 45 with one yard to go. This time he elected to keep the ball and probably wished he hadn't. The 6'2", 205 pound "Golden Boy," called by many the most versatile quarterback in the history of Notre Dame football, charged into the SC line like a wounded Cape Buffalo and was stopped in his tracks. But not for long. The surest way of stopping Paul Hornung in his prime would have been the effective use of a 90mm cannon.

He took to the air and found end Gene Kapish on the 24. By this time the bells had stopped ringing, so with atavistical glee he threw himself once more into the center of the SC line. This time he bulled his way to the 11 and another first down. The Trojan defense stiffened and held on the 8. Fourth down and one to go. Field goal? Not on your life. Hornung took the snap from center, broke two tackles on the ten, cut to his right and battered his way into the end zone carrying two more tacklers on his back. He made the extra point to tie the score 7-7.

Now it was SC halfback Jon Arnett's turn for some heroics. He returned the Notre Dame kickoff 31 yards to his 43. Then alternating runs with right half Ron Brown, worked the ball to the Irish 15 at the end of the quarter.

It took just one play . . . a pass from Kissinger to Roberts to score. Arnett converted to make it 14-7.

Now Lady Luck, who had kept her gaze averted from Jesse Hill's eager face for most of the season, suddenly turned and smiled upon him. Notre Dame fullback Dick Fitzgerald fumbled on the first play after kickoff. George Galli recovered for the Trojans on the Irish 21 but it took Arnett and Brown three plays to make just 4 yards, so on fourth down there were six long yards to go.

Coach Hill sent field goal kicker Bob Isaacson in, Kissinger knelt to hold. But when the pass from center came, Kissinger jumped up and fired a quick pass to Arnett on the left flank and Jon raced to the ten for a first down. Two plays later he waltzed over for the Trojans, third score. Isaacson converted and the University of Southern California led 21-7 three minutes into the second quarter of the game. It was hard to tell who was more surprised, the Trojans or the Irish.

The SC defense proved to be very stingy and it looked as though the half would end with no further scoring, but Hornung had other ideas. The Notre Dame defense had been no more generous than the Trojans', so with only minutes to go in the third quarter, SC was forced to punt. It was a beauty. Frank Hall boomed a classic spiral deep into Irish territory. It was downed on the Notre Dame 22 and the Trojan fans had visions of going into the second half with a 14 point lead. The vision turned out to be myopic. Hornung on first down faded

Jon Arnett of Troy beats Paul Hornung to end zone

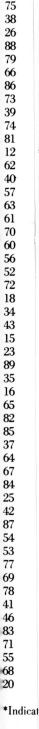
back and uncorked a bomb. It flew like a homesick passenger pigeon straight into the waiting arms of Slim Jim Morse (remember him, SC's nemesis in 1954?) on the 45 yard line and no one even got close to him. A 78 yard pass play for the second Notre Dame touchdown. Even so, after Hornung's conversion attempt went wide, the Trojans trotted into the dressing room with what would appear to be a comfortable 21-13 lead.

To underestimate the Fighting Irish can be fatal, regardless of score or time remaining to play. Coach Hill and the Trojan team were keenly aware of this. They may have remembered the old sourdough '49er saying, "It seems a man always gets lucky just before he dies." They took no chances and played the entire third quarter close to the vest. Neither team scored, but there were some sticky minutes for both.

The Irish recovered an SC fumble, but then Leon Clarke bobbed up to intercept Hornung's pass. Roberts, with Doug Krantz assisting, worked the ball to the Irish 5, but fumbled. Gene Kapish of Notre Dame recovered and Hornung drove the Irish all the way back to Southern Cal's 3 and it seemed certain that Brennan's boys would score before the end of the quarter.

They didn't. What's more they fumbled in the first play of the fourth quarter and Brown of SC recovered in the end zone for a touchback.

But Hornung was far from through. He and Morse clicked

for a 60 yard gain the next time the Irish got the ball and parlayed it into a third Notre Dame touchdown. The Golden Boy's conversion attempt was good and left the Irish just one point shy at 20-21 with 12 minutes remaining.

The Men of Troy however had caught the scent of victory . . . and it was as intoxicating as it was unfamiliar. It had been five long years.

Jim Contratto came in at quarterback and almost immediately found Arnett on the Notre Dame 26 with one of his celebrated southpaw passes. Jon didn't hesitate. He flew all the way. He scored his second touchdown and followed it up with his third successful conversion, and the score was now 28-20 and the SC fans began to breath a little easier. The Trojan team and Jess Hill did not. Revenge had been a long time coming and it savored sweet. With sanguinary zeal, the men of Troy launched themselves against the invaders like the Assyrians coming down on the fold.

Substitute guard Baird Willot harrassed Hornung so ferociously that big Paul was forced into making mistakes . . . something he rarely did. The first came on the SC 44. Hornung, pressed into hurrying a pass, bobbled one into the arms of Trojan end Bing Bordier. Now with Contratto alternately pitching and handing off to MacFarland, Brown and Arnett, the interception resulted in the Trojans' fifth touchdown and Arnett's fourth conversion. 35-20, Southern California.

Willot was having too much fun to stop. A few plays later

NOTRE DAME ROSTER — 1955

NO.	NAME	POS.	HT.	WT.	AGE	CLASS	HOME TOWN (H.S.)
71	Beams, Byron	T.	6'4"	233	22	Jr.	Ada, Okla.
79	Bihn, Joseph	T.	6'2"	210	20	Jr.	San Jose, Calif.
62	**Bisceglia, Pat	L.G.	5'10"	190	25	Sr.	Worcester, Mass.
74	Bosse, Joseph	R.T.	6'2"	207	21	Jr.	Lawrence, Mass.
6	Cooke, Larry	Q.	6'0"	190	20	Jr.	Ennis, Tex.
45	Cunningham, Tom	G.	6'0"	200	19	Jr.	Pomona, Calif.
64	Djubasak, Paul	G.	6'0"	200	19	Soph.	Cleveland, Ohio
46	Dolan, Pat	L.T.	6'3"	210	20	Soph.	Throop, Pa.
82	**Edmonds, Wayne	L.T.	6'0"	210	22	Sr.	Canonsburg, Pa.
32	**Fitzgerald, Dick	F.	5'11"	190	22	Sr.	Chicago, Ill.
63	Francis, Al	C.-G.	6'0"	210	19	Soph.	San Jose, Calif.
68	Gaydos, Bob	R.G.	6'0"	200	20	Soph.	Donora, Pa.
76	Groble, George	T.	6'2"	212	19	Jr.	Chicago, Ill.
8	Hebert, Carl	Q.	5'11"	170	19	Soph.	Lafayette, La.
65	Hedrick, Eugene	L.G.	6'0"	190	19	Soph.	Canton, Ohio
49	Hendricks, Dick	F.	6'1"	180	21	Sr.	Danville, Ill.
5	*Hornung, Paul	Q.	6'2"	205	19	Jr.	Louisville, Ky.
67	Hughes, Tom	L.G.	6'0"	190	20	Jr.	Portland, Ore.
89	*Kapish, Gene	R.E.	6'1"	190	20	Sr.	Barberton, Ohio
20	Kiley, Roger	H.	5'11"	178	19	Soph.	Chicago, Ill.
54	Kuchta, Frank	C.	6'1"	205	19	Soph.	Cleveland, Ohio
72	**Lemek, Ray	R.T.-G.	6'1"	205	21	Sr.	Sioux, City, Iowa
23	Lewis, Aubrey	L.H.	6'0"	185	20	Soph.	Montclair, N.J.
48	Lima, Chuck	F.	6'2"	190	19	Soph.	Cincinnati, Ohio
85	*Loncaric, Lou	C.-E.	6'3"	190	20	Jr.	Battle Creek, Mich.
25	Lynch, Dick	R.H.	6'0"	185	19	Soph.	Clinton, N.J.
70	*Martell, Gene	R.G.-T.	6'3"	215	21	Sr.	Midland, Pa.
11	McDonnell, John	H.-Q.	5'11"	175	20	Jr.	Sterling, Ill.
61	McMullan, John	R.G.	5'10"	203	22	Sr.	Hoboken, N.J.
51	*Mense, James	C.	5'11"	206	20	Sr.	Hamilton, Ohio
19	Milota, James	H.	5'10"	165	20	Jr.	Park Ridge, Ill.
73	Mondron, Bob	T.	6'3"	210	20	Jr.	Charleston, W.Va.
17	*Morse, Jim	R.H.	5'11"	175	20	Jr.	Muskegon, Mich.
80	Munro, Jim	L.E.	6'0"	193	20	Jr.	Chicago, Ill.
77	*Nicula, George	L.T.	6'2"	210	21	Sr.	Warren, Ohio
50	Noznesky, Pete	E.	6'0"	180	21	Jr.	Lansdowne, Pa.
87	Prendergast, Dick	L.E.	6'2"	195	18	Soph.	Homewood, Ill.
37	*Raich, Nick	G.	5'10"	188	21	Sr.	Milwaukee, Wis.
57	Regan, Michael	E.	6'2"	212	20	Sr.	Buffalo, N.Y.
83	*Scannell, Bob	R.E.	6'0"	190	20	Jr.	South Bend
9	**Schaefer, Don	F.	5'11"	190	21	Sr.	Pittsburgh, Pa.
86	Schramm, Paul	R.E.	6'2"	200	20	Jr.	Cincinnati, Ohio
39	Shulsen, Richard	G.	6'0"	190	19	Soph.	Salt Lake City, Utah
12	*Sipes, Sherrill	H.	6'0"	185	20	Jr.	Louisville, Ky.
69	Stanitzek, Frank	G.	5'10"	205	20	Jr.	Grand Rapids, Mich.
22	*Studer, Dean	L.H.	5'11"	180	19	Jr.	Billings, Mont.
52	Sullivan, Ed	R.T.-C.	6'0"	190	20	Soph.	McKeesport, Pa.
7	Trapp, Harold	Q.	6'0"	180	19	Soph.	Sycamore, Ill.
35	Ward, Robert	L.H.	5'8"	160	20	Jr.	Lamberton, Pa.
33	Wilkins, Dick	R.H.-F.	5'11"	190	21	Soph.	Duncan, Okla.
84	Wilson, George	L.E.	5'11"	190	21	Sr.	Polo, Ill.
88	Zajeski, Benedict	E.	6'3"	205	21	Sr.	Chicago, Ill.

*Indicates varsity letters won

1956
CHAPTER 29

". . . THE SPIRIT WAS WILLING, BUT THE TEAM WAS WEAK."
A Cleveland priest . . . 1956

As far as the Notre Dame family was concerned, the 28th meeting of the Trojans and the Irish in the Coliseum was almost anti-climactic. Another battle had started the day before, but this was was verbal, and Heaven forbid . . . *between two Notre Dame men!*

This internecine strife erupted when former coach Frank Leahy, in a newspaper interview, accused the Irish team under 27-year-old Coach Brennan of having lost their fight and will to win.

"It's not the losses that upset me," said Leahy. "It's the attitude."

"This is a personal thing," Brennan replied. "Something came up between Leahy and me a couple of days ago. I'll have something to say after the game."

The "something" that came up was Brennan's refusal to allow Paul Hornung to appear with Leahy on a television show on the eve of the game. It was a routine request, and a routine refusal. Something Coach Leahy also would have done the evening before an important game. It has been suggested that this incident exposed just the tip of an iceberg of resentment that had been mostly submerged since Leahy had been eased out to make room for a 25 year old philosophy student. Certainly Leahy's bitterness had been no secret among his friends, but it took the disagreement over Hornung's appearance to make it public.

"If any Notre Dame man is critical of what I've said, I can only say: 'Isn't it true?'," Leahy continued. "Teams like Notre Dame lose games, but they've always gone down swinging. But this team quit cold in the fourth quarter of the tough Iowa game."

"I think if Leahy's interest in Notre Dame was sincere, he would not have said such things," said Brennan.

The line-up of participants in the intramural squabble grew.

Said former coach Elmer Layden, "Leahy's statement in Los Angeles was in very poor taste. Leahy's publicity hungry. He's trying to keep his name in the newspapers. He should remember that when he was playing with inexperienced youngsters in 1950, he lost four games. Sure he had great teams . . . after the war when he had returning servicemen that were seven years older when they graduated than when they enrolled. Being able to coach men is damned nice if you can get it."

Paul Hornung Notre Dame All American

Jim Conroy picks up yardage behind Hillard Hill's block

Said Notre Dame athletic director Moose Krause, "Fighting spirit? That's one thing we haven't lost. The boys have been trying 60 minutes of every game."

Said Hunk Anderson, "I love that old place down there too much to add fuel to the fire."

Probably the most sensible statement in this Golden Dome donnybrook was made by veteran Notre Dame publicist Charley Callahan. "None of these things happen when you're winning," he mused.

He was right. The two years preceding the disastrous 1956 season when Coach Brennan had posted 9-1-0 and 8-2-0 back to back, he was a boy wonder. The galahad of the gridiron, he was called. But now, facing SC in the last game of the season, the once nearly invincible Irish had won 2 and lost 7 . . . the worst season since 1887 when they played one game and lost that.*

The gold in Terry Brennan's halo had begun to tarnish a little, but most observers thought Leahy was being unfair. Of the 38 man squad suited up for the crushing 48-8 defeat by Iowa, 22 were sophomores. Only Hornung, Jim Morse, Dean Struder, Ed Sullivan and a handful of others could be considered seasoned talented performers and some of them were on the disabled list. And the schedule had been tough . . . Oklahoma, Michigan State, Navy and Iowa all had better than usual teams.

On the other hand, Jess Hill, coaching his last game for the Trojans, was having his best season since 1952, having lost only to Stanford and Oregon . . . a remarkable achievement considering the fact that USC was playing under a Pacific Coast Conference penalty that limited a number of players to only five games, among them All American Jon Arnett.

The reason for the penalty was the Southern California Education Foundation's unauthorized financial assistance to players during 1955-56. The amount was only around $45 a month, but the penalty was costly . . . a $10,000 fine, probation until July 1, 1958, forty-two football players deprived of a year's eligibility, and the Trojans were barred from the next two Rose Bowl games. Nor were they alone.

It's a wonder any team from the Pacific coast got to the Rose Bowl that year. Washington was cited first for illegal financial aid, then UCLA drew a three-year probationary period, and California was fined $25,000 and placed on probation until July 1, 1957. A fine mess.

But Coach Hill had weathered the storm and brought the Trojans to the Coliseum with a 7-2 record to try for their ninth win over the Irish in 28 games. The oddsmakers thought they could do it. The University of Southern California was a solid 14-point favorite, even without Jon Arnett.

For the first few minutes of the game it looked as though the bookmakers were right. Trojan halfback Don Hickman returned the opening kickoff 14 yards to the SC 34, then sophomore quarterback Jim Conroy, mixing his plays like a vet-

*To Michigan, 0-8 when touchdowns counted four points.

Bob Williams passes out of own end zone

eran, sent Ernie Zampese (Arnett's replacement) over right tackle for five, then handed off to Hickman on a cross buck for 19 more. Hickman and C. R. Roberts took turns terrorizing the Irish line and six plays later the Trojans were on the Notre Dame 10 and knocking on the door. Zampese failed to gain, so Conroy, behind beautiful blocking, took it around right end to score. Kissinger converted and it looked like a runaway. Eighty yards in the first ten plays of the game and the Trojans led 7-0.

But the Irish, obviously stung by Leahy's accusation of lying down in the Iowa game, answered with a ten-play 76-yard march of their own. They had a little help from whichever saint watches over the football fortunes of Our Lady. On his own 24, Irish halfback Dick Lynch hit tackle for four yards, and then bobbled the ball. Just as though they had practiced such a play, end Dick Royer plucked it out of the air and raced 36 more yards. The Irish kept pecking away to the 6, where on second down, quarterback Bob Williams sneaked over for the score. Hornung's extra point attempt was wide and the score was 7-6 SC, but the Irish had shown no inclination toward surrender so the Trojans decided on a quick riposte.

From the SC 23 C. R. Roberts slammed through right tackle and made it all the way to the Trojan 41. Roberts and Zampese picked up 17 yards between them. Then Conroy faded back to pass on the Irish 40 and found himself trapped. But not for long. He escaped around right end and drove 16 yards to the

Irish 24 behind murderous blocking by end Hillard Hill. Tony Ortega got four more, Zampese picked up another five, and the Trojans were threatening from the Irish 15.

Razzle dazzle time. Conroy decided to go with a play that had beaten UCLA the week before. He pitched out to Roberts who threw a perfect strike to Hill in the end zone. Sophomore tailback Rex Johnston converted and the SC partisans watched for the Irish to crumble. They had reckoned without Paul Hornung and had taken Frank Leahy too seriously.

Early in the second quarter Hornung took a Zampese punt on the Notre Dame 16 and breezed 35 yards to the Trojan 49, but the Irish suffered their third clipping penalty on the next play and had to start all over again from their 34.

Ortega was called for pass interference on Bob Wetoska on the Trojan 41, and the Irish started to march. They gained eight yards only to have it wiped out by still another clipping penalty. They were undaunted. Hornung connected with Royer for a 25-yard gain, Williams hit halfback Bob Ward with a short pass for a first down on the 25-yard line of Southern Cal. It took only six more plays for Williams to work close enough to find Wetoska in the end zone with a 10-yard pass and the score was 14-13.

In the third quarter Notre Dame was again found guilty of clipping and was forced to punt from their own goal line. Zampese grabbed it on the Irish 45 and returned it to the 35. Conroy confidently and smoothly moved the Trojans to the 15

161

where he capped the drive with a touchdown pass to Don Voyne to score. Kissinger converted. The score was now 21-13, but the Irish showed no signs of quitting . . . at this point it's doubtful anyone expected them to.

Waving a white flag was certainly the furthest thing from Hornung's mind as he gathered in Zampese's punt and raced 95 yards for another Notre Dame touchdown, and then booted his own conversion to narrow the score to 21-20 with less than two minutes to play in the quarter.

Going into the final period of a game against Notre Dame holding only a shaky one point lead is courting disaster. Any Notre Dame team. If that Irish team happens to have Paul Hornung in the backfield, even Lloyd's of London would back down.

Fortunately Ernie Zampese didn't. Forty-six seconds into the fourth quarter on the Notre Dame 38, fourth down and one to go, Ernie decided to gamble. It worked. He cut through right tackle and never looked back. Kissinger converted, the Trojans held on and the game ended 28-20, USC.

So the bookies were wrong by 6 points and Frank Leahy was wrong by a country mile. But still a loss is a loss and the Irish dragged home with them the worst season record in Notre Dame history . . . a dreary 2-8-0.

In Cleveland, a priest who wishes to remain anonymous* even used the Notre Dame season as a subject for a sermon on charity. Gently chiding Leahy on his lack of it he paraphrased, "I think in this instance it was a case of, '. . . the spirit was willing, but the team was weak.' "

It was Jess Hill's last game as SC's head football coach; he was promoted to Athletic Director to replace retiring Willis O. Hunter. He had batted .722 in his six years as coach. Since 1951 when he was drafted to replace Jeff Cravath, he had posted 45 victories, 17 defeats and one tie. He had coached SC to a 7-0 triumph over Wisconsin in the Rose Bowl in 1953 . . . the only Pacific Coast Conference victory of the series. He finished his last season 8-2-0 and beat Notre Dame and UCLA the same season . . . the Trojans hadn't done that since 1938. Nor had they whipped the Irish two years in a row since 1939. Not bad for a track coach pressed into service because apparently no one else wanted the job. After the Notre Dame game reporters asked Hill if he might be persuaded to stay on for one more season. He replied, "I'd want a fifty year contract."

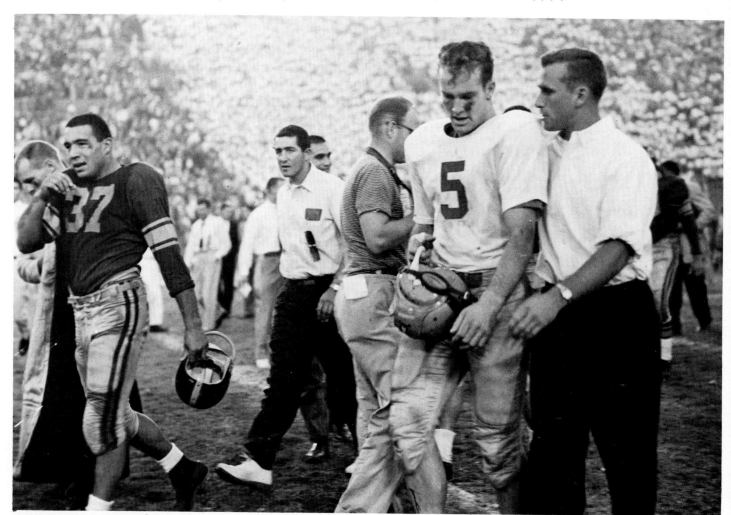

Tony Ortega, Paul Hornung and Jon Arnett walk off field after Trojan victory

SOUTHERN CALIFORNIA ROSTER — 1956

NAME	POS.	HT.	WT.	AGE	EXP.	CLASS	HOME TOWN (H.S.)
*Abram, Fabian	R.T.	6'3"	225	21	1V	Sr.	Redondo Beach
Agapay, Joe	R.H.	5'10"	182	20	1JV	Soph.	Upland (Chaffey)
Antle, Ken	C.	6'0"	184	19	Fr.	Soph.	Watsonville
**Arnett, Jon	L.H.	5'11"	185	21	2V	Sr.	L.A. (Manual Arts)
Bahrman, Don	Q.	5'8"	155	26	2JC	Jr.	Gardena
Belnap, Roger	C.	5'11½"	205	20	1JV	Soph.	Laguna Beach
**Belotti, George	L.T.	6'3"	228	22	2V	Sr.	Oxnard
Bronson, Dick	L.G.	6'2"	215	19	1JV	Soph.	El Cajon
Byrd, Lou	R.G.	6'1"	208	24	1JV	Soph.	New Orleans, La.
Clark, Lyle	L.T.	6'3"	222	19	1JV	Soph.	Corcoran
Clark, Monte	R.T.	6'5"	246	19	Fr.	Soph.	Kingsburg
Conroy, Jim	Q.	6'0"	197	19	Fr.	Soph.	Baldwin Park
**Decker, Jim	L.H.-F.	5'9"	176	24	2V	Sr.	San Pedro
Debovsky, Phil	L.T.	6'3"	215	19	1JV	Soph.	San Francisco (Poly)
DeMartini, Ed	L.T.	6'1½"	220	22	1JV	Jr.	San Francisco (Galileo)
Dorsey, Dick	L.E.	6'2½"	199	20	HS	Soph.	Santa Monica
**Enright, Dick	L.T.	6'1½"	225	22	2V	Sr.	Gardena
Fiorentino, Frank	R.G.	5'10"	199	19	1JV	Soph.	Fresno (San Joaquin)
**Fletcher, Ron	R.T.	6'3"	214	21	2V	Sr.	L.A. (LAHS)
Gorrell, Walt	C.	5'11"	195	20	1V	Jr.	Covina
Gurasich, Walt	L.G.	6'1"	230	20	1JV	Soph.	Sherm. Oaks (Notre Dame)
Hagy, Jerry	L.G.	6'2"	216	21	1JV	Jr.	San Bernardino
**Hall, Frank	Q.	6'0"	188	21	2V	Sr.	San Francisco (Poly)
Henry, Mike	L.T.	6'2"	218	20	1JV	Soph.	L.A. (Bell)
*Hickman, Don	R.H.	5'10"	174	23	1V	Jr.	Monterey Park (Keppel)
Hill, Hillard	L.E.	6'1"	179	20	2JC	Jr.	Pasadena
Hubby, Lindsy	R.E.	6'2"	204	22	1V	Jr.	San Bernardino
Humeniuk, Rod	L.T.	6'2"	209	19	1JC	Soph.	L.A. (LAHS)
*Isaacson, Bob	F.	6'1"	201	20	2V	Sr.	Gardena
Isherwood, Ed	F.	5'10½"	186	20	1JV	Soph.	Lynwood
Johnston, Rex	L.H.	6'1"	182	19	Fr.	Soph.	Bellflower (Compton)
Kasten, Don	F.	6'0"	191	20	1JV	Soph.	Torrance
Keehn, Ludwig	L.E.	5'11"	173	24	1V	Sr.	L.A. (Belmont)
**Kissinger, Ells	Q.	5'10"	183	21	2V	Sr.	York, Pa. (Penn)
*Kranz, Doug	L.H.-R.H.	5'11"	177	20	1V	Jr.	Covina
*Kurlak, Wayne	Q.	5'11"	190	21	1V	Jr.	Colton
*Lardizabal, Ben	L.G.	5'11"	216	31	2V	Jr.	L.A. (Manual Arts)
**Leimbach, Chuck	L.E.	6'4½"	193	21	2V	Sr.	Fresno (Roosevelt)
Neal, Dean	L.G.	6'0"	214	20	1JV	Soph.	Venice
Ortega, Tony	R.H.	5'11"	194	19	Fr.	Soph.	L.A. (Cathedral)
Perpich, Chuck	L.E.	6'2"	189	26	1V	Jr.	Oakmont, Pa.
Petrisky, Phil	C.	6'1"	202	20	1JC	Soph.	Allentown, Pa.
Pierce, Fred	L.H.-R.H.	5'11½"	184	22	2V	Sr.	Rosemead
Reagan, Pat	R.G.	5'10½"	202	20	2JC	Jr.	Hawthorne (Serra)
*Roberts, C. R.	F.	6'1"	207	21	1V	Jr.	Oceanside
Rosendahl, Bob	R.E.	6'1"	185	21	1V	Jr.	Lynwood
*Rubke, Karl	C.	6'4"	231	20	1V	Jr.	L.A. (Mt. Carmel)
Shubin, Pete	R.H.	6'4"	210	20	1JV	Soph.	San Pedro
Slade, Hank	R.G.	5'7"	182	21	1V	Jr.	Santa Barbara
Voiles, Bob	R.E.	6'1"	194	21	1V	Jr.	El Monte
Voyne, Don	L.E.	6'1"	182	19	1JC	Soph.	L.A. (No. Hollywood)
**Willott, Laird	R.G.	6'0"	202	21	2V	Sr.	Glendale (Hoover)
*Zampese, Ernie	L.H.	5'9"	160	20	1V	Jr.	Santa Barbara

*Indicates varsity letters won

NOTRE DAME ROSTER — 1956

NO.	NAME	POS.	HT.	WT.	AGE	CLASS	HOME TOWN
53	Burke, Kevin	C.	6'2"	200	19	Soph.	Richland, Wash.
77	Ciesielski, Richard	R.T.	5'11"	210	19	Soph.	South Bend
41	Colosimo, Jim	E.	6'1"	198	19	Soph.	Eveleth, Minn.
6	*Cooke, Larry	Q.	6'0"	190	21	Sr.	Ennis, Texas
45	Cunningham, Tom	C.	6'0"	200	20	Sr.	Pomona, Calif.
46	Dolan, Pat	L.T.	6'3"	210	21	Jr.	Throop, Pa.
1	Dugan, Mike	Q.	6'1	181	19	Soph.	Omaha, Neb.
60	Ecuyer, Al	R.G.	5'10"	195	19	Soph.	New Orleans, La.
68	*Gaydos, Bob	R.G.	6'0"	200	21	Jr.	Donora, Pa.
66	Geremia, Frank	L.T.	6'3"	215	19	Soph.	Sacramento, Cal.
8	Hebert, Carl	Q.	5'11"	170	20	Jr.	Lafayette, La.
65	*Hedrick, Gene	L.G.	6'0"	190	20	Jr.	Canton, Ohio
37	Hickman, William	F.	5'11"	190	19	Soph.	Oak Park, Ill.
5	**Hornung, Paul	Q.-F.	6'2"	205	20	Sr.	Louisville, Ky.
67	Hughes, Tom	G.	6'0"	190	21	Sr.	Portland, Ore.
44	Just, Jim	F.	6'1"	190	19	Soph.	Milwaukee, Wis.
56	King, Joseph	C.	6'2"	190	19	Soph.	Cinn., O.
54	Kuchta, Frank	C.	6'1"	205	20	Jr.	Cleveland, Ohio
72	Lawrence, Don	R.T.	6'1"	215	19	Soph.	Cleveland, Ohio
23	*Lewis, Aubrey	L.H.	6'0"	185	20	Jr.	Montclair, N.J.
48	Lima, Chuck	F.	6'2"				
85	**Loncaric, Lou	C.	6'3"	195	21	Sr.	Battle Creek, Mich.
25	*Lynch, Dick	R.H.	6'0"	185	20	Jr.	Clinton, N.J.
90	Manzo, Lou	E.	6'2"	205	18	Soph.	Old Forge, Pa.
11	McDonnell, John	H.	5'11"	175	21	Sr.	Sterling, Ill.
75	McGinley, John	R.G.	6'2"	195	19	Jr.	Indianapolis
78	Meno, Charles	T.-G.	6'0"	200	18	Soph.	Gillespie, Ill.
19	Milota, James	L.H.	5'10"	170	21	Sr.	Park Ridge, Ill.
17	**Morse, Jim	R.H.	5'11"	175	21	Sr.	Muskegon, Mich.
79	Mosca, Angelo	L.T.	6'4"	230	19	Soph.	Waltham, Mass.
80	Munro, Jim	L.E.	6'0"	195	21	Sr.	Chicago, Ill.
82	Myers, Gary	R.E.	6'1"	195	19	Soph.	Spokane, Wash.
70	Nagurski, Bronko	R.T.	6'1"	215	18	Soph.	International Falls, Minn.
50	Noznesky, Pete	E.	6'0"	180	22	Sr.	Lansdowne, Pa.
71	O'Brien, Tom	T.	6'4"	220	23	Jr.	Danielson, Conn.
18	Odyniec, Norm	F.	5'11"	180	19	Soph.	Greensboro, N.C.
49	Pietrosante, Nick	F.	6'2"	205	19	Soph.	Ansonia, Conn.
87	*Prendergast, Dick	L.E.	6'2"	200	19	Jr.	Homewood, Ill.
27	Reynolds, Frank	L.H.	5'11"	170	19	Soph.	Oak Park, Ill.
84	Royer, Dick	L.E.	6'2"	190	19	Soph.	Cincinnati, Ohio
83	**Scannell, Bob	L.E.	6'0"	190	21	Sr.	South Bend
82	Schaaf, Jim	L.G.	6'0"	195	18	Soph.	Erie, Pa.
88	Seaman, Neil	E.	6'1"	198	19	Soph.	Power Hill, Pa.
10	Selcer, Dick	Q.	5'9"	173	19	Soph.	Cincinnati, Ohio
39	Shulsen, Dick	L.G.	6'0"	190	20	Jr.	Salt Lake City, Utah
12	Sipes, Sherrill	R.H.	6'0"	185	21	Sr.	Louisville, Ky.
22	**Studer, Dean	F.-H.	5'11"	180	20	Sr.	Billings, Mont.
52	*Sullivan, Ed	C.	6'0"	190	21	Jr.	McKeesport, Pa.
35	*Ward, Bob	L.H.	5'8"	160	21	Sr.	Lamberton, Pa.
89	Wetoska, Bob	R.E.	6'3"	215	19	Soph.	Minneapolis, Minn.
9	Williams, Bob	Q.	6'2"	185	19	Soph.	Wilkes Barre, Pa.

*Indicates varsity letters won

1957
CHAPTER 30
"HOPE SPRINGS ETERNAL . . ."
Alexander Pope 1688-1744

In 1957 the Trojan Horse was hollow indeed . . . the evisceration was started by the PCC and finished by the natural evolutionary process of graduation. Of the 71 candidates, only 14 were lettermen. C. R. Roberts and seven other seniors were declared ineligible by the Conference. Arnett, Kissinger, Willot, Isaacson, and Hickman had picked up their diplomas and left to make their mark on the world; Zampese had dropped out*, and Jess Hill had graduated to athletic director.

At the end of the previous season, Los Angeles Times columnist Frank Finch had observed, ". . . nobody in his right mind would want the SC (coaching) job next year, what with nothing but a handful of sophs, frosh, and transfers available for action." Apparently most people agreed with him. Especially the big time coaches to whom the job was offered. Finally, after a year's search, the dubious distinction of becoming head football coach of the Trojans was inherited by 33 year old Don Clark, Hill's line coach since 1951. Clark played guard under Jeff Cravath on the 1945-46-47 team, then played pro ball for the San Francisco '49ers for two years before starting his coaching career under Eddie Erdelatz at Navy.

Coach Clark was given a four year contract at $17,000 a year, but by mid-season must have wondered if it was all worth it . . . he hadn't won a game. He scrapped the single wing and converted to the split-T and straight-T formation and beat Washington 19-12. It turned out to be a winning streak of one. The Trojans lost the next three games and journeyed east to meet a much improved Irish team on the frozen wastes of Notre Dame stadium with a bleak 1-8-0 record.

In 1957 the longest winning streak in College football came to an end. On November 16, Bud Wilkinson's mighty Oklahoma after five years and 47 straight victories was upset 7-0 . . . and by whom? Notre Dame.

Terry Brennan's fourth season as coach of the Irish started the way Notre Dame seasons are supposed to start. Four straight wins over Purdue, Indiana, Army (on the schedule for the first time since 1947), and Pitt did a lot to restore the Notre Dame fans' confidence in their young coach. But then came successive losses to Navy and 3rd ranked Michigan State and the love affair began to cool. The upset win over Oklahoma fanned the embers to life once more however, and the flame of passion nearly obscured the following week's 13-

21 loss to Iowa, and the fact that the Irish were going into the USC game with a mediocre 5-3 record.

Even without the services of leading ground gainer Nick Pietrosante, and leading scorer Dick Lynch, both sidelined by injuries, the Irish trotted onto the field 14 point favorites.

54,793 frozen fans sat in the 20 degree temperature and peered through a swirling blizzard waiting to watch the Irish put a merciful end to the worst USC football season in the school's history.

The scoring began early when Irish quarterback Bob Williams intercepted a Trojan pass and ran it back to the SC 27 yard line. Six plays later, Ron Toth rolled in from seven feet out to score. Big Monty Stickles missed the point after, and the Irish led 6-0.

USC Head Coach, Don Clark

Rex Johnson gets 6 points for Men of Troy

By the middle of the first quarter the blizzard had begun to peter out. So, it seemed, had the Trojans. They fumbled on their own 32, Irish tackle Charles Puntillo recovered and Bob Williams, sensing SC's vulnerability to air attack, pitched first to Frank Reynolds for a first down on the 17, then to Monty Stickles in the end zone for the second tally. This time Monty's conversion was good and the lead lengthened to 13-0.

Halfway through the second quarter, fortune smiled briefly on the frozen Californians when Trojan guard Walt Gurasich recovered a Notre Dame fumble on the Irish 22 after SC had been forced to give up the ball on the 8. This time they knew what to do with it. After an offside penalty moved the ball back to the 27, the Trojans moved the ball to the 10, and Rex Johnston boomed over right tackle for the touchdown. The point after was missed, but at least SC was on the scoreboard.

Notre Dame struck back with serpentine swiftness. USC kicked off and halfback Pat Doyle returned it 92 yards for the third Irish score. So much for the first half . . . it ended 19-6, Notre Dame.

Notre Dame continued the slaughter in the third quarter with a 66-yard march from kickoff. Irish halfback Jim Crotty, playing his first game of the year, carried the ball on five of the 13 plays needed to score. This time Monty Stickles' kick didn't miss and the game was all but iced . . . figuratively and literally . . . 26-6.

The Trojan game plan had been to keep the ball in the air . . . a strategy no doubt born of desperation rather than choice. The previous week they had attempted to run against UCLA and had been squashed 20-9. Official and unofficial advisors counciled, "Keep the ball in the air." Clark tried it; he might as well have . . . nothing else worked that season

anyway . . . and of course it didn't work in the sub-freezing wind of South Bend. The Trojans, fresh from the Mediterranean climate of Southern California, couldn't have held on to the football that day even if it had had handles. The linemen were wearing mittens, but you could have sworn the quarterbacks and pass receivers were too. The stats show seven passes completed out of 29 attempts.*

In the final quarter, the Trojans, outgunned as they were, refused to quit. Tom Maudlin climaxed a 67-yard drive with a quarterback sneak from about six inches out for SC's final score.

In the final quarter Williams lobbed a seven yard pass to Stickles to complete a 70-yard march for six, and George Izo, a sophomore quarterback, directed the Irish offensive 81 yards and capped it with a pass to Dick Prendergast for the final touchdown (it seems that boys from places with names like Manistique, Michigan or International Falls, Minnesota have better luck hanging on to frozen footballs). Both conversions were good . . . the score 40-12. Mercifully the gun sounded. To the Trojans it must have seemed a little like euthanasia. You couldn't accuse the Irish of cruelty. Brennan used 41 players and made no concerted effort to run up the score. It just happened. It was the highest score ever tallied by Notre Dame against USC.

The following week the Irish beat SMU 54-21 to end the season with a respectable 7-3-0 record and were ranked ninth in the nation by UPI and tenth by AP.

The University of Southern California started playing football in 1888. They had winning seasons until 1891 when the Olive Club whipped them 12-16 and Loyola won by the unlikely score of 2-0. The Trojans ended that season 1-2. 1896 was a bummer too. USC played three games and lost all three . . . the last one to Whittier Reform (they got even in 1905 however, 75-0); but the season of 1957 was and is to this day the most disastrous in the 88-year history of Southern California football. One win, nine losses. But the wounded don't cry, at least not when the lights are on and the alumni are watching. Besides there is always next year, and in the breast of every lover, gambler, and football coach . . . hope springs eternal.

The officials and alumni of USC were understandably quiet. They had not expected too much. When Coach Clark was hired, everyone in the Trojan family realized that he had inherited a young inexperienced team, but it's doubtful anyone anticipated only one win in ten games, so perhaps the silence was born of shock. At any rate, Clark had three more years to go on his contract, and it was unlikely that SC would pay him off to the tune of $51.000 and search for another coach. In addition, recruiting was beginning to pay off again and in the words of Braven Dyer, ". . . we can assume that things will be better in 1958. Certainly they can't get any worse."

Monty Stickles, Notre Dame All American End

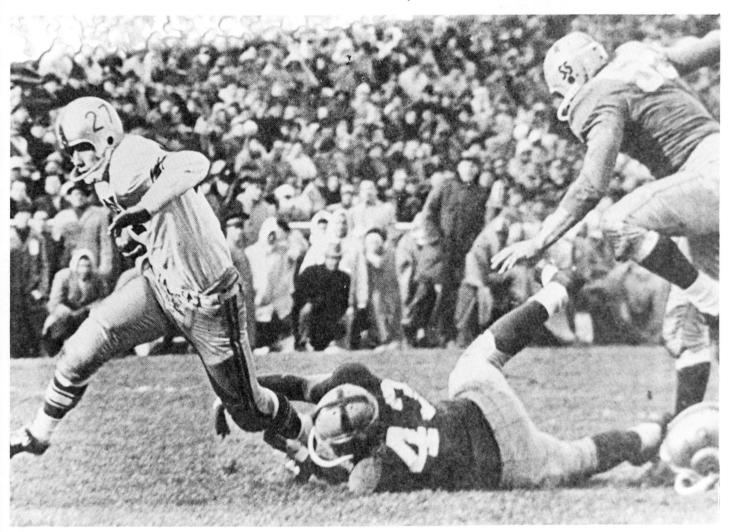

Johnson almost gets away again

UNIVERSITY OF SOUTHERN CALIFORNIA 1957 VARSITY ALPHABETICAL ROSTER

NO.	NAME	POS.	AGE	HT.	WT.
64	Ane, Gil	L.G.	21	5'9"	219
57	*Antle, Ken	C.	20	5'11"	191
89	Boies, Larry	R.E.	20	6'0"	209
60	Botelho, Rod	L.G.	19	5'9"	213
12	Brodie, Bill	Q.B.	19	6'3"	185
67	Bronson, Dick	R.T.	21	6'2"	220
20	Buford, Don	L.H.	20	5'5"	154
72	Byrd, Lou	L.G.	25	5'11"	209
52	Chuha, Joe	C.	20	6'3"	218
71	*Clark, Monte	L.T.	20	6'5"	255
42	Clayton, Hal	R.H.	19	5'10"	185
19	*Conroy, Jim	Q.B.	19	6'0"	197
18	Crockett, Bob	Q.B.	19	6'0"	172
77	Debovsky, Phil	R.G.	20	6'2"	208
81	Douglas, Don	R.E.	21	6'0"	200
76	Finneran, Gary	L.T.	23	5'2"	219
62	*Fiorentino, Frank	R.G.	20	5'10"	203
66	*Gurasich, Walt	L.G.	21	6'1"	230
68	Hagy, Jerry	L.T.	22	6'2"	209
31	Han, Paul	L.H.	20	5'8"	173
21	Harling, Russ	L.H.	21	5'9"	163
78	*Henry, Mike	R.T.	21	6'2"	229
80	*Hill, Hillard	L.E.	21	6'2"	182
43	Holden, Clark	R.H.	18	5'10"	193
40	Howard, Bill	R.H.	20	5'9"	154
84	*Hubby, Lindsy	L.E.	23	6'0"	206
74	*Humenuik, Rod	R.T.	19	6'1"	20
27	*Johnston, Rex	L.H.	20	6'1"	18
45	*Isherwood, Ed	F.B.	21	5'10"	18
44	Kasten, Don	F.B.	20	6'0"	19
82	Kubas, John	R.E.	21	6'1"	18
65	**Lardizabal, Ben	L.G.	32	5'10"	21
75	Mattson, Don	L.T.	19	6'3"	22
15	Maudlin, Tom	Q.B.	21	6'2"	17
63	Mietz, Roger	R.G.	18	5'10"	20
85	Mix, Ron	R.E.	19	6'3"	20
73	Naukana, George	R.T.	19	6'0"	21
37	*Ortega, Tony	R.H.	20	5'10"	19
34	Page, Mike	F.B.	20	5'10"	19
35	Persinger, Jerry	F.B.	19	5'9"	18
53	Plutte, Ed	C.	21	6'1"	20
61	*Reagan, Pat	R.G.	21	5'10"	20
79	Seinturier, John	L.T.	21	6'0"	26
88	Shubin, Pete	R.E.	21	6'4"	21
56	Slade, Hank	C.	22	5'7"	17
41	Steel, Gerry	R.H.	20	6'0"	19
83	*Voiles, Bob	R.E.	22	6'1"	19
86	Voyne, Don	L.E.	20	6'1"	20
87	Wilder, Glenn	L.E.	23	6'0"	18
26	Willis, Jack	L.H.	22	5'9"	16
16	Wood, Willie	Q.B.	20	5'9"	17

NOTRE DAME 1957 VARSITY ALPHABETICAL ROSTER

NO.	NAME	POS.	WT.
67	Adamson, Kenneth	G.	200
51	Beschen, Richard	C.	190
53	Burke, Kevin	C.	200
41	Colosimo, James	E.	198
69	Corson, Robert	C.	205
40	Costa, Donald	G.	195
24	Crotty, James	H.B.	185
2	DeNardo, Ronald	F.B.	195
64	Djubasak, Paul	G.-T.	200
46	Dolan, Patrick	T.	210
32	Doyle, Patrick	H.B.	190
1	Dugan, Michael	Q.B.	180
60	*Ecuyer, Allen	G.	195
83	Flor, Oliver	E.	202
38	Frederick, Charles	E.	187
68	**Gaydos, Robert	G.	200
66	*Geremia, Frank	T.	215
78	Gorham, Michael	T.	215
22	Healy, Patrick	H.B.	212
7	Hebert, Carl	Q.B.	170
37	Hickman, William	H.B.	190
50	Hurd, David	C.	215
3	Izo, George	Q.B.	205
44	*Just, James	H.B.	188
54	*Kuchta, Frank	C.	205
72	*Lawrence, Donald	T.	212
23	**Lewis, Aubrey	H.B.	185
48	*Lima, Charles	F.B.	190
74	Lodish, Michael	E.-T.	210
31	Loop, Paul	G.	208
25	**Lynch, Richard	H.B.	185
90	Manzo, Louis	T.	205
73	McAllister, Donald	T.	225
75	*McGinley, John	G.	195
16	McGinn, Douglas	F.B.	195
82	*Myers, Gary	E.	195
63	Muehlbauer, Michael	G.	200
70	*Nagurski, Bronko	T.	230
86	Nebel, Edward	E.	195
76	Nicolazzi, Robert	T.	215
18	Odyniec, Norman	F.B.	180
81	Owens, William	E.	190
49	Pietrosante, Nick	F.B.	205
61	Pietrzak, Robert	G.	215
87	**Prendergast, Richard	E.	205
33	Pring, Larry	G.	190
57	Puntillo, Charles	T.	205
27	*Reynolds, Frank	H.B.	170
21	Rini, Thomas	H.B.	185
84	*Royer, Richard	E.	190
65	Sabal, Albin	G.	205
29	Salsich, Peter	H.B.	175
62	Schaaf, James	G.	195
55	Scholtz, Robert	C.	225
88	Seaman, Neil	T.	198
10	Selcer, Richard	H.B.	173
39	*Shulsen, Richard	G.	190
26	Steckler, Gary	G.	200
80	Stickles, Monty	E.	215
52	**Sullivan, Edward	C.	195
43	Toth, Ronald	F.B.	205
35	**Ward, Robert	H.B.	156
91	Weber, Paul	E.	196
89	*Wetoska, Robert	E.	215
6	White, Donald	Q.B.	190
4	Wilke, Henry	Q.B.	200
9	*Williams, Robert	Q.B.	190

1958
CHAPTER 31

WAR HAS NO FURY LIKE THAT OF A NON-COMBATANT
. . . Montague

For the first time since 1912 scoring values in collegiate football were changed. The two point conversion rule was introduced and there were mixed reactions even in the same camp. On November 28, the eve of the SC game, Moose Krause, the athletic director of Notre Dame, said, "I like the two point try because it adds excitement to the game." Said Terry Brennan on the same day, "I don't think the two point conversion is a good rule, and I think they should establish what the majority wants which wasn't the case when the rule was put in . . ." Coach Don Clark had no comment that evening . . . he was attending the annual Alumni Men's football dinner at the Town and Gown on the SC Campus where the Trojan varsity of 1933 and the fathers of the current SC squad were guests of honor. Entertainment chairman Pierre Cosette had lined up Buddy Bregman and his orchestra, Treniers, Mamie Van Doren, the Andrew Sisters, Edgar Bergen and Charlie McCarthy, and Doodles Weaver. It's a sure bet the USC athletic staff enjoyed themselves more that evening than they did the following day.

On paper the teams didn't seem unmatched, as a matter of fact the two came to the thirtieth meeting nearly even so far as their season records were concerned. Notre Dame with five wins and four defeats, USC with a four, four and one record. The main difference was in the quality of opponents. The Irish had met four of the nation's top ranking teams and lost, but might have won any of them with a little help from that sometime inconstant patron saint who was supposed to be watching over Terry Brennan. They had lost to tough Army 2 to 14, but then Army ranked number three. Notre Dame was unranked. They lost to Purdue on a rainy October day, but by only 7 points. The Boilermakers were unranked also, but had been the spoilers of the Big Ten. Pittsburgh managed to squeeze out a 29-26 victory in the last 11 seconds, and number two ranked Iowa downed the Irish 31-21.

In the waning days of the Pacific Coast Conference (they disbanded at the end of the year), USC was less than a power. Oregon had blanked them 25-0, California put them away 14-12 . . . Don Clark, in his second year, could take little comfort in the fact that Michigan and North Carolina had defeated the Trojans by only one point. Coaches are not paid to lose, even by one point. The newspapers and the alumni were still charitable of mind and patient of heart. "Don Clark's team,"

wrote Braven Dyer in the Los Angeles Times, "while greatly improved over last year's team, has a nasty habit of committing too many errors."* Dick Hyland wrote, "The Irish are pegged to defeat El Trojan, handily. But will they? Or, even, should they?" It was a case of home team loyalty or simply whistling in the dark. Every football fan in Southern California knew that Notre Dame and SC had met one common foe that season: North Carolina. SC bowed to the Tarheels by a single point, but Notre Dame devoured them 34-24.

The Trojan forward wall was considered capable, even formidable, with the McKeever twins, Marlin and Mike, Ken Antle, Dan Ficca, Frank Fiorentina, Lou Byrd, and Hilliard Hill. They had played well all season but were outweighed by the Irish nearly ten pounds per man. Nor had they encoun-

Notre Dame All American, Nick Pietrosante

tered a quarterback with George Izo's passing skill. Some students of Notre Dame football called him the greatest passer in Irish history. His record that year was 59 completions out of 112 attempts for nine touchdowns. Monty Stickles, a 6-4, 225-pound sophomore end was Izo's favorite target, and he hit him often. Twenty pass receptions for seven touchdowns. And just in case Izo got tired, there was Bob Williams waiting in the wings. Nick Pietrosante, the Irish top ground gainer was back again to plague the Trojans at fullback. The Trojans saw a lot of familiar faces that day. Coach Terry Brennan came to town with a squad of 39 men and 23 of them were seniors, among them All American guard Al Ecuyer.

Coach Clark had only 15 seniors on his roster and had to rely on the experience of quarterback Tom Maudlin and the explosive speed of 5-5, 155-pound halfback Don Buford to mount any kind of offensive action. The bookmakers didn't think they could do it.

So on the 29th of November, 1958, the fighting Irish of Notre Dame trotted on the field in the Coliseum to meet the Trojans of USC for the thirtieth time, solidly installed as 11-point favorites. The series now stood at 18-9-2, and you had to give the Trojans a lot of credit for perseverance . . . and courage. Of course, as Emerson observed, "A great part of courage is having done the thing before." And in this case the thing was losing to Notre Dame.

And they lost again, but they did not go gently into that good night. They fought and struggled every yard, every step, every inch of the way. But the Irish, known for their affection for trench warfare, also struggled every yard, every step, every inch of the way and in the end they prevailed. Since 1926, when little infirm, southpaw Art Parisien confounded the Trojans with a fourth quarter passing attack to win the first game 13-12, fans of the Irish and USC have expected a pier nine brawl when the two met. Rarely have they been disappointed . . . certainly not in this year's battle.

Braven Dyer's lead in the Los Angeles Times the next day went like this, "Sometime, somewhere some football team may have staged a greater goal line stand than the Fighting Irish of Notre Dame did in the fourth quarter of yesterday's heart stopper with the Trojans of Southern California. But I doubt it."

With only inches separating the underdog Trojans from a touchdown that might have sent them into a 20-21 lead with only minutes to play, the Irish dug in like the Spartans at the battle of Thermopylae and refused to surrender.

It was obvious from the opening whistle that this would be another no holds barred, give no quarter, take no quarter, alley fight. Another Gandy Dancer's Ball, where the little guy says to the big guy, "You may whip me, but by God you'll know you've been in a fight."

Notre Dame took the lead in the first six minutes of the game, 6-0, when Pietrosante smashed in from one yard out.

But a scant two minutes later the Trojans were in the lead 7-6 thanks to a 41-yard pass by little Don Buford, who turned out to be a giant that day. The Bantam Buzzsaw they called him. He kicked off, he tackled, he ran interference, he ran for yardage, he intercepted, and he threw that long touchdown pass to Hilliard Hill for the first SC score of the game. Yet, he had occupied a position on the bench for a good portion of the season. SC alumni later asked why.

Early in the second quarter sophomore halfback Jerry Traynham scooted in from one yard out to cap a 34-yard drive. Don Zachik converted. 13-6, and the Trojans looked like anything but 11-point underdogs. They didn't enjoy that seven point lead very long. The Irish answered with a 70 yard drive, Bob Williams took it in to score, but Monty Stickles missed the conversion attempt for the second time and the score at halftime was 13-12 USC.

George Izo just couldn't get started that day. He had only one completion out of six attempts and had gained a measly four yards. Brennan sent in veteran Bob Williams at quarterback. He guided the Irish 69 yards in eight plays, found big Bob Wetoska in the end zone and sent Notre Dame ahead 18-13. The Irish coach hadn't thought too much of the two point conversion rule before the game, but it's reasonable to assume that he changed his mind in the next few minutes. Williams flipped a two pointer to Jim Crotty and made up for one missed conversion attempt. 20-13 Notre Dame.

SC quarterback Tom Maudlin weighed only 175, but it was 175 pounds of tempered steel. For the second successive Saturday he played 58 minutes of the game, and in the final minutes of the third quarter of the Notre Dame game he put on a passing show that brought fans from both sides of the field to their feet a half dozen times. First he hit towering Luther Hayes for a first down on the Irish 24, a gain of 33 yards. Buford got two on the ground then snagged a pass for five more. Clark Holden, the Trojan leading ground gainer that day (he was not thrown for a loss during the entire game) drove through right tackle for a 14 yard gain and a first down. Maudlin then angled to his right and at the last minute flipped a perfect lateral to Buford for another 9 yards. This was the last play of the quarter, but the heroics were just beginning and the crowd sensed it. When at the beginning of the fourth quarter the teams charged to the "home plate" end of the field, the roar was deafening.

From 5 yards out Holden smashed through right tackle and damn near made it to the promised land . . . but not quite. But he did make it to the two foot for a first down. At this point there were few people in the Coliseum who doubted that Jim Maudlin could drive the Trojans into the end zone from twenty-four inches out with four tries. But among those few were eleven Irishmen on the goal line. Doubt is a poor choice of words. They were determined to bar the way, and they did.

USC's Don Buford returns Notre Dame punt

On the next play both teams were offside, then Holden fumbled, but Maudlin recovered on the one yard line. Three downs to make three feet. Tom cut left on the next play and found a hole in the Irish line. He tucked his chin into his chest and charged with the ferocity of a rutting honey badger straight into 6-2, 225 pound center Bob Scholz. Maudlin bounced backward and lost a half a yard, but he bounced Big Bob right out of the game. Tom then tried right tackle, but Bob Reynolds playing a tight secondary read the play and stopped him dead. Maudlin then asked Buford to try over the same spot. Don cut back, and thinking he saw daylight between two Notre Dame defenders and operating on the theory that where the needle goes the thread must follow, ducked his head and hurled himself into the breach. But when he got there there was no breach, the gap had slammed shut like a dungeon door, locking the Trojans outside. When the officials pulled some fifteen men off of little Don's body, they found he was still inches from the goal line. It was kind of like having your bride stolen on your wedding night.

The Bantam Buzzsaw was not finished. Four plays later, after SC held and forced Notre Dame to punt, Buford fielded the kick on the 42 and raced to the Irish 21. There was still enough time for another Trojan assault, but SC was penalized for clipping and the ball was returned to mid-field. That ended Troy's offensive threat for the day. They did make a determined goal line stand of their own, however, when Bob Williams, still playing brilliantly, directed an Irish attack all the way to the 7 yard line of SC where Pietrosante's capable replacement,* Norm Odyniec was hit hard and fumbled. Tro-

jan tackle Dan Ficca recovered on the two and prevented a fourth Notre Dame touchdown. The gun barked and the game was over. Notre Dame 20-13.

"A few more inches and a two point conversion and it would have been SC 21 Notre Dame 20 . . . why did SC charge into the big Notre Dame line instead of trying to run wide?" This seemed to be the question every Trojan fan was asking. It's the prerogative of every football fan to do a little quarterbacking on Monday morning. Even the newspaper got in on the act. "Would anyone, even the most rabid Irish rooter believe that . . . Holden or Buford on DIRECT DRIVE PLAYS behind that big Trojan line could not have gained the distance in three tries after the initial bobble?" ". . . Offensive Trojan thinking was somewhat mysterious in other ways too . . ." ". . . The Trojans chose to fool around and so stop themselves . . ." "Why was not a single pass thrown to Luther Hayes until the third quarter, he hauled that one in for a 33-yard gain." Coach Clark fielded all questions gracefully and graciously, made explanations, complimented his team and the victorious opponent while muttering under his breath the words of the philosopher Montague, "War has no fury like that of a non-combatant."

Bob Williams got the game ball, Terry Brennan got the gate. There were other changes at the end of the season. Red Blaik resigned at Army, Eddie Erdelatz left Navy, and Bump Elliot went to Michigan and the University of Southern California hired a thirty-six-year-old assistant coach from the University of Oregon, named John McKay.

SOUTHERN CALIFORNIA ROSTER — 1958

NO.	NAME	POS.	HT.	WT.
54	Anderson, Chuck	C.	6'1"	196
57	**Antle, Ken	C.	5'11"	185
29	*Arnett, Bob	L.H.	5'11"	185
89	*Boies, Larry	R.E.	6'0"	200
69	Botelho, Rod	R.G.	5'10"	206
32	Bloom, Bill	Q.	6'1"	195
23	Brown, Bill	Q.	5'9"	170
20	*Buford, Don	L.H.	5'5"	154
61	*Byrd, Lou	L.G.	5'11"	209
18	Charles, Ben	Q.	6'0"	195
71	**Clark, Monte	R.T.	6'5"	249
21	Coia, Angie	L.H.	6'2"	195
81	*Douglas, Don	R.E.	6'0"	195
56	Edwards, Bob	C.	6'0"	195
78	Ficca, Dan	L.T.	6'1"	230
76	*Finneran, Gary	L.T.	6'2"	219
62	**Fiorentino, Frank	L.G.	5'10"	203
84	Hayes, Luther	L.E.	6'3"	198
80	*Hill, Hillard	R.H.	6'1"	175
43	*Holden, Clark	F.	5'10"	190

NO.	NAME	POS.	HT.	WT.
31	Hren, Jerry	R.H.	5'10"	165
53	Johnson, Skip	R.G.	6'1"	185
44	Kasten, Don	L.H.	6'0"	195
60	Lewis, Mike	R.G.	5'11"	193
47	Livesay, Mike	F.	5'9"	175
75	*Mattson, Don	L.T.	6'3"	222
15	*Maudlin, Tom	Q.	6'2"	175
85	McKeever, Marlin	R.E.	6'1"	210
64	McKeever, Mike	R.G.	6'1"	210
63	Mietz, Roger	R.G.	5'10"	206
74	*Mix, Ron	R.T.	6'3"	203
35	Persinger, Jerry	F.	5'9"	188
12	Prukop, Al	Q.	6'1"	175
26	Traynham, Jerry	R.H.	5'10"	180
55	Treier, Jack	C.	6'3"	215
70	Tysell, Reuben	R.T.	6'4"	250
82	Van Vliet, George	L.E.	6'2"	193
86	*Voyne, Don	L.E.	6'0"	203
16	*Wood, Willie	Q.	5'9"	173
19	Zachik, Don	P.-K.	5'8"	156

*Indicates varsity letters won

NOTRE DAME ROSTER — 1958

NO.	NAME	POS.	HT.	WT.
67	*Adamson, Ken	R.G.	6'2"	200
85	Baer, Mike	L.E.	6'2"	200
51	Beschen, Dick	C.	6'1"	190
54	Boyle, Richard	C.	6'1"	200
53	Burke, Kevin	C.	6'2"	200
77	*Ciesielski, Dick	L.T.	5'11"	210
25	Clark, Bill	L.H.	5'11"	175
24	*Crotty, Jim	R.H.	5'10"	180
32	*Doyle, Pat	L.H.	6'0"	180
1	Dugan, Mike	Q.	6'1"	180
60	**Ecuyer, Al	R.G.	5'10"	205
83	Flor, Oliver	R.T.	6'2"	200
66	**Geremia, Frank	L.T.	6'3"	225
46	Griffith, Daniel	F.	5'10"	185
7	Henneghan, Bill	Q.	6'2"	190
50	*Hurd, Dave	C.	6'2"	215
3	*Izo, George	Q.	6'2"	205
44	**Just, James	R.H.	6'2"	190
72	**Lawrence, Don	R.T.	6'1"	220
74	Lodish, Mike	R.E.	6'0"	210
31	Loop, Paul	L.T.	6'1"	210
5	Luecke, Dan	Q.	6'0"	175
23	Mack, William	L.H.	6'0"	175
63	Muehlbauer, Mike	R.G.	5'10"	200
82	**Myers, Gary	R.E.	6'1"	195

NO.	NAME	POS.	HT.	WT.
70	**Nagurski, Bronko	R.T.	6'1"	225
86	Nebel, Ed	R.E.	6'3"	195
69	Nissi, Paul	L.G.	6'0"	205
18	Odyniec, Norm	R.H.-F.	5'11"	180
49	*Pietrosante, Nick	F.	6'2"	215
61	Pietrzak, Bob	L.G.	6'3"	215
75	Pottios, Myron	C.	6'2"	215
57	*Puntillo, Chuck	R.T.	6'2"	200
35	Ratkowski, Ray	L.H.	6'1"	185
27	**Reynolds, Frank	L.H.	5'11"	170
21	Rini, Tom	R.H.	5'9"	185
84	**Royer, Dick	L.E.	6'2"	190
65	*Sabal, Al	R.G.	5'11"	210
37	Scarpitto, Bob	R.H.	5'11"	180
62	*Schaaf, Jim	L.G.	6'0"	203
55	*Scholtz, Bob	C.	6'2"	225
79	Scibelli, Joe	L.T.	6'0"	235
10	*Selcer, Dick	R.H.	5'9"	173
39	*Shulsen, Dick	L.G.	6'0"	200
80	*Stickles, Monty	L.E.	6'4"	225
43	*Toth, Ron	F.	6'1"	205
89	**Wetoska, Bob	R.E.	6'3"	225
6	*White, Don	Q.	5'11"	190
4	Wilke, Henry	F.	6'0"	195
9	**Williams, Bob	Q.	6'2"	200

*Indicates varsity letters won

172

1959
CHAPTER 32
I NEVER INTENDED MAKING COACHING MY LIFE WORK
. . . Don Clark, 1959

In 1959 the self-destructive course the Pacific Coast Conference had charted for itself ended where nearly everyone knew it would, and where nearly no one cared . . . on the rocks. As early as 1956 it was apparent that the only thing the conference could agree on was to disagree. Correction . . . they did agree to disband. In 1915 California, Oregon, Oregon State, and Washington banded together to form the PCC. Stanford and Washington State joined a year later. In 1922 USC and Idaho became members, and in 1927 UCLA was admitted. Montana State had joined in 1924, but dropped out in 1950. It was ill-fated from the start. Petty jealousy led to petty arguments. Vendettas and surreptitious sniping turned inward and destroyed the main body like a cancer growing from the inside out. The whole thing was upside down. Football was holding the league together . . . it should have been the other way around. At any rate the disease was terminal and in the spring of 1959 the PCC silently passed on. Before the body was cold there were plans to organize a new conference. USC, California, UCLA, and Washington were enthusiastic. Stanford liked the idea, Washington State decided to give it another try in 1963 . . . Oregon and Oregon State joined in 1968 to make it the Pacific Eight.

But in 1959 the Trojans and the Fighting Irish had other problems. The Irish had a new coach and the Trojans had mischievous Mike McKeever.

Mike and Marlin McKeever were 19 year old identical twins from Los Angeles. Mike was a guard, Marlin was an end. The only way you could tell them apart was by the number on the jersey. When the McKeevers converged on the attack, the opposing quarterback never quite knew whether Coach Clark had opened up the gorilla cages in nearby Griffith Park and suited up a pair of simians or he, the quarterback, was suffering from acute diplopia. Both were 6-1, 218 pounds and playful. In the Trojan 14-7 victory over California, Mike got too playful and hit Cal halfback Steve Bates a little too hard and a little too late. "Dirty football," screamed California coach Pete Elliot.

"Just hard football, that's the way we teach them to play at USC," countered Coach Clark.

"It was deliberate," said Elliot. "McKeever hit Bates out of bounds with an elbow to the face." Mike didn't say anything and Steve couldn't . . . he had a broken nose and cheekbone.

USC president Norm Topping believed both McKeever and Clark and stated, "California has insisted on bringing this into public and when it's over I firmly believe we'll be in a favorable light. These outlandish accusations have been insulting to the university, the football team, and myself."

Topping took the game movies with him to Berkeley where he was met by a group of California officials with a passle of photographs under their arms. Photos, they said, which showed Bates lying on his back on the sideline just before McKeever landed on him, elbow crooked and extended.

"Hmmmm," said Topping, "The University of Southern California is truly sorry for this most regrettable incident." He did not specifically mention McKeever.*

Students at the University of California were so angered that there was talk of taking SC off the schedule, but cooler heads and the comptroller's office prevailed and they still play.

A couple of thousand miles to the east the University of Notre Dame was weathering a storm that had been gathering since 1956 but burst a few days before Christmas of 1958. It had been raging ever since, and now threatened to grow into a full-blown hurricane . . . and in its eye, young Terry Brennan.

The Notre Dame family is a tight family. Naturally, there are sibling rivalries and occasional squabbles, but as in all close families, if outsiders interfere or even pay too much attention, the clan closes ranks. But now for the second time in two years, they had left the curtains to the bedroom open, they had put their business on the street . . . it was almost like leaving the door to the confessional ajar, everyone wanted to listen in and judge.

The faculty board in control of athletics had fired Terence Patrick Brennan. To the pro-Brennan faction the very fact that he had been asked to resign was shocking enough, but the timing made it a tragedy. At a time of year when children gather on street corners to sing Silent Night, when you stumble over skinny Santas guarding every block with bells and kettles, when nearly every young father is staggering home through the snow laden with Christmas gifts or Christmas cheer . . . this young Catholic father of four was out of a job.

Brennan's supporters, among them Father Hesburgh, pointed out that the scholarship quota had been tightened making it difficult to replace the star quality players he had inherited from Frank Leahy. For his first two seasons he was 17-3, and then the well of talent ran dry. In 1956 he was 2-8. The old line alumni who had been horrified when Leahy had been permitted to step down in favor of a 25-year-old youth got busy looking for a replacement. They quieted down in 1957 when Terry posted a 7-3, but 1958's 6-4 made him vulnerable again.

Brennan's firing occupied the sports columns for weeks. Arthur Daley in the New York Times wrote, "Never before has Notre Dame plummeted to such low esteem and it was the timing that made such an outrageous botch of the job. The damage is irreparable."

Syndicated columnist Red Smith: "Again and again the firing of Brennan has been interpreted as an official statement of policy: win or else. . . . Nobody questioned Brennan's fitness as a leader of young men. In short, there seems to have been no conceivable reason for his dismissal except that his team did not win all the time. "This seems to leave the University without a defense for its action."

Perhaps the school had no defense for its action, but the alumni did and they made no bones about it . . . they wanted a winner. They thought they had found one. Before the beginning of the 1957 season a story surfaced that alumni groups had approached Joe Kuharich, a Notre Dame alumnus who had played guard for Elmer Layden in 1935-36-37. In 1957 he was the successful head coach of the Washington Redskins but Our Lady can be a siren . . . Joe Kuharich listened to her song and came home to the Golden Dome with a clear mandate to win.

It wasn't that easy.

Joseph Lawrence Kuharich was a South Bend kid who used to watch the Notre Dame team practice when Rockne was coaching. He played on sandlots and later at Riley High. He was small but tough and determined.

In 1934 he matriculated at Notre Dame and in his sophomore year became a regular guard. He gave the impression that he lived and breathed only football, but he left Notre Dame with a master's degree.

After graduation in 1938, he played guard two years with the Chicago Cardinals, then to the Pittsburgh Steelers as line coach, then to the University of San Francisco for four years where he won 26 and lost 14. His last season he was undefeated, 9-0. He went back to the Cardinals as head coach, then to Washington in '54, was named Pro Coach-of-the-Year, then back to Notre Dame December 22, 1958.

He was forty-one years of age and had twenty years of experience; he brought with him from the pros new ideas and furthered some others brought by Brennan's assistants who had also come from pro ball. He stressed offense and elaborate plays, but they take time to perfect even with experienced players and he had only twelve lettermen who were returning.

George Izo and halfback Red Mack were injured in a pre-season practice session, so he started the season without his passer and best receiver. After the second game, Myron Pottios came up lame and Jim Crotty injured an ankle. By mid-season he had lost three and won two with what one writer called, "A patchwork quilt of a team." A surprise win over tough Navy, then a hard fought loss to Georgia Tech, another to Pittsburgh and a 20-19 upset win over Iowa.

New Coach, Joe Kuharich, as he looked at guard for Irish in 1935, 36, 37

So Joe Kuharich approached the end of his first year as head coach of the Fighting Irish with less than even a mediocre season record. He needed this win to bat .500. Notre Dame and her proud sons are not pleased with coaches who win only 50% of their games. They are not pleased with coaches who win only 75% of their games. When you walk along the paths of Rockne and Leahy and under the watchful eye of their shades, nothing less than 100% is expected. The dismal season certainly wasn't caused by a lack of labor or concentration on the part of Coach Kuharich. The week prior to the USC game he had been scheduled to speak before the annual Chicago banquet for 200 prep coaches. With the Trojan game just around the corner, he felt he couldn't take the time and sent his regrets . . . thus incurring the wrath of Chicago's mayor

Richard Daley. Joe may have lost more than that. When he decided he couldn't make the engagement, he suggested Duffy Daugherty from Michigan State as a replacement. Now, the annual Chicago prep school banquet is a college recruiter's dream, and sending that silver tongued Irishman to speak to a bunch of eager high school prospects who haven't decided on a college is like setting a fox to guard a hen house. You can bet Michigan State won that day.

With an 8-1 record, Don Clark was on his way to the best USC record since Jess Hill's 10-1 record in 1952. Much to everyone's surprise he had been able to pull the team together and go into the UCLA game favored and with 8-0 record. The Bruins upset the Trojans 10-3, but after the last couple of years, eight out of nine looked pretty good to the Southern California rooters.

The Trojans and the Irish had collided with two mutual foes, California and Pitt. USC crushed Pitt 23-0, while the best the Irish could do was 13 points against Pitt's 28. USC beat California 14-7, the Irish rolled over Cal 28-6 . . . but it was the consensus that the disparity in score was due to the Bears' five fumbles at crucial points during the game. At any rate, the bookmakers were sufficiently impressed to install the Trojans as two-point favorites.

Even two points looked good to the frozen Trojan team and their fans as they trotted on the field that November 29. Over 48,000 frost-bitten football maniacs huddled in the bleachers to see if the University of Southern California could whip Notre Dame on her own ground for the first time in twenty years.

It had been so cold that once more both teams were forced

The All American McKeever twins—Marlin (86) and Mike (68)

to practice indoors. The weather was cold, but the Trojans were colder. The Irish scored in the first four minutes of the game and were never in danger after that. On the fourth play of the game the Trojans forced the Irish to kick, and from the Notre Dame 40 George Sefcik got off a beauty that rolled dead on the SC 8 and the Trojans could never seem to get out of the hole. Notre Dame's massive line choked off every offensive move then rushed Clark Holden's punt and the ball rolled out of bounds on the Trojan 38. Gerry Gray, 195-pound sophomore fullback, broke through left tackle, picked up some blockers and galloped all the way to the 13 before he was caught by Jerry Traynham. It didn't work out the way it should have for SC. Jerry hit Gerry so hard that the ball squirted out of his arms and the forward momentum carried it crazily to the three yard where Nick Buoniconti, a sophomore Irish guard, fell on it. Gray repeated the same play and bulled his way over for the first touchdown. Monty Stickles connected with this 15th conversion of the season and the score was 7-0, Notre Dame.

If it hadn't been for *bad* luck, the Trojans wouldn't have had any at all. Bob Levingston, SC sophomore halfback, intercepted one of George Izo's long passes and ran it back 32 yards to the Irish 38 . . . Wilie Wood flipped a little screen pass to Traynham. Jerry got all the way to the 5-yard line behind some beautiful blocking, but a penalty for clipping brought the ball back to the 29 and seemed to take the heart out of the Trojan offensive. Traynham got to the 26 for a first down finally, but apparently the retreat had unnerved SC quarterback Willie Wood. He threw three wild passes and it was late in the second quarter before the Trojans could put anything together again. The threat, such as it was, was set up on the next to last play of the first quarter, when Levingston again intercepted George Izo on the 13. Wood managed to marshall his forces and direct a drive from the Trojan 38 to the Irish 23, but on fourth and two, Luther Hayes couldn't handle Wood's pass, so the Irish took over on their own 13 with just enough time to run one play before the half ended.

Halfway through the third quarter the sun came out but instead of thawing out the beach boys of California, it awakened a hibernating bear. 6-2, 210 Irish quarterback, Izo, was aching to get even for the humiliation suffered at the hands of the Trojans the previous year. And even he got. He drove the Irish 49 yards for their second and deciding touchdown in less time than it would take to find an Irish name on the Irish roster. He found Stickles first, then Jim Crotty, then Pat Heenan

and two plays later, Gray crashed in again over left tackle. Stickles converted and it was 14-0, with five minutes to play in the third quarter, plenty of time for the Trojans to formulate some kind of attack, but they seemed numb . . . from the weather or shock. It didn't really matter, nothing was going according to plan anyhow. Angelo Coia, Traynham's replacement at halfback for SC found himself trapped on the next kickoff and in a futile effort to escape eleven bloodthirsty Irishmen, retreated back into the end zone. He should have kept going right to the airport. He was attacked and captured and the safety boosted the score to 16-0.

At this juncture the two-point spread suggested by the bookies didn't look too good. It never got to look much better. Ben Charles came in at quarterback for SC and did a smooth job of commanding an 84-yard assault on the Irish stronghold. He hit Luther Hayes on the 28, then found Coia on the 13 and on the next play he faded right and flipped a little screen pass to Coia in the end zone for SC's first and only score. Charles figured that perhaps with a two point conversion the Trojans could get back in the game. We'll never know . . . he rolled out looking for a receiver but dropped the ball.

The Trojans tried an onside kick, but that didn't work any better than any other strategy that day. The final score, 16-6, Notre Dame.

Don Clark resigned. There were those who said he was annoyed at the fact that President Topping had not supported him as strongly in the McKeever incident as he had expected. But after all, with a record of 1-9 the first year, 4-5-1 the second, and then in the third year 8-2 . . . why not quit on top? Besides, "I never intended to make coaching my life's work," he said.

The score might have been a little different had the mischievous McKeever twins been able to play. Marlin had a broken hand and had to play with a cast. Mike played only five minutes of the game . . . the injury is not known. Perhaps a sore elbow. Don Clark took a job as executive vice president of a southern California corporation. President Topping accepted his resignation with the statement ". . . Clark has done an outstanding job . . ." and hired an assistant coach to take his place and had enough confidence in the 36 year old coach to give him a one-year contract. His name was John McKay.

---

*Not everybody was upset with Mike. The Newspapers Enterprises Association named him All American guard, and named Marlin on the third team. The New York Times named Marlin an All American end, but didn't mention Mike. Maybe they didn't like the way he bent his elbow.

SOUTHERN CALIFORNIA ALPHABETICAL ROSTER — 1959

NO.	NAME	POS.	HEIGHT	WEIGHT	HOMETOWN
61	Anderson, Chuck	G.	6'2"	203	Whittier, Cal.
62	Bansavage, Al	G.	6'2"	205	Union City, N.J.
79	Bundra, Mike	T.	6'2"	235	Catasaugua, Pa.
88	Carleton, Will	E.	6'5"	201	Oakland, Cal. (Castlemont)
18	Charles, Ben	Q.B.	6'2"	190	Lancaster, Pa. (Catholic)
71	Clark, Roger	T.	6'2"	232	Inglewood, Cal. (Lennox)
21	*Coia, Angelo	H.B.	6'2"	182	Philadelphia, Pa. (Northeast)
40	**Conroy, Jim	F.B.	6'0"	185	Baldwin Park, Cal.
66	Coones, Ken	G.	5'10"	214	Wilmington, Cal. (Banning)
67	Delaney, Gary	G.	6'0"	205	Whittier, Cal.
56	*Edwards, Bob	C.	6'0"	205	Montebello, Cal.
80	Edwards, Mel	E.	6'1"	191	Houston, Tex. (Wheatley)
78	*Ficca, Dan	T.	6'1"	230	Atlas, Pa. (Mt. Carmel)
76	**Finneran, Garry	T.	6'3"	222	Los Angeles, Cal. (Cathedral)
31	Gaskill, Lynn	H.B.	6'0"	175	Wilmington, Cal. (Banning)
84	Hayes, Luther	E.	6'3"	195	San Diego, Cal. (Lincoln)
43	**Holden, Clark	F.B.	5'10"	200	Los Angeles, Cal. (Marshall)
32	Levingston, Bob	H.B.	6'0"	185	Los Angeles, Cal. (L.A.)
33	Maples, Jim	H.B.	5'11"	181	Bakersfield, Cal. (E. B'field)
70	Marinovich, Marv	T.	6'3"	220	Watsonville, Cal.
83	Matern, Dick	E.	6'3"	220	Oakland, Cal. (Castlemont)
75	*Mattson, Don	T.	6'4"	210	Port Chicago, Cal. (Mt. Diablo)
86	McKeever, Marlin	E.	6'1"	218	Los Angeles, Cal. (Mt. Carmel)
68	*McKeever, Mike	G.	6'1"	218	Los Angeles, Cal. (Mt. Carmel)
15	Merrill, Ron	Q.B.	6'0"	184	Maywood, Cal. (Bell)
63	*Mietz, Roger	G.	5'11"	211	San Leandro, Cal.
74	**Mix, Ron	T.	6'4"	224	Inglewood, Cal. (Hawthorne)
42	Mollett, Jerry	F.B.	6'1"	202	Van Nuys, Cal.
57	Morgan, Dave	C.	6'3"	197	Natick, Mass.
53	Petrisky, Phil	C.	6'1"	206	Allentown, Pa.
12	*Prukop, Al	Q.B.	6'1"	183	Los Angeles, Cal. (Mt. Carmel)
81	Rosin, Ben	E.	6'2"	193	Los Angeles, Cal. (Garfield)
19	Schmidt, Bob	Q.B.	6'4"	196	Bakersfield, Cal.
52	Schmidt, Denny	C.	6'1"	204	Bakersfield, Cal.
27	Shields, Alan	H.B.	6'0"	183	Eagle Rock, Cal.
29	Skvarna, Carl	H.B.	5'9"	160	Upland, Cal. (Chaffey)
34	Stephenson, Warren	H.B.	6'0"	170	Los Angeles, Cal. (Dorsey)
26	*Traynham, Jerry	H.B.	5'10"	185	Woodland, Cal.
55	*Treier, Jack	C.	6'3"	202	Lancaster, Pa. (Catholic)
82	*Van Vliet, George	E.	6'3"	208	Whittier, Cal.
85	Washington, Dave	E.	6'3"	198	Oroville, Cal.
87	Wilder, Glenn	E.	6'0"	175	Van Nuys, Cal.
72	Wilkins, John	T.	6'4"	225	Newport News, Va.
64	Williams, Britt	G.	6'1"	205	Walnut Creek (Las Lomas)
44	Winston, Lloyd	F.B.	6'2"	201	Merced, Cal.
16	**Wood, Willie	Q.B.	5'9"	177	Washington, D.C. (Armstrong)
20	Zachik, Don	H.B.	5'8"	155	Linden, N.J.

*Number of varsity letters won

NOTRE DAME ALPHABETICAL ROSTER — 1959

NO.	NAME	POS.	AGE	HT.	WT.	HOMETOWN
67	**Adamson, Ken (Capt.)	G.	21	6'2"	205	Colo. Springs, Colo.
87	Augustine, Charles	E.	19	6'3"	205	San Rafael, Calif.
71	Bill, Robert	T.	18	6'2"	220	Garden City, N.Y.
54	Boyle, Richard	C.	20	6'1"	200	Chicago, Ill.
79	Brown, Tom	T.	19	6'4"	235	Norwalk, Ohio
64	Buoniconti, Nicholas	G.	19	5'11"	210	Springfield, Mass.
85	Burnell, Max	E.	20	6'3"	195	Evanston, Ill.
90	Candido, Don	E.	18	5'11"	195	St. Louis, Mo.
73	Carollo, Joseph	T.	19	6'2"	230	Wyandotte, Mich.
2	Castin, John	Q.B.	20	6'0"	175	Okmulgee, Okla.
77	*Ciesielski, Richard	T.	22	5'11"	210	South Bend, Ind.
25	Clark, William	H.B.	20	5'11"	180	Youngstown, Ohio
57	Clements, William	C.	18	6'4"	220	Philadelphia, Pa.
41	*Colosimo, James	E.	22	6'1"	195	Eveleth, Minn.
24	**Crotty, James	H.B.-F.B.	21	5'10"	185	Seattle, Wash.
44	Dabiero, Angelo	H.B.	19	5'8"	165	Donora, Pa.
20	De Luca, Raymond	H.B.	20	6'0"	180	Pueblo, Colo.
32	**Doyle, Patrick	H.B.	21	6'0"	180	Sioux, City, Iowa
72	Flor, Oliver	T.	21	6'2"	200	Seattle, Wash.
88	Ford, William	E.	19	6'2"	200	Benton H'bor, Mich.
39	Gargiulo, Frank	F.B.	20	6'0"	190	North Bergen, N.J.
66	Giacinto, Michael	G.	19	6'1"	215	Bayside, N.Y.
33	Gray, Gerry	F.B.	18	6'2"	195	Baltimore, Md.
11	Haffner, George	Q.B.	18	6'0"	180	Chicago, Ill.
30	Healy, Patrick	H.B.	23	6'1"	210	Baltimore, Md.
53	Hecomovich, Thomas	C.	19	6'3"	205	Bovey, Minn.
83	Heenan, Patrick	E.	21	6'2"	190	Detroit, Mich.
7	Henneghan, William	Q.B.	20	6'2"	190	Detroit, Mich.
69	Hinds, Robert	G.	19	6'0"	215	Cincinnati, Ohio
3	**Izo, George	Q.B.	21	6'2"	210	Barberton, Ohio
1	Jorling, Thomas	Q.B.	19	6'1"	200	Cincinnati, Ohio
28	Kane, James	G.	20	5'6"	175	Bloomington, Ill.
68	Koreck, Robert	T.	20	6'2"	210	Philadelphia, Pa.
48	Liggio, Thomas	H.B.	19	5'11"	195	W. New York, N.J.
51	Linehan, John	T.-C.	20	6'0"	205	Tulsa, Okla.
74	Lodish, Michael	E.	21	6'0"	210	Detroit, Mich.
62	Loula, James	G.	19	6'0"	195	Rock Island, Ill.
5	Luecke, Daniel	Q.B.	20	6'0"	175	Los Angeles, Calif.
23	*Mack, William	H.B.	22	6'0"	175	Allison Pk., Pa.
70	Magnotta, Mike	G.	19	5'10"	210	Albion, Mich.
84	Mikacich, James	E.	18	6'2"	205	Sacramento, Calif.
89	Monahan, Tom	E.	21	6'2"	185	Arcola, Ill.
63	Muehlbauer, Michael	G.	21	5'10"	200	Buffalo, N.Y.
36	Naab, Richard	F.B.	18	6'0"	190	Rock Island, Ill.
86	Nebel, Edward	E.	21	6'3"	195	Mt. Clemens, Mich.
26	O'Leary, Richard	H.B.	20	6'0"	180	Terre Haute, Ind.
38	Perkowski, Joseph	F.B.	19	6'0"	200	Wilkes Barre, Pa.
61	Pietrzak, Robert	G.	20	6'3"	215	Hamtramck, Mich.
75	*Pottios, Myron	C.	20	6'2"	215	Van Voorhis, Pa.
56	Powers, John	C.	19	6'2"	215	Harvard, Ill.
35	Ratkowski, Ray	H.B.	20	6'1"	185	Ridgewood, N.Y.
21	Rini, Thomas	H.B.	21	5'9"	185	Cleveland, Ohio
59	Roth, Richard	T.	21	6'5"	225	Toledo, Ohio
60	Roy, Norbert	G.	19	5'10"	195	Baton Rouge, La.
65	**Sabal, Albin	G.-T.	21	5'11"	210	Chicago, Ill.
37	*Scarpitto, Bob	H.B.	20	5'11"	180	Rahway, N.J.
55	**Scholtz, Bob	C.	21	6'2"	235	Tulsa, Okla.
9	Schulz, Clay	Q.B.	19	6'1"	190	Schofield, Wis.
22	Sefcik, George	H.B.	19	5'8"	170	Cleveland, Ohio
80	**Stickles, Monty	E.	21	6'4"	225	Poughkeepsie, N.Y.
81	Traver, Leslie	E.	19	6'2"	190	Toledo, Ohio
52	Viola, Gene	C.	19	6'1"	215	Scranton, Pa.
6	**White, Don	Q.B.-F.B.	21	5'11"	190	Haverhill, Mass.
82	Wilke, Henry	E.	21	6'0"	195	Hamilton, Ohio
78	Wilke, Roger	T.	19	6'1"	230	Hamilton, Ohio
76	Williams, George	T.	19	6'2"	220	Marshfield, Mass.
58	Zmarzly, Ted	G.	19	5'10"	215	Cleveland, Ohio

1960
CHAPTER 33

"I DON'T HAVE ANY ASSURANCE THAT HE'LL (JOE KUHARICH) BE BACK, BUT THEN I HAVE NO ASSURANCE HE WON'T BE." . . .Father Edmund Joyce, 1960

John McKay inherited a somewhat lame Trojan horse in 1960. True, it was not as hollow as the 1957 model (1-9), but nevertheless the condition was critical. To McKay's credit, he not only refused to blame Don Clark for the lack of team talent, he defended Clark and his record . . . and he was probably right. After all, Clark had also inherited a crippled team, thanks to the PCC. Yet in three years he had brought USC from 1-9 to an 8-2 season record. In 1959 he had lost only to Notre Dame and UCLA. Yet the attack of the alumni was relentless and merciless. Don Clark is a proud man and had at that time seven children to feed. The $17,000 a year salary of head coach was hardly enough compensation to bear both pressures. In addition, he had a good job waiting. His brother John wanted him to take over a successful business he had started, but was no longer in physical shape to run. Don did, and is a successful businessman today.

John McKay was quite another breed of cat. It's quite possible that he was also sensitive to criticism; most coaches are . . . but if he was, not many people knew. He may also have been a little apprehensive over the one-year contract at SC. He had four children to support and was 36 years old, the same age Don Clark was when he became head coach. And if McKay failed, he had no lucrative job waiting. But then, as now, showing fear or indecision is not a McKay characteristic. He once said, "There's not a man that takes his first head coaching job, that's not scared." But he also said, ". . . no decision scares me . . . I'll make all the big ones on and off the field."

Making decisions came naturally to John H. McKay, a result of early maturation. His father was a supervisor in the coal mines of West Virginia, and although not well-to-do by most standards, the McKays, all seven of them, were comfortable. But in 1936, John senior died at the age of 45. Young John was 12, and the second eldest son. He went to work early but still found time for football and basketball at Shinnston High and was named All State running back in 1939.

After graduation he went into the mines for a year, and then joined the Army Air Corps. In 1946 he was a freshman defensive back at Purdue. In 1943 he transferred to Oregon and was a two way starter in '48 and '49. McKay and quarterback Norm Van Brocklin led the 1948 Ducks to a 9-1 season and

into the Cotton Bowl where they lost to SMU. He scored eight touchdowns that season, a team high . . . he still holds two Oregon records, most rushing touchdowns in one game (three) and his average of 6.4 yards per carry has not been bettered.

He could have gone to the New York Yankees of the All American Conference, but decided to coach instead. After nine years as assistant at Oregon, he came to USC as Don Clark's backfield coach.

New Head Coach John McKay with Bill Nelson and Ben Wilson

Darle Lamonica hands off to Angelo Dabiero

When President Topping named McKay as Clark's successor, the alumni were not pleased. They were weary of the "promoting from within" theory and wanted a name coach. So, when Coach McKay came to the Coliseum to meet Notre Dame for the thirty-second conflict, with a 4 and 5 record, the alumni felt vindicated. But their feelings were ambivalent, because the week before, the Trojans had upset UCLA 17-6. Now if SC could slip by Notre Dame . . . and they were slim favorites . . . the season would be a success. Johnny McKay* seemed unflappable. He is a tough and highly intelligent man. He also has an intuitive sense that told him that if SC can beat Cal, UCLA and Notre Dame in the same season, you can lose the rest and still have a certain amount of job security. Cal and UCLA had been taken care of with Stanford thrown in for good measure, and the bookmakers were confident enough to make the Trojans 6-point favorites over the Irish.

And no wonder. The Trojans had won four of their last six games and the Irish were wallowing in the trough of an eight-game losing streak. A loss to USC would bring them in at 1 and 9 . . . the worst season since 1887. Joe Kuharich would have the dubious distinction of breaking Terry Brennan's 1956 record, and becoming the "losingest" coach in Notre Dame's modern football history.

So, on the 26th of November at two o'clock, the Trojans of SC and the Fighting Irish of Notre Dame lined up in the Coliseum and faced each in a drizzling rain to see which team would have the least disastrous season. The fans were underwhelmed. Sixty thousand were expected, 45,000 tickets were sold, and 28,297 showed up.

Some of the sportswriters had predicted a wide open rolling contest, probably because of the giveaway game both teams had played all season. SC had fumbled the ball 23 times thus far and had given it away by interception another eight times. Notre Dame, not to be outdone, had fumbled 16 times and presented the ball to their opponents 21 times by way of interception. Both teams, however, had been able to engineer spectacular scoring drives with thrilling runs and heart stopping long passes. But not on this day . . . as one Los Angeles sportswriter put it, "The weather was sloppy, but the Trojans were sloppier." Al Wolf in the Times: "It was a dreary day — and for the Trojans an equally dreary performance." They were right. Neither team did the expected. "Shoddy, sloppy tackling . . . non-existent defense" was said of USC, the favorite. "Feather-footed, sticky fingered Notre Damers," was the description of the underdog Irish who had lost eight in a row.

The outcome was never in doubt. The Irish assumed total command from the opening kickoff and never relinquished it. Angelo Dabiero saw to that. In the first play of the game, he ran the kickoff to the 29, then, guided by the steady leadership of Daryle Lamonica, the invaders from South Bend pressed on 57 yards to the Trojan 14 . . . all on the ground . . . they

*It was Johnny McKay until he started having winning seasons. Then it became John McKay.

180

Bill Nelson on a keeper around left end

didn't have to take to the air. The Trojan defense jelled long enough to slow the attack, but they couldn't stop it. Joe Perkowski came on to boot a field goal from the 21 yard line and the score was 3-0 with little more than five minutes of the game played. For the Trojans it never got any better. SC kicked off and on the second play quarterback Bill Nelson lofted a long pass intended for Jim Bates. Irish fullback Bill Ahern tipped it, Lamonica grabbed it, and brought it back 18 yards to the 45-yard line of Southern California. The Irish threw only two passes that day and completed just one, but it was enough. The one completion was on the next play. Lamonica threw an eighteen yard pass, then capped the drive with a quarterback sneak from the one; Perkowski converted, and the score was 10-0. The game was not 11 minutes old.

Notre Dame looked like anything but 6 point underdogs who had lost eight games in a row. Halfway through the second period they drove 80 yards to the Trojan nine. Irish halfback Bob Scarpitto sidestepped Al Prukop, outran Dave Washington, and plunged over. Perkowski did it again to make it 17-0.

Up until this time the Trojan rooters had little to root about. But there was still a minute left in the half and time for one more thrill. Trojan quarterback Bill Nelsen swept out for thirteen yards to give the men of Troy their first first down of the game. Ben Wilson bulled his way to midfield . . . Nelsen then completed his first pass, a sixteen yarder to Wilson. Another to Marlin McKeever was good for 20 more. Time was running

out but momentum and luck seemed to have turned in favor of USC. The Irish were guilty of holding, and the Trojans had time for one more play. But with the ball on the 19 yard of Notre Dame and a chance to hit the locker room at halftime with at least some kind of talley on the scoreboard, Nelsen was rushed. He fumbled and the half was over . . . so was the game, so far as the University of Southern California was concerned. The game ended that way 17-0. There was no score in the second half and very little action. Jim Bates, USC's speediest halfback nearly broke loose with the opening kickoff of the half, but after a thirty-yard gallop up the middle he collided with the ubiquitous Mr. Lamonica on the 45-yard line of USC and that ended that. SC managed to work from its own 37 to Notre Dame's 19 late in the game, but Jim Maples dropped the touchdown pass on a third down play and the game was over.

The most thrilling action in the last half of the game was when Nelsen and Dabiero agreed to disagree and squared off. Nelsen at 6-0 and 190, Dabiero at 5-8 and 165 . . . the referee declared it a mismatch and stopped the bout. On the next play Bob Floro at 6-2 and 223 decided to renew hostilities with Dabiero. The officials, recognizing the difference between a mismatch and mayhem, penalized the Trojans fifteen yards for their tackle's warlike zeal and the game just sort of faded away. At the end, combatants on both sides were too wet, cold and tired to consider any exacerbation.

So John McKay, in his first season as head coach of the Trojans of USC, failed to bat .500. He ended the season with four wins and six losses. For Joe Kuharich it was a sort of reprieve. At least with the 17-0 upset of Southern Cal he finished the season 2-8-0, and was saved from infamous immortality. He would not go into the record books alone as Notre Dame's most unsuccessful coach. He tied Terry Brennan. There was little joy in Notre Dame, Indiana, in the autumn of 1960. But Joe Kuharich refused to leave the light of hope behind and bravely stated, "I've got two years to go on my contract, and I always live up to my contracts."

Said the Reverend Edmund P. Joyce, executive vice president of Notre Dame and chairman of the faculty board in control of athletics, "I have no doubt Joe will be back." And then elaborated with a statement that would have made any corporate choreographer in the advertising business flush with pride.

"I don't have any assurance that he will be back," Joyce said, "But then I have no assurance that he won't be . . ."

A few days before the game, Notre Dame president Father *Theodore Hesburgh announced that henceforth the University of Our Lady would concentrate on "academic excellence." Most students interpreted that statement as a precursory move toward the de-emphasis of football at Notre Dame, and they weren't buying it. On the twenty-third of November the students demonstrated carrying placards which boldly proclaimed, "Down with excellence, we want football players."*

In Los Angeles John McKay smiled. You had to give him credit for guts. He had finished his first season losing six and winning only four, he was facing next season bereft of twelve seniors, including Mike and Marlin McKeever, and no one had mentioned anything about renewing his one-year contract. But he had an undefeated freshman team, patience, and a hell of a lot of confidence.

And he could sell. USC bought and signed him for another year. He was witty, bright, sometimes caustic, but always good copy . . . something USC had never had. Even the somewhat jaded Los Angeles sportswriters went along with it. "Watch Troy travel in 1961," warned the Times.

Bob Scarpitto starts on 9 yard scoring jaunt

SOUTHERN CALIFORNIA ROSTER — 1960

NO.	NAME	POS.	HT.	WT.	AGE	EXP.	CLASS
61	Anderson, Chuck	R.G.	6'2"	220	21	1V	Jr.
25	Aubrey, Truman	L.H.-R.H.	6'0"	176	21	1JV	Soph.
37	Bates, Jim	L.H.	6'2"	199	19	1JV	Soph.
74	Bishop, John	R.T.	6'4"	240	20	2JC	Jr.
89	Buncom, Frank	L.E.	6'1"	218	20	2JC	Jr.
79	*Bundra, Mike	R.T.	6'4"	235	21	1V	Jr.
87	Butcher, Ron	R.E.	6'2"	211	19	Fr.	Soph.
83	Carleton, Will	L.E.	6'5"	208	20	2JV	Jr.
18	*Charles, Ben	Q.	6'2"	200	22	1V	Jr.
56	Cox, Chuck	C.	5'11"	205	19	Fr.	Soph.
65	Clark, Roger	R.T.	6'2"	242	19	1JV	Soph.
67	Delaney, Gary	R.G.	6'1"	220	19	1V	Jr.
20	Del Conte, Ken	R.H.	5'11"	184	18	Fr.	Soph.
78	**Ficca, Dan	L.T.	6'1"	243	21	2V	Sr.
80	Fisk, Bob	R.E.	6'3"	205	19	1JV	Soph.
70	Floro, Bob	R.T.	6'2"	223	21	1JV	Jr.
31	*Gaskill, Lynn	R.H.	6'0"	178	20	1V	Jr.
84	**Hayes, Luther	L.E.	6'3"	203	21	2V	Sr.
54	Johnson, Skip	C.	6'0"	190	21	2JV	Jr.
40	Jones, Ernie	F.	6'0"	198	20	Fr.	Soph.
32	*Levingston, Bob	R.H.	6'0"	187	20	1V	Jr.
35	Livesay, Mike	F.	5'9"	186	21	2JV	Jr.
69	Mabry, Ed	R.G.	6'1"	200	21	1JV	Soph.
33	*Maples, Jim	R.H.	5'11"	185	20	1V	Jr.
86	**McKeever, Marlin	R.E.	6'1"	230	20	2V	Sr.
68	**McKeever, Mike	L.G.	6'1"	230	20	2V	Sr.
36	McLean, Nick	R.H.	6'0"	190	19	Fr.	Soph.
63	**Mietz, Roger	L.G.	6'0"	225	21	2V	Sr.
42	*Mollett, Jerry	F.	6'1"	210	21	1V	Jr.
57	*Morgan, Dave	C.	6'3"	222	20	1V	Jr.
66	Neidhardt, Dave	L.G.	6'1"	212	19	Fr.	Soph.
16	Nelsen, Bill	Q.	6'0"	190	19	1JV	Soph.
53	O'Brien, Bill	L.G.	6'0"	220	21	1JV	Jr.
88	Potter, Gary	L.E.	6'2"	195	19	Fr.	Soph.
12	**Prukop, Al	Q.	6'1"	185	20	2V	Sr.
81	*Rosin, Ben	L.E.-R.E.	6'3"	205	19	1V	Jr.
60	Samuel, Jim	L.G.	6'2"	220	20	1JV	Soph.
77	Sanzo, Tony	L.T.	6'2"	205	20	1JV	Jr.
19	Schmidt, Bob	Q.	6'4"	210	21	1V	Sr.
52	Schmidt, Denny	L.T.	6'2"	218	20	1JV	Soph.
76	Shea, Pat	R.T.	6'1"	227	21	1JV	Soph.
27	*Shields, Alan	L.H.	6'0"	185	20	1V	Jr.
29	Skvarna, Carl	L.H.	5'9"	158	21	1V	Jr.
34	Stephenson, Warren	F.	5'11"	177	20	1V	Jr.
45	Tobin, Hal	F.	5'11"	201	20	1JV	Soph.
26	**Traynham, Jerry	L.H.	5'10"	185	21	2V	Sr.
55	**Treier, Jack	C.	6'3"	215	23	2V	Sr.
82	**Van Vliet, George	L.E.	6'3"	216	21	2V	Sr.
85	Washington, Dave	R.E.	6'3"	207	20	1V	Jr.
72	*Wilkins, John	L.T.	6'4"	230	23	1V	Sr.
64	*Williams, Britt	R.G.	6'1"	220	20	1V	Jr.
49	Wilson, Ben	F.	5'11"	223	21	Fr.	Soph.
21	*Zachik, Don	P.-K.	5'8"	155	25	2V	Sr.

*Indicates number of varsity letters won

NOTRE DAME ROSTER — 1960

NO.	NAME	POS.	HT.	WT.	AGE	CLASS
40	Ahern, Bill	F.	6'0"	200	19	Soph.
63	Augustine, Charlie	R.G.	6'3"	205	20	Jr.
71	*Bill, Bob	R.T.-L.T.	6'2"	220	20	Jr.
86	Boulac, Brian	L.E.	6'4"	195	19	Soph.
64	*Buoniconti, Nick	L.G.	5'11"	210	20	Jr.
72	Burke, Ed	L.T.	6'1"	225	18	Soph.
85	*Burnell, Max	R.E.	6'3"	195	20	Jr.
73	*Carollo, Joe	R.T.	6'2"	230	20	Jr.
2	Castin, Jack	Q.	6'0"	175	21	Sr.
57	Clements, Bill	C.	6'4"	215	19	Jr.
44	*Dabiero, Angelo	R.H.	5'8"	165	20	Jr.
67	DePola, Nick	R.G.	6'2"	210	19	Soph.
88	Ford, Bill	L.E.	6'2"	200	20	Jr.
58	Grau, Francis	R.G.	6'2"	210	20	Jr.
11	*Haffner, George	Q.	6'0"	180	19	Jr.
30	Henneghan, Bill	F.	6'2"	190	21	Sr.
54	Hoerster, Ed	C.	6'1"	210	18	Soph.
91	Kolski, Steve	R.E.	6'3"	200	19	Soph.
68	Koreck, Bob	L.T.	6'2"	210	21	Sr.
55	Kutzavitch, Bill	C.	6'2"	205	18	Soph.
3	Lamonica, Daryle	Q.	6'2"	205	19	Soph.
48	Liggio, Tom	R.H.	5'11"	195	20	Jr.
32	Lind, Mike	F.	6'1"	195	20	Soph.
51	Linehan, John	C.	6'0"	205	21	Sr.
62	Loula, James	L.G.	6'0"	195	20	Jr.
5	Luecke, Dan	Q.	6'0"	175	21	Sr.
70	Magnotta, Mike	L.G.	5'10"	205	20	Jr.
41	Maxwell, Joe	F.	5'11"	188	19	Soph.
84	Mikacich, Jim	L.E.	6'2"	205	19	Jr.
28	Minik, Frank	L.H.	5'7"	165	19	Soph.
92	Monahan, Tom	E.	6'2"	185	22	Sr.
83	Murphy, Dennis	R.E.	6'2"	200	19	Soph.
36	Naab, Richard	F.	6'0"	190	19	Jr.
69	Nissi, Paul	R.G.	6'0"	205	21	Sr.
21	O'Hara, Chuck	L.H.	6'0"	190	19	Soph.
38	*Perkowski, Joe	F.	6'0"	200	20	Jr.
61	*Pietrzak, Bob	R.T.	6'3"	215	21	Sr.
75	**Pottios, Myron	L.G.	6'2"	215	21	Sr.
6	Rascher, Norb	Q.	6'1"	180	18	Soph.
35	*Ratkowski, Ray	L.H.	6'1"	185	21	Sr.
60	*Roy, Norb	R.G.	5'10"	195	20	Jr.
1	Rutkowski, Ed	L.H.	6'1"	195	19	Soph.
37	**Scarpitto, Bob	R.H.	5'11"	180	21	Sr.
9	*Schulz, Clay	Q.	6'1"	190	20	Jr.
22	*Sefcik, George	L.H.	5'8"	170	20	Jr.
87	Sherlock, Jim	R.E.	6'0"	200	19	Soph.
81	*Traver, Les	L.E.	6'2"	190	20	Jr.
52	Viola, Gene	C.	6'1"	210	20	Jr.
78	Wilke, Roger	L.T.	6'1"	225	20	Jr.
76	*Williams, George	R.T.	6'2"	215	20	Jr.

*Indicates number of varsity letters won

1961
CHAPTER 34

"WE WANT A COACH, NOT A COMEDIAN"
. . . Alum 1961

Well, Troy traveled in 1961, but not far. By the time they met Notre Dame in mid season* they had lost to Georgia Tech and Iowa, and had narrowly squeaked by SMU 21-16. They had about as much chance to upset Notre Dame as they would have had to beat the Green Bay Packers. It's tough enough to go against a big fast Notre Dame team with a healthy squad, but the team that Coach McKay brought to Notre Dame that year looked like the survivors of the Bataan death march. Half-back Willie Brown made the trip east, but wasn't expected to start. Tackle Mike Eaton and fullback Rich McMahon, end Phil Hoover and halfback Alan Shields were left in Los Angeles because of injuries. Fullbacks Hal Tobin and Ernie Jones, halfback Lynn Gaskill and guards Chuck Anderson and Harold Beach were below par physically, but traveled with the squad to Notre Dame. After all, you have to put somebody on the field. The only positions not threatened by injuries were center and quarterback, and a few days before the game, center Skip Johnson developed a bad knee and was listed as a doubtful starter . . . quarterback Bill Nelsen managed to stay healthy, as did 6-5 end Hal Bedsole. Fortunately for the Trojans so did tackle Mike Bundra at 6-3 and 230 pounds. They needed all the size they could get on the line. At tackle the Irish had Bob Bill at 6-2 and 228 and Joe Carollo, 6-2 and 235 and still growing. In case of any unexpected fragility, they were backed up by 6-3, 240-pound sophomore George Bednar and a couple of 230-pound seniors, Roger Wilke and George Williams. All American guard Nick Buoniconti, the Irish co-captain, had 6-1, 240-pound Ed Burke waiting in the wings. Spindly little fullback Joe Perkowski at 6-0 and 200 pounds had Jim Snowden to help out. Big Jim was 6-4 and 235. Even their quarterback Daryle Lamonica at 6-2 and 200 pounds could hardly be called small. The Irish had won the first two games of the season against Oklahoma and Purdue, but still there was trouble in Paradise. Notre Dame had given Joe Kuharich the same vote of confidence it had given Brennan after his first bad year and even extended his contract two extra years, but the optimism of Father Hesburgh and the Holy Cross fathers was not matched by the Notre Dame alumni. Not all Irish eyes were smiling. New York columnist Jimmy Powers, whose brother had attended Notre Dame, fired this broadside. ". . . Little wonder the subway alumni are bewildered

. . . Taken by any measure — personality, charm, attendance, or won-lost records — Kuharich comes out on the bottom." Then this zinger: "I'm aware that it rained the final game of (last) season in California, but in the past, rain and sub-zero temperatures failed to dampen the ardor of Notre Dame rooters. For the record, Notre Dame completed this past season in a contest with a major opponent and played to 20,000 empty seats." That's hitting where it hurts . . . in the box office.

Joe Kuharich may have been even a little less lucky than SC's Jeff Cravath during his coaching tenure. According to Francis Wallace, the playing field in Notre Dame stadium had been reseeded with an "improved grass' that was good for golf courses, but couldn't hold up under the stress and strain of a football contest. The result was knee injuries . . . to George Izo, Red Mack, and Gerry Gray. They were lost to Kuharich for most of his first two seasons. The field was reseeded after the 1960 season, but it was too late to help old Joe . . . he was 7-13-0 and trying to play catch-up.

At the start of the 1961 season it looked as though he might pull it off. He beat Oklahoma and Purdue and by the time the Irish met the Trojans for their third game of the season on the 16th of October, the Notre Dame alumni, real and subway, had begun to have visions of a return to the Rockne-Leahy seasons of unbeaten teams and greater gridiron glory.

Nor were they disappointed in the Irish performance that afternoon. They roared onto the field at Notre Dame stadium like winners. Those who were there said there could be no doubt of the outcome from the first play. Notre Dame all the way. Al Wolf, covering the game for the L.A. Times, put it this way in his lead the following day: "You could sense the impending slaughter when the Irish of Notre Dame trotted out on the field here Saturday."

And that's what it was . . . slaughter.

USC was completely outclassed. The huge powerful linemen ripped through the Trojan line to dump Bill Nelsen before he could even cock his arm to pass. It was clearly a case of cruel and unusual punishment for the Trojan quarterback. He had made the trip to South Bend to play football, not to be maimed. Al Wolf again: "The punching bag at the old Main Street Gym never got hit more than Troy's quarterback did

Saturday." He was there and he saw it. And yet, he reported that at the end of the game Nelsen was still ". . . full of fight at the final gun. And so were his battered and bruised teammates."

Even under such brutal attack, Nelsen and his sub Pete Beathard managed to complete 14 of 28 passes for 199 yards. Notre Dame connected only twice in eleven attempts for eighteen . . . but their ground game was rolling, 322 yards. The Trojan ground game? More of that later.

The weather forecast of a sunny and warm afternoon brought out 50,427 fans to watch the debacle. The Southern Californians should have suspected the gods were against them that day when Indiana's unpredictable weather turned sour and it began to rain. Kickoff time was 10:30 A.M. By 10:47 it was 14-0 Notre Dame.

By 11 o'clock it was 20-0 Notre Dame.

Before the end of the first half, the Irish had managed to mount drives of 55, 74, and 84 yards for their three touchdowns.

With Willie Brown out of the lineup, Uncle Joe knew Coach McKay would be forced to take to the air and employed an umbrella defense four deep and it worked. Three times the Irish defenders knocked down long passes which would have resulted in Trojan touchdowns. McKay tried everything, but nothing worked. He switched Hal Bedsole from end to halfback, and Pete Beathard from quarterback to flanker, but it was like hunting elephants with buckshot.

Lamonica scored first on a 12-yard run, Perkowski converted . . . Lamonica threw a 19-yard pass to Jim Kelly, who scored. Perkowski did it again. A few minutes later Rutowski topped off an 84-yard drive with a six-yard push, but Perkowski missed, one of the few times he did that year.

In the third quarter Lamonica again guided the Irish to the USC one-yard line and finished it off himself with a one-yard smash into the end zone. Perkowski added the extra point. 27-0. Five minutes and fifty seconds into the final quarter the Irish once bulled their way to the Trojan 49 and on fourth down Joe Pernowski kicked a 49-yard field goal to complete the scoring of the day.* A 30-0 rout.

"We really missed Willie Brown," said Coach McKay. "He's far and away our best player. With him hurt and Hal Bedsole hurt, our receiving really suffered. Ben Wilson did a good running job though." Probably true on all counts. Willie Brown, later an assistant coach at USC and now McKay's assistant at Tampa, was the Big Five's leading rusher with 282 yards and an average of 8.1 yards per carry. Hal Bedsole carried only once for 12 yards, and received twice for 59 before he was sidelined with a chest injury. And Ben Wilson did do a good running job when the Irish allowed it. But they were stingy. They let Ben make 11 yards in six carries and receive five passes for 58 yards.

By now those SC fans who remembered Braven Dyer's gloomy prediction in 1953 that ". . . it is doubtful that anyone who sat in on yesterday's track meet will live long enough to see it (the series) evened up," were becoming believers. The 30-0 victory gave Notre Dame its third straight victory of the season, its eighth straight over SC at Notre Dame Stadium, and the fifth straight win in the intersectional rivalry which was not becoming a classic. The record now stood at 22-9-2.

The stats, as usual, told the story. First downs were nearly even. Sixteen for Notre Dame, 13 for SC. Notre Dame gained only 18 yards passing, but they didn't even need that . . . they gained 322 yards on the ground. USC's net yardage was minus 4.

"I never had a team with that much minus yardage," lamented McKay.

The Trojans ended the season with 4 wins, 5 losses, and one tie. At the end of McKay's second year as head coach his record stood at 8-11-1. Not very impressive. But he was recruiting, and still perfecting his I formation offense. Despite the fact that some critics said the I stood for *ineffective, incompetent, or intolerable.* Coach McKay had faith . . . and a sense of humor.

"We have become," he said, "specialists in the incomplete pass."

"We want," growled the alumni, "a coach, not a comedian."

One sportswriter who covered the game wrote, "But nothing was going to stop Joe Kuharich's great club Saturday, in fact nothing may top it all season." That seemed to be the consensus in October. But by December they had skidded right back to where they had begun, all even. Joe Doyle, writing for the South Bend Tribune wrote, "It's hard to believe the same football team played the various parts of the schedule. One moment the Notre Dame team of 1961 seemed to be an eager, husting squad that believed it could lick any opponent. At other times it was lethargic . . . indifferent . . . and unable to cope . . ." The Irish finished 5-5-0. Nick Buoniconti, who played a brilliant defensive game against USC, was named All American . . . Daryle Lamonica who went on to a long and successful career in the pros was not even mentioned.

Nor was anyone on the Southern Cal roster. Of course, that's not unusual when you end a season winning 4, losing 5 and tying 1. "We're a better team than we look," said Coach McKay. "I'm proud of our boys, they didn't give up."

Neither did John McKay, he was already looking forward to 1962.

*When Jess Hill became athletic director he decided to propose a schedule change. When the game was played at Notre Dame, it should be in October, when played in Los Angeles, late autumn, to take advantage of the good weather . . . Notre Dame agreed.

Notre Dame Captain Nick Buoniconti was only All American for either team

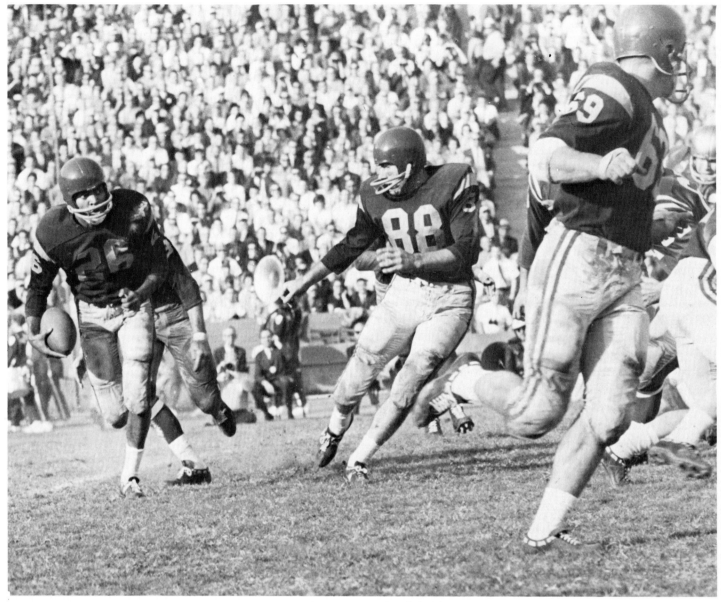

The great Willie Brown sweeps right end behind the blocking of John Brownwood and Pete Lubisich

guard Jim Carroll slowed him but couldn't stop him. Gerry Gray did that on the 18. It was a beautiful 34 yard run . . . the longest of the afternoon. Enter Big Ben Wilson, SC's 225-pound 6-0 fullback, called by Daryle Lamonica, "the best fullback we've faced so far." Ben drove over right tackle to the ten, then got three more to move the Trojans to the ten. The Irish were penalized half the distance to the goal line for being offside and Beathard bulled his way to the one. On the next play Wilson dove over. Tom Lupo converted, and the score was 7-0, five minutes into the first quarter.

The Irish tried to strike back in the last part of the period and the first few minutes of the second, but the entire team was a little off that day and Lamonica, a strong leader, was not having his sharpest afternoon. Nevertheless, two short runs by Don Hogan and two short passes by Lamonica to his favorite receiver, All American end Jim Kelly, brought the Irish to the SC 28 for a first down, but on the next play Joe Farrell bob-

bled the ball and Trojan end Hal Bedsole, all 6-5 and 213 pounds, pounced on the ball like a hungry cat on a field mouse. As if to teach the invaders a lesson, the Trojans took the ball from the 22 all the way home on the ground. Seventy-eight yards in nine plays. Beathard rolled out for 28 yards, Brown on a pitchout picked up another 21 that moved to the Notre Dame 14, then Wilson punched and punched his way into the end zone. The two-point conversion attempt failed, so the score at half time was 13-0, USC.

Notre Dame managed to chalk up six first downs in the third quarter, but was never able to get past the Trojan 45. Penalties hurt. The Irish did get to the SC 35 which would have been a first down, but the play was called back because they had an ineligible receiver downfield . . . they had to punt from their 40. Frank Budka made the mistake of trying to stop bull moose Ben from the wrong angle and was carried from the field with a fractured leg. Irish halfback Denny Phil-

Third string quarterback, Craig Fertig scores last touchdown to make it 25-0

lip injured an arm and these casualties forced Coach Kuharich to bring in 5-7 Frank Minik to cover All American Hal Bedsole (6-5, remember?). Oddly enough, little Frank was quite effective. Hal drew a blank.

In the fourth period Pete Lubisich, considered the best lineman on the field that day, threw Lamonica for a 16-yard loss back to the Irish 11. Notre Dame was forced to punt, and Ken Del Conte ran it back to the Irish 40. Rich McMahon, Jay Clark, Bill Nelsen and of course, Ben Wilson, hammered their way to the Notre Dame 14. Nelsen rifled a flat pass over the middle to Fred Hill, who took it off his shoe tops and scored from the one.

It was a long afternoon for Daryle Lamonica. He completed only seven of twenty-four passes . . . had one intercepted and ended up with a minus ten yards in the rushing department. The interception came in the last quarter when SC center Armando Sanchez snagged one on the Trojan twenty. Craig

Fertig, Troy's third string quarterback found Gary Hill on the seven, Ernie Jones crashed for a yard, and Fertig, a sophomore, made the final six yards over right tackle and scored. There were 55 seconds of the game remaining and SC was using the last eleven of the 41 players they had used that day. Once again the two-point conversion attempt failed and the score was 25-0, USC. But that was enough. In the thirty-four year history of the Notre Dame-USC rivalry it was the greatest point spread for the University of Southern California. It was only their ninth win, nevertheless the Californians were ecstatic. ". . . USC's defense was phenomenal. Lubisich, Marinovich, Pye, Sanchez, and Fisk, Svihus, All American guard Damon Bame, Beathard and Brown," wrote Sid Ziff in the Times, ". . . it was a roll call of heroes."

"A new Southern California Thundering Herd stampeded on the turf of Memorial Coliseum Saturday afternoon . . . It trampled Notre Dame, 25-0."

A pall descended over the Notre Dame campus. Another 5-5-0 year. Joe Kuharich's four-year record of 17 wins and 23 losses was hardly in the Rockne tradition. Joe's contract had three years to run, but it was rumored that certain alumni groups were attempting to buy up the contract. It has been said that "Notre Dame doesn't expect to win them all, but it always tries. It has never told its coaches win-or-else." Maybe Notre Dame doesn't tell its coaches that, but the alumni, who pay a good portion of the bills, do.* At any rate, the move to purchase the contract was supposedly blocked by the University administration, which wanted to avoid any more publicity. It didn't really matter Joe quit anyway. On March 13, just before the spring practice sessions started, Joe said, "This insatiable appetite to win has become so strong it is ludicrous." And he packed it in.

So "Uncle Joe" went back to the pros and became head coach and later general manager of the Philadelphia Eagles, and John McKay went to the Rose Bowl. There the new Thundering Herd defeated favored Wisconsin 42-37. The University of Southern California had an undefeated season and a national championship for the first time in 30 years. The coach got a thousand dollar raise, and the McKay family got a new swimming pool.

After the Iowa game when SC was 2-0 for the season, the coach, bowing to some family pressure, had blithely promised to put in a swimming pool if he had a perfect season. After he beat Stanford 39-14 the seventh game and with only three more to go, he was once more reminded not just by eight-year-old Terri, who had instigated the action, but by Johnny, Michele and Richie as well. After the Notre Dame game he began to hedge a little. After all, his salary as head coach of one of the major universities was only $16,500. "Root us in once more against Wisconsin in the Rose Bowl," he told the kids, "and we'll see about the pool."

A grateful alumni put in the pool.

**McKay's method turned out in the long run to be better than Dr. Topping's. In the twelve years that followed the two first disastrous seasons, McKay's teams won three national championships, had three undefeated seasons, made seven Rose Bowl appearances, and won eight Pac Eight championships . . . and during those winning years private sources donated more than $200 million to USC.

*Re-gilded that year for the eighth time in eighty years. The 1/1000 inch thick 24 karat gold leaf cost $50,000.

*They may have been wondering why a team with both Lamonica and John Huarte in the lineup could score only 159 points and lose half of the games scheduled. They probably still do.

Fred Hill scores on Nelson pass to make it 19-0 USC

Ben Wilson gets first TD of day on 1 yard plunge

SOUTHERN CALIFORNIA ROSTER — 1962

NO.	NAME	POS.	HGT.	WGT.	AGE	EXP.	CLASS
80	Austin, Joe	L.E.	6'2"	200	19	Fr.	So.
64	Bame, Damon	L.G.	5'11"	187	19	2JC	Jr.
12	*Beathard, Pete	Q.B.	6'1"	191	20	1V	Jr.
19	*Bedsole, Hal	L.E.	6'5"	213	20	1V	Jr.
26	*Brown, Willie	L.H.	5'11"	170	20	1V	Jr.
88	Brownwood, John	R.E.	6'2"	205	19	Fr.	So.
87	*Butcher, Ron	L.T.	6'3"	205	21	2V	Sr.
68	Byrd, Mac	L.G.	6'1"	184	20	Fr.	So.
23	Clark, Jay	L.H.	6'0"	175	21	2JC	Jr.
34	Crow, Harvey	R.H.	5'10"	175	19	Fr.	So.
20	**Del Conte, Ken	R.H.	5'11"	185	20	2V	Sr.
75	Eaton, Mike	R.T.	6'2"	205	19	1JV	So.
15	Fertig, Craig	Q.B.	6'1"	174	20	1JV	So.
61	Fisk, Bill	R.G.	6'0"	203	18	Fr.	So.
82	*Gale, Mike	L.T.	6'2"	205	21	1V	Jr.
63	Gonta, Stan	R.G.	6'0"	200	20	1V	Jr.
33	Heller, Ron	R.H.	6'2"	190	22	1JC	So.
81	Hill, Fred	R.E.	6'2"	197	18	Fr.	So.
31	Hill, Gary	L.H.	6'0"	185	19	Fr.	So.
85	*Hoover, Phil	L.E.	6'2"	183	23	1V	Sr.
57	Houck, Hudson	C.	6'0"	200	19	1JC	So.
35	*Hunt, Loran	R.H.	6'0"	187	20	1V	Jr.
79	Johnson, Tom	L.G.	6'0"	185	20	2JC	Jr.
40	*Jones, Ernie	F.B.	6'0"	200	21	1V	Jr.
74	Jones, Randy	R.T.	6'4"	222	19	Fr.	So.
72	Kirner, Gary	L.T.	6'3"	200	20	2JC	Jr.
69	*Lubisich, Pete	R.G.	6'1"	205	20	1V	Jr.
18	Lupo, Tom	Q.B.	6'1"	190	18	Fr.	So.
70	**Marinovich, Marv	R.T.	6'3"	217	22	2V	Sr.
36	McLean, Nick	R.H.	6'0"	185	21	1V	Jr.
43	*McMahon, Rich	F.B.	6'1"	195	20	1V	Jr.
16	**Nelsen, Bill	Q.B.	6'0"	192	21	2V	Sr.
84	Potter, Gary	R.E.	6'1"	195	21	1V	Sr.
47	Pye, Ernie	F.B.	5'11"	200	19	1JC	So.
66	*Ratliff, John	L.G.	6'0"	206	23	1V	Jr.
71	Reade, Lynn	R.T.	6'2"	255	21	1V	Jr.
55	Sagouspe, Larry	C.	6'0"	212	20	2JC	Jr.
54	Sanchez, Armando	C.	5'11"	195	20	2JC	Jr.
52	Schmidt, Denny	C.	6'2"	200	22	2V	Sr.
65	*Smedley, Ron	R.G.	5'10"	200	22	1V	Sr.
67	Svihus, Bob	L.G.	6'4"	215	19	Fr.	So.
89	Thurlow, Toby	L.E.	6'1"	195	21	1V	Jr.
77	Vihlene, Vern	L.T.	6'0"	205	19	1JV	So.
83	Viltz, Theo	R.H.	6'2"	190	19	1JC	So.
49	*Wilson, Ben	F.B.	6'0"	225	22	2V	Sr.
32	Winslow, Gary	L.H.	5'11"	180	19	1JV	So.
21	Yamamoto, Teruo	R.H.	5'10"	175	20	1JV	So.

*Indicates number of varsity letters won

NOTRE DAME ROSTER — 1962

NO.	NAME	POS.	AGE	HT.	WT.	CLASS
40	*Ahern, William	F.B.	21	6'0"	195	Sr.
59	Allen, Wayne	G.	20	6'1"	205	Jr.
79	Anton, John	T.	20	6'1"	220	Jr.
25	Antongiovanni, John	H.B.	19	6'0"	175	So.
48	Barnard, John	H.B.	20	5'10"	185	Jr.
76	Bednar, George	T.	20	6'3"	234	Jr.
22	Bliey, Ronald	H.B.	20	6'1"	190	So.
8	Bonvechio, Alex	Q.B.	19	5'10"	185	So.
86	*Boulac, Brian	E.	21	6'4"	205	Sr.
71	Brocke, James	T.	18	6'2"	220	So.
2	*Budka, Frank	Q.B.	20	6'0"	190	Jr.
51	**Burke, Edward	T.	20	6'1"	240	Sr.
57	Burns, William	C.	19	6'1"	204	Jr.
60	Carroll, James	G.	19	6'1"	202	So.
68	Dennery, Vincent	G.	18	6'2"	205	So.
69	DiCarlo, Michael	G.	20	5'10"	200	Jr.
20	Dupuis, Richard	H.B.	20	5'10"	180	So.
78	Etten, Nicholas	T.	20	6'0"	220	Jr.
42	Farrell, Joseph	F.B.	20	6'0"	201	So.
93	*Goberville, Tom	E.	18	6'3"	197	Jr.
33	**Gray, Gerard	F.B.	22	6'2"	198	Sr.
61	Harnisch, James	G.	19	5'11"	215	So.
54	**Hoerster, Ed	C.	20	6'1"	216	Sr.
44	Hogan, Donald	H.B.	19	5'11"	182	So.
7	Huarte, John	Q.B.	18	6'0"	180	So.
75	Humenik, David	T.	20	6'3"	233	Jr.
89	*Kelly, James	E.	20	6'2"	204	Jr.
52	Kostelnik, Thomas	C.	19	6'2"	200	So.
3	**Lamonica, Daryle	Q.B.	21	6'2"	202	Sr.
65	*Lehmann, Robert	G.	21	6'0"	212	Jr.
32	**Lind, Mike	F.B.	21	6'1"	203	Sr.
23	*MacDonald, Thomas	H.B.	19	5'11"	172	Jr.
62	Maglicic, Kenneth	G.	19	5'10"	211	So.
72	Mattera, Vincent	T.	19	6'3"	220	So.
41	Maxwell, Joseph	F.B.	21	5'11"	182	Sr.
63	Meyer, John	G.	19	6'2"	210	So.
28	**Minik, Frank	H.B.	21	5'7"	161	
83	**Murphy, Dennis	E.	21	6'2"	203	Sr.
92	Murray, John	E.	21	6'1"	205	Jr.
50	Nicola, Norman	C.	19	6'0"	235	So.
74	Olosky, Martin	T.	20	6'1"	228	Jr.
34	O'Rourke, James	F.B.	20	5'11"	185	Jr.
12	O'Shaughnessy, Pat	Q.B.	19	6'2"	190	So.
38	Paolillo, Leonard	F.B.	19	5'10"	195	So.
73	Penman, Eugene	T.	19	6'2"	223	So.
11	Pfeiffer, William	Q.B.-H.B.	20	6'0"	196	Jr.
43	Phillips, Dennis	H.B.	21	6'0"	186	Jr.
80	Pivec, David	E.	19	6'3"	215	So.
47	Rakers, James	H.B.	19	6'4"	196	So.
64	Ruel, John	G.	18	6'1"	210	So.
1	*Rutkowski, Edward	H.B.	21	6'1"	202	Sr.
95	Schrader, Joseph	E.	19	6'3"	190	So.
31	Selzer, Jack	H.B.	19	6'0"	189	So.
87	*Sherlock, James	E.	21	6'0"	201	Sr.
94	*Simon, John	E.	19	6'3"	210	Jr.
56	Slafkosky, John	T.	21	6'4"	234	Sr.
85	Snow, Jack	E.	19	6'2"	210	So.
84	Stephens, Clay	E.	19	6'3"	205	Jr.
5	Szot, Denis	Q.B.	20	6'0"	185	Jr.
79	Telfer, Robert	T.	19	6'2"	230	So.
68	Wood, Gregory	G.	19	6'0"	192	Sr.

*Indicates varsity letter won

1963
CHAPTER 36

" SHOULD BE WITH US A LONG TIME, AFTER ALL HE SIGNED TWICE."
. . . Moose Krause, 1963

And so in 1963 Joe Kuharich slipped suddenly and silently into the past tense at the University of Notre Dame. His replacement was an old war horse by the name of Hugh Devore. Coach Devore was no stranger to Notre Dame. In 1933, his senior year, he had co-captained the Irish for "Hunk" Anderson. He had played right end on the same line with Moose Krause. In the 1933 Notre Dame-USC program the mini-bio under his picture reads, "Hugh J. (Hughey) Devore. His County Donegal-County Limerick background may explain why he is the most fearless man on the squad. Expert swimmer. Strong and silent." That was to his advantage over his many years of coaching, especially in 1963.

Coach Devore had served a long apprenticeship . . . he was one of the vagabond assistants during the Thirties, Forties, and Fifties. After his graduation in '34, he served one year under Elmer Layden as assistant line coach, then went to Fordham as one of Sleepy Jim Crowley's assistants where he helped Frank Leahy carve the Seven Blocks of Granite. He went to Providence in 1938 as head coach. Then to Holy Cross in 1942 and back to Notre Dame in 1943 to assist Frank Leahy once more. When Leahy went into the Navy in 1944, Devore was one of the two interim coaches. In 1945 he led the Irish to a 7-2-1 season. When Leahy came marching home, Devore moved on to St. Bonaventure as head coach. He stayed there three years, then journeyed on to NYU where he headed the coaching staff until football fell from grace to New York University three years later. He then decided to try the professional ranks for one season with the Green Bay Packers, but returned to college football at Dayton University and stayed there for three years. In 1956, back to the pros to coach the Philadelphia Eagles. But in 1958 he came home again . . . to Notre Dame. Four years later he was head coach. "I don't know why they picked me," Hugh said, "but I'm going to make it the best football season I've ever had."

By the time the USC game rolled around on October 12 that year, Coach Devore was trying to figure out how to make that promise come true. In the season opener he was only minutes away from victory over Wisconsin, but the Badgers pulled it out with a last minute desperation drive and won 14-9. Against Purdue the Irish carried a 6-0 lead into the final period, but lost 7-6.

The Trojans were coming to Notre Dame with 26 lettermen left over from the 1962 national championship team that defeated the Irish 25-0, and beat powerful Wisconsin 42-37 in the Rose Bowl.

By this time Coach John McKay was a genius. He was now called witty instead of comic. "Vigorous, bright, colorful . . . innovative," they said. And he was. He took the old I-formation, or shifting T, and installed 32 variations. He called it his

Hugh Devore, Notre Dame head coach for 1963 only

"I-bone." He divided his squad into three platoons, the Red Team, which played both offense and defense, the Green Team, which played only offense . . . and the Gold Team, which played defense only. The innovation seemed to be working. After last season's perfect record, the Trojans took the opener against Colorado 14-0, and managed to hold number one ranked Oklahoma to a five point victory. The Sooners won 17-12.

Despite the fact that the Trojans won only three times out of fifteen played at Notre Dame in the 37-year history of the contest (the last in 1939), they were the bookmakers' choice by six points.

But Coach Devore had a few surprises. Frank Budka, who had been carried from the field in last year's SC game had had recurring leg problems and had played a total of only three minutes in the first two games. Today however, he was starting as offensive quarterback. Jim Kelly, two time All American, was suited up. It was reported the day before that he was hospitalized with the flu. Coach Devore also chose this game to take the wraps off of a 195-pound third string sophomore halfback, Bill Wolski. The last of Devore's little surprises was a left end named Ken Ivan. He had a hell of a toe. After the game the Trojans referred to him as Ivan the Terrible.

The 59,135 shirtsleeved fans who crowded into Notre Dame Stadium on Saturday afternoon on October 12 knew they were in for an afternoon of hard football from the opening play. Early in the first period SC's Damon Bame tackled Ron Biley with a head-on charge that jarred the ball out of the Irish halfback's hands. Mike Garrett recovered on the Notre Dame 45. Beathard passed to Bedsole . . . complete, but out of bounds. They tried again on the next play, but the pass was too high and bounced off Bedsole's fingers into Tom MacDonald's. The fleet-footed Irish halfback took off and with some good blocking by Norm Nicola, went all the way. Ivan converted. Score 7-0, 9:46 in the first quarter.

Ernie Jones's 57-yard punt kept Notre Dame deep in its own territory, and when the Trojans took over, Beathard, Pye, Brown and Garrett marched 74 yards in nine plays . . . Dick Brownell made the point after, and the Trojans pulled to a 7-7 tie.

There were still over ten minutes to play in the second period, but the Irish didn't need that much time to regain the lead. Wolski returned the kickoff 30 yards and three plays later shot over the middle for another 36 yards to the Trojan eight where Loran Hunt and Tom Lupo brought him down. Budka got two more and Wolski rammed over the left side for the final six yards and again Ivan scored the extra point. The whole series took a little over a minute.

Willie Brown fumbled on the first play after the kickoff and Irish end Tom Goberville recovered on the USC 47. Notre Dame powered its way to the Trojan 7, but then Brown got

even and creamed Wolski on the screen pass attempt. Ivan tried a field goal from the 27, but it was blocked. Trojan fullback Ed King grabbed it in the air and brought it out to the 15. A penalty brought the ball back to the 7, and they started all over from there. Then they began to look like champions again. They drove the 93 yards in nine plays, Brownelli converted again before the halftime gun, and both teams went into the locker room locked in a 14-14 tie.

In the third quarter the Trojans couldn't get anything started, the Irish defense saw to that. They had one chance, but couldn't make it pay. Right end John Thomas put a savage rush on Budka, causing him to hurry his throw. As a result Mike Garrett picked it off on the Trojan 40. Willie Brown made a spectacular one handed catch for a 21-yard gain. But after the Trojans had worked their way to the Notre Dame 12, Irishmen John Simon and Norm Nicola dropped Beathard back on the 26 for a 14 yard loss. On the next play Pete hit Hal Bedsole on the 2, but Tom MacDonald, who seemed to be everywhere that afternoon, managed to jar the ball loose. Incomplete. Beathard tried again but overthrew big Hal in the end zone. That made it fourth and twenty-four on the 26. The Trojans figured, what the hell, and went for broke. And they went broke. Beathard tried a screen pass to Willie Brown. He couldn't shake loose and was cut down on the 17.

By now the game was well into the fourth period. Notre Dame moved down to the 15-yard line of SC where Ivan the Terrible kicked a 33-yard field goal with 6 minutes and 28 seconds left to play. And it ended that way. The Trojans were unable to move against the Irish defense. Notre Dame 17, USC 14.

So once again the Fighting Irish of Notre Dame made suckers of the seers and it suited them. They had upset USC. They also whipped UCLA, but that was it for the season. They ended with a dismal 2-7 year. Devore, it turned out, was once again an interim coach. Everyone second guesses the coach. If all the games played in the 1963 season had ended after the third quarter, it would have been a 7-2 season. Why did Huarte play only 45 minutes that season? He could pass, and he had Jack Snow, All American Jim Kelly and Pat Costa for receivers . . . and so on.

No one in the coaching profession was more respected or loved than Hughie Devore. The university administration and everyone associated with football was hoping he could pull it out. When it became obvious he couldn't, the search was on once more.

Devore became assistant athletic director and for the first time in 46 years the University of Notre Dame went outside its immediate family for a head coach. Their choice was an Armenian French Presbyterian by the name of Ara Parseghian, the current head coach of Northwestern University.

A press conference was called for the formal announce-

USC's Willie Brown, halfback

Notre Dame's Frank Budka—Quarterback

ment, so everyone assumed that everything was finalized. Everyone but Ara, that is. He walked out and went back to Northwestern. Father Joyce stated simply that a few minor points had not been agreed upon. Later Ara explained, "Father Joyce wanted a shamrock on the new helmets, and I wanted a camel." The disagreements were not serious and quickly were ironed out. Ara returned in a few days, another press conference was set up. He signed the contract, posed for pictures and became an adopted son of Our Lady of the Lake. Somewhere Father Sorin must have smiled. At an alumni meeting soon after, Moose Krause said as he introduced Ara, "He should be with us a long time, after all he signed twice."

Defeat can bring on a certain amount of paranoia. The day after the game the SC coaching staff told sportswriter Charlie Park that they suspected they had been spied upon. It seems that a student manager spotted a man with binoculars in a third story classroom building overlooking the practice field the week before the game. "He also had a notebook and he was writing things down," assistant coach Dave Levy was quoted as saying. "The suspect scrammed when he noticed he had been observed. I think we were watched all week." Notre Dame's instant reaction to a screen pass play that SC had never used in a game before strengthened their suspicion at the time, but years later John McKay remembers it a little differently.

According to McKay in his biography, Levy said, "Coach, there's a man up there in the window who appears to be spying and he won't leave."

"I'll get him to leave," growled McKay. As the coach approached he got hotter with every step. "You Goddamn spy, get out of that window! And I mean right now!"

The man fled, and the next day Jess Hill, obviously more than a little upset, sought out McKay and asked, "John, did any of your assistants swear at the dean of the religion department yesterday?"

"Oh no, Jessie," replied McKay, "you know how it is out there. The coaches get a little riled up sometimes. Someone must have yelled at one of the players and that poor man misunderstood."

The defeat by Notre Dame bumped the Trojans from ninth place in the national standings right off the chart. Texas took over first and Oklahoma dropped to fifth. Coach McKay and his new Thundering Herd narrowly missed a repeat invitation to the Rose Bowl. Washington, with an inferior record, but with a win over SC, got the nod.

Hugh Devore stuck around the school he loved for a few more years, locked behind a desk, but early in 1966 the clarion call of battle sounded in his ears and the old warhorse galloped off to combat on the side of the Houston Oilers.

USC ALPHABETICAL ROSTER — 1963

NO.	NAME	POS.	AGE	HT.	WT.
70	Arrobio, Chuck	L.T.	19	6'4"	223
80	Austin, Joe	R.E.	20	6'2"	198
64	*Bame, Damon	L.G.-L.B.	21	5'11"	192
74	Barry, Steve	L.T.	19	6'1"	209
12	**Beathard, Pete	Q.B.	21	6'1"	197
19	**Bedsole, Hal	L.E.	21	6'5"	221
38	Blecksmith, Ed	L.E.	20	6'2"	195
26	**Brown Willie	R.H.	21	5'11"	172
41	Brownell, Richard	P.K.	19	6'0"	185
88	*Brownwood, John	R.E.	20	6'2"	207
78	*Byrd, Mac	L.T.	21	6'1"	196
86	Cerjak, Joe	R.E.	21	6'0"	215
27	Champion, Bill	L.H.	21	5'11"	200
23	*Clark, Jay	R.H.	22	6'0"	178
39	Crisell, Bob	R.H.	20	5'10"	185
34	Crow, Harvey	L.H.	20	5'10"	183
15	*Fertig, Craig	Q.B.	21	6'1"	176
61	*Fisk, Bill	R.G.	19	6'0"	215
20	Garrett, Mike	L.H.	19	5'9"	182
77	Giers, Mike	L.T.	21	6'0"	225
63	*Gonta, Stan	R.G.	20	6'0"	210
73	Hayhoe, Jerry	R.T.	20	6'4"	225
33	*Heller, Ron	L.H.	23	6'2"	203
81	*Hill, Fred	L.E.	20	6'2"	197
31	*Hill, Gary	R.H.	20	6'0"	187
57	Houck, Hudson	R.T.	20	6'0"	205
35	**Hunt, Loran	L.H.	21	6'0"	187
25	Johnson, Don	L.H.	20	6'0"	195
52	Johnson, Paul	C.	19	6'2"	213
68	*Johnson, Tom	L.G.	21	6'0"	194
40	**Jones, Ernie	F.B.	22	6'0"	197
87	Kaiser, Bob	L.E.	19	6'0"	172
46	King, Ed	F.B.	19	6'2"	200
72	*Kirner, Gary	R.T.	21	6'3"	213
49	Lockwood, John	F.B.	21	6'0"	210
62	Lopez, Frank	R.G.	19	6'1"	203
69	**Lubisich, Pete	L.G.	20	6'1"	210
18	*Lupo, Tom	Q.B.	20	6'1"	205
43	**McMahon, Rich	F.B.	21	6'1"	192
16	Mills, Pat	Q.B.	19	6'1"	195
67	Moore, Denis	R.T.	19	6'4"	214
29	Moss, Bob	L.H.	20	6'2"	208
82	Moton, Dave	L.E.	19	6'0"	201
47	*Pye, Ernie	F.B.	20	5'11"	202
66	**Ratliff, John	L.G.	24	6'0"	210
71	*Reade, Lynn	R.T.	21	6'2"	250
36	Renison, Bill	R.H.	20	5'8"	170
85	Richman, Dennis	R.E.	21	6'3"	215
60	Rowe, Mike	L.G.	20	6'1"	215
55	*Sagouspe, Larry	C.	21	6'0"	224
54	*Sanchez, Armando	C.	20	5'11"	200
65	Shirk, John	L.G.	20	5'8"	206
76	*Svihus, Bob	R.T.	20	6'4"	220
84	Thomas, John	R.E.	20	6'1"	202
89	*Thurlow, Toby	L.E.	22	6'1"	199
83	Viltz, Theo	L.E.	20	6'2"	184
32	Winslow, Gary	R.H.	20	5'11"	180
10	Winslow, Troy	Q.B.	19	6'0"	160
21	Yamamoto, Teruo	R.H.	21	5'10"	175
45	Zirbel, Bob	C.	20	6'2"	218

NOTRE DAME ALPHABETICAL ROSTER — 1963

NO.	NAME	POS.
25	Andreotti, Pete	H.B.
60	Anton, John	T.-G.
63	Arrington, Dick	T.
66	Atamian, John	G.
48	Barnard, Jack	H.B.
76	*Bednar, George	G.-T.
59	Billy, Frank	C.
22	*Bliey, Ron	H.B.
8	Bonvechio, Alex	Q.B.
71	Brocke, Jim	T.
2	**Budka, Frank	Q.B.
57	*Burns, Bill	C.
1	Carey, Tony	Q.B.
54	*Carroll, Jim	G.-C.
26	Conway, Dennis	H.B.
75	*Costa, Paul	T.
68	Dennery, Vince	G.
69	*DiCarlo, Mike	G.
20	Dupuis, Richard	H.B.
32	Duranko, Pete	F.B.
78	*Etten, Nick	T.
42	*Farrell, Joe	H.B.
90	Geraghty, John	E.
93	**Goberville, Tom	E.
56	Harding, Tom	C.-T.
44	*Hogan, Don	H.B.
58	Hribal, Larry	G.-T.
7	Huarte, John	Q.B.
87	Ivan, Ken	E.
31	Kantor, Joe	F.B.
89	**Kelly, Jim	E.
67	Kolasinski, Dan	T.
52	Kostelnik, Tom	C.
65	**Lehmann, Bob (Capt.)	G.
37	Loboy, Alan	F.B.
86	Long, Harry	E.
49	Longo, Tom	H.B.
23	**MacDonald, Tom	H.B.
62	*Maglicic, Ken	G.
53	Mattera, Vince	C.
34	Mauch, Larry	H.B.
3	McGinn, Dan	Q.B.
51	Meeker, Bob	T.
72	Meyer, John	T.
28	Mittelhauser, Tom	F.B.
50	*Nicola, Norm	C.
21	O'Hara, Charlie	H.B.
74	*Olosky, Marty	T.
81	Papa, Bob	E.
11	*Pfeiffer, Bill	H.B.
43	*Phillips, Denny	F.B.-E.
80	*Pivec, Dave	E.
47	Rakers, Jim	F.B.
27	Rassas, Nick	H.B.
70	Seymour, Herb	T.
83	Sheridan, Phil	E.
46	**Simon, John	H.B.-E.
64	Smith, Jim	G.
40	Snow, Jack	H.B.
73	*Snowden, Jim	E.-T.
84	**Stephens, Clay	E.
55	Sullivan, Tom	T.-G.
5	Szot, Denis	Q.B.
82	Talaga, Tom	E.
77	Telfer, Bob	T.
24	Tubinis, Jerry	H.B.
36	Vasys, Arunas	H.B.
61	Wadsworth, Mike	G.-T.
79	Webster, Mike	T.
35	Wolski, Bill	H.B.
6	Zloch, Bill	Q.B.

1964
CHAPTER 37

"ANYONE WHO REALLY WANTS TO BE HEAD COACH OF ANY KIND OF FOOTBALL TEAM MUST HAVE A PROPENSITY FOR PSYCHOLOGICAL FLAGELLATION."
. . . the author

Thousands of young men (and recently a few women) have matriculated at and graduated from the University of Notre Dame, fully believing in football miracles, and with good cause. The whole history of Notre Dame football is just a little short of miraculous. Few other universities have been so blessed. But when you walk daily on a campus with the shades of Harper, Rockne, Layden, and Leahy, under the watchful eye of touchdown Jesus (a mosaic on the west wall of the new library), or Moses with the tablets in one hand and reminding you with the other that you're number One . . . or past the graven image of Father Corby standing in all his statuesque dignity with his right arm upraised signaling a fair catch . . . you expect miracles. And sometimes you get them.

Nineteen-sixty-four was one of those years. With the same basic personnel that had gone 2-7-0 the previous year, tough, vibrant, volatile and brilliant Ara Parseghian came to Los Angeles with nine straight wins. Unbeaten so far this year and favored by 12 points to say that way, it's small wonder he was called "The Miracle Worker."

And he managed that miracle with little help from above. Most of it was done with hard work and the native cunning of a middle east camel trader. "He gave each of us a chance to show what we could do," said Jack Snow. "He'd be in there with us, doing exercises . . . showing us how to block and run. He told us we were good . . . gave us confidence." The coach also recognized the inherent and untapped ability of a senior quarterback from Anaheim, California. It was his third year on the squad, but he hadn't played much. His name was John Huarte, and he was named All American and won the Heisman trophy that year.

In Los Angeles John McKay waited, but not idly. Taking a page from Rockne's book, he publicly and loudly lamented that it was impossible to run against Notre Dame, and would be impossible to keep the Irish from running on the Trojans. Privately, of course, he thought no such thing. His game plan was to slow down the Irish running attack with what he called "a confusion rush," and guard against the long pass by playing his secondary deep. As far as running against Notre Dame was concerned, Pitt had done it so it was not impossible . . . and he had Mike Garrett. He also had more confidence in his aerial attack than he led most people to believe. McKay called his quarterback Craig Fertig "the best pure passer I've ever coached." The records bore him out. Fertig, later McKay's assistant at SC,* held the school's record for yards gained in a season, 1446; most completions, 94. He had sparkled in his last two winning games against Stanford and UCLA.

Nevertheless, the bookmakers, balancing Huarte and Snow and an unbeaten string against Fertig, Garrett, and a 6-3 record, made the Irish 12-point favorites.

So for the thirty-sixth time since 1926 Notre Dame and SC faced each other on the gridiron and eighty-three thousand-eight hundred and forty fans jammed the L.A. Memorial Coliseum to see if the unranked Trojans could topple number one Notre Dame and win a bid to the Rose Bowl. They did and they didn't. They did topple the Irish, but they didn't go to the Rose Bowl.

For the first half, the players pretty well followed the script. The Irish were a little slow in starting, but they gained momentum when Huarte began to treat the customers to his expected passing show. After the opening kickoff the Irish could gain only eight yards in three rushes, so Snow punted 52 yards to the Trojan 10. SC made it to their 45 with Ron Heller doing most of the rushing, but Rod Sherman fumbled when he was hit hard by Tom Longo, and Irishman Don Gmitter recovered on the Trojan 46.

Then Huarte tossed a 16-yarder to Phil Sheridan, a 22-yarder to Nick Eddy on the eight . . . fullback Joe Kantor (an Irish Kantor?) gained two more, but Eddy lost them, hit by Mac Byrd and Mike Giers. Enter Ken Ivan "the Terrible" to attempt a twenty-five yard field goal. Naturally he made it and after 9 minutes and 33 seconds of the game gone the score was Notre Dame 3, Troy 0.

SC lost the ball on a clipping penalty after the kickoff, and the Irish began to flex their muscles. Even after a clipping

Heisman winner John Huarte, picks apart SC defense in first half

penalty of their own which pushed them back to the 27 and a fifteen yard penalty for having an illegal receiver downfield, the Irish scored in 11 plays. Huarte alternated four passes to Snow and Sheridan for 70 yards after two plays and a minute and six seconds of the second quarter, he found Snow in the end zone . . . Ivan clicked again, and the score was 10-0.

Now the hometown crowd began to understand how the dynamic duo of Huarte and Snow had averaged thirty points per game and wiped our 11 school records.

Huarte had quick hands and quick feet and had passed for 1790 yards and 18 touchdowns, just two of his four single game records and three season records. Big Jack Snow, 6-2 and 225, owned the record of most yards on receptions caught in one game, 217, plus three season records: Most passes caught, 50; most yards on reception, 956; and most touchdown passes caught, 8.

They were awe-inspiring. The ease with which they committed such atrocities on opposing teams was shameful . . . unless of course you're Irish.

Rod Sherman ran the kickoff back 22 yards to the Trojan 25, then Garrett, Heller, and Homer Williams proved to be surprisingly effective against the big Notre Dame line which had permitted opponents just 61.3 yards per game. They worked the ball down to the 20, but Fertig threw a wild lateral and by the time Mike Garrett recovered it, they were back on the 33. Craig lined a 17-yard pass to Sherman which made it fourth down, four to go, on the 16-yard line. Dave Morton was open in the end zone, but Fertig overthrew him, and the Trojans had to give up the ball.

The Irish mobilized and began to march. Then Huarte made one of the few mistakes he had made all season. Jim Walker intercepted his pass intended for Jack Snow and ran it back to the 33 of Notre Dame. On fourth and three, Fertig still gambling, tried a pass play, but Tom Longo broke it up and the Irish took over on their twenty-eight . . . and the press gang went to work again. Huarte couldn't miss, and they covered the distance in eleven plays with Wolski capping the drive by taking a pitchout the remaining five yards for the TD. Ken Ivan converted once more and at halftime it was 17-0 Notre Dame. The Trojans did give the Irish a scare in the waning

Mike Garrett picks up big gain for USC

moments of the period. Garrett returned the kickoff 40 yards, Sherman made an amazing catch to move the ball to Notre Dame's 9. Fertig found Hill in the end zone, but Longo hit with such fury that the ball was dropped. An offensive penalty moved the ball back to the 23, and the Irish took over on their twenty as the half ended.

But the Trojans had found out they could move on the Irish. They were tough, but not invincible. After taking the kickoff, the men of Troy, directed by Fertig, pushed 66 yards in ten plays. A personal foul against the Irish moved the ball from the 13 to the Notre Dame 6. On third down Mike Garrett crashed through from the one. Dick Brownell made the point after. They had used only four minutes of the second half and suddenly that 17-7 lead didn't seem insurmountable. The Irish were well aware of that as well. They bounced back with an assault that brought them all the way down to the Trojan nine. There Huarte made his second mistake of the day . . . a wobbly pitchout intended for Wolski. It never got there. SC fullback John Lockwood pounced on it, but the Trojan offensive never got off the ground. Literally and figuratively. Another

pass interference call stopped them in their tracks. The Irish took over on their 34 and rolled the length of the field. From one yard out Kantor plunged into the end zone for another six . . . or so the Irish thought. The touchdown was called back by a holding penalty, and the Notre Damers decided to go for it on fourth down. But the gamble didn't pay off and they turned the ball over to SC on the 12.

Now it was Craig Fertig's turn to become a virtuoso.

In ten plays he guided the Trojans 88 yards for their second score. He passed to Hill for 28, Sherman for 18, then Hill again for 14. The final play was another pin-point pass to Hill from twenty three yards out. Then came a breakdown in communications. Coach McKay sent Ron Heller in to ask for time, and instruct Fertig to go for the two-point conversion. Ron got a late start and rushed on the field just as Brownell, in the confusion, missed the kick. The score remained at 17-13 Notre Dame.

But with little over five minutes left in the game and only a five-point lead, you'd better hold onto the ball. Control it. The Irish hadn't really been stopped all day, only slowed a little in

Rod Sherman catches winning TD pass from Craig Fertig in waning minute of game

the first quarter; but now they couldn't get anything started. The Irish machine had bogged down on its own 40 and SC took over with two minutes and 10 seconds left to play. The momentum had shifted, now it was the Trojans of SC that looked like national champions. Their confidence was apparent to every hysterical fan in the stands.

Fertig, who had completely outplayed Huarte in the second half, calmly took command and with a pass to Hill gained a fast 23 yards. Two plays later he got one through to Fred in the end zone, but the officials ruled it out of bounds. On the next play 6-5, 230-pound Alan Page slammed into Fertig as he dropped back to pass. "Fumble," screamed the Irish fans.

"Incomplete pass," ruled the officials.

SC got a second chance and they made it count. Fertig got one to Sherman on the three and Rod danced over. This time Brownell didn't miss. The score was 20-17 USC with 1:33 left to play. But for Notre Dame the rhythm was gone, the Irish jig was up, the dance was over. Time to pick up the shillelaghs and go home. And they did . . . a few yards shy of a perfect season.

There was, of course, hysteria bordering on madness in the stands as well as the Trojan locker room. McKay and the assistants were tossed in the showers. The pummeling the team gave each other in the dressing room made the game look like a tea dance.

"BEAT MICHIGAN" was scrawled on the blackboard. They were ready for the Rose Bowl before their bruises had

started to turn blue. "Now we've got something to do on New Year's Day," said Craig Fertig.

"I'll show you around Pasadena, it's my home town," said Rod Sherman.

"It'd be a disgrace to keep us out of the Rose Bowl now," said Jess Hill. "But still, you never know. Strange things happen."

A strange thing did. Less than two hours after USC's upset defeat of Notre Dame, the AAWU announced that the Beavers of Oregon State would meet Michigan in the Rose Bowl. USC and Oregon State had identical 3-1 conference records, but had not played each other. SC's defeat over Notre Dame gave them a 7-3 season. Oregon State finished 8-2.

When he heard of the selection, Jess Hill said, "It's the rankest injustice that ever occurred in the field of intercollegiate athletics."

"I'm not going to worry about it," said John McKay before he knew of the decision. "I'm going out and enjoy the evening." Still, when he learned of the vote, he was disappointed. Naturally.

So was Ara Parseghian that evening. Notre Dame's first national championship since 1949 had just gone down the tubes. It was said of Ara that the only time he ever took off work was to make a speech. Even after his position was secure he arose at 5:30, was in his office at 7, and worked every night until 10. Sunday is a light day . . . he doesn't start work until 2 P.M. Then he and his staff studied game films until nine,

Heisman Trophy Winner—John Huarte

All American Jack Snow

with a half hour out for dinner. In 1964 he worked even harder.

Yet he missed his undefeated season and McKay, who worked just as hard, missed the Rose Bowl for the second straight year.

Anyone who really wants to be a head football coach must have some kind of propensity for psychological flagellation.

Craig Fertig was voted the outstanding back of the game. In the second half he completed 10 for 14 passes and two touchdowns. Even though he was overshadowed in the first half by Huarte, he finished the day with 15 for 20 and 225 yards. In this, his final year, he passed for 1671 yards, a new SC record. Also his 1695 yards total offense put him ahead of "Racehorse Russ" Saunders who set his mark in 1929.

Mike Garrett was the only Trojan to mar the all opponent's team. Huarte won the Notre Dame Alumni Club's award as the foremost Irish performer. He too extended his records at Notre Dame . . . most yards gained passing, 2,082, and most touchdowns responsible for, 19. He, Jim Carroll and Jack Snow, were named consensus All Americans. Snow also added a little more lustre to his record book. Most receptions in a season, 60 . . . most yards on catches, 1,114, and most TDs scored on passes, 9. He also received one of the nicest awards any college football player can receive . . .

He was first round draft choice of the Minnesota Vikings, and seventh round pick of the San Diego Chargers. "I'll go with whoever makes me the best offer," he said. He ended up with the L.A. Rams in 1965.

Mike Garret, Heisman Trophy winner

Notre Dame students vent their feelings

year either.

McKay, of course, didn't know that ton the Saturday morning they boarded the team bus for Notre Dame Stadium . . . but he must have suspected that the stars were not in his heaven that day. He looked at the name tag on the sun visor above the driver. Cheerfully it proclaimed, "Your bus driver today is Fred Loser." In his biography McKay stated, "That figured."

On a bleak, cheerless October afternoon on a field swept by wind, rain and hail, the Irish defense all but put Mike Garrett in a bottle. Pete Duranko, Tom Rhoads, Mike McGill, Jim Lynch, John Horney, and Dave Martin obviously had been told to key on Garrett. As all football fans know, "key" is a euphemism for clobber, and clobber they did. The first half, Iron Mike, who had averaged 170 per game in the first five, netted seven yards . . . in his first nine carries he was thrown for losses three times; held to no gain three times . . . there hadn't been an ambush like that since Sitting Bull surprised George Armstrong Custer at the Little Big Horn. The longest runs he made all day were to and from huddles. He averaged 43 yards that long afternoon. That was his usual average for the first three carries, and he was a pretty sure bet to win the Heisman trophy that year . . . USC's first player to be recog-

nized and so honored. Notre Dame had had six.

A nineteen year old fullback from Harrisburg, Pennsylvania, by the name of Lawrence James Conjar, surely did everything he could that October 23rd to make the sportswriters and the downtown N.Y. Athletic Club forget about Mike Garrett. He wasn't even trying for the Heisman Trophy; he just wanted a permanent place on the team. He got it . . . he scored four touchdowns and gained 116 yards, that's 73 more than Garrett made and 122 more than Rod Sherman, and as a matter of fact it was 42 yards more than the whole USC team made.

The Trojans never got started. They did get one first down after the opening kickoff, and they were lucky to get that. With the predominantly Notre Dame crowd shouting, "Remember, Remember, Remember," the Irish kickoff sailed toward the Trojan deep man, Mike Hunter. He got the ball on the eight and made it to the thirteen where he slipped and fell like a ____. For a few seconds he didn't move. "Oh, Christ," breathed McKay, "they shot him!" It wasn't fatal, and of course Hunter wasn't shot, he wasn't even hurt, but he and the Trojans were off to a lousy start. Quarterback Troy Winslow managed a ten yard pass to John Thomas, but the Irish defense

Larry Conjar #32, and Nick Eddy #47—Notre Dame's top running backs

hounded Garrett with the tenacity of a Chinese praying mantis and all but consumed him. "Everywhere I went in the first half," he said after the game, "even when I was faking without the ball, I had a couple of fists in my face." They stopped him colder than the north wind that threatened to turn the field into an ice rink that day. Rod Sherman did start, but his knee got progressively worse, and he jammed an elbow on a pass play . . . he tried but he wasn't much help.

It's doubtful anything could have helped USC that afternoon. It was clearly Notre Dame's day, or more specificially, Larry Conjar's. He and Wolski ripped up the middle for 45 yards in ten plays for the first touchdown when the game was just eight minutes old. Ivan made the point after. The next time the Irish got their hands on the ball, they did it again. Aided by a 15-yard penalty for roughness, they moved 40 yards in eight plays and Conjar slammed in once more, Ivan converted once more. Thirteen minutes and five seconds of the first quarter and the score was 14-0. How sweet is revenge!

It began to look as though Conjar could handle the entire Trojan team alone. Early in the second period he did most of the ground gaining on a 67-yard march for another six. Ivan as usual couldn't miss; 21-0 at the half.

A well known and successful writer was once asked why he never changed his plot line. "Why tamper with success?," he replied. Coach Parseghian also subscribed to that theory. Five minutes and 36 seconds into the third quarter with Conjar leading the way, the Irish covered another 67 yards for touchdown number three. The Crushing Croat capped his own drive with a one yard plunge, Ivan trotted onto the field, and the score became 28 zip.

On the first play of the final quarter, the Trojans began to look like a football team. Starting on their own 24, they drove 76 for their only score. Winslow made 12 then seven on keepers, he then passed to Sherman for 13 . . . John Thomas made a spectacular catch for 21 and on the next play an even more dramatic diving catch in the end zone for the tally. Tim Rossovich made the extra point and the Trojans were finally on the scoreboard, but time was running out.

In the closing minutes they did manage to move the ball again, but unfortunately most of the yardage was made in the wrong direction. Garrett got 12, Mickey Upton got ten, Winslow hit Sherman with a short pass that netted 13 and put SC on the nine-yard line with a first and goal to go. From there they marched steadily backward and were able to reach the 39-

yard line before the gun sounded.

L.A. Times staff writer Jim Murray wrote the next day in reference to Conjar's conquest, "Of course he only had the USC line to run through. You have heard of the seven blocks of granite? Well this day we had the seven chips of potato."

After the game Coach Parseghian said, "I think all of us will recognize that Southern Cal is a very dangerous team." Murray wasn't through. "True," he agreed, "they're apt to do real harm to themselves."

Before the game it was rumored that Notre Dame was so concerned about Mike Garrett's running ability that they had a player in practice imitating all of Mike's moves. When asked about it, Parseghian said, "Listen, if we had a guy who could imitate Mike Garrett, we'd suit him up and start him. The only thing our guy can do as well as Garrett is eat. He wears number 20 . . . there the resemblance ends."

On the Notre Dame roster number 20 was a back by the name of Butash, but you kind of have to wonder if Ara pulled a Rockne switch and had Conjar in that jersey during practice.

There is no doubt that the slippery rainsoaked turf slowed Garrett down, but then it was just as wet and slippery on both sides of the line. He won the Heisman Trophy anyway and was named All American for the second time. He ended the season gaining 1,440 yards rushing, which broke Morley Drury's record of 1,163 set in 1927. His 267 rushing attempts broke Drury's 223. His career total of 3,221 broke Orv Mohler's record of 2,025 set in 1930, 31 and 32.

McKay and Parseghian ended the season with identical records, 7-2-1 . . . well matched, wouldn't you say?

Notre Dame students with Mike Garrett coffin

1965 SOUTHERN CALIFORNIA ALPHABETICAL ROSTER

NO.	NAME	POS.	AGE	HT.	WT.	HOMETOWN	SCHOOL
51	Allmon, Dick	R.L.B.	19	6'0"	204	La Jolla, Calif.	La Jolla
70	**Arrobio, Chuck	R.T.	21	6'4"	243	Glendale, Calif.	Glendale
55	*Bain, Marv	L.L.B.	20	6'1"	197	Santa Ana, Calif.	Mater Dei
64	Barry, Steve	R.G.	21	6'1"	210	Los Angeles, Calif.	Loyola
38	*Blecksmith, Ed	R.S.	22	6'2"	196	Covina, Calif.	Charter Oak
31	Bowie, Wilson	R.H.	19	6'1"	183	New Orleans, La.	Carver
26	Cahill, Ray	L.E.	20	6'1"	203	Los Angeles, Calif.	Manual Arts
72	Conroy, Jerry	R.G.	20	6'1"	206	Montclair, Calif.	Montclair
60	Crane, Dennis	R.T.	20	6'5"	240	Colton, Calif.	Colton
18	Cunerty, Bill	P.K.	19	5'10"	160	Torrance, Calif.	No. Torrance
81	Curtis, Mike	D.E.	19	6'1"	205	Los Angeles, Calif.	Loyola
19	Elliott, Dick	Q.B.	20	6'4"	182	Temple City, Calif.	Temple City
40	Fite, Gary	F.B.	24	6'0"	217	San Jacinto, Calif.	San Jacinto
59	Fluet, Dennis	C.	20	6'2"	200	Arcadia, Calif.	St. Francis
20	**Garrett, Mike	L.H.	21	5'9"	185	Los Angeles, Calif.	Roosevelt
21	Grady, Steve	D.H.B.	20	6'0"	201	Los Angeles, Calif.	Loyola
85	Hayhoe, Bill	L.E.	19	6'8"	227	Van Nuys, Calif.	Birmingham
73	*Hayhoe, Jerry	L.T.	21	6'4"	228	Van Nuys, Calif.	Birmingham
90	Hoffman, John	R.E.	22	6'6"	240	Studio City, Calif.	Western (Anaheim)
69	Homan, Jim	R.G.	20	6'2"	221	Long Beach, Calif.	St. Anthony
23	Hull, Mike	F.B.-L.H.	20	6'4"	205	La Crescenta, Calif.	Crescenta Valley
25	Hunter, Mike	R.H.	21	5'9"	155	Newport Beach, Calif.	Anaheim
52	*Johnson, Paul	C.	21	6'1"	205	Long Beach, Calif.	St. Anthony
39	Kaiser, Bob	D.H.B.	21	6'1"	190	Inglewood, Calif.	Inglewood
46	*King, Ed	L.S.	21	6'3"	209	Fresno, Calif.	Bullard
37	Kochinas, Tony	R.S.	18	5'9"	175	Los Angeles, Calif.	Lincoln
28	Lawrence, Jim	R.H.	19	5'11"	190	Buena Park, Calif.	Buena Park
27	*Lee, Phil	D.H.B.	20	5'11"	173	Stockton, Calif.	Edison
49	*Lockwood, John	M.G.	23	6'1"	218	Burbank, Calif.	Burbank
62	*Lopez, Frank	L.G.	21	6'1"	206	Whittier, Calif.	Sierra
36	McCall, Don	L.H.	21	5'11"	192	Los Angeles, Calif.	Fremont
75	Magner, Gary	D.T.	20	6'3"	216	Costa Mesa, Calif.	Mater Dei
67	May, Ray	D.E.	20	6'2"	225	Los Angeles, Calif.	Los Angeles
86	Miller, Bob	R.E.	19	6'4"	212	Compton, Calif.	Dominguez
16	Mills, Pat	Q.B.	21	6'1"	196	Santa Monica, Calif.	Santa Monica
54	Moore, Denis	D.E.	21	6'5"	217	Los Angeles, Calif.	Westchester
29	Moss, Bob	F.B.	23	6'2"	221	Los Angeles, Calif.	Narbonne
82	**Moton, Dave	L.E.	21	6'1"	222	Stockton, Calif.	Franklin
32	Nyquist, Paul	R.S.	20	5'10"	172	Glendale, Calif.	Glendale
79	O'Malley, Jack	D.T.	19	6'4"	243	Wilmington, Calif.	Banning
15	Page, Toby	Q.B.	19	6'0"	182	Santa Ana, Calif.	Mater Dei
63	*Patrick, Doug	D.T.	21	6'4"	204	South Pasadena, Calif.	So. Pasadena
61	Petrill, Larry	M.G.	20	6'0"	204	Redondo Beach, Calif.	Morningside
56	Rippen, Bob	C.	20	6'2"	196	Alhambra, Calif.	Alhambra
88	Rossovich, Tim	D.E.	19	6'5"	215	Mt. View, Calif.	St. Francis
80	*Salness, Ty	L.S.	20	6'1"	199	Anaheim, Calif.	Anaheim
76	Scarpace, Mike	L.T.	19	6'1"	245	Van Nuys, Calif.	Birmingham
89	*Shaw, Nate	D.H.B.	20	6'2"	201	San Diego, Calif.	Lincoln
12	Sherman, Rod	R.H.	20	6'0"	189	Pasadena, Calif.	Muir
35	Sims, Leonard	D.H.B.	19	5'11"	190	Garden Grove	Santiago
53	Slattery, Dennis	R.E.	20	6'2"	223	West Covina	Arroyo
74	*Smith, Jeff	L.L.B.-D.E.	21	6'1"	236	Long Beach, Calif.	Poly
65	Snow, Jim	L.L.B.	18	5'11"	206	San Diego, Calif.	San Diego
84	**Thomas, John	R.E.	22	6'1"	210	Alhambra, Calif.	Alhambra
87	Truman, Phil	L.E.	19	6'5"	191	Rosemead, Calif.	Rosemead
33	Upton, Mickey	R.S.	21	5'10"	174	Rialto, Calif.	Stillwater, Okla.
83	Viltz, Theo	L.S.	22	6'1"	185	Los Angeles, Calif.	Serra
78	*Vellone, Jim	L.T.	21	6'2"	255	Whittier, Calif.	California
66	Walker, Jim	R.L.B.	22	6'2"	210	Los Angeles, Calif.	Hadley Tech (St. Louis, Mo.)
71	Westphal, Mike	D.T.	20	6'6"	250	Long Beach, Calif.	Jordan
44	*Williams, Homer	F.B.	22	6'1"	222	Long Beach, Calif.	St. Anthony
10	Winslow, Troy	Q.B.	21	6'0"	183	Inglewood, Calif.	Inglewood
58	Wood, Don	R.G.	19	6'1"	216	San Francisco, Calif.	St. Ignatius
68	Woudenberg, Dana	L.G.	19	6'1"	216	Scottsdale, Ariz.	Arcadia, Phoenix
57	Wojcik, Greg	C.	19	6'5"	245	Huntington Beach, Calif.	Huntington Beach
77	Yary, Ron	D.T.	19	6'6"	252	Bellflower, Calif.	Bellflower
50	Young, Adrian	R.L.B.	19	6'1"	198	La Mirada, Calif.	Bishop Amat

*Denotes lettermen

1965 NOTRE DAME ALPHABETICAL ROSTER

NAME	POS.	AGE	HT.	WT.	HOMETOWN	SCHOOL
Alexander, Harry	T.	20	6'1"	240	Wilmington, Del.	Salesianum
*Andreotti, Peter	H.B.	21	5'9"	178	Chicago, Ill.	Mendel
**Arrington, Richard	G.	23	5'11"	232	Erie, Pa.	Erie East
Azzaro, Joseph	K.	19	5'11"	190	Pittsburgh, Pa.	Central Catholic
Bleier, Robert	H.B.	19	5'11"	185	Appleton, Wisc.	Xavier
Burgener, Michael	H.B.	19	5'10"	185	Marion, Ill.	Marion
*Carey, Anthony	D.H.B.	22	6'0"	190	Chicago, Ill.	Mount Carmel
Conjar, Lawrence	F.B.	19	6'0"	205	Harrisburg, Pa.	Bishop McDevitt
Conway, Dennis	H.B.	21	5'9"	165	Sioux City, Iowa	Heelan Catholic
Dainton, William	G.	18	6'2"	220	Gary, Ind.	Andrean
*Duranko, Peter	D.T.	21	6'2"	225	Johnstown, Pa.	Bishop McCort
*Eddy, Nicholas	H.B.	21	6'0"	190	Lafayette, Calif.	Tracy (California)
Fournier, Louis	T.	19	6'3"	240	Cheboygan, Mich.	Cheboygan Catholic
*Gmitter, Donald	E.	20	6'2"	210	Pittsburgh, Pa.	South Hills Cath.
Goeddeke, George	C.	20	6'3"	225	Detroit, Mich.	St. David's
Gorman, Timothy	G.	20	5'11"	205	Hoboken, N.J.	St. Joseph's
Grable, Charles	G.-T.	19	6'0"	210	Oshkosh, Wisc.	Lourdes
Hagerty, Robert	T.-F.B.	19	6'3"	230	Mingo Junction, Ohio	Steubenville Catholic
Haley, David	H.B.	18	5'11"	185	Hingham, Mass.	Archbishop Williams
*Hardy, Kevin	D.T.	20	6'5"	270	Oakland, Calif.	St. Elizabeth's
Harshman, Daniel	H.B.	19	6'0"	185	Toledo, Ohio	St. Francis DeSales
Horney, John	L.B.	19	5'11"	205	Youngstown, Ohio	Cardinal Mooney
*Ivan, Kenneth	D.H.B.-K.	20	6'1"	185	Massillon, Ohio	Massillon
Jeziorski, Ronald	L.B.	20	5'10"	205	South Bend Ind.	St. Joseph's
Kelly, Gerald	C.	19	6'1"	210	Los Angeles, Calif.	Mount Carmel
Koenings, Daniel	Q.B.	19	6'2"	185	Racine, Wisc.	St. Catherine's
Konieczny, Rudy	T.	18	6'0"	235	Fairview, Mass.	Chicopee
Kuzmicz, Michael	E.T.	18	6'4"	230	South Bend, Ind.	Central
Lium, John	C.	20	6'4"	230	Bronx, N.Y.	Cardinal Farley
Loboy, Alan	F.B.-L.B.	21	6'0"	195	Park Ridge, Ill.	Notre Dame (Niles)
Long, Harold	D.E.	21	6'0"	205	LaGrange, Ill.	Fenwick
**Longo, Thomas	D.H.B.	23	6'1"	195	Lyndhurst, N.J.	Lyndhurst
*Lynch, James	L.B.	20	6'1"	215	Lima, Ohio	Central Catholic
Marsico, Joseph	G.	20	6'0"	210	River Forest, Ill.	Fenwick
Martin, David	E.-L.B.	18	6'0"	200	Kansas City, Kan.	Bishop Miege
May, Paul	F.B.	19	5'10"	200	Alexandria, Va.	St. John's College
McGill, Michael	L.B.-E.	18	6'2"	220	Hammond, Ind.	Bishop Noll
McGinn, Daniel	K.-Q.B.	21	5'11"	180	Omaha, Nebr.	Cathedral
*Meeker, Robert	T.	21	6'2"	235	Akron, Ohio	St. Vincent's
Merkle, Robert	F.B.	21	6'1"	210	Brandywine, Md.	St. Leo Prep
O'Leary, Thomas	H.B.	19	5'10"	185	Columbus, Ohio	St. Charles Prep
O'Malley, Hugh	Q.B.	20	5'10"	178	South Bend, Ind.	St. Joseph's
Orians, Ronald	H.B.	19	5'11"	187	Tiffin, Ohio	Mohawk
*Page, Alan	D.E.	20	6'5"	230	Canton, Ohio	Central Catholic
Pergine, John	L.B.-Q.B.	18	6'0"	190	Norristown, Pa.	Plym.-Whitemarsh
Quinn, Steve	C.-G.	19	6'1"	207	Northfield, Ill.	Loyola Academy
*Rassas, Nicholas	S.	21	6'0"	185	Winnetka, Ill.	Loyola Academy
*Regner, Thomas	G.	21	6'1"	245	Kenosha, Wisc.	St. Joseph's
Rhoads, Thomas	D.E.	20	6'2"	210	Cincinnati, Ohio	St. Xavier
Ryan, James	K.	21	5'10"	185	Shreveport, La.	Byrd
Sack, Allen	D.E.	20	6'3"	200	Boothwyn, Pa.	Chichester
Sauget, Richard	L.B.	21	6'3"	205	Belleville, Ill.	Cathedral
Schoen, Thomas	Q.B.	19	5'11"	178	Euclid, Ohio	St. Joseph
Seiler, Paul	T.-C.	19	6'4"	235	Algona, Iowa	Bishop Garrigan
*Sheridan, Philip (C)	E.	21	6'4"	215	Rutherford, N.J.	St. Mary's
Smithberger, James	H.B.-S.	18	6'1"	185	Welch, W.Va.	Weich
Sullivan, Thomas	T.	21	6'2"	230	Berkeley, Calif.	Bishop McGuinness
Swatland, Richard	T.-G.	19	6'2"	218	Stamford, Conn.	Stamford Catholic
Talaga, Thomas	E.	21	6'5"	220	Chicago, Ill.	St. Patrick's
Thornton, Peter	G.	22	6'2"	210	Portland, Me.	Cheverus
VanHuffel, Alan	E.-L.B.	19	6'2"	215	South Bend, Ind.	St. Joseph's
*Vasys, Arunas	L.B.	22	6'2"	220	Cicero, Ill.	Saint Phillip
*Wadsworth, Michael	D.T.	22	6'3"	240	Toronto, Ont.	DeLaSalle
*Webster, Michael	T.	21	6'1"	250	Vancouver, B.C.	Gladstone
Wengierski, Timothy	H.B.	20	6'0"	185	River Forest, Ill.	Fenwick
**Wolski, William	H.B.	21	5'11"	195	Muskegon, Mich.	Muskegon Catholic
Zloch, William	Q.B.	20	6'3"	190	Ft. Lauderdale, Fla.	St. Thomas Academy
Zurowski, David	H.B.	20	6'3"	190	Oxon Hill, Md.	Gonzaga

1966
CHAPTER 39

"FORGET IT GUYS, DO YOU REALIZE THAT THERE ARE 700 MILLION CHINESE WHO DON'T EVEN KNOW THE GAME WAS PLAYED?" . . . John McKay, 1966

In 1966 the series stood Notre Dame 24, USC 11 and two ties. And as had happened many times before, both teams were closing the season with much more at stake than a single game win or loss. For the fighting Irish it meant number one national ranking . . . for the Trojans it meant that the Pac 8 had not been mistaken when they pinned their hopes on SC in the Rose Bowl. They had been chosen the previous Monday to represent the west coast in the New Year's day classic.

It began to shape up as a game of replacements. Notre Dame's Terry Hanratty had been injured against Michigan State and Coley O'Brien was expected to replace him.

USC quarterback Troy Winslow was hurt in a freak practice accident, and Toby Page was expected to start. On the surface that looked good for the Californians. Page had as his top receivers Ron Drake, Rod Sherman, and Bob Klein and he had a 60% completion record. Notre Dame's O'Brien hadn't played much until Hanratty was hurt, and then had only a 42% completion average, but he was recognized as a superior runner. He also had Jim Seymour, an absolutely sensational sophomore end. At 6-4 and 2-5 Seymour seemed almost indestructible. He had caught 37 passes that season, 6 for touchdowns. All American Nick Eddy was also there to help . . . and Larry Conjar. Conjar and Eddy had accounted for half of the Irish ground attack that season.

Coley O'Brien also had something more important than good receivers. He had monumental courage. Before the Navy game in late October, it was discovered that he was diabetic. With the typical determination of a dedicated athlete (he won ten letters at St. John's prep) he simply adjusted his schedule and kept on playing. He increased his caloric intake up to 5,000 per day by eating five meals, learned to give himself insulin shots, and carried candy bars to ward off occasional dizzy spells when the blood sugar level got too low. In the Michigan State game, a particularly rough one that was fought to a 10-10 tie, he came off the field feeling weak and light-headed. He gobbled a chocolate bar, gulped some orange juice, and trotted back on the field and finished the game.

USC expected to be at full strength in the running department with Don McCall back in form and Jim Lawrence at left halfback. Homer Williams had been out all season with a knee injury but seemed to be in shape for Notre Dame. The Trojans needed all the strength and depth they could muster to penetrate the awesome Irish defense, and they knew it . . . they had scouts and they could read the newspapers. The Notre Dame defense had given up just 38 points the entire season. USC's main hope was that their big interior line averaging 235 pounds, and headed by All American Ron Yary at 6-6 and 275, could intimidate the Irish defensive unit, but it didn't seem likely. The Trojans had other worries. The rugged Notre Dame offensive line averaged 223 pounds and had rushed for an average of 422 yards per game and had scored a season total of 311 points . . . and they were undefeated.

The Trojans were going into the game with a 7-2 record. They were in for a long, hard November afternoon, they suspected that . . . but if they had known just how long and hard they might not even have shown up.

The morning of the game, Paul Zimmerman, sports editor of the L.A. Times wrote: "It could be a low scoring contest, bringing together two of the top ranked defensive units of the land. The Irish also boast a high scoring offense . . ."

Well he was half right anyway.

The Trojans managed to get past midfield only twice . . . the second time in the fourth quarter they made it to the 34 against the Irish reserves.

Notre Dame took the opening kickoff and never really gave up the ball for more than a few minutes. They organized drives of 80, 72, 64, 41, 39 and 38 yards. Two pass interceptions of 44 and 33 yards contributed to the seven touchdowns scored by the Irish, Joe Azzaro kicked six extra points and a 38-yard field goal.

That's right . . . 51-0.

Notre Dame started with the kickoff on their 20 and started to chip away. The wheels of the Irish offense ground slowly, but they ground exceedingly small. Seventeen plays later they were in the end zone. Conjar plunged the last two yards over center. Azzaro converted.

USC took over with Toby Page at quarterback, but couldn't get past midfield before being forced to punt. Notre Dame's attack also bogged down at about the same place and they had to punt . . . the first of only two for the day. It worked out for

Jim Lynch—Notre Dame Captain and All American

Nick Eddy breaks through for large gain

them anyway. Page threw a pass intended for Bob Klein, but Tom Scheon, an Irish defensive safety, got there first. He intercepted at the 44, got a key block from 6-5, 270-pound Kevin Hardy, and galloped all the way home. One of the few light moments for the SC fans that day was when a frustrated Trojan booster stood up in the stands and cried, "Schoen, Schoen . . . come back Schoen!"

It was now 14 to nothing and only the first quarter. But the Irish hadn't really started yet. They were slowed a little, but not stopped . . . well, they paused briefly on the SC 38-yard line, but Azzaro kicked a field goal to make the score 17-0. Now O'Brien and Seymour decided to impress the Trojans and they did it with all the authority and finality of a company of Gurkha mercenaries attacking a Tibetan monastery. They also did it with great glee, and utter disdain for the Trojan defense. "We could even tell when he was going to pass," said John McKay later, "but when we shot our linebackers, there was no place for them to go. They just couldn't get to the passer." He had that right. A 66-yard drive in eight plays, all passes, capped by a 13-yard pass from O'Brien to Seymour for the TD. Less than a minute later Seymour grabbed another pass, this one 39 yards from O'Brien, with only eight seconds remaining in the half. Seymour was beginning to enjoy leaping between SC safety Mike Battle and Pat Cashman and/or defensive halfback Nate Shaw. They went into the locker room 31-0.

They could have stopped right there. The interception by Schoen seemed to have taken the wind out of the sails of

Southern Cal . . . wind? More like a gentle zephyr. "I think the pass interception was the turning point," said McKay. Kevin Hardy agreed. "You could feel the letdown in them . . . they seem to wilt."

On the second play after the second half kickoff, Mike Hull fumbled and gave the Irish possession on the USC 42 yard line. Six plays later O'Brien found Don Harshman on the goal line, tossed him a 23-yard pass and the score was 38-0 after Azzaro's conversion.

After SC's Adrian Young intercepted an Irish pass and returned it 43 yards, the Trojans tried to mount some kind of an offense. It nearly resulted in a face saving touchdown, but on November 26, 1966, the Irish defense would have locked out Bart Starr and the Green Bay Packers. Page did manage to complete passes to Ron Drake, Bob Klein and Ray Cahill, before Jim Smithberger nearly intercepted on the nine. If he had been able to hold onto the ball he could have gone all the way. Even if he had, it wouldn't have affected the outcome much . . . on the next play Drake dropped the ball in the end zone, the Irish took over and drove 71 yards for touchdown number six . . . Eddy brought it in from nine yards out. Point after attempt unsuccessful, Notre Dame 44, USC 0, and there was one more quarter to play.

In 1905 Notre Dame played American Medical at Notre Dame. After a 25-minute first half the Irish led 121 to 0. The second half was shortened to eight minutes to give the "Doctors" enough time to eat before catching a train back to Chi-

Rod Sherman meets Notre Dame defense

cago. Notre Dame scored 27 touchdowns, but missed 20 extra points. The final score was 142-0.* At the start of the fourth quarter, John McKay must have felt like that poor benighted coach of the "Doctors" whose name, fortunately, has gone down in anonymity.

Coach Parseghian apparently felt that the game was safe enough to send in his reserves. It's doubtful that he wanted to run up the score, but who knows? As Coach Leahy observed years before, it's hard to drill into a player six days a week, "Win! Win! Win!" and then on the seventh tell him to go out and play the game hard, but don't score. At any rate the Irish were not through. The subs drove 46 yards to the USC 14 before they lost the ball on a fumble. They weren't without it long. Linebacker Dave Martin picked off another of Page's passes at the 33, snuggled behind a couple of blockers, and skipped merrily to the seventh Irish touchdown of the day. Azzaro added one more and that's the way it ended . . .51-0.

To Coach McKay the final gun must have sounded like a death knell . . . but there must have been something merciful about the sound. At least the carnage was over.

And now second guess time. Before the Irish had finished chanting, "We're number one" and before Ara Parseghian's clothes had dried from his being tossed in the shower by his exuberant players, the Monday morning quarterbacks were plucking away at John McKay's flesh.

"Now they're thinking if McKay could have held the score down as he said he could, he should have done it," said one columnist. "The stigma is on the 1966 Trojans."

"How's McKay taking it?" asks the first guy. "Oh, he's hanging in there," says the second. First guy peers into the Trojan locker room to see from which rafter . . . another bit of humor from the Los Angeles Times.

"Well, USC will show up in the Rose Bowl January 2nd all right, but first we'll have to put 'em in the sack for you . . . It may take time to find all the pieces." No wonder head coaches develop ulcers. Coaches that is, without senses of humor. McKay's never seems to desert him. It has probably saved him from complete lunacy. When asked what in particular he was going to have his team work on for the Rose Bowl game against Purdue, he said "Everything."

Concerning the Notre Dame game, he said, "We did a good job of moving the ball nowhere." After the disaster he talked to his disconsolate players in the dressing room.

"Forget it guys, do you realize there are 700 million Chinese who don't even know the game was played?"

The following week he got three letters from China complaining about the way he coached the game.

*In 1905 touchdowns scored 5 points, field goals 4 points, and conversions 1.

Coach McKay talks with Toby Page

The coach with the second best win record in modern SC football history had coached the Trojans to their worst defeat, and as he stood on the sidelines in the fourth quarter he was reminded of that fact no fewer than fourteen times. But McKay is a gambler; unfortunately he was gambling against one of the great college teams of all times. But after all's said and done, a loss is a loss regardless of score and why not take a chance. Nobody ever accused McKay of not having the guts to roll the dice. That day they just seemed to come up craps. He had the class to say to his players after the game, "You didn't play well, but you didn't play poorly enough to get beaten 51-0. I got you beat that badly and I'll never make that mistake again."

The echoes of the Notre Dame victory march drifted away and one by one the lights of the Coliseum winked and went dark. McKay sat looking at the tips of his shoes. With him was Dave Levy, his assistant, and his son John, then thirteen years old. That evening he was scheduled to speak before a group of SC's most generous athletic donors, in a banquet room several miles from the stadium. He and Levy walked the first few miles, and then because he had that paranoid feeling that defeat can bring, said to Levy, "I feel like everybody's watching us, let's take a cab." They did and he made his speech. For coach John McKay it must have been a feté worse than death.

He also lost to Purdue in the Rose Bowl . . . 13-14. It just wasn't his year.

1966 USC VARSITY ALPHABETICAL ROSTER

NO.	NAME	POS.	HT.	WT.	AGE	CLASS
52	Adams, Bill	C.	6'2"	211	20	Jr.
66	Allmon, Dick	D.E.	6'0"	220	20	So.
54	Baccitich, John	C.	6'1"	222	21	Jr.
64	*Barry Steve	R.G.	6'2"	210	22	Sr.
17	Battle, Mike	S.	5'11"	164	19	So.
63	Blanche, John	L.G.	6'2"	215	19	So.
78	Born, Dennis	L.T.	6'1"	235	20	Jr.
31	Bowie, Wilson	L.H.	6'1"	190	20	So.
26	Cahill, Ray	L.E.	6'1"	208	21	Sr.
30	Cashman, Pat	ROV.	5'11"	175	19	Jr.
79	Crane, Dennis	D.T.	6'5"	257	21	Jr.
33	Dale, Steve	L.H.	5'11"	185	19	So.
83	Drake, Ron	L.E.	6'0"	172	20	Jr.
59	Ferguson, Jim	L.B.-C.	6'4"	224	24	Jr.
65	Garland, Cal	R.G.	6'1"	203	20	So.
21	Grady, Steve	L.H.	6'0"	200	21	Jr.
85	Hayhoe, Bill	R.E.	6'8"	239	20	So.
73	*Hayhoe, Jerry	L.T.	6'4"	243	22	Sr.
69	*Homan, Jim	R.G.	6'2"	225	21	Sr.
16	Hough, Dick	Q.B.	6'0"	175	20	Jr.
23	*Hull, Mike	F.B.	6'4"	219	21	Jr.
25	*Hunter, Mike	R.H.	5'9"	154	22	Sr.
41	Jaroncyk, Bill	D.H.	6'1"	176	19	Jr.
39	Kaiser, Bob	D.H.	6'0"	190	22	Sr.
46	**King, Eddie	ROV.	6'3"	220	22	Sr.
84	Klein, Bob	R.E.	6'5"	230	19	So.
37	Kochinas, Tony	D.H.	5'9"	175	19	So.
28	Lawrence, Jim	R.H.	5'11"	182	20	So.
82	Leon, Rich	L.E.	6'1"	177	19	Jr.
36	*McCall, Don	L.H.	5'11"	189	22	Sr.
22	McCullouch, Earl	S.	5'11"	168	20	Jr.
75	*Magner, Gary	D.T.	6'3"	215	21	Jr.
67	*May, Ray	D.E.	6'2"	221	21	Sr.
86	Miller, Bob	R.E.	6'4"	220	20	So.
71	*Moore, Denis	D.T.	6'5"	231	22	Sr.
24	Motley, Marv	L.H.	5'9"	180	20	Jr.
18	Nungesser, Kendall	D.H.	6'2"	195	19	So.
32	Nyquist, Paul	S.	5'10"	180	21	So.
53	Oliver, Ralph	M.G.	6'1"	215	22	Jr.
92	O'Malley, Jack	R.T.	6'4"	261	20	Jr.
15	Page, Toby	Q.B.	6'0"	190	20	Jr.
61	*Petrill, Larry	M.G.	6'0"	214	21	Sr.
88	*Rossovich, Tim	D.E.	6'5"	220	20	Jr.
80	*Salness, Ty	D.E.	6'1"	200	21	Jr.
76	*Scarpace, Mike	L.T.	6'1"	239	20	Jr.
38	Scott, Dan	F.B.	5'10"	200	19	So.
89	**Shaw, Nate	D.H.	6'2"	192	21	Sr.
12	**Sherman, Rod	R.H.	6'0"	190	21	Sr.
43	Skarg, Ken	F.B.	6'1"	205	19	So.
55	Snow, Jim	L.B.	5'11"	215	19	So.
14	Sogge, Steve	Q.B.	5'10"	178	19	So.
58	Swanson, Steve	L.B.	5'10"	200	20	Jr.
74	Taylor, Mike	D.T.	6'5"	240	20	Jr.
70	*Wells, Harry	R.G.	6'1"	240	21	Jr.
44	*Williams, Homer	F.B.	6'1"	220	22	Sr.
10	*Winslow, Troy	Q.B.	6'0"	180	22	Sr.
68	Woudenberg, Dana	L.G.	6'1"	224	20	So.
77	*Yary, Ron	R.T.	6'6"	272	20	Jr.
50	*Young, Adrian	L.B.	6'1"	205	20	Jr.

*Indicates number of varsity letters won.

NOTRE DAME ALPHABETICAL ROSTER — 1966

NO.	NAME	POS.	HT.	WT.	AGE	CLASS
77	*Alexander, Harry	T.	6'1"	240	21	Sr.
90	Azzaro, Joe	K.	5'11"	190	20	Sr.
2	Belden, Bob	Q.B.	6'2"	205	19	So.
28	*Bleier, Bob (Rocky)	H.B.	5'11"	185	20	Jr.
33	Burgener, Mike	H.B.	5'10"	182	20	Jr.
32	*Conjar, Larry	F.B.	6'0"	212	20	Sr.
21	Criniti, Frank	H.B.	5'8"	173	19	So.
64	**Duranko, Pete	T.	6'2"	235	22	Sr.
38	Dushney, Ron	F.B.	5'11"	195	20	So.
47	**Eddy, Nick	H.B.	6'0"	195	22	Sr.
68	Fox, Roger	G.	5'11"	230	19	So.
20	Gladieux, Bob	H.B.	5'11"	185	19	So.
80	**Gmitter, Don	E.	6'2"	210	21	Sr.
54	*Goeddeke, George	C.	6'3"	228	21	Sr.
57	Gorman, Tim	G.	5'11"	220	21	Sr.
22	Haley, Dave	H.B.	5'11"	190	19	Jr.
5	Hanratty, Terry	Q.B.	6'1"	190	18	So.
74	*Hardy, Kevin	T.	6'5"	270	21	Jr.
34	Harshman, Dan	H.B.	6'0"	190	20	Jr.
84	Heaton, Mike	E.	6'2"	205	19	Jr.
86	Heneghan, Curt	E.	6'3"	190	18	So.
44	Holtzapfel, Mike	F.B.	6'1"	200	19	So.
51	*Horney, John	L.B.	5'11"	205	20	Sr.
65	Jeziorski, Ron	G.	5'10"	210	21	Sr.
58	Kelly, Gerald	C.	6'1"	205	20	Sr.
73	*Konieczny, Rudy	T.	6'0"	225	19	Jr.
75	Kuechenberg, Bob	T.	6'2"	225	18	So.
82	Kuzmicz, Mike	T.-E.	6'4"	235	19	Jr.
93	Lauck, Chuck	E.	6'1"	220	18	So.
41	Lavin, John	L.B.	6'4"	200	19	So.
61	**Lynch, Jim (Captain)	L.B.	6'1"	225	21	Sr.
69	Marsico, Joe	G.	6'0"	220	21	Sr.
56	*Martin, Dave	L.B.	6'0"	210	19	Jr.
31	*May, Paul	F.B.	5'10"	205	20	Jr.
79	McKinley, Tom	T.-G.	6'1"	218	19	So.
55	Monty, Tim	C.	6'0"	198	19	So.
72	Norri, Eric	T.	6'2"	240	19	So.
3	O'Brien, Coley	Q.B.	5'11"	173	19	So.
40	*O'Leary, Tom	H.B.	5'10"	185	20	Jr.
81	**Page, Alan	E.	6'5"	238	21	Sr.
50	Pergine, John	L.B.	6'0"	210	19	Jr.
62	*Quinn, Steve	C.	6'1"	215	20	Jr.
19	Quinn, Tom	H.B.	6'1"	192	19	So.
1	Rassas, Kevin	H.B.-E.	6'1"	190	20	Jr.
76	**Regner, Tom	G.	6'1"	245	22	Sr.
87	*Rhoads, Tom	E.	6'2"	220	21	Sr.
11	Ryan, Jim	K.	5'10"	185	22	Sr.
88	Sack, Allen	E.	6'3"	205	21	Sr.
70	Schnurr, Fred	T.	6'3"	245	20	Sr.
7	*Schoen, Tom	H.B.	5'11"	178	20	Jr.
71	Seiler, Paul	T.	6'4"	235	20	Sr.
85	Seymour, Jim	E.	6'4"	205	19	So.
25	Smithberger, Jim	H.B.	6'1"	190	19	Jr.
92	Snow, Paul	E.	6'1"	180	18	So.
91	Stenger, Brian	E.	6'4"	210	19	So.
59	*Swatland, Dick	G.	6'2"	225	20	Sr.
89	VanHuffel, Alan	L.B.	6'2"	210	20	Jr.
35	Vuillemin, Ed	L.B.-E.	6'1"	205	18	So.

*Denotes number of varsity letters won

1967

CHAPTER 40

"O JESUS, THERE HE GOES AGAIN."
. . . Roger Valdiserri, 1967

The afternoon of November 26 *was* long for John McKay, but it was nothing compared to the winter of '66. Everywhere he went he was reminded of 51-0. He said later, "If Notre Dame had as many students and alumni as I met that year, the school must have had an annual enrollment of about two million." This year with the record standing at 25 wins for Notre Dame, 11 for USC, and two ties, the Trojans were scheduled to meet the Irish in Notre Dame, Indiana, where they hadn't won since 1939.

But Coach McKay doesn't believe in jinxes. He didn't have to that year. He had a 4-0 record going into the contest and was ranked number one in the nation and he had acquired a running back of some ability. He came to USC from a junior college, City College of San Francisco. There he was a defensive safety . . . when one of the halfbacks was injured, he switched to offense to fill in. In two years he shattered every scoring record in junior collegiate football history. He scored 54 touchdowns and gained 2552 yards . . . he was 6-2, 205 pounds of solid muscle, and could run the hundred in 9.4. His name was Orenthel James Simpson.*

Notre Dame was 2-1, due to an upset by Purdue, but had started breathing fire again the previous week . . . they had beaten Iowa by fifty points and were ranked fifth.

McKay may not have believed in hexes, but the oddsmakers did, and they established the Irish as 13-point favorites. The Trojans took off for Notre Dame, Indiana, with 71 players, 16 of whom were seniors that had been outscored by Notre Dame the last two years 79-7. The juniors still had vivid memories of 51-0. Eight of the defensive starters had played in that game.

The night before the game, at one of Notre Dame's famous frenetic pep rallies, Irish defensive coach John Ray delivered a fiery speech in pure Rocknese.

"Southern California has an outstanding football team, and a big back by the name of O. J. Simpson."

"Who's he, who's he, who's he?" chanted the crowd.

By the time the game was over the following day they knew.

McKay had some bitter memories of the 1965 game, aside from the obvious pain of losing. That game, of course, had been played at Notre Dame and the Irish had kept the Trojan

team waiting on the field cooling off and taking abuse from the Notre Dame fans. This year he vowed not to be the first on the field. It nearly cost him the game. As he and the team waited in the dressing room the referee came in and warned the coach to have his team on the field in five minutes. McKay snapped, "We aren't going out on the field until Notre Dame does."

"I'll call the game," said the official.

"What does that mean?" asked McKay.

"That means Notre Dame will win 2-0 on a forfeit."

"That," growled McKay, "would be the best deal we've ever gotten in this stadium." Clearly the coach was not in one of his better moods that afternoon. He was also annoyed by the extreme noise of the crowd which drowned out SC's offensive signals. "If you can't be heard," he told quarterback Steve Sogge, "walk away from center. I don't care if they penalize you all the way to the end zone. You have a right to be heard." The crowd was raucous all right, but Sogge got more cooperation from the officials than McKay had anticipated. They simply called time until the din subsided.

The first half was sloppy, both teams banging away like a couple of heavyweights with a lot of strength and little direction. Hanratty did manage to score in the second quarter on a three yard keeper, so the Irish led at half time 7-0.

McKay had told his men before the game, "To lose this game would be a crime. You're too good. This time you're better than Notre Dame. If you lose you'll know you've lost to an inferior team." At half time he reminded them.

It must have worked. After Notre Dame's Chuck Landolfi fumbled the opening half kickoff on his own 20 and linebacker Steve Swanson recovered for the Trojans on the 18, it was Southern Cal all the way. Seven plays later Simpson smashed over left tackle from the one, Rikki Aldridge converted, and the score was tied. Seven minutes later O. J. swept around left end for 36 yards and another score. Aldridge added the extra point, and a few minutes later kicked a 22 yard field goal.

In the fourth quarter Mike Battle intercepted a Hanratty pass and brought it to the Irish 17. From there it took Simpson just once to slam into the end zone. The final score, 24-7.

Coach Parseghian gave most of the credit for SC's win to an

While in college he discovered that on his birth certificate his name was spelled Orenthel rather than Orenthal. But as every football fan knows, it has always been O.

OJ Simpson dives for first touchdown

inspired Trojan defense. Terry Hanratty, one of the best quarterbacks in the country, could complete only ten passes out of 23 and had five picked off. Coley O'Brien, his substitute and engineer of last year's humiliation, was 4 for 16 and was robbed twice. The only real Irishman on the field, SC's Adrian Young, born in Dublin, had four interceptions and 12 tackles. His partner linebacker, Jim Snow, had 14. Simpson had 38 carries for 150 yards and had scored all three touchdowns. Now the Irish knew who he was. Eastern sportswriters had nicknamed O. J. "The Orange Juice Kid." "Nonsense," said Roger Valdiserri, Notre Dame publicist.

"The O. J. should stand for O Jesus, as in O Jesus, there he goes again."

Back in Los Angeles a cheering crowd of three thousand greeted the conquering Trojans as they arrived at the airport. O. J. stepped off the plane wearing a big grin and a big round button which proudly commanded, "Kiss me, I'm Irish."

For Coach John McKay it was a moment of triumph. It was his biggest win as head coach up to that date, and it helped to erase the nightmare of 1966. But what must have seemed even sweeter was that he had just handed Coach Parseghian the worst beating he had received since Ara took over at Notre Dame. And he had whipped the jinx.

The last time USC had beaten Notre Dame on their own home ground, Johnny McKay was a sixteen-year-old schoolboy in Shinnston, West Virginia. The 28-year-old reign of terror had ended. McKay had killed 'em.

. . . But in every reign a little life must fall.

Quarterback Steve Sogge sets Trojan team

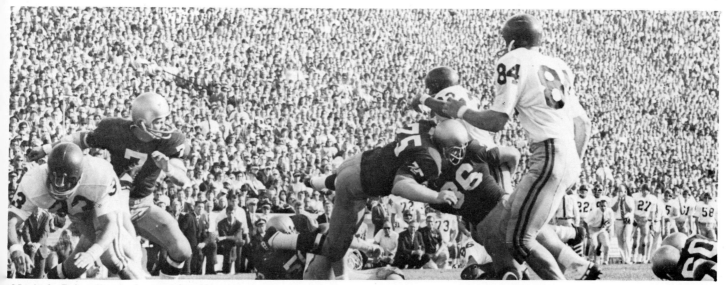
OJ is hit by Robert Kuechenberg and Curt Henegan

1967 NOTRE DAME ALPHABETICAL ROSTER

NO.	PLAYER	POS.	WT.
90	*Azzaro, Joe	K.	190
2	Belden, Bob	Q.B.	205
28	**Bleier, Bob (Captain)	H.B.	195
64	Brennan, Terry	O.T.	235
33	*Burgener, Mike	D.B.	182
21	Criniti, Frank	H.B.	180
81	deArrieta, Jim	O.E.	190
10	Devine, Edgar	LB	195
49	Donohue, Pete	H.B.	193
38	Dushney, Ron	F.B.	195
53	Fischer, Ray	G.	230
57	Freebery, Joe	L.B.	207
83	Furlong, Nick	O.E.	200
88	Furlong, Tom	D.E.	205
46	Gasser, John	D.B.	185
20	*Gladieux, Bob	H.B.	185
6	Gores, Tom	Q.B.	180
22	Haley, Dave	H.B.	190
5	*Hanratty, Terry	Q.B.	200
74	**Hardy, Kevin	D.E.	270
34	*Harshman, Dan	H.B.	190
84	Heaton, Mike	O.E.	205
86	Heneghan, Curt	D.B.-	190
51	Holtzapfel, Mike	C.	215
14	Hurd, Bill	O.E.	180
70	Jockisch, Bob	D.T.	260
71	Kelly, George	D.T.	220
76	Kennedy, Charles	O.T.	240
48	Kiliany, Dennis	L.B.	205
73	*Konieczny, Rudy	O.T.	225
75	*Juechenberg, Bob	O.T.	245
78	Kunz, George	O.E.	240
39	Lambert, Steve	D.E.	210
17	Landolfi, Chuck	F.B.	210
41	Lavin, John	L.B.	205
93	Lauck, Chuck	D.E.	225
87	Lawson, Tom	O.E.	230
56	**Martin, Dave	L.B.	210
77	McCoy, Mike	D.T.	270
60	**McGill, Mike	L.B.	225
79	*McKinley, Tom	G.	235
30	Merlitti, Jim	L.B.	205
55	*Monty, Tim	C.	220
37	Nash, Tom	F.B.	225
23	Ness, Rick	L.B.	215
72	Norri, Eric	D.T.	245
3	*O'Brien, Coley	Q.B.	180
40	**O'Leary, Tom	D.B.	185
36	Olson, Bob	L.B.	225
50	*Pergine, John	L.B.	215
80	Poskon, Dewey	D.E.	225
62	*Quinn, Steve	C.	225
19	Quinn, Tom	D.B.	200
65	Racanelli, Vito	G.	210
89	Rassas, Kevin	D.E.	218
11	Reid, Don	D.B.	185
61	Reilly, Jim	G.-O.T.	230
12	Reynolds, Tom	L.B.	193
63	Ruzicka, Jim	G.	235
43	Ryan, Kevin	H.B.	200
7	**Schoen, Tom	D.B.	178
24	Schumacher, Larry	L.B.	205
85	*Seymour, Jim	O.E.	205
18	Slettvet, Tom	F.B.	202
25	*Smithberger, Jim	D.B.	190
92	Snow, Paul	O.E.-F.L.	180
91	*Stenger, Brian	D.E.	215
59	**Swatland, Dick	G.	235
68	Swearingen, Tim	O.T.	235
13	Torrado, Rene	K.	170
69	Tuck, Ed	O.T.	235
27	VanHuffel, Alan	L.B.	210
35	Vuillemin, Ed	D.E.	205
54	Vuillemin, Larry	C.	230
96	Winegardner, Jim	O.E.	225
67	Wisne, Gerry	D.T.	235
32	Ziegler, Ed	F.B.	213

1967 USC VARSITY ALPHABETICAL ROSTER

NO.	NAME	POS.	HT.	WT.
27	Aldridge, Rikki	R.H.	6'1"	185
66	Allmon, Dick	C.	6'0"	220
17	*Battle, Mike	S.-D.H.	6'1"	175
63	*Blanche, John	M.G.	6'2"	220
78	Born, Dennis	L.T.	6'1"	237
31	Bowie, Wilson	L.H.	6'1"	193
44	Brown, Bob	F.B.	6'3"	211
30	*Cashman, Pat	D.H.	5'11"	180
57	Coleman, John	C.	6'4"	225
82	Curtis, Mike	D.E.	6'0"	205
33	Dale, Steve	R.H.	5'11"	193
83	*Drake, Ron	L.E.	6'0"	170
60	Dunn, Brodie	C.	6'1"	240
16	Durko, Sandy	S.-D.H.	6'1"	170
62	Fielder, Reg	M.G.	5'10"	200
21	*Grady, Steve	L.H.	6'3"	201
56	Gunn, Jim	D.E.	6'1"	200
85	Hayhoe, Bill	D.E.	6'8"	254
7	Holmgren, Mike	Q.B.	6'4"	220
41	*Jaroncyk, Bill	D.H.	6'1"	188
51	Jensen, Bob	L.B.	6'0"	223
64	Khasigian, Fred	L.G.	5'11"	215
84	*Klein, Bob	R.E.	6'5"	235
28	*Lawrence, Jim	R.H.	5'11"	185
68	Lehmer, Steve	L.G.	6'2"	225
70	McArthur, Gary	D.T.	6'4"	245
22	McCullouch, Earl	L.E.	5'11"	170
75	**Magner, Gary	D.T.	6'3"	220
59	Melillo, Jim	L.T.	6'3"	235
86	*Miller, Bob	R.E.	6'5"	225
18	Nungesser, Kendall	D.H.	6'2"	195
90	Obbema, Joe	D.E.	6'2"	210
53	*Oliver, Ralph	M.G.	6'1"	220
73	O'Malley, Jack	D.T.	6'4"	255
15	*Page, Toby	Q.B.	6'0"	190
26	Robinson, Skip	R.H.	5'11"	175
88	**Rossovich, Tim	D.E.	6'5"	235
80	**Salness, Ty	ROV.	6'1"	185
76	**Scarpace, Mike	R.G.	6'1"	250
38	*Scott, Dan	F.B.	5'10"	205
71	Scott, Bubba	D.T.	6'1"	235
46	Shaw, Jerry	ROV.	6'0"	190
32	Simpson, O. J.	L.H.	6'1"	202
72	Smith, Sid	R.T.	6'5"	257
55	*Snow, Jim	L.B.	5'10"	210
12	Sogge, Steve	Q.B.	5'10"	170
54	Stahr, Dallas	L.B.	6'2"	215
58	Swanson, Steve	L.B.	5'10"	200
74	*Taylor, Mike	L.T.	6'5"	238
81	Terry, Tony	D.T.	6'3"	220
77	**Yary, Ron	R.T.	6'5"	245
50	**Young, Adrian	L.B.	6'1"	220
61	McConnell, Steve	M.G.	6'2"	235
93	Gregg, Mike	D.T.	6'2"	215

1968
CHAPTER 41
". . . WOULD YOU CONSIDER WINNING THIS GAME FOR THE COACHING STAFF'S EIGHT WIVES AND THEIR TWENTY-THREE CHILDREN?"
. . . John McKay, 1968

The Trojans went on to a 10-1 season in 1967, their only loss was to Oregon State. They defeated Indiana in the Rose Bowl and McKay had his second national title. O. J. Simpson was named All American, as was Adrian Young, Tim Rossovich, and for the second time, Ron Yary.

Parseghian's 1967 team captained by "Rocky" Bleier* boasted seven All Americans. Three of them, Tom Schoen, Kevin Hardy and Jim Seymour for the second year, mentioned for the first time; Mike McGill, John Pergine, Dick Swatland, and Jim Smithberger. All but Jim Seymour were gone in 1968 and the Irish were ranked number nine, but they still had Terry Hanratty and Coley O'Brien, now a halfback, but still capable of filling in at quarterback if needed. They also had a sophomore quarterback named Joe Theisman who showed some promise. He was needed . . . by game time on November 30, Hanratty was out of commission and 19-year-old Theisman was the starting quarterback.

United Press International rated USC tops in the nation, but Associated Press picked Ohio State number 1 . . . and they were to meet the Trojans in the Rose Bowl. McKay knew that a win over Notre Dame would probably give him undisputed possession of first place in all the polls. But he had more than a mythical poll position at stake. He had within his grasp what every coach covets. A perfect season. So far it had been just that. They had been undefeated in nine games and were expected to win over Notre Dame, but by only two points . . . an opinion of the oddsmakers which confounded the Trojan fans and most of the west coast. What made it even more confusing was that in the same week O. J. Simpson had been named Back of the Year for the second straight season as well as All American, and earlier had been named the Heisman Trophy winner. He was within 25 yards of breaking Mike Garrett's three year NCAA rushing record of 3,221 in only *two* seasons.

"He's absolutely fantastic," said Parseghian. "Probably the most outstanding runner of our time."

Maybe the bookmakers were looking at the Notre Dame stats which showed them second in the nation on offense with

OJ Simpson, USC's greatest runner, All American and Heisman Trophy Winner says goodby in last game of his career

OJ sweeps left for short gain

an average of 511.3 yards a game. They didn't have an O. J. but they managed with rather unspectacular runners to rush an average 309 yards per game and score an average of 39.4 points a game. Their defense had allowed only 82.3 yards per game on the ground.

The bookies turned out to be wrong, but not by much. On November 30th, 82,659 men, women and children poured into the Coliseum to see if Notre Dame could stop O. J. Simpson.

They could. In twenty-one carries he couldn't get more than 55 yards.

Using a six man front with two linebackers in tight, the Irish displayed hubris bordering on contempt for the Heisman Trophy winner and grudgingly allowed him 55 yards on 21 carries. His longest run of the afternoon was seven yards . . . the lowest single game score for the Juice in his career at USC.

At half time with the Irish leading 21-7, the SC coaching staff and quarterback Steve Sogge began to suspect that Simpson might not be too successful against the big Notre Dame line. Good thinking. At halftime he had gained only twenty-three yards.

The game had started out as though the Trojan Horse might run away. Joe Theisman threw a pass to Jim Seymour, but SC's Sandy Durko intercepted and sprinted 21 yards for the touchdown. Ron Ayala made a successful conversion and after only 40 seconds the score was USC 7, Notre Dame 0. But Notre Dame answered with an 86 yard attack in 18 plays with Ron Dushney going in from the three. Scott Hempel converted and the score was tied.

Three and a half minutes before the first quarter ended, Bob Gladieux topped off a 77-yard drive in four plays with a 57-yard run on a pitchout to score another 6 . . . Hempel added another. 14-7 Notre Dame.

In the second period Joe Theisman and quarterback-turned-halfback Coley O'Brien (by then it must have seemed to the Trojans that Coley had been at Notre Dame for seven years) decided to put on their own little show. It was, to say the least, spectacular, and it sure fooled the Trojans. With thirty sec-

OJ scores from 1 yard out on forth down

onds left in the half, from the 13-yard line of SC Theisman pitched out to flanker O'Brien. Coley put on the brakes and threw back to the left to Theisman who had put a move on Trojan tackle Tony Terry. Theisman didn't even have to break stride . . . he merrily skipped into the end zone for another 6 . . . a few moments later Hempel made it 21-7.

At half time McKay made some changes. He had to . . . the attack had been built around Simpson, and Simpson had been stopped. Adjustments had to be made. Simpson was not just double covered, he was quadruple covered. McKay decided to use O. J. as a decoy and have Sogge fake to him but throw to Terry De Kraii, Sam Dickerson or Bob Chandler. He bolstered the defense and in the third quarter the strategy began to pay off. Dickerson made 11 on a pass from Sogge, then De Kraii made 18 for a first down on the 38. Chandler got to the 13 and Simpson carried it the rest of the way in three running plays and with Ayala's help the 65-yard drive netted another seven points. The Trojans had some help from the Irish on a pass interference call that gave them a first down on their own 27

and kept the drive alive.

Gerry Shaw, the Trojan defensive roverback, probably saved the season for USC. He intercepted Joe Theisman's pass intended for O'Brien at the Trojan 24, and raced to the 46. A few plays later Sogge fired a pass to Dickerson on the line, he stepped in, Ayala made the point after good, and the score was tied 21-21.

There was plenty of time for both teams to break the tie and win the game . . . over ten minutes . . . but both teams muffed it. The Irish missed two field goals of 47 and 33 yards and Steve Sogge passed to Simpson over the middle for a first down at the Trojan 39, but there were only 29 seconds to play by that time and the Trojans were getting a little nervous. Dickerson got behind the Irish secondary, but Sogge's pass was about two feet short . . . the game ended 21-21.

Naturally, neither coach was overjoyed. "Give SC credit for coming back," said Coach Parseghian. "At least we didn't lose to number one."

"I'd play out there 'til midnight," said Coach McKay. "I

OJ stopped cold

SC quarterback, Steve Sogge

just don't like ties. Ties are what men get for Christmas and never wear."

Nor were the players pleased.

"Down deep in my heart," said Joe Theisman, "I think we should have won it. We had them on the run."

Said O. J. Simpson, ". . . I'm a little disappointed. I wanted to go out a winner."

He did. He just didn't feel like it that afternoon. In only two years he set eleven Southern California records, including records talented and determined Mike Garrett had labored three years to set. After the Notre Dame game, Dr. Topping announced that O. J.'s number would be retired. No other Trojan will ever wear a jersey with number 32 on it . . . that belongs to Orenthel James Simpson . . . permanently. One hell of a football player, and one hell of a man.

McKay relates in his biography, *A Coach's Story*, that at half time he knew his team was in trouble. He also sensed they were, in the vernacular, uptight. He looked at his players. "Men," he said, "it's obvious you're not going to win this game for yourselves. In that case, would you consider winning it for the coaching staff's eight wives and 23 children."

So SC ended its season with a 9-1 record, and lost its number one rank in the nation. Then to add insult to injury, Ohio State beat them 27-16 in the Rose Bowl, despite O. J.'s 80 yard touchdown run in the opening few minutes and the 171 yards he gained that New Year's day.

Notre Dame had seven wins, two losses and, of course, the tie with USC. Associated Press sportswriters ranked them number five, UPI thought number 9 was more like it. Both coaches vowed to get even next year, and even they got. Very even.

Another tie.

Left to right, Jeff Zimmerman, Bob Gladieux, Terry
Hanratty, Jim Seymour, Ara Parseghian

1968 NOTRE DAME VARSITY ALPHABETICAL ROSTER

NAME	POS.	WT.
Allan, Dennis	H.B.	190
Belden, Robert	Q.B.	205
Brennan, Terence	O.T.	230
Buches, Stephen	C.	235
*Criniti, Frank	H.B.	180
deArrieta, James	D.H.B.-P.	190
*Dushney, Ronald	F.B.	195
Eaton, George	S.E.	200
Fischer, Raymond	O.G.-T.	220
Freebery, Joseph	L.B.	207
Gasser, John	D.H.B.	178
**Gladieux, Robert	H.B.	185
Gores, Thomas	Q.B.	180
**Hanratty, Terrence	Q.B.	200
Hempel, Scott	L.B.-K.	235
Heneghan, Curtis	D.H.B.	190
Holtzapfel, Michael	C.	215
Jackson, Ernest	D.H.B.	182
*Jockisch, Robert	D.T.	260
Johnson, Ronald	L.B.	208
Kelly, Timothy	L.B.	212
*Kennedy, Charles	O.T.	240
Kondrla, Michael	L.B.	215
Kos, Gary	D.T.	234
**Kuechenberg, Robert	D.E.	245
*Kunz, George (Co-Capt.)	O.T.	240
Lambert, Stephen Wayne	D.E.	210
Landolfi, Charles	H.B.-F.B.	205
*Lauck, Charles	D.E.	225
Lawson, Thomas	T.E.	230
Martin, Michael	O.T.	260
*McCoy, Michael	D.T.	270
**McKinley, Thomas	O.G.	235
Merlitti, James	L.B.	205
**Monty, Timothy	C.	220
Mudron, Patrick	D.T.	240
Nash, Thomas	D.E.	225
*Norri, Eric	D.T.	245
**O'Brien, Coleman	H.B.	180
*Olson, Robert (Co-Capt.)	L.B.	230
Poskon, Dewey	T.E.	220
*Quinn, Thomas	D.H.B.	200
Reid, Donald	D.H.B.	185
*Reilly, James	O.G.	230
Schumacher, Lawrence	L.B.	205
**Seymour, James	S.E.	205
*Snow, Paul	S.E.	180
Standring, John	D.H.B.	190
Theismann, Joseph	Q.B.	170
*Tuck, Edward	O.G.-T.	235
Wack, Stephen	D.H.B.	190
*Winegardner, James	T.E.	225
Wisne, Gerald	D.T.	230
Wright, James	L.B.	220
Wittliff, Philip	L.B.	205
Ziegler, Edward	H.B.	213
Zilly, John	O.T.	240
*Zimmerman, Geoffrey	F.B.	205
Ziznewski, Jay	D.T.	250
Zloch, Charles	D.H.B.	180

1968 USC VARSITY ALPHABETICAL ROSTER

NO.	NAME	POS.	HGT.	WGT.
58	*Allmon, Dick	C.	6'1"	230
8	Ayala, Ron	S.-K.	5'9"	171
17	**Battle, Mike	D.H.	6'1"	175
23	Berry, Mike	L.H.	5'9"	192
67	Berry, Bob	L.G.	6'1"	225
54	Blanche, John	L.B.	6'2"	217
31	Bowie, Wilson	L.H.	6'1"	189
82	Brucker, Bill	D.E.	6'2"	216
9	Chandler, Bob	R.H.	6'1"	174
79	Clark, Ron	D.T.	6'1"	221
39	Covington, Humphrey	F.B.	5'11"	198
72	Cowlings, Al	D.T.	6'5"	250
33	Dale, Steve	L.H.	5'11"	191
19	DeKraai, Terry	L.E.	5'10"	188
18	Dickerson, Sam	L.E.	6'2"	190
16	Durko, Sandy	D.H.	6'2"	173
14	Failor, Walt	ROV.	6'2"	196
62	Fielder, Reg	L.B.	5'10"	202
24	Franklin, Herman	R.H.	5'11"	174
81	Gallaher, Ron	R.E.	6'3"	207
65	George, Greg	L.G.	6'0"	216
88	Grissum, Jim	D.E.	6'1"	228
83	*Gunn, Jim	D.E.	6'1"	208
50	Haluchak, Mike	L.B.	5'11"	195
85	*Hayhoe, Bill	D.E.	6'8"	250
42	Holland, Bill	F.B.	6'1"	204
7	Holmgren, Mike	Q.B.	6'4"	220
43	Hudson, Tyrone	R.H.	6'0"	175
51	Jensen, Bob	L.B.	6'0"	215
64	*Khasigan, Fred	L.G.	6'0"	222
84	**Klein, Bob	R.E.	6'5"	238
28	**Lawrence, Jim	R.H.	6'0"	179
68	*Lehmer, Steve	R.G.	6'2"	230
70	McArthur, Gary	D.T.	6'5"	235
57	McConnell, Steve	D.T.	6'2"	221
61	Melillo, Jim	R.G.	6'2"	219
86	**Miller, Bob	R.E.	6'5"	229
78	Montgomery, Marv	L.T.	6'6"	229
67	Mooers, Doug	D.T.	6'4"	245
22	Morgan, Mike	R.H.	6'1"	170
76	Mullins, Gerry	L.T.	6'3"	228
75	Neilsen, Carl	R.T.	6'6"	255
34	Obbema, Joe	F.B.	6'2"	220
59	Oberreuter, Rich	C.	6'2"	225
37	Olszewski, Bob	L.B.-P.	6'1"	190
73	O'Malley, Jack	L.T.	6'4"	243
12	Orcutt, Gary	R.H.	6'1"	176
29	Pharris, Ron	R.H.	6'0"	170
48	Ray, Terrel	D.H.	5'11"	169
56	Redding, Bill	M.G.	6'1"	213
26	Robinson, Skip	D.H.	6'0"	169
38	**Scott, Dan	F.B.	5'10"	207
71	*Scott, Willard	M.G.	6'1"	240
46	*Shaw, Gerry	ROV.	6'0"	194
32	*Simpson, O. J.	L.H.	6'2"	207
45	Sims, Leonard	ROV.	6'0"	185
36	Smith, Martin	F.B.	5'9"	198
77	Smith, Sid	R.T.	6'4"	251
55	**Snow, Jim	L.B.	5'10"	212
6	*Sogge, Steve	Q.B.	5'10"	175
63	Stirling, Bob	L.G.	6'2"	210
74	*Terry, Tony	D.T.	6'3"	245
60	Yary, Wayne	R.G.	6'1"	216
15	Young, John	ROV.-P.	6'2"	185

CHAPTER 42
"GOD WAS A TROJAN ON THAT KICK"
. . . John McKay, 1969

One of the problems with a tie is that it is a little like artificial insemination. The game gets played, there are some results, but no one has much fun. A dead heat on a merry-go-round. Duffy Daugherty, former head coach of Michigan State, once observed that playing to a tie is like kissing your sister. If nobody wins, everybody loses a little. Especially coaches . . . a very competitive breed.

It is quite probable that two more competitive men than Ara Parseghian and John McKay do not exist. And that quality more than any other single characteristic contributed to their coaching genius . . . so imagine their frustration when for the second consecutive year they played to a tie. McKay, the gambler, felt that in 1968 the Trojans had tied Notre Dame, but in 1969 the Irish and a cautious Parseghian tied Southern Cal. It looked that way. With less than seven minutes to play in the game, Notre Dame scored as a result of a blocked punt. When asked later whether he had considered going for a two point conversion and a possible 15-14 win, Ara replied, "I wasn't even tempted. I noticed that Big Ten statistics show that their teams are 91% successful kicking conversions, but they have made only three of seventeen tries for two points."

Competitive yes . . . but cautious . . . and remember he still had six and a half minutes. In the final two he nearly did it. Football is a game of inches. If the goal posts had been four inches lower or Scott Hempel's kick from 48 yards out four inches higher, it would have been 17-14 Notre Dame and no one would have second guessed the Irish head coach. If . . . but then if the hound hadn't stopped to scratch a flea, he would have caught the rabbit.

Notre Dame and the University of Southern California went to war again on a windy, chilly, lead gray autumn afternoon in an old brick stadium at Notre Dame, Indiana. On October 18, 1969 these two ancient and honored enemies faced each other on the field of combat for the forty-first time.

It was the fifth game of the season for John McKay's Trojans and they were unbeaten and ranked 3rd. They were called the "Wild Bunch." The Fighting Irish had lost one game to very tough Purdue, and had won three, including an impressive 45-0 pasting of Army the week before. They were ranked 10th. Nevertheless, the Irish, according to the wizards of odds, were three point favorites.

"How can we be favored?" asked Coach Parseghian. "USC is without question a much better team than it was offensively with O. J. Jimmy Jones gives them a fourth dimension in the backfield." Rockne, thou art mighty yet.

SC All American, Clarence Davis

Jones was a poised sophomore quarterback who had already thrown seven touchdown passes so far that season, and junior halfback Clarence Davis, the nation's number two rusher, had gained 56 more yards than O. J. had when he came to Notre Dame two years ago, and Clarence was just one of a crew of fleet-footed Trojan receivers.

Of course, the Irish were hardly bereft of talent. They had Mike McCoy, 6-5, 275 pound All American tackle (McKay said he looked as though he had come out of a dinosaur egg) who contained O. J. last year, and he led a defensive line that outweighed the Trojans by five pounds per man . . . Mike Kadish, 6-4, 249 at tackle, Bob Olsson 6-0 and 230 and Larry Schumacher, 6-0, 216 were quick and capable linebackers. They also had a big offensive line. Jim Reilly at 6-2, 247, guard Larry Di Nardo, 6-1, 230, and center Mike Oriard, 6-3, 221. And they still had quarterback Joe Theisman, whose favorite target had become sophomore split end Tom Gatewood. No . . . Notre Dame could hardly be declared a football disaster area.

And they did it to USC again. In 1965 it was Mike Garrett, in 1968 it was O. J. Simpson . . . in 1969 it was Clarence Davis they put in a bottle. He gained only 75 yards in thirty carries. The Irish seemed able to throttle SC's great running backs. In the first quarter Davis broke loose for a fifteen yard touchdown run, but it was called back. A holding penalty against SC nullified the score. "Questionable," said McKay later. Even before Davis' run the Trojans had worked their way down to the eight yard line of Notre Dame only to have Charlie Evans fumble the ball.

At the half the game was scoreless.

In the third quarter Theisman started to move his team. He did it well, 74 yards in eleven plays. Ed Ziegler caught one of his passes for 16 and a first down on the SC 46, tight end Dewey Poskon grabbed another for a first down at the 21. Poskon again receiving for another first down on the Trojan 7. Bill Barz finished the drive with a one yard plunge, Hempel converted and the score at 4:51 of the second half was 7-0.

Six minutes later Jimmy Jones had directed the Trojans 75

USC's "The Wild Bunch" Jim Gunn, Tody Smith, Bubba Scott, Al Cowlings, Charlie Weaver

yards in eleven plays to tie the score. De Kreii capped it with a 19 yard pass reception, but Dickerson, Davis and Jones all contributed. Ayata made it 7-7 and the third period ended.

Before the fourth quarter was one minute old, Tyrone Hudson intercepted Joe Theisman's pass and ran it back 25 yards to the Irish 15. From there Jones threw to Dickerson for another score, and the Trojans were ahead 14-7. But not for long. USC couldn't move the ball against Notre Dame's rock ribbed defense and was forced to punt. At the 33 John Young waited for the ball. On the other side of the line Mike McCoy waited over SC's center and right guard for a chance to annihilate John Young. When the snap came from center, McCoy nearly destroyed two linemen and charged Young. Young cooly and gracefully punted the ball right into the jaw of Mike McCoy. Big Mike didn't even blink. And to this day they say Mike McCoy has a face resembling a blocked punt. Walt Patulski recovered on the seven for the Irish and moments later Denny Allen snaked his way over, Hempel hit again, and the score was tied once more, 14-14, and that's the way the cookie

crumbled that day. During the first half Jimmy Jones was a little less than accurate with his passes. He sharpened up in the second half, but his receivers dropped the ball. It was an exercise in frustration for both teams. With two minutes left to play, the Irish were on the SC 31. Scott Hempel was poised for a field goal attempt. Joe Theisman held. The moment Scott kicked it you could tell it was well hit and accurate. Theisman and Hempel grabbed each other and started a war dance. John McKay closed his eyes.

The cheers and screams of the Notre Dame fans gurgled to moans and McKay opened his eyes. The first thing he saw was the ball bouncing around on the field, it had hit the crossbar squarely in the middle and rebounded back nearly to the twenty yard line. The second thing he saw was a white bedsheet, lettered in green, of course, and probably left over from the pep rally of the night before. "God made Notre Dame number one!" it screamed.

"Maybe," breathed John McKay, "but God was a Trojan on that kick."

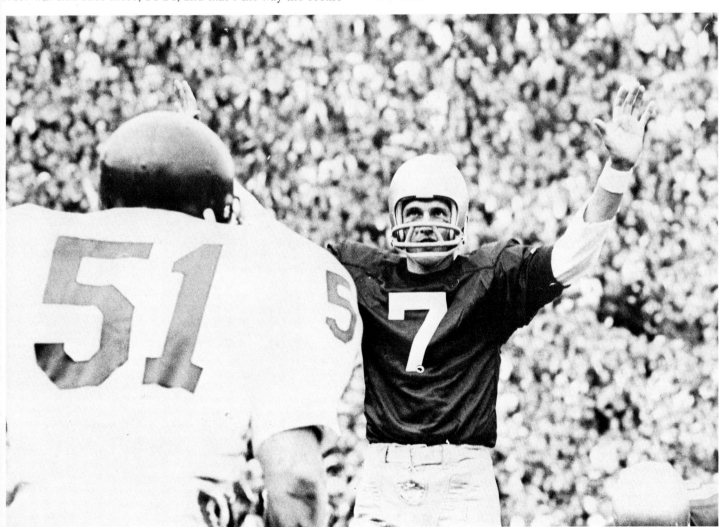

Joe Theisman asks for quiet as SC's Bob Jensen looks on from the defensive center

229

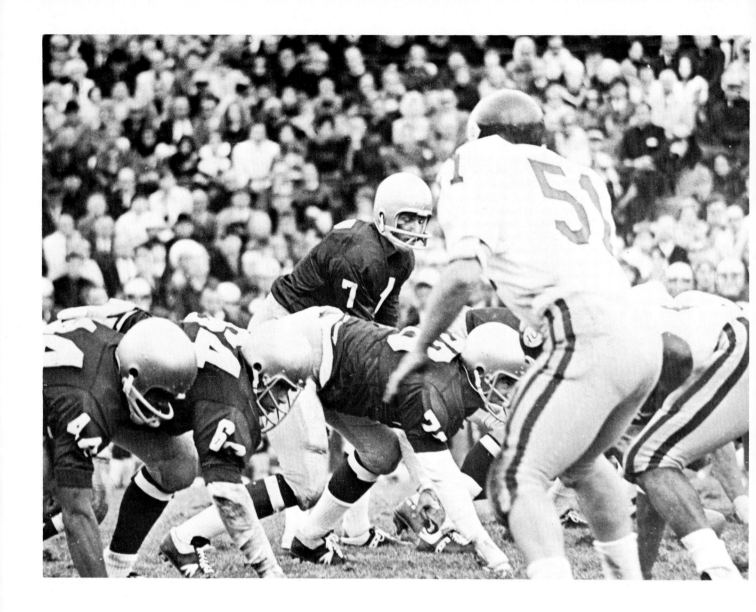

McKay said he never felt worse over a tie game . . . he was reasonably happy with the Trojan defense, but was damned unhappy with the pass receiving and nearly livid over some of the official judgments. He had every right to be happy with the defense. Al Cowlings made 14 tackles, Tody Smith got nine. Linebacker Greg Slough who had become a father just four days before the game, made seven unassisted tackles and helped to shut off the Irish running game. The tie cost USC the national championship, but the Trojans went unbeaten that year, beat Michigan 10-3 in the Rose Bowl, and ended up third in the national ratings.

Ara didn't say much after the game. Just the usual things . . . he was proud of his team, they fought well and hard. SC was a gallant foe and he was looking forward to next year's confrontation. You're damned right he was. He was already plotting something before the echo of the final gun had died away.

The Irish ended the 1969 season with an 8-1-1 record. Good, but for Ara Parseghian and Notre Dame that wasn't quite good enough.

Coach Parseghian and Joe Theisman

TROJANS — 1969

No.	Name	Info	No.	Name	Info
17	Ayala, Ron Junior	D.H.B.-K., 5'9", 180 Lakewood	7	Holmgren, Mike Senior	Q.B., 6'4", 227 San Francisco (Lincoln)
81	Bain, John Sophomore	L.B., 6'2", 210 St. Bernard's	43	Hudson, Tyrone Junior	D.H.B., 6'0", 177 Los Angeles (Roosevelt)
23	Berry, Mike Junior	L.H.B., 5'10", 199 Minneapolis (Central)	11	Jenkins, Bill Junior	D.H.B., 6'3", 172 Huntington Beach
9	Briner, Greg Sophomore	Q.B., 5'10", 177 Gardena	51	Jensen, Bob Senior	L.B., 6'0", 215 Anaheim (Magnolia)
57	Brown, Dave Sophomore	C., 6'1", 202 Eagle Rock	8	Jones, Jimmy Sophomore	Q.B., 6'1", 190 Harrisburg, Pa. (J. Harris)
10	Chandler, Bob Junior	R.H.B., 6'1", 180 Whittier	64	Khasigian, Fred Senior	L.G., 5'11", 223 Selma
62	Churchill, John Sophomore	L.B., 6'1", 223 Whittier (La Serna)	68	Lehmer, Steve Senior	R.G., 6'2", 238 Anaheim (Loara)
92	Clark, Ron Sophomore	D.T., 6'1", 232 San Diego (Morse)	70	McArthur, Gary Senior	D.T., 6'5", 234 Oregon (Mt. Vernon)
39	Covington, Humphrey Senior	F.B., 6'0", 196 San Diego (Lincoln)	78	Montgomery, Marv Junior	L.T., 6'6", 246 Sylmar
72	Cowlings, Al Senior	D.T., 6'5", 249 San Francisco (Galileo)	22	Morgan, Mike Sophomore	H.B., 6'0", 168 Santa Ana (Mater Dei)
54	Culbreath, Cliff Sophomore	L.B., 6'3", 218 San Bernardino (Pacific)	86	Mullins, Gerry Junior	R.E., 6'3", 235 Anaheim
28	Davis, Clarence Junior	L.H.B., 5'11", 194 Los Angeles (Washington)	73	Nielsen, Carl Junior	R.T., 6'6", 259 San Francisco (Lowell)
19	DeKraai, Terry Junior	O.E., 5'11", 185 Long Beach (Wilson)	59	Oberreuter, Rich Junior	C., 6'1", 230 San Diego (Kearny)
18	Dickerson, Sam Junior	O.E., 6'2", 194 Stockton (Franklin)	12	Orcutt, Gary Senior	L.E., 6'1", 185 Buena Park
16	Durko, Sandy Senior	D.H.B., 6'1", 176 West Covina	67	Papadakis, John Sophomore	L.B., 6'0", 230 Rolling Hills
21	Dyer, Bruce Sophomore	O.E., 6'0", 172 Dearborn Hts. (Riverside) Mich.	56	Redding, Bill Senior	M.G., 6'1", 217 Michigan (Grosse De)
68	Eriksen, Bob Sophomore	D.E., 6'2", 214 Fresno (Bullard)	31	Rollinson, Bruce Sophomore	D.H.B., 5'9", 186 Garden Grove (Mater Dei)
33	Evans, Charlie Junior	F.B., 6'1", 215 Gardena	79	Ruppert, Dick Sophomore	T., 6'4", 240 Palos Verdes
14	Failor, Walt Junior	ROV., 6'2", 199 Aberdeen, Wash.	71	Scott, Willard Senior	M.G., 6'1", 237 Los Angeles (Manual Arts)
6	Fassel, Jim Junior	Q.B., 6'2", 199 Anaheim	46	Shaw, Gerry Senior	ROV., 6'0", 180 Claremont
34	Fitzpatrick, Tom Sophomore	F.B., 6'0", 207 Anaheim	53	Slough, Greg Junior	L.B., 6'3", 237 San Diego (Point Loma)
24	Franklin, Herman Junior	D.H.B., 6'0", 170 Los Angeles (Jordan)	52	Smith, Martin Senior	L.B., 5'9", 198 Los Angeles (Fremont)
80	Gallaher, Ron Junior	R.E., 6'4", 220 Sylmar	77	Smith, Sid Senior	R.T., 6'4", 254 Long Beach (Wilson)
76	Gallaher, Allen Sophomore	T., 6'3", 225 Sylmar	93	Smith, Tody Junior	D.T.-M.G., 6'5", 237 Beaumont, Texas (Charlton)
30	Garrison, Edesel Sophomore	O.E., 6'0", 184 Compton (Centenial)	58	Stirling, Bob Sophomore	R.G., 6'2", 228 Santa Ana (Westminster)
65	George, Greg Junior	L.G., 5'11", 220 Corona Del Mar	74	Terry, Tony Senior	D.T., 6'3", 250 Long Beach (St. Anthony)
25	Giorgetti, Robert Sophomore	R.H.B., 5'9", 170 San Francisco (St. Ignatius)	75	Vella, John Sophomore	L.T., 6'4", 245 Sherman Oaks (Notre Dame)
61	Graf, Allan Sophomore	G., 6'2", 233 San Fernando	36	Walsh, Jim Sophomore	ROV., 6'1", 203 San Francisco (Riordan)
83	Gunn, Jim Senior	D.E., 6'1", 213 San Diego (Lincoln)	84	Weaver, Charles Junior	D.E., 6'2", 204 Richmond
50	Haluchak, Mike Junior	L.B., 5'11", 209 Concord (Clayton)	85	Weber, Scott Sophomore	D.E., 6'5", 204 Modesto
29	Harris, Lou Sophomore	H.B., 5'10", 194 Sacramento	60	Yary, Wayne Junior	R.G., 6'1", 219 Bellflower
38	Holland, Bill Sophomore	F.B., 6'1", 209 Los Angeles	15	Young, John Junior	D.H.B., 6'2", 186 La Mesa (Helix)

NOTRE DAME — 1969

22	*Allan, Dennis Junior	H.B., 5'11", 188 Ashtabula, Ohio (St. John's)
33	Barz, Bill Junior	F.B., 6'2", 216 Country Club Hills, Ill. (Rich Central)
64	*Brennan, Terry Senior	O.T., 6'4", 254 Chicago, Ill. (Weber)
58	Buches, Steve Junior	C., 6'3", 235 Clairton, Pa. (Jefferson)
29	Cloherty, John Sophomore	L.B., 6'0", 199 Pittsburgh, Pa. (Churchill)
60	Cotter, Bob Junior	D.T., 6'2", 215 Chicago, Ill. (St. Patrick)
17	Crotty, Mike Sophomore	H.B., 5'9", 178 Seattle, Wash. (Glacier)
81	deArrieta, Jim Senior	H.B.-S.E., 6'1", 188 Winnemucca, Nev. (Humboldt)
51	DePremio, Dennis Sophomore	C., 6'1", 212 Greensburg, Pa. (Central Catholic)
56	*DiNardo, Larry Junior	O.G., 6'1", 230 Queens, N.Y. (St. Francis)
89	*Eaton, Tom Junior	S.E., 6'3", 197 Lancaster, Ohio (Bishop Fenwick)
39	Eckman, Mike Sophomore	K., 6'0", 190 Lafayette, Ind. (Central Catholic)
23	Ellis, Clarence Sophomore	D.H.B., 6'0", 176 Grand Rapids, Mich. (Central)
2	Etter, Bill Sophomore	Q.B., 6'2", 185 Spokane, Wash. (Lewis & Clark)
83	*Furlong, Nick Senior	S.E., 6'1", 200 Pelham, N.Y. (Iona Prep)
4	Gardner, John Junior	Q.B., 6'2", 188 Colorado Springs, Colo. (St. Mary's)
70	Gasseling, Tom Junior	D.T., 6'2", 235 Wapato, Wash. (Wapato)
46	*Gasser, John Senior	D.H.B., 6'2", 186 Logan, Ohio (Logan)
44	Gatewood, Tom Sophomore	H.B.-S.E., 6'2", 203 Baltimore, Md. (City College)
6	Gores, Tom Senior	Q.B., 6'1", 182 Seattle Wash. (Seattle Prep)
91	Grenda, Ed. Sophomore	D.T., 6'2", 230 Masontown, Pa. (Albert Gallatin)
12	Gulyas, Edward Sophomore	D.H.B., 5'11", 190 San Carlos, Calif. (Carlmont)
68	Gustafson, Phil Sophomore	O.G., 6'2", 238 Galesburg, Ill. (Galesburg)
95	Hartzel, Nick Junior	T.E., 6'4", 233 White Bear Lake, Minn. (White Bear Lake)
52	*Hempel, Scott Junior	K., 6'0", 235 Copley, Ohio (Copley)
97	Hooten, Herman Sophomore	D.T., 6'2", 231 Tuskegee, Ala. (Tuskegee Institute)
20	Huff, Andy Sophomore	H.B., 5'11", 192 Toledo, Ohio (St. Francis)
53	Humbert, Jim Sophomore	O.G., 6'2", 225 Cincinnati, Ohio (Roger Bacon)
31	Johnson, Ron Junior	L.B., 6'1", 208 Seattle, Wash. (Seattle Prep)
72	Kadish, Mike Sophomore	D.T., 6'4", 249 Grand Rapids, Mich. (Central Catholic)
42	*Kelly, Tim Junior	L.B., 6'1", 212 Springfield, Ohio (Catholic Central)
76	**Kennedy, Charles Senior	O.T., 6'3", 240 Claymont, Del. (Salesianum)
34	Kondrla, Mike Junior	L.B., 6'0", 215 Oaklyn, N.Y. (Camden Cath.)
62	Kos, Gary Junior	O.G., 6'2", 234 Minneapolis, Minn. (DeLaSalle)
43	McHale, John Junior	L.B., 5'11", 181 Montreal Queb. (Atlanta Marist)
30	Merlitti, Jim Senior	L.B., 6'0", 205 Akron, Ohio (St. Vincent's)
14	Merritt, Tom Sophomore	H.B., 5'10", 190 Tacoma, Wash. (Fife)
18	Minnix, Bob Sophomore	H.B., 5'11", 184 Spokane, Wash. (Lewis & Clark)
74	Mudron, Pat Junior	D.T., 6'0", 240 Joliet, Ill. (Joliet Catholic)
59	Nash, Tom Senior	D.E., 6'1", 235 Flushing, N.Y. (Holy Cross)
88	Neidert, Bob Junior	L.B., 6'0", 216 Akron, Ohio (Archbishop Hoban)
28	Nightingale, Chuck Junior	H.B., 5'10", 165 Valparaiso, Ind. (Valparaiso)
50	Novakov, Dan Sophomore	C., 6'2", 226 Cincinnati, Ohio (Moeller)
36	**Olson, Bob, Co-captain Senior	L.B., 6'0", 230 Superior, Wis. (Superior)
54	*Oriard, Mike, Co-captain Senior	C., 6'3", 221 Spokane, Wash. (Gonzaga Prep)
45	Patton, Eric Sophomore	L.B., 6'2", 215 Santa Ana, Calif. (Mater Dei)
85	Patulski, Walt Sophomore	D.E., 6'5", 235 Liverpool, N.Y. (Christian Brothers)
3	Peiffer, Mike Sophomore	Q.B., 6'1", 190 South Bend, Ind. (St. Joseph's)
96	Pope, Al Sophomore	D.T., 6'3", 250 Iselin, N.Y. (J.F.K. Memorial)
80	Poskon, Dewey Senior	T.E., 6'4", 220 Elizabeth, Pa. (Forward)
41	Raterman, John Sophomore	L.B., 6'1", 200 Cincinnati, O. (Elder)
11	*Reid, Don Senior	D.H.B., 6'1", 191 Flint, Mich. (St. Mary's)
61	**Reilly, Jim Senior	O.T., 6'2", 247 Yonkers, N.Y. (Hackley Prep)
63	Ruzicka, Jim Senior	O.T., 6'1", 242 Portland, Ore. (Jesuit)
24	*Schumacher, Larry Senior	L.B., 6'0", 216 East Orange N.J. (Essex Catholic)
16	Sheahan, Jim Junior	D.H.B., 5'11", 188 Bellevue, Wash. (Bellevue)
92	*Snow, Paul Senior	S.E., 6'1", 190 Long Beach, Calif. (St. Anthony's)
15	*Standring, Jay Senior	D.H.B., 5'10", 190 Chicago, Ill. (Leo)
90	Stark, Craig Junior	S.E., 6'5", 210 South Bend, Ind. (St. Joseph's)
21	Stepaniak, Ralph Sophomore	D.H.B., 6'2", 195 Alpena, Mich. (Central Catholic)
93	Swendsen, Fred Sophomore	D.E., 6'4", 230 Tacoma, Wash. (Fife)
7	*Theismann, Joe Junior	Q.B., 6'0", 170 South River, N.J. (South River)
38	Thomann, Rick Sophomore	L.B., 6'1", 206 Akron, Ohio (Archbishop Hoban)
82	Trapp, Bill Sophomore	S.E., 6'3", 197 Chicago, Ill. (Mt. Carmel)
94	Williams, Scott Sophomore	T.E., 6'2", 225 Baltimore, Md. (Calvert Hall)
66	Witchger, Jim Sophomore	L.B., 5'10", 190 Indianapolis, Ind. (Brebeuf Prep)
26	Wittliff, Phil Senior	L.B., 6'2", 201 Port Huron, Mich. (Catholic Central)
40	Wright, Jim Junior	L.B., 6'1", 220 Sparta, N.J. (Sparta)

1970
CHAPTER 43

". . . YOU JUMP HIGHER, YOU DIVE DEEPER, YOU EVEN COME UP DRIER."
. . . Darrell Royal, 1970

Now it was McKay's turn to rain on Parseghian's parade, literally and figuratively. The Irish arrived in Los Angeles unbeaten in nine starts. They were ranked third and on their way to the Cotton Bowl. The last time Notre Dame brought an unbeaten team to Los Angeles was in 1964. The Trojans upset the favored Irish, knocked them out of the national championship, and sent them home with a 9-1-0 record.

In 1970 the Trojans upset the favored Irish, knocked them out of the national championship, and sent them home with a 9-1-0 record.

The Trojans had looked good the early part of the season. They had defeated Alabama in the opener, tied tough Nebraska, then gone on to decisive wins over Iowa and Oregon State. Then somewhere, somehow, something turned upside down. They lost to Stanford, beat Washington by only three points, then lost to Oregon and California; rolled over a weak Washington State team, but then went down before a rather ordinary UCLA 45-20 in what McKay called the worst defensive game any team of his ever played.

The Trojans were 5-4-1, the worst season since 1961 and 11 point underdogs. The point spread would probably have been wider except that it was generally conceded that the USC schedule had been tougher than Notre Dame's. Even so the stats on the Irish season were awe-inspiring. With Joe Theisman running and throwing, Tom Gatewood receiving (he caught 79 passes that season), the Irish offense had scored 302 points while giving up only 59. Aye . . . there was the rub. The Notre Dame defense. Stingy was no word for it . . . they were downright miserly. They were so finely honed and conditioned to attack, it's a wonder they didn't tackle each other. You kind of had the feeling as Ara prowled the sidelines that instead of merely sending in his defensive unit, he unleashed them and commanded, "Kill, White Fangs, kill!"

"They're strong where we're weak," said McKay. "Right up the middle. Notre Dame isn't as good as everyone says . . . they're better."

"It all shapes up to be a dreary afternoon for the Trojans," wrote Times staff writer Jeff Prugh.

It was dreary alright, but not for the Trojans.

The 28th of November dawned dull and overcast and by game time the sky was as black as a pawnbroker's heart, and it started to rain. At first just a California drizzle.

It didn't bother the men from Notre Dame, Indiana. Midwesterners are used to weather like that. They took the opening kickoff 80 yards in twelve plays for the first score of the game. Gatewood and Cieszkowski received passes from Theisman, Gulyas drove three yards for a crucial first down at the USC 28. Theisman took it in on a 25 yard run. Hempel converted. It was four minutes into the first quarter, and the 64,694 damp fans (88,000 tickets were sold) looked at each other and nodded . . . this is what they expected to see, which made what they saw next all the more unbelievable. In the next ten minutes Jimmy Jones guided the Trojans to three touchdowns. Charlie Evans and Bob Chandler both gained 19 yards on passes from Jones, Clarence Davis ran for a 16 yard gain, then took the ball in on a three yard run. Ayala converted. A 70 yard drive in seven plays. There were penalties on both sides, but against Notre Dame it was defensive holding and against SC just a five yard offside call. That helped a little.

On the next series they didn't need any help. Davis caught a 31 yard pass from Jones, Chandler grabbed one for ten which gave the Trojans a first down on the 5, and Davis carried it in. Ayala missed the kick and the score was 13-7. 51 yards in five plays. By now the fans weren't nodding their heads, they were shaking them in disbelief. They hadn't seen anything yet.

The rain started falling a little faster, the air became a little chillier, and Jimmy Jones got hotter. He hit Sam Dickerson with a 45 yard bomb that actually hit Notre Dame defender Clarence Ellis first, but bounced off his shoulder straight into Sam's eager hands. The two point conversion, a pass from Jones to Chandler was good, and the Trojans led at the half 21-14. The Irish were in a state of shock . . . so, for that matter were the Trojans.

Jones didn't throw a single incomplete pass in the first period. Seven passes for 143 yards and 21 points in fourteen minutes. No other Notre Dame opponent had scored more than 14 points in four quarters that season.

In the third quarter it all came down . . . the rain, Joe Theisman's hope of bettering Greg Cook's 554 yard passing mark, and Notre Dame's hope of an undefeated season and a national championship.

Joe Theisman was having an incredible day. Handling a rain slick ball he was able to complete 33 of 58 passes for 526 yards . . . a new Notre Dame record. One more completion and he might have had that record. But playing catch-up with a wet football is rough and what happened to Notre Dame the next few minutes is almost unbelievable.

On the first play of the second half, SC defensive end Willie Hall crashed into Darryll Dewan hard enough to make him fumble. Ken Carter recovered on the Irish 17. Three plays later the Trojans were at the one. Then tailback Mike Berry fumbled in the end zone but SC tackle Pete Adams recovered for a Trojan touchdown. Ayala's conversion attempt was good, and USC led 31-14. Just 42 seconds later under relentless pressure from Trojan defensive end Willie Hall, Theisman retreated all the way to the end zone where Hall tackled him and forced a fumble. Tackle John Vella fell on it for another Trojan touchdown. They now led 38-14 . . . 24 points!

The Southern Cal fans were astonished and the Notre Dame fans were aghast.

Later in the quarter Theisman passed the Irish to another touchdown. A 72 yard drive in just five plays. Larry Parker took it over after receiving a 46 yard pass from Joe, who on the __28th__ of __Nov__ couldn't make a mistake. Notre Dame scored again in the last quarter, but the momentum was on the other side. Theisman ploughed through on a one yard run after a 69 yard aerial attack in 17 plays with Cieszowski doing most of the catching and Theisman most of the running. There was only a minute and eight seconds gone in the fourth quarter, but for the Irish time had run out. In a teeming rain the Trojan defense refused to give ground. That was the final score . . . 38-28.

Parseghian was desolate. "How much chance would anyone have given USC after that performance against UCLA last week (UCLA destroyed the Trojans 45-20)."

Texas coach Darrell Royal was there scouting Notre Dame. "Emotion," he said, "was the difference. When that adrenalin flows you get there faster, you jump higher, you dive deeper, and you even come up drier."

John McKay just smiled. For the fourth time in forty years an unbeaten Notre Dame team had been knocked out of contention

Notre Dame quarterback evades Charlie Weaver of the "Wild Bunch"

for a national championship by the University of Southern California.

In the Cotton Bowl the Irish beat Royal's Texas Longhorns 24-11, and snapped a 30 game winning streak. If they had won the USC game, they would have been ranked first by Associated Press after the Cotton Bowl. Instead, Nebraska was ranked first (SC had played them to a 21-21 tie early in the season) and the Irish second. So it was tears, tears, for old Notre Dame.

McKay kept smiling . . . and plotting. There was next year to plan for and he hadn't forgotten 51-0. The season hadn't been great, but the upset victory over Notre Dame would "make the winter livable."

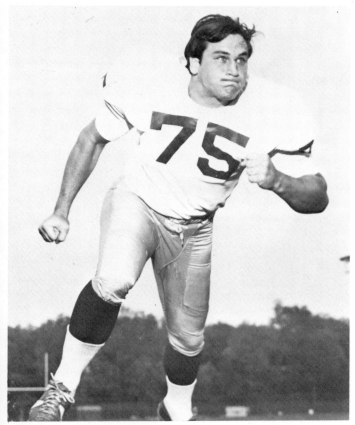

All American tackle — Greg Marx

USC halfback, Rod McNeil

UNIVERSITY OF NOTRE DAME 1970 TEAM ROSTER

NO.	NAME	POS.	WT.	NO.	NAME	POS.	WT.	NO.	NAME	POS.	WT.
22	**Allan, Dennis	H.B.	188	52	**Hempel, Scott	K.	235	26	Parker, Larry	H.B.	185
33	*Barz, Bill	F.B.	216	20	*Huff, Andy	F.B.	192	45	Patton, Eric	L.B.	220
69	Bossu, Frank	G.	187	53	*Humbert, Jim	O.G.	225	85	*Patulski, Walt	D.E.	235
58	Buches, Steve	T.-C.	235	65	Johnson, Ron	L.B.	208	41	*Raterman, John	L.B.	200
4	Bulger, Jim	Q.B.	200	72	*Kadish, Mike	D.T.	249	68	Schivarelli, Pete	D.T.	235
35	Cieszkowski, John	F.B.	218	42	**Kelly, Tim	L.B.	225	16	Schlezes, Ken	D.H.B.	185
91	Creaney, Mike	T.E.	215	77	Kondrk, John	D.T.	250	11	Steenberge, Pat	Q.B.	175
17	*Crotty, Mike	D.H.B.	180	34	Kondrla, Mike	L.B.	215	21	*Stepaniak, Ralph	D.H.B.	195
67	Dampeer, John	O.T.	235	62	*Kos, Gary	O.G.	235	93	*Swendsen, Fred	D.E.	235
51	DePremio, Dennis	G.	220	76	Marciag, Dick	D.T.	250	90	Tereschuk, John	C.	205
10	Dewan, Darryll	H.B.	195	73	Martin, Mike	O.T.	250	7	**Theismann, Joe	Q.B.	170
56	**Dinardo, Larry	O.G.	235	75	Marx, Greg	D.T.	235	38	↓f Thomann, Rick	L.B.	205
59	Drew, Dave	C.	215	43	McHale, John	L.B.	200	82	*Trapp, Bill	S.E.	195
89	**Eaton, Tom	S.E.	197	18	Minnix, Bob	H.B.	185	61	Webb, Mike	L.B.	200
23	*Ellis, Clarence	D.H.B.	178	74	Mudron, Pat	D.T.	240	40	*Wright, Jim	L.B.	220
96	Freistroffer, Tom	D.E.	235	47	Musuraca, Jim	L.B.	210	9	Yoder, Jim	H.B.	178
70	Gasseling, Tom	O.T.	235	88	*Neidert, Bob	D.E.	220	79	*Zikas, Mike	D.T.	240
44	*Gatewood, Tom	S.E.	208	28	Nightingale, Chuck	H.B.	175	84	Zilly, John	O.T.	226
12	Gulyas, Ed	H.B.	190	50	*Novakov, Dan	C.	225	27	**Zloch, Chuck	D.H.B.	185
64	Hagopian, Gary	O.G.	215	81	O'Malley, Jim	L.B.	210				

UNIVERSITY OF SOUTHERN CALIFORNIA 1970 TEAM ROSTER

NO.	NAME	POS.	HT.	WT.	NO.	NAME	POS.	HT.	WT.
77	Adams, Pete	O.T.	6'3"	269	27	McNeill, Rod	T.B.	6'2"	220
5	*Ayala, Ron	D.B.-K.	5'9"	175	66	Meier, Jack	O.G.	6'1"	230
23	*Berry, Mike	T.B.	5'10"	197	78	*Montgomery, Marv	O.T.	6'6"	255
7	Boulware, Dave	Q.B.	6'1"	194	22	Morgan, Mike	S.E.	6'1"	175
57	Brown, Dave	C.	6'0"	221	86	*Mullins, Gerry	T.E.	6'3"	236
87	Carter, Kent	D.E.	6'3"	215	59	Oberreuter, Rich	C.	6'1"	237
10	**Chandler, Bob	F.L.	6'1"	176	67	Papadakis, John	L.B.	6'0"	230
15	Chaney, Chris	F.L.	6'2"	184	54	Perryman, Pat	L.B.	5'10"	225
39	Cunningham, Sam	F.B.	6'3"	212	51	Preston, Ron	L.B.	6'1"	208
28	*Davis, Clarence	T.B.	5'11"	195	90	Pultorak, Steve	D.T.	6'3"	245
18	*Dickerson, Sam	S.E.	6'2"	194	6	Rae, Mike	Q.B.	6'1"	190
21	Dyer, Bruce	D.B.	6'0"	178	31	Rollinson, Bruce	D.B.	5'9"	193
88	Eriksen, Bob	D.E.	6'2"	207	73	Ruppert, Dick	-O.T.	6'4"	242
33	*Evans, Charlie	F.B.	6'1"	212	68	Ryan, Mike	O.G.	6'1"	237
14	Failor, Walt	D.B.	6'1"	194	71	Skiles, John	D.T.	6'3"	230
70	Follett, George	D.T.	6'4"	240	53	*Slough, Greg	L.B.	6'3"	230
76	Gallaher, Allen	O.T.	6'3"	234	93	*Smith, Tody	D.T.	6'5"	247
65	George, Greg	L.B.	5'11"	221	58	Stirling, Bob	O.G.	6'2"	230
61	Graf, Allan	O.G.	6'1"	244	92	Stone, Jim	D.E.	6'2"	232
94	Grant, John	D.T.	6'4"	222	46	Thomas, Alonzo	D.B.	6'2"	205
55	Grissum, Jim	D.E.	6'1"	220	45	Timmons, Curtis	D.B.	5'11"	172
83	Hall, Willie	D.E.	6'3"	220	81	Vella, Chris	C.-T.E.	6'3"	225
50	**Haluchak, Mike	L.B.	6'0"	200	75	*Vella, John	O.T.-D.T.	6'4"	245
29	Harris, Lou	T.B.	5'11"	190	84	*Weaver, Charlie	L.B.	6'2"	214
38	Holland, Bill	F.B.	6'2"	205	85	Weber, Scott	D.E.	6'5"	214
43	*Hudson, Tyrone	D.B.	6'0"	175	60	*Yary, Wayne	O.G.	6'2"	230
8	*Jones, Jim	Q.B.	6'1"	193	89	Young, Charles	T.E.	6'4"	216
16	McAuley, Mike	D.B.	6'0"	180					
74	McGirr, Mike	O.T.	6'5"	268					

CHAPTER 44

"IF I FOUGHT ANYONE, IT WOULD BE PARSEGHIAN . . ."
. . . McKay, 1971

For John McKay, the winter of '70 may have been "liveable" but the autumn of '71 was damned near unbearable. He had a problem . . . as a matter of fact he had two . . . or three, or maybe more.

Marcus Aurelius, the great Roman Emperor-philosopher, once noted that "problems come not in single spies, but in legions."

The coach's first problem and most serious, was that he had team divided. And against itself it could not stand. As a matter of fact, it hadn't been able to stand against anyone but Rice and Illinois. The Trojans were 2 and 4 when they went to Notre Dame on October 23rd. The dissension was caused primarily because there were two quarterbacks, each with a following within the team. There were ugly racial overtones. Jimmy Jones, who had led the Trojans to an unbeaten season in 1969 and a victory over Michigan in the Rose Bowl, had a disappointing year in 1970 (except for Notre Dame) and 1971 looked worse. And he was black. McKay was under tremendous pressure to bench him. He refused, for two reasons. Number one, the coach is tough and would not bow to that kind of constraint. Number two, the coach is loyal. He had faith in Jimmy and felt he was the best quarterback. He also resented the implication that the team was losing because Jimmy was black.

Mike Rae was white, and also good. He led the Trojans to a national title in 1972. But in 1971 he was still a junior quarterback, but with friends on the team and among the fans who thought he could move the team better than Jones. McKay, with characteristic savvy, decided to alternate them and bring back some semblance of unity to the Southern California team. One problem solved, but he still had another . . .

Notre Dame, with five straight wins, ranked sixth and favored by 14 points. Their defensive front four would have caused Torquemada and the Spanish Inquisitors to blanch with fear. Someone had dubbed them the "Stormin' Shamrocks." That's like calling Alabama's Crimson Tide the "Crushin' Creek" or the Pittsburgh Panthers the "Pushin' Pussycats."

So obdurate were they, that they allowed but 16 points to be scored against them in the first five games and hadn't given up a touchdown for 14 quarters. They had allowed opponents an average of only two yards per carry. They looked as though they should be fed raw meat and exercised in a cage. They had a combined weight of a little over a half ton and averaged 6 ft. 5.

The University of Southern California, on the other hand, had a defensive unit noted for its generosity. The Trojans had allowed 94 points in the last three games, and seemed to want to make friends of its enemies . . . they didn't wish to be too rough.

John McKay is not a locker room speaker in the image of Rockne. He is much better on the banquet circuit or in a booth at Julie's. This time he made an exception and it may have won him the game.

"We've been disgraceful this season," he began, "and it's a crime. If we're going to play this game, let's play it as well as we can. For just one day, let's forget about who should be quarterback . . . forget about yourselves and play as a team, as men, and if you don't, it may be the last goddamn time some of you ever get a chance to play — if I have to play nobody."

At the risk of being repetitious, when John McKay says something seriously, he means it. And when he gets sentimental no one doubts his sincerity. "This is what it's all about . . . Notre Dame, this is what I've believed in since I was a little kid. And I still believe in it."

Ara Parseghian looks disgusted

He should have tried that earlier in the season. His team went crashing through the dressing room doors onto the field and keelhauled the favored Irish 28-14.

And they made it look almost easy.

The Trojans had a secret weapon . . . secret because he had never even worn a football uniform in high school. 6-1, 185 pound split end Edesel Garrison, a junior. That afternoon he caught five passes for 127 yards, scored twice, set up a third touchdown, and completely out-maneuvered All American cornerback Clarence Ellis.

About midway through the first quarter defensive end Glenn Byrd intercepted Notre Dame's quarterback Cliff Brown and returned the ball to the Irish 48. Two plays later the Trojans were on the 31. Jimmy Jones found Garrison open on the three. Ellis, covering, slipped on the rain slick turf and fell. Garrison danced into the end zone, Mike Rae came in and made the point after. 7-0, SC.

Irish halfback Gary Diminick answered right back with a 66 yard kickoff return that set up Notre Dame's first touchdown. In seven plays they covered the remaining 34 yards . . . Mike Parker ran 15 yards for a first down on the three, and Andy Huff took it in for the score. Bob Thomas converted to tie the game.

Charlie Hinton must have been studying Diminick's moves, the Trojan tailback returned the Irish kickoff 65 yards to the Notre Dame 35. McKay had begun to alternate quarterbacks, but galloping Garrison was still in there, much to the consternation of Clarence Ellis, who let him get free in the end zone. Mike Rae threw a perfect strike to Edesel in the left corner, and then kicked the conversion to send the Trojans ahead at the end of the first quarter, 14-7.

In the second quarter the Trojans continued their passing attack, they had to . . . the Notre Dame defense would have pulled the legs off their running backs if they had tried to buck

Edesel Garrison surprises Notre Dame with long pass catch for TD.

that line. Brian Dougherty, an Irish sophomore quarterback, helped the Trojan cause by booting a punt that traveled only 28 yards. Jimmy Jones, back in at quarterback, completed a 42 yard pass play to Garrison for a first down at the four, and Sam ("Bam") Cunningham, who should have been called "the Diver," launched himself into that big Notre Dame line three times, and on the last attempt went over from the one. "Into the line" is probably not quite correct. Sam had a theory . . . with a line that tough you don't plow into them, you go over them. And that's what he did to give SC a 21-7 lead 2:12 into the second quarter.

Two minutes later Dyer got his second interception and raced 53 yards down the sidelines for another SC touchdown. Rae's third point after attempt was good and the Trojans led 28-7.

The Irish never recovered. They still had Tom Gatewood to receive, but they didn't have Joe Theisman to throw, and Cliff Brown, a sophomore, was having an erratic day. They did get one more touchdown when Jim Musuraca recovered Mike Rae's fumble and Brown completed a 41 yard pass to Mike Creany to give the Irish a first down at the 13. John Cieszkowski ran it in from the four and Thomas got the extra point. The Trojan defense using three linemen and four linebackers, proved to be as tough that day as the Irish had been all year. They held and the game ended 28-14.

For the second year the Irish *and* the bookmakers were stunned. The Notre Damers for obvious reasons and the odds-makers . . . well that's obvious too. They had the point spread right, but they gave it to the wrong team.

They might have had better luck making book on the fight in the second quarter. It was a beauty. SC assistant coach Craig Fertig felt his team was ahead on points in that conflict too when the official stopped it. The brawl was triggered when Mike Rae fumbled and SC recovered, but the referee awarded

Coach Craig Fertig breaks up the fight

the ball to the Irish. It had been a hard fought game and tempers were short. Insults were traded first and then blows. The main event was a matchmaker's dream. In USC's corner was 6-4, 225 pound tackle Chris Vella, wearing the blue and gold was Greg Marx, 6-5 and weighing in at 249 . . . also a tackle. Vella was a little smaller than Marx, but he had an edge. His coach. When the benches emptied, McKay headed for the center of the fray.

"I ended up pushing this guy," he told the Times the next day, "and I looked up and the guy I was pushing was Marx. If he would have hit me he would have killed me. If I wanted to find someone to fight, I'd go fight Parseghian, not Marx."

Of course he would have his chance next year. For his Trojans it was a mediocre season in some ways, a success in others. They finished 6-4-1. But any time USC beats California 28-0, *and Notre Dame 28-14, and didn't lose to UCLA (they played to a 7-7 tie), it's a reasonably good year. The prickliest burr under Coach McKay's saddle was a 33 to 18 loss to 10th ranked (AP) Stanford. Stanford is not one of his favorite schools. He would almost rather lose to Notre Dame than the Cardinals of Stanford.*

Coach Parseghian ended the season with an 8-2-0 record and was ranked number 15th by the United Press, and 13th by Associated Press. The only other Irish loss was to LSU, ranked 10th by UPI. Tom Gatewood and Clarence Ellis were named All American for the second time. Defensive tackle Mike Kadish was mentioned, and defensive end Walt Patulski was a unanimous selection on all official teams . . . unfortunately for Ara, none of them would be back next year.

But a college football coach learns to live with that.

#	Name	Pos., Ht., Wt. / Class	Hometown
7	Adams, Pete	O.T., 6'3", 265	San Diego, Calif. (University)
	Junior		
9	Adolph, Robyn	Q.B., 6'0", 180	Dinuba, Calif.
	Sophomore		
5	Anthony, Charles	L.B., 6'1", 218	Fresno, Calif. (Edison)
	Sophomore		
3	Berg, Darryl	D.B., 6'1", 198	Westminster, Calif.
	Sophomore		
0	Blanche, Dave	D.E., 6'6", 232	Claremont, Calif.
	Sophomore		
9	Bohlinger, Tom	L.B., 6'2", 212	Santa Ynez, Calif.
	Sophomore		
7	Boulware, Dave	D.B., 6'2", 202	Downey, Calif. (Warren)
	Sophomore		
3	Bratonia, Mark	T.B., 5'11", 194	Bremerton, Wash. (East)
	Sophomore		
7	Brown, Dave	C., 6'0", 228	Glendale, Calif. (Eagle Rock)
	Junior		
4	Byrd, Glenn	D.E., 6'3", 216	Oakland, Calif. (McClymonds)
	Sophomore		
7	Cantwell, Phil	S.E., 6'1", 186	Covina, Calif. (Bishop Amat)
	Sophomore		
7	Carter, Kent	L.B., 6'3", 216	Los Angeles, Calif. (Cathedral)
	Senior		
0	Carter, Russ	C., 6'4", 229	Santa Barbara, Calif.
	Sophomore		
5	Chaney, Chris	S.E., 6'2", 187	West Covina, Calif. (Bishop Amat)
	Junior		
2	Clark, Avery	L.B., 6'3", 200	San Diego, Calif. (Morse)
	Sophomore		
0	Cunningham, Sam	F.B., 6'3", 212	Santa Barbara, Calif.
	Junior		
4	Culbreath, Cliff	O.T., 6'2", 240	San Bernardino, Calif. (Pacific)
	Junior		
2	Doris, Monte	D.E., 6'3", 242	Fresno, Calif.
	Sophomore		
4	Dyer, Bruce	D.B., 6'0", 179	Dearborn Hts., Mich. (Riverside)
	Senior		
3	Eriksen, Bob	L.B., 6'2", 210	Fresno, Calif. (Bullard)
	Senior		
7	Fate, Steve	D.B., 6'2", 193	Anaheim, Calif. (Servite)
	Junior		
9	Follett, George	D.T., 6'4", 233	Huntington Beach, Calif
	Junior		
3	Follmar, Ken	O.G., 6'2", 232	Los Gatos, Calif.
	Sophomore		
0	Gallaher, Allen	O.G., 6'3", 255	Sylmar, Calif.
	Junior		
3	Garrison, Edesel	S.E., 6'1", 185	Compton, Calif. (Centennial)
	Junior		
1	Graf, Allan	O.G., 6'0", 246	San Fernando, Calif.
	Junior		
4	Grant, John	D.E., 6'5", 229	Boise, Ida. (Capital)
	Junior		
3	Hall, Willie	D.E., 6'3", 214	New Britain, Conn. (Pulaski)
	Senior		
3	Hancock, Mike	D.T., 6'3", 241	Norwalk, Calif. (St. Paul's)
	Sophomore		
0	Harris, Lou	T.B., 5'10", 205	Sacramento, Calif.
	Senior		
0	Henderson, Glen	L.B., 6'3", 195	Los Angeles, Calif. (Hamilton)
	Junior		
	Hinton, Charles	T.B., 5'11", 184	E. Orange, N.J.
	Junior		
3	Holland, Bill	F.B., 6'1", 210	Los Angeles, Calif.
	Senior		
	Ivey, Randy	O.G., 6'2", 253	Burbank, Calif.
	Sophomore		
	Johnson, Eddie	D.B., 5'11", 165	Oceanside, Calif.
	Junior		
	Jones, Jim	Q.B., 6'1", 192	Harrisburg, Pa. (Harris)
	Senior		
16	McAuley, Mike	D.B., 6'2", 199	Simi Valley, Calif.
	Junior		
73	McCaffrey, Bob	D.T., 6'2", 243	Bakersfield, Calif. (Garces)
	Sophomore		
74	McGirr, Mike	D.T., 6'5", 265	Walnut, Calif. (Rowland)
	Junior		
27	McNeill, Rod	T.B., 6'2", 220	Baldwin Park, Calif.
	Junior		
93	Marderian, Greg	D.E., 6'4", 234	Granada Hills, Calif.
	Sophomore		
12	Meyer, John	Q.B., 6'0", 201	Bricktown, N.J. (Bricktownship)
	Sophomore		
80	Miller, Ron	D.T., 6'2", 226	Los Angeles, Calif. (Locke)
	Sophomore		
44	Moore, Manfred	T.B., 6'1", 187	San Fernando, Calif.
	Sophomore		
22	Morgan, Mike	F.L., 6'1", 182	Santa Ana, Calif. (Mater Dei)
	Senior		
91	Morrison, Don	O.G., 6'2", 245	Los Angeles, Calif. (Washington)
	Junior		
18	Moses, Greg	S.E., 6'1", 195	Los Angeles, Calif. (Manual Arts)
	Sophomore		
50	Olmstead, Sherm	L.B., 5'11", 207	Ventura, Calif. (Moorpark)
	Junior		
67	Papadakis, John	L.B., 6'0", 235	Rolling Hills, Calif.
	Senior		
14	Parker, Artimus	D.B., 6'4", 207	Sacramento, Calif.
	Sophomore		
48	Pekarcik, Al	D.B., 5'11", 186	Anaheim, Calif. (Loara)
	Junior		
51	Preston, Ron	L.B., 6'2", 206	El Paso, Tex. (Belair)
	Senior		
6	Rae, Mike	Q.B., 6'1", 186	Lakewood, Calif.
	Junior		
53	Raymond, Al	L.B., 6'1", 223	Fresno, Calif. (San Joaquin Mem.)
	Sophomore		
23	Revelle, Bob	D.B., 6'2", 197	Gardena, Calif. (Serra)
	Sophomore		
78	Riley, Steve	O.T., 6'4", 244	Chula Vista, Calif. (Castle Park)
	Sophomore		
68	Ryan, Mike	O.G., 6'2", 235	San Francisco, Calif. (St. Ignatius)
	Junior		
62	Shaputis, Bob	O.T., 6'4", 234	Norwalk, Calif. (St. John Bosco)
	Sophomore		
65	Shaw, Mike	C., 6'2", 216	Pasadena, Calif. (Blair)
	Sophomore		
71	Skiles, John	D.T., 6'3", 220	Bakersfield, Calif. (North)
	Junior		
56	Springer, Marc	L.B., 6'1", 233	Downey, Calif. (Warren)
	Sophomore		
58	Stirling, Bob	C., 6'2", 241	Westminster, Calif.
	Senior		
92	Stone, Jim	L.B., 6'2", 222	Whittier, Calif. (California)
	Junior		
24	Swann, Lynn	F.L., 6'0", 180	Foster City, Calif. (Serra)
	Sophomore		
86	Sweany, Bruce	T.E., 6'2", 232	Rolling Hills, Calif.
	Sophomore		
46	Thomas, Alonzo	D.B., 6'2", 205	Kansas City, Calif. (Wyondotte)
	Senior		
45	Timmons, Curt	D.E., 5'11", 180	Norwalk, Calif. (St. Paul's)
	Junior		
81	Vella, Chris	T.E., 6'", 225	Van Nuys, Calif. (Notre Dame)
	Junior		
75	Vella, John	O.T., 6'4", 256	Van Nuys, Calif. (Notre Dame)
	Senior		
66	Walsh, Scott	OG, 6'3", 238	Santa Clara, Calif.
	Sophomore		
34	Washmera, Ray	F.B., 6'1", 210	San Francisco, Calif. (St. Ignatius)
	Sophomore		
10	Watson, Nery	F.L., 5'10", 168	Los Angeles, Calif. (Manual Arts)
	Junior		

NOTRE DAME — 1971

52	Alvarado, Joe Sophomore	C., 6'1", 218 East Chicago, Ind. (Hammond Noll)
78	Briick, Herb Junior	O.T., 6'4", 240 Hinsdale, Ill. (Hinsdale Township)
8	Brown, Cliff Sophomore	Q.B., 6'0", 185 Middleton, Pa. (Middletown Area)
4	Bulger, Jim Junior	Q.B., 6'5", 200 Pittsburgh, Pa. (Central Catholic)
88	Casper, Dave Sophomore	T.E., 6'3", 228 Chilton, Wis.
35	*Cieszkowski, John Junior	F.B., 6'2", 218 Detroit, Mich. (University of Detroit H.S.)
48	Clemente, Brian Sophomore	L.B., 6'2", 215 Loudonville, N.Y. (Christian Bros.)
91	*Creaney, Mike Junior	T.E., 6'4", 215 Towson, Md. (Loyola)
17	**Crotty, Mike Senior	D.H.B., 5'9", 180 Seattle, Wash. (Glacier)
67	*Dampeer, John Junior	O.T., 6'4", 240 Kermit, Texas
51	*DePrimio, Dennis Senior	O.G., 6'1", 220 Greensburg, Pa. (Central Catholic)
43	Devine, Tom Sophomore	L.B., 6'3", 210 Jackson, Mich. (Lumen Christi)
10	*Dewan, Darryll Junior	H.B., 6'0", 195 Danbury, Conn.
23	**Ellis, Clarence Senior	D.H.B., 6'0", 178 Grand Rapids, Mich. (Central)
89	Frazier, Algery Sophomore	S.E., 6'5", 195 Calvert, Texas
96	Freistroffer, Tom Junior	D.E., 6'4", 235 Fort Wayne, Ind. (Central Catholic)
19	Gallagher, Bill Senior	H.B., 5'11", 183 Philadelphia, Pa. (Father Judge)
5	Garner, Terry Junior	D.H.B., 6'2", 185 Canton, Ohio (Central Catholic)
44	**Gatewood, Tom Senior	S.E., 6'2", 208 Baltimore, Md. (City College)
12	*Gulyas, Ed Senior	H.B., 5'11", 190 San Carlos, Calif. (Carlmont)
33	Haggar, Joe Junior	D.H.B., 5'8", 170 Dallas, Texas (Jesuit)
64	Hagopian, Gary Senior	O.G., 6'0", 215 Colorado Springs, Colo. (Wasson)
95	Hayduk, George Sophomore	D.E., 6'3", 225 Factoryville, Pa. (Lackawanna Trail)
99	Hein, Jeff Sophomore	D.E., 6'1", 210 Cincinnati, Ohio (Oakwood Canton)
22	Hill, Greg Sophomore	H.B., 6'1", 180 Pilot Mountain, N.C. (North Stokes)
97	Hooten, Herman Senior	D.T., 6'2", 239 Tuskegee, Ala. (Tuskegee Institute)
20	*Huff, Andy Junior	F.B., 5'11", 192 Toledo, Ohio (St. Francis)
53	**Humbert, Jim Junior	O.G., 6'2", 225 Cincinnati, Ohio (Roger Bacon)
72	**Kadish, Mike Senior	D.T., 6'5", 260 Grand Rapids, Mich. (Central Catholic)
77	*Kondrk, John Junior	O.T., 6'5", 260 Hopelawn, N.J. (Woodbridge Senior)
54	Lane, Garry Sophomore	L.B., 6'0", 230 Kalamazoo, Mich. (Comstock)
76	Maciag, Dick Junior	D.T., 6'5", 250 Buffalo, N.Y. (H. C. Technical)
69	Mailey, Kevin Sophomore	O.T., 6'3", 221 Jenkintown, Pa. (Abington)
30	Mariani, John Junior	L.B., 5'11", 195 Philadelphia, Pa. (Archmere Academy)
75	*Marx, Greg Junior	D.T., 6'5", 249 Redford, Mich. (Catholic Central)
74	McBride, Mike Sophomore	O.T., 6'5", 230 Michigan City, Ind. (Elston)
18	*Minnix, Bob Senior	H.B., 5'11", 185 Spokane, Wash. (Lewis & Clark)
66	Morrin, Dan Sophomore	D.T., 6'4", 230 Croydon, Pa. (Bishop Egan)
47	Musuraca, Jim Junior	L.B., 6'0", 210 East Liverpool, Ohio
49	Naughton, Mike Sophomore	D.H.B., 6'3", 180 Bloomfield Hills, Mich. (Assumption)
50	**Novakov, Dan Senior	C., 6'2", 225 Cincinnati, Ohio (Moeller)
81	O'Malley, Jim Junior	L.B., 6'2", 210 Youngstown, Ohio (Chaney)
39	O'Toole, Dan Junior	D.H.B., 6'1", 180 Oklahoma City, Okla. (Casady)
26	*Parker, Larry Junior	H.B., 6'1", 185 Cincinnati, Ohio (Elder)
34	Parker, Mike Sophomore	D.H.B., 5'10", 175 Cincinnati, Ohio (Elder)
45	*Patton, Eric Sophomore	L.B., 6'2", 235 Santa Ana, Calif. (Mater Dei)
85	**Patulski, Walt Senior	D.E., 6'6", 260 Liverpool, N.Y. (Christian Brothers)
87	Peiffer, Mike Senior	S.E., 6'1", 190 South Bend (St. Joseph)
41	*Raterman, John Senior	L.B., 6'1", 200 Cincinnati, Ohio (Elder)
83	Robinson, Tyrone Junior	D.E., 6'2", 220 Philadelphia, Pa. (Olney)
6	Roolf, Jim Junior	D.H.B.-P., 6'0", 185 Sewickley, Pa. (Quaker Valley)
7	Rudnick, Tim Sophomore	S., 5'10", 170 Chicago, Ill. (Notre Dame)
16	Schlezes, Ken Junior	D.H.B., 6'3", 185 Rochelle, Ill. (Heelan (Sioux City, Ia.))
3	Smith, Scott Junior	K., 5'10", 165 Dallas, Texas (Jesuit)
11	Steenberge, Pat Junior	Q.B., 6'1", 175 Erie Pa. (Cathedral Prep)
21	**Stepaniak, Ralph Senior	D.H.B., 2'2", 195 Alpena, Mich. (Central Catholic)
42	Sullivan, Tim Sophomore	L.B., 6'3", 217 Des Moines, Iowa (Dowling)
93	**Swendsen, Fred Senior	D.E., 6'4", 235 Tacoma, Wash. (Fife)
65	Szatko, Greg Sophomore	T.E., 6'4", 220 Western Springs, Ill. (Lyons Twp.)
90	*Tereschuk, John Junior	T.E.-C., 6'0", 200 Long Beach, Calif. (Pius X)
38	*Thomann, Rick Senior	L.B., 6'1", 225 Akron, Ohio (Archbishop Hoban)
98	Thomas, Robert Sophomore	K., 5'10", 175 Rochester, N.Y. (McQuaid Jesuit)
27	Townsend, Mike Sophomore	D.H.B., 6'3", 178 Hamilton, Ohio (Garfield)
80	Townsend, Willie Junior	S.E., 6'3", 190 Hamilton, Ohio (Garfield)
82	*Trapp, Bill Senior	S.E., 6'3", 195 Chicago, Ill. (Mount Carmel)
31	Washington, Bob Sophomore	S.E., 6'0", 175 Steubenville, Ohio
61	Webb, Mike Junior	L.B., 6'2", 220 New Castle, Del. (Salesianum)
36	Wright, Tom Junior	H.B., 5'11", 190 Sparta, N.J. (Sparta)
37	Zielony, Dick Senior	F.B., 6'0", 200 Vancouver, Wash. (Jesuit Portland)
79	**Zikas, Mike Senior	D.T., 6'4", 240 Dolton, Ill. (Thornridge)

1972

CHAPTER 45

"I'VE GOT TO LOOK AT ANTHONY DAVIS FOR TWO MORE YEARS."
. . . Ara Parseghian, 1972

In 1970 Coach McKay had his worst season in eight years, 6-4-1. Naturally he was not pleased. In 1971 he had the second worst season in nine years, 6-4-1. McKay was not just displeased . . . he was a little short of furious. So, when most college coaches were golfing in the summer sun or weeding the garden or simply lying in a hammock wondering if their jobs were secure for one more year, John McKay spent those months of the spring of '72 in the stifling darkness of a projection room and pondered. The more he reflected, the more he realized that the Trojans needed more speed on defense, but more importantly the USC offense had become predictable.

Darrell Royal of Texas once said, "If you've got a cannon, shoot it." McKay had had a series of cannons . . . tailbacks Garrett, Simpson and Clarence Davis. But, he had come to rely too heavily on this artillery, and had fired the cannon so often that the enemy knew the emplacement and had learned how to spike the gun and muzzle the offense.

The coach had other worries. The defensive unit had only four starters returning, so speed had to be combined with simplicity. In retrospect one has to wonder why McKay suffered such trepidation. At the end of the season he called the defensive team the quickest he had ever watched, college or pro. All American tackle John Grant had such football sense that his uncanny ability to read the opponent's offense amazed even McKay. Another All American, Richard Wood, ran the 40 in 4.5 and safety Artimus Parker in the secondary made All American the following year.

And he had what may have been the most athletically talented group ever assembled on one football team in the history of collegiate sports.

Edsel Garrison was a world class quartermiler, Mike Rae starred in both baseball and basketball, Sam Cunningham was a shot putter, flanker Lynn Swann was good enough at the long jump to have once beated Olympic champion (and fellow Trojan) Randy Williams at his own game. Linebacker Ray Rodriguez could high jump 6'6" and fellow linebacker Wood in addition to that 4.5 40-yard dash was a standout at basketball and was a heavyweight wrestler. There was another wrestler on the team who also played varsity baseball. His name was Anthony Davis.

However, at the beginning of the season this awesome collection of jocks failed to fill Coach McKay with confidence. The offensive line was made up mostly of seniors who were capable of playing well but had been somewhat erratic the last two years, the sophomores were still an unknown quantity, and both Sam Cunningham and starting tailback Rod McNeill were recovering from injuries.*

McKay made changes. He returned to some of the formations of a few years earlier where the flankers shadowed the tailbacks and could carry the ball on reverses or counter plays. When you have a flanker like Lynn Swann, this makes good sense . . . simply a cannon of a different calibre to be fired when needed.

By the time spring practice had ended, the Coach's professional pessimism (an occupational hazard, it seems) had been replaced by cautious optimism. Cunningham and McNeill had healed, his new formation which he called his "I-bone" had proved effective, the offensive line had steadied down and the sophomores proved to be a surprise. By mid-season they had surprised every opponent they had faced . . . unpleasantly.

Quarterback Pat Haden showed that he could share responsibility with senior quarterback Mike Rae. His favorite receiver, J. K. McKay, the coach's son, although not very big and not very fast, proved he could do two things well. He could get open and he could catch a football under almost any condition and hang onto it. Linebacker Richard Wood had terrorized the enemy offense in every game. Fullback Allen Carter at 5-11 and 205 had the size and speed to back up Rod McNeill and Anthony Davis at tailback. Oh yes, Anthony Davis . . .

Coach McKay relates that even in practice A. D., which Davis prefers to be called, ran every play as though he were playing in the Rose Bowl. So when McNeill's hip injury slowed him to a mere gallop, A. D. was ready.*

Although A. D. started only the last four games, he gained 1,191 yards, averaged 5.8 yards per carry and scored 19 times as a sophomore. By the time December 2 and the Fighting Irish arrived in southern California, the Trojans were unbeaten, untied and had risen from a shaky ninth place in the national ratings to number one. It had not been easy. SC had had one of the roughest schedules of John McKay's career. Fifth ranked Arkansas was the opener and the Trojans were

USC's great wide receiver and All American Lynn Swann

Anthony Davis — All American

six-point underdogs. They won 31-10. Tough Illinois and always dangerous Michigan State . . . Stanford, UCLA . . . all disposed of. After the 44 to 3 destruction of a much better than average Washington team, Couger coach Jim Sweeney told McKay, "I don't think you're number one, John . . . I think the Miami Dolphins are a little better." Now there remained only Notre Dame.

Coach Ara Parseghian's Fighting Irish, though unranked and 14 point underdogs, brought an enviable record to the Coliseum. They, too, had beaten Michigan State (although by only 16-0 compared to the 51-6 thrashing administered by SC) and rolled over a determined Pittsburgh team 42-16. Missouri, the perennial spoilers, pulled off the major upset of the year and handed the Irish a 30-26 defeat. It was Notre Dame's only loss . . . until they ran into Anthony Davis and the reincarnation of the Thundering Herds of the early thirties.

Irish co-captain Greg Marx, the huge defensive tackle, had no fear of A. D., at least before the game started. "They've beaten us two years in a row and we've got something to prove," he said. "We have to stop the pass and make them run . . ." He probably still wishes he hadn't said that.

USC won the toss and elected to receive. Cliff Brown kicked off and waiting on the three yard line with arms outstretched

like a lonesome lover stood Anthony Davis. With Charles Hinton and Ed Powell supplying key blocks, A. D. exploded into the clear, cut left and galloped the remaining 97 yards for a touchdown. Greg Marx did get a measure of revenge . . . he blocked the point after and held the Trojans to a 6-0 lead seconds after the opening whistle.

The Irish were not intimidated . . . yet. Quarterback Tom Clements, a sophomore who had completed 50% of his passes and rushed for 356 yards, guided his team down the field to retaliate. Andy Huff and leading rusher Eric Penick, a sophomore halfback who needed just 12 more yards to add to his 703 total to become Notre Dame's top rusher in the last eighteen years, maneuvered close enough for Bob Thomas to attempt and make a 45 yard field goal. 6-3.

On the next series Mike Rae passed deep to Lynn Swann, incomplete, but pass interference was called on Irish defensive halfback Reggie Barnett and USC had a first down and goal to go on the one yard line. Davis took it in. This time Rae's extra point was not blocked and the Trojans led 13-3.

With 25 seconds still left in the first quarter, Davis scored his third touchdown. Penick fumbled on the Trojan nine, Dale Mitchell recovered and A. D. took it in on a sweep from the five.

Richard "Batman" Wood directs the defense for Troy

The score remained 19-3 during most of the second quarter, but before the half ended Tom Clements put together a ten play offensive covering 73 yards to narrow the gap to 19-10. The Irish quarterback alternated running plays with passes to tight end Mike Creany and halfback Gary Diminick, then found Willie Townsend with a five yard scoring pass and Bob Thomas converted.

The Irish charged on the field for the beginning of the second half cocked and primed, but their first shot misfired. Trojan defensive back Chuck Hinton picked off a Clements pass at the Trojan 41, then Rae passed to Swann for a gain of 16 . . . with All American Pete Adams blocking, A. D. picked up 11 more and capped the attack with a four yard run into the end zone for touchdown number four. The two point conversion attempt failed, but even so the 25-10 lead looked comfortable . . . to anyone that is, who has not faced Notre Dame. After an exchange of punts it was Irish defensive halfback Mike Townsend's turn to defuse a Trojan attack. He intercepted Mike Rae's pass at the SC 47 yard line, and it took Clements only six plays to hit Diminick in the end zone with an 11 yard pass. The point after was good and suddenly the Trojan lead didn't look so comfortable. Eight point leads seldom do. It looked even less comfortable a few mintues later when Mike

Townsend again intercepted one of Mike Rae's passes and Clements took the field and with all the poise and confidence of a Prussian Field Marshall and directed his troops on another assault which was almost an instant replay of the first. Halfback Art Best gained nine yards, then five. Third and two at the Trojan 20 yard line. Best hit the line for ten more yards and a first down at the ten. Clements rifled a pass to Creany who was waiting in the end zone. Now the score was USC 25, Notre Dame 23. Clements attempted a two point conversion to Willie Townsend, but SC's Steve Fate batted the ball loose and the score remained unchanged.

Time was running out in the third quarter and the Irish needed to regain possession of the ball. Since A. D.'s opening kickoff return, Coach Parseghian had instructed his kicker to squib the ball anywhere Anthony Davis wasn't. Cliff Brown did just that, and the ball rolled out of bounds just a few feet from the goal line, but the kick was called back because of a penalty. Brown kicked off once more, this time from the 35. For some reason Ara had ordered a deep kick . . . it was a mistake. It was a beautiful kick, deep, high, and it floated down like the last leaf of autumn into the waiting hands of Anthony Davis. As A. D. waited under the ball, SC's offensive guard Allen Graff turned to reserve lineman Bob Shaputlis,

"Bob," he shouted, "I'll bet A. D. can do it again." A. D. could and did. He gathered the football in on the five, headed straight up the field into the blocking wedge and through it, headed for the left sideline, eluded the Notre Dame tackler Tim Rudnick at the 25, slid into the end zone to do his little knee dance that all Notre Dame fans had come to know and love that afternoon.

Touchdown number five and Rae's successful conversion brought the score to 32-23 USC with a minute and seven seconds remaining in the third quarter. Only a minute and 25 seconds later, Davis got touchdown number six on a sweep to the right side and an eight yard run. Rae was accurate once more and the score was not 39 to 23. From the sidelines A. D. watched Sam Cunningham dive in from the one yard line for the final Trojan score. 45-23.

Davis had hit the Irish for 368 yards that day . . . 99 yards rushing, 51 yards on pass receptions, and 218 yards on kickoff returns. He had smashed five USC records which had survived assaults by some of the most gifted running backs in college football history . . . most touchdowns in one game, most points scored in one game. Longest kickoff return (97 yards) and most kickoff return yardage in one season, 468.

In the locker room after the game John McKay was asked how he compared Davis to Heisman trophy winners Mike Garrett and O. J. Simpson.

"Favorably," he said, "Favorably."

In the Notre Dame dressing room, a disconsolate Ara Parseghian sat, brooding.

"Cheer up, Coach," said one of the reporters from the Chicago Tribune, "there's still the Orange Bowl, and there's always next year. This is only one game."

"That's not it," growled Ara, "don't you realize I've got to look at Anthony Davis for two more years?"

So, the Trojans of Southern California won over Notre Dame for the third year in a row . . . and the series now stood Notre Dame 26, USC 15, 3 ties. Notre Dame still clearly ahead . . . in more ways than one. 75,243 fans were in the Los Angeles Coliseum on that December day, and that represents a lot of money: Notre Dame made $203,000 from the television rights and their share of the gate receipts amounted to $223.00; The University of Notre Dame du Lac, an independent school, make $426,000 that Saturday afternoon. It works this way, when Notre Dame plays SC on national television, 6% off the top goes to the NCAA. Notre Dame receives 50% of the balance. SC gets four-tenths of the remaining 50% and one of eight shares of the other six-tenths. USC netted $319,000. It had cost them $107,000 in television money in just one day to be in the Pac 8.

The Trojans beat third-ranked Ohio State in the Rose Bowl to win the undisputed national title . . . for John McKay, it was that perfect season. 12 wins, no losses, no ties. He attributed it to team unity. A large part of that unity he attributed to a mascot.

Anthony Davis breaks loose again

The University of Southern California has as its official mascot a large white horse named Traveler III. But, in 1972 the football team had a mascot all its own . . . a dog named Turd, a small furry canine of questionable parentage whose father was no doubt a street cur named desire. Turd was a stray that had adopted Pete Adams, SC's All American tackle. He followed Pete into practice one day and became a part of the Trojan football team. He slept in the dorm during the two-a-day drills, ate at the training table, and ran wind sprints with the team every night. Sometimes his interest would wander and he fell behind, and when he did Marv Goux would shout at him and accuse him of dogging it. If he got too tired, he would simply jump up into Coach McKay's golf cart and ride. Turd went everywhere the team went . . . even into the huddle with the offensive team. Somewhere from that circle of 22 muscular legs you could see a furry tail protruding. When the huddle broke up, he would trot to the sideline and watch the play. The players enjoyed him and he kept them loose, probably because it was the first time any USC team had a mascot that could join them in practice . . . after all, a 1400 pound white horse in a huddle? Wind sprints maybe, but . . . at any rate Pete Adams went to the NFL the following year and Turd went with him. He is now a pro dog. The amount of his contract is not known.

UNIVERSITY OF SOUTHERN CALIFORNIA 1972 ALPHABETICAL ROSTER

NO.	NAME	POS.	HT.	WT.	AGE	CLASS	HOMETOWN (HIGH SCHOOL)
77	Pete Adams	O.T.	6'4"	256	21	Sr.	San Diego (University)
8	Rob Adolph	Q.B.	6'0"	187	20	So.	Dinuba
55	Charles Anthony	L.B.	6'0"	235	19	Jr.	Fresno (Edison)
69	Tom Bohlinger	D.E.	6'2"	221	21	Jr.	Santa Ynez
7	Dave Boulware	F.L.	6'1"	192	21	Jr.	Downey (Warren)
63	Booker Brown	O.G.	6'3"	255	20	Jr.	Santa Barbara
57	Dave Brown	O.C.	6'0"	229	21	Sr.	Glendale (Eagle Rock)
50	Kevin Bruce	O.G.	6'1"	225	17	Fr.	La Canada (St. Francis)
82	Glen Byrd	D.T.	6'3"	234	20	So.	Oakland (McClymonds)
16	John Cantwell	W.R.	6'1"	174	18	So.	San Pedro (Fermin Lasuen)
17	Phil Cantwell	W.R.	6'1"	188	20	So.	San Pedro (Fermin Lausen)
21	Allen Carter	T.B.	5'11"	205	18	So.	Bonita
15	Chris Chaney	F.L.	6'2"	187	21	Sr.	West Covina (Bishop Amat)
24	Marvin Cobb	D.B.	6'0"	178	18	So.	Carson (Notre Dame, R.)
42	Pat Collins	D.B.	6'2"	188	21	Jr.	San Diego (St. Augustine)
71	James Cordell	O.T.	6'5"	250	18	Fr.	Long Beach (Wilson)
54	Cliff Culbreath	O.G.	6'2"	239	21	Sr.	San Bernardino (Pacific)
39	Sam Cunningham	F.B.	6'3"	218	21	Sr.	Santa Barbara
28	Anthony Davis	T.B.	5'9"	185	20	So.	San Fernando
64	Joe Davis	O.T.	6'4"	249	18	Fr.	Claremont
72	Monte Doris	D.G.	6'3"	232	19	Jr.	Fresno
47	Steve Fate	D.B.	6'1"	199	20	Sr.	Anaheim (Servite)
70	George Follett	D.T.	6'4"	249	22	Sr.	Huntington Beach
76	Allen Gallaher	G.-T.	6'3"	261	21	Sr.	Sylmar
19	Edsel Garrison	S.E.	6'1"	204	20	Sr.	Compton (Centennial)
88	James Givehand	D.E.	6'2"	218	19	So.	Los Angeles (Verbum Dei)
61	Allan Graf	O.G.	6'2"	243	22	Sr.	San Fernando
94	John Grant	O.T.	6'5"	237	21	Sr.	Boise, Idaho (Capital)
37	Ken Gray	L.B.	6'0"	216	18	So.	San Pedro
10	Pat Haden	Q.B.	6'0"	172	18	So.	West Covina (Bishop Amat)
95	Mike Hancock	D.G.	6'3"	239	21	So.	Norwalk (St. Paul's)
26	Charles Hinton	D.B.	5'10"	198	21	Sr.	E. Orange, New Jersey
11	Eddie Johnson	D.B.	5'11"	168	21	Sr.	Oceanside
96	Jim Lee	D.T.	6'5"	217	21	Jr.	Granada Hills (Monroe)
86	Dean Lingenfelter	T.E.	6'4"	233	20	Jr.	Pomona (Ganesha)
79	Karl Lorch	D.T.	6'3"	226	21	Sr.	Honolulu (Kamehameha)
40	James Lucas	D.B.	6'3"	192	18	Fr.	Arcadia
58	Bob McCaffrey	C.	6'2"	237	20	So.	Bakersfield (Garces)
25	J. K. McKay	S.E.	6'0"	175	18	So.	Covina (Bishop Amat)
27	Rod McNeill	T.B.	6'2"	218	21	Jr.	Baldwin Park
85	Dale Mitchell	L.B.	6'2"	213	18	So.	Carlsbad
44	Manfred Moore	T.B.	6'1"	188	21	Jr.	San Fernando
14	Artimus Parker	D.B.	6'3"	212	20	Jr.	Sacramento
48	Al Pekarcik	D.B.	5'11"	186	20	Sr.	Anaheim (Loara)
49	Charles Phillips	D.B.	6'2"	203	18	So.	Pasadena (Blair)
87	Ed Powell	D.E.	6'2"	213	18	So.	Richmond (Kennedy)
6	Mike Rae	Q.B.	6'1"	190	20	Sr.	Lakewood
78	Steve Riley	O.T.	6'4"	261	19	Jr.	Chula Vista (Castle Park)
52	Ray Rodriguez	L.B.	5'11"	193	20	Jr.	Los Angeles (Roosevelt)
68	Mike Ryan	O.G.	6'2"	252	21	Sr.	San Francisco (St. Ignatius)
62	Bob Shaputis	O.T.	6'4"	245	20	Jr.	Norwalk (St. John Bosco)
41	James Sims	D.E.	6'0"	198	20	Jr.	Los Angeles (Locke)
56	Mike Smith	O.T.	6'4"	230	18	So.	Montebello
90	George Stewart	O.T.	6'4"	219	17	Fr.	Pasadena
22	Lynn Swann	W.R.	6'0"	179	20	Jr.	Foster City (Serra)
81	Chris Vella	T.E.	6'4"	227	21	Sr.	Van Nuys (Notre Dame)
34	Ray Washmera	F.B.	6'1"	212	20	Jr.	San Francisco (St. Ignatius)
92	Jeff Winans	D.T.	6'4"	245	20	Sr.	Turlock
83	Richard Wood	L.B.	6'2"	220	18	So.	Elizabeth, N.J. (Jefferson)
89	Charles Young	T.E.	6'4"	228	21	Sr.	Fresno (Edison)

UNIVERSITY OF NOTRE DAME 1972 ALPHABETICAL ROSTER

NO.	NAME	POS.	HT.	WT.	CLASS	HOMETOWN
52	Alvarado, Joe	C.	6'1"	224	Jr.	E. Chicago, Mich.
14	Barnett, Reggie	D.H.B.	5'11"	180	So.	Flint, Mich.
62	Bolger, Tom	O.G.	6'2"	225	Jr.	Cincinnati, Ohio
63	Borbely, Joe	O.G.	6'1"	232	Sr.	Akron, Ohio
78	Briick, Herb	O.T.	6'4"	230	Sr.	Hinsdale, Ill.
8	Brown, Cliff	Q.B.	6'0"	196	Jr.	Middletown, Pa.
68	Casper, Dave	O.T.-T.E.	6'3"	240	Jr.	Chilton, Wisc.
35	Cieszkowski, John	F.B.	6'2"	220	Sr.	Detroit, Mich.
2	Clements, Tom	Q.B.	6'0"	180	So.	McKees Rocks, Pa.
50	Collins, Greg	L.B.	6'3"	216	So.	Troy, Mich.
91	Creaney , Mike	T.E.	6'4"	232	Sr.	Towson, Md.
67	Dampeer, John	O.T.	6'4"	237	Sr.	Kermit, Texas
10	Dewan, Darryll	H.B.	6'0"	204	Sr.	Danbury, Conn.
28	Diminick, Gary	H.B.	5'9"	168	Jr.	Mt. Carmel, Mich.
72	Dinardo, Gerry	O.G.	6'1"	240	So.	Howard Beach, N.Y.
9	Doherty, Brian	Q.B.-B.	6'2"	188	Jr.	Portland, Ore.
59	Drew, Dave	C.	6'2"	220	Sr.	Vestal, N.Y.
19	Etter, Bill	Q.B.	6'2"	185	Sr.	Spokane, Wash.
88	Fanning, Mike	D.E.	6'6"	260	So.	Tulsa, Okla.
32	Fiber, Ed	L.B.	5'11"	185	Sr.	Fremont, Ohio
96	Freistroffer, Tom	D.E.	6'4"	234	Sr.	Fort Wayne, Ind.
5	Garner, Terry	S.	6'1"	185	Sr.	Canton, Ohio
25	Gutowski, Dennis	D.B.	5'10"	181	Sr.	Hobart, Ind.
33	Haggar, Joe	D.H.B.	5'11"	172	Sr.	Dallas, Texas
53	Hartman, Pete	C.	6'1"	233	Jr.	San Francisco, Calif.
95	Hayduk, George	D.E.	6'3"	240	Jr.	Factoryville, Pa.
99	Hein, Jeff	D.E.	6'1"	224	Jr.	Cincinnati, Ohio
22	Hill, Greg	H.B.	6'1"	185	Jr.	Pilot Mountain, N.C.
20	Huff, Andy	F.B.	5'11"	210	Sr.	Toledo, Ohio
77	Kondrk, John	O.G.	6'5"	257	Sr.	Hopelawn, N.J.
69	Lozzi, Dennis	T.	6'3"	253	Jr.	Whitman, Mich.
76	Maciag, Dick	D.T.	6'5"	277	Sr.	Buffalo, N.Y.
45	Mahalic, Drew	L.B.	6'4"	213	So.	Birmingham, Mich.
31	Mariani, John	L.B.	5'11"	195	Sr.	Chester Heights, Pa.
75	Marx, Greg	D.T.	6'5"	260	Sr.	Redford, Mich.
74	McBride, Mike	O.T.	6'5"	256	Jr.	Michigan City, Ind.
46	McGraw, Pat	L.B.	6'1"	221	Sr.	Ft. Collins, Colo.
66	Morrin, Dan	O.G.	6'4"	230	Jr.	Croydan, Pa.
47	Musuraca, Jim	L.B.	6'0"	214	Sr.	East Liverpool. Ohio
49	Naughton, Mike	D.H.B.	6'3"	186	Jr.	Bloomfield Hills, Ohio
60	Nosbusch, Kevin	D.T.	6'4"	267	So.	Milwaukee, Wisc.
81	O'Mally, Jim	L.B.	6'2"	221	Sr.	Youngstown, Ohio
44	Penick, Eric	H.B.	6'1"	195	So.	Cleveland, Ohio
56	Pomarico, Frank	O.G.	6'1"	238	Jr.	Howard Beach, N.Y.
40	Potempa, Gary	L.B.	6'0"	225	Jr.	Niles, Ill.
90	Quehl, Steve	T.E.	6'4"	220	So.	Cincinnati, Ohio
83	Robinson, Tyrone	D.E.	6'2"	226	Sr.	Philadelphia, Pa.
6	Roolf, Jim	S.E.	6'0"	185	Sr.	Sewickly, Pa.
7	Rudnick, Tim	D.H.B.	5'10"	185	Jr.	Chicago, Ill.
24	Samuel, Al	S.E.	6'1"	178	So.	Newport News, Va.
16	Schlezes, Ken	D.H.B.	6'3"	192	Sr.	Rochelle, Ill.
3	Smith, Scott	K.	5'10"			
55	Smith, Sherman	L.B.	6'2"	208	So.	Chillicothe, Mo.
42	Sullivan, Tim	L.B.	6'3"	219	Jr.	DesMoines, Iowa
71	Sylvester, Steve	O.T.	6'4"	248	So.	Milford, Ohio
65	Szatko, Greg	D.T.	6'4"	251	Jr.	Western Springs, Ill.
98	Thomas, Robert	K.	5'10"	178	Jr.	Rochester, N.Y.
27	Townsend, Mike	D.H.B.	6'3"	183	Jr.	Hamilton, Ohio
80	Townsend, Willie	S.E.	6'3"	196	Jr.	Hamilton, Ohio
34	Zanot, Robert	D.B.	6'0"	183	Fr.	Riverton, Ill.

1973
CHAPTER 46

"SHOULD I, TOM?, SHOULD I?"
. . . Ara Parseghian, 1973

In the early days of vaudeville, theatre managers had a rather unique way of informing performers that their act was not going all too well. They simply posted a note on the call board, DON'T SEND OUT ANY LAUNDRY. In the college football business the story is told that the day after a disastrous season ended a well known coach sat moping at the breakfast table. Finally, for want of something to do, some distraction . . . he said to his wife, "Well, I guess I'll go out and rake the leaves and fertilize the roses for next year."

"My dear," replied his long suffering wife, "If you heard what I heard in the stands yesterday, you wouldn't even start a short story."

There's an old adage also bandied about the coaching circuit. "Coaches don't build houses." Ara did . . . and before his team had played game number one. He had that kind of confidence.

Another characteristic he and McKay had in common. Supreme confidence in their own ability. All successful coaches seem to possess that quality. Makes sense. If you don't have it, you're not successful . . . if you're not successful you don't remain a head coach very long. Bear Bryant has that kind of iron clad confidence. McKay likes to tell the story of the time he was visiting the Bear at his home in Alabama.

"John," said Bear, "I have a lovely surprise for you. Tomorrow morning we are going to arise at 3:30 A.M., have some ham, eggs, biscuits, gravy and grits and get down to the duck blind by 4:30, watch the sun come up and get us some ducks."

"Bear," moaned McKay, "I wouldn't get up at 3:30 in the goddamn morning to see the last supper with the original cast, and I am a Catholic."

But Bear Bryant is a most persuasive man. The following morning, according to McKay, he, Bryant and Jack Daniels sat in a duck blind waiting for some unsuspecting flock to blunder into their murderous trap. None did. They waited . . . and waited . . . and waited. After three hours or more, a solitary duck, either lost or as disoriented as the coaches were by that time, happened to wander by. The Bear aimed and fired. The duck flapped nonchalantly on his way and probably made it to Fort Lauderdale without any further harassment. With a jaundiced eye, Bryant watched the duck slowly disappear in the morning haze and turned to McKay and announced,

Lynn Swann catches TD pass from Pat Haden

Tom Clements directs Irish air attack

"John, you are witnessing a genuine, bona fide miracle. There flies a dead duck."

"That," says McKay, "is confidence."

By October 27th, 1973, Coach Ara Parseghian's home had been lived in for nearly ten years, he had won 78 games, tied 4 and lost only 13. He was 5-0 on his way to his second unbeaten season. He made it and he was confident he would.

As a kind of fringe benefit along the way he acquired the national championship, and the Associated Press ranked the Irish number one. United Press International, who has agreed with AP 19 times out of the 24 times they have both voted, disagreed this time. They judged the Irish to be fourth.*

But Southern California was no pushover. They were 5-0-1 and AP thought they were good enough to be rated 4th, UPI thought 6th. The oddsmakers were only mildly impressed, the Trojans were favored by a single point. After the 1966 shellacking, it was reported that McKay vowed publicly never to lose to Notre Dame again. He never said such a thing. He's much too smart for that . . . but you can bet your junior varsity jock strap he was thinking it. He also had a 23 game unbeaten streak going. And he still had Anthony Davis. For A. D. to simply de-plane in South Bend, Indiana had to take the same kind of foolhardy courage it took for Horatio to stand alone on that bridge a few centuries ago . . . or for that idiotic commander of the Light Brigade to shout, "CHARGE," and ride into the valley of death with the other 599 unfortunates.

Davis was about as welcome in Notre Dame, Indiana as an Arab in Miami Beach or a mother-in-law on a honeymoon. They had his picture taped to the sidewalks in South Bend so

Eric Pennick is off on his TD jaunt. This was the turning point for Irish

they could step on his face . . . he was hanged in effigy by semi-hysterical mobs of Notre Dame students screaming, "REMEMBER . . . REMEMBER . . . REVENGE . . . REVENGE." Those of more religious persuasion prayed for divine intercession.

"Our Father Who Art in Heaven," "Don't Let Anthony Davis Score Seven."

He didn't. He scored one on a one yard sweep.

Under the sullen skies of a northern Indiana autumn, John McKay's win streak came to an end. Nearly 60,000 screaming fans, most of them pro-Irish of course, watched the Trojans go down to a 23-14 defeat. Their first loss to Notre Dame in six years.

Notre Dame scored first on a 32 yard field goal by Bob Thomas, after Jim Lucas' punt was partially blocked by Tim

Rudnick and traveled only 15 yards. Lucas had a lousy day and Bob Thomas had a good one. That was the real difference in the game. Both teams scored two touchdowns, but Notre Dame scored three field goals and in the first half, SC whose kicking game had been good thus far this season, couldn't punt out of its own way. Lucas couldn't get more than 33 yards and presented the Irish with the ball on the Trojan eight the first time, then the Irish 41, then the USC 47. All the short punts led to Irish scores in the first half.

But at the end of the first quarter the Trojans led. Anthony Davis made 22 yards in six carries. Lynn Swann caught a 26 yard pass from Haden, and Davis went the final yard. 65 yards in nine plays. Chris Limahelu contributed the extra point to put Southern Cal in the lead 7-3.

*In the Associated Press poll the teams are selected by the sportswriters. The UPI choices are rated by college coaches. Since UPI got into the act in 1950, they have agreed on Notre Dame's standing five times . . . on USC's only twice, in 1967 and 1972. They hadn't agreed on Notre Dame since 1966. At game time in 1973 the Irish were rated 7th by AP and 8th by UPI.

1973 NOTRE DAME FOOTBALL TEAM

1st Row (l to r): Joe Alvarado, Tom Creevey, George Hayduk, Bob Thomas, Brian Doherty, Lew Miskowitz, Dave Casper, Mike Townsend, Frank Pomarico, Dan Morrin, Willie Townsend, Tim Rudnick, Tim Sullivan, Gary Potempa, Mike Naughton.

2nd Row: John Gambone, Larry Susko, Max Wasilevich, Tom Bolger, Mike McBride, Jim Zloch, Gary Lane, Kevin Kinealy, Gary Diminick, Cliff Brown, Bob Washington, Mike Parker, Greg Hill, Mark Brenneman, Pete Hartman, Dennis Lozzi, Mike Webb, Ed Scales, Greg Szatko.

3rd Row: Sherman Smith, Steve Quehl, Bob Sweeney, Drew Mahalic, Frank Allocco, Kevin Nosbusch, Tom Clements, Tim Miller, Tom Bake, Steve Sylvester, Andrew Rohan, Tom Laney, Pete Demmerle, Bill Arment, Steve Bossu, John Audino, Steve Neece, John O'Donnell, Gerry DiNardo.

4th Row: Mike McGuire, Jeff Hein, Paul Sawicz, Jim Chauncey, Bob McGreevey, Eric Penick, Wayne Bullock, Al Samuel, Ron Goodman, Reggie Barnett, Tom Fine, Mike Fanning, Greg Collins, Tom Parise, Tony Brantley, Kurt Horton, Pat Sarb, Al Wujciak, John Galanis, Pat Pohlen, Joe Pszeracki.

5th Row: Ivan Brown, Bob Zanot, Randy Payne, Bob Walls, Fred Trosko, Kevin Doherty, Art Best, Jay Achterhoff, Bob Messaros, Tom Lopienski, Frank Rutkowski, Calvin Balliet, Ken Andler, Nick Fedorenko, Jim Stock, Tony Novakov, Rick Slager, Steve Niehaus, Tom Maschmeier, Russ Kornman, Fran McDonald, Robin Weber.

6th Row: Luther Bradley, Kerry Moriarty, Tom Eastman, Mike Ostrander, Ed Sharkey, Tony Zappala, John Rufo, Drew Pattyn, Ross Bonder, Tom Gullickson, Ed Gleckler, John Soutner, Stan Bobowski, Mike Kafka, Mike Banks, Steve Humbert, Marvin Russell, John Likovich, Elton Moore, Jack Lloyd, Doug Buth, Don Rodenkirk, Don Malinak.

7th Row: Ross Browner, John Harchar, Tom Katenkamp, Dan Knott, Mark Ewald, Al Hunter, Roy Henry, Tom Unis, Gene Smith, Willie Fry, Bill Sohan, Jim Weiler, Rich Allocco, Terry Leary, John Dubenetzky, Tim Simon, Dan Kelleher, Vince Klees, Dave Buck.

8th Row: Joe Sweeney, Kevin Flanagan, Gene O'Neill, Mike Creaney, Greg Blache, John Murphy, Joe Yonto, George Kelly, Paul Shoults, Ara Parseghian, Tom Pagna, Wally Moore, Brian Boulac, Mike Stock, Denny Murphy, Bill Hickey, Larry DiNardo, Gene Paszkiet, Gary Bockrath.

NOTRE DAME — 1973

79	Achterhoff, Jay Sophomore	D.T., 6'4", 249 Muskegon, Mich. (Muskegon)
12	Allocco, Frank Junior	Q.B., 6'1", 178 New Providence, N.J. (New Providence)
52	Alvarado, Joe Senior	C., 6'1", 232 East Chicago, Ind. (Hammond Noll)
63	Balliet, Calvin Sophomore	O.G., 6'4", 220 Moorestown, N.J. (North Allegheny)
14	Barnett, Reggie Junior	D.H.B., 5'11", 182 Flint, Mich. (Central)
23	Best, Art Sophomore	H.B., 6'1", 200 Gahanna, Ohio (Bishop Hartley)
62	Bolger, Tom Senior	O.G., 6'2", 229 Cincinnati, Ohio (Elder)
20	Bradley, Luther Freshman	D.H.B., 6'2", 194 Muncie, Ind. (Northside)
4	Brantley, Tony Sophomore	P., 6'0", 200 Oklahoma City, Okla. (Putnam City)
59	Brenneman, Mark Senior	C., 6'4", 230 York, Pa. (West York Area)
8	Brown, Cliff Senior	Q.B., 6'0", 193 Middletown, Pa. (Middletown Area)
46	Brown, Ivan Sophomore	D.E., 6'3", 220 LeRoy, Ill. (LeRoy High)
89	Browner, Ross Freshman	D.E., 6'3", 218 Warren, O. (Reserve)
30	Bullock, Wayne Junior	F.B., 6'1", 210 Newport News, Va. (G. W. Carver)
86	Casper, Dave Senior	T.E., 6'3", 240 Chilton, Wisc. (Chilton)
13	Chauncey, Jim Junior	D.H.B., 6'0", 174 Wheat Ridge, Colo. (Wheat Ridge)
2	Clements, Tom Junior	Q.B., 6'0", 185 McKees Rocks, Pa. (Canevin)
50	Collins, Greg Junior	L.B., 6'3", 220 Troy, Mich. (Bro. Rice, Birmingham)
41	Creevey, Tom Senior	D.E., 6'3", 210 Mishawaka, Ind. (Marian)
85	Demmerle, Pete Junior	S.E., 6'1", 190 New Canaan, Conn. (New Canaan)
28	Diminick, Gary Senior	H.B., 5'9", 166 Mt. Carmel, Pa. (Mt. Carmel Area)
72	DiNardo, Gerry Junior	O.G., 6'1", 242 Howard Beach, N.Y. (St. Francis Prep)
9	Doherty, Brian Senior	P., 6'2", 186 Portland, Ore. (Jesuit)
32	Doherty, Kevin Sophomore	S.E., 6'0", 174 Portland, Ore. (Jesuit)
88	Fanning, Mike Junior	D.T., 6'6", 254 Tulsa, Okla. (Edison)
93	Fine, Tom Junior	T.E., 6'5", 234 Apple Valley, Calif. (Apple Valley)
94	Fry, Willie Freshman	D.E., 6'3", 220 Memphis, Tenn. (Northside)
96	Galanis, John Sophomore	D.E., 6'4", 223 Ipswich, Mass. (Ipswich High)
35	Gambone, John Senior	F.B., 6'1", 207 Canton, Ohio (St. Thomas Aquinas)
21	Goodman, Ron Junior	H.B., 5'11", 192 Mt. Sinai, N.Y. (Port Jefferson)
53	Hartman, Pete Senior	C., 6'1", 244 San Francisco, Calif. (St. Ignatius)
95	Hayduk, George Senior	D.T., 6'3", 240 Factoryville, Pa. (Lackawanna Trail)
99	Hein, Jeff Senior	F.B., 6'1", 235 Cincinnati, Ohio (Oakwood, Canton)
25	Hunter, Al Freshman	H.B., 5'11", 189 Greenville, N.C. (J. H. Rose)
92	Miskowitz, Lew Senior	D.T., 5'11", 234 Rock Island, Ill. (Rock Island)
57	Moore, Elton Freshman	O.G., 6'1", 230 Portland, Ore. (Jesuit)
66	Morrin, Dan Senior	O.G., 6'3", 235 Croydan, Pa. (Bishop Egan)
49	Naughton, Mike Sr.	D.H.B., 6'3", 185 Bloomfield Hills, Mich. (Assump., Ont., Can.)
64	Neece, Steve Junior	O.T., 6'3", 253 Janesville, Wisc. (Craig)
60	Nosbusch, Kevin Junior	D.T., 6'4", 259 Milwaukee, Wisc. (Pius X)
38	Novakov, Tony Sophomore	L.B., 5'11", 195 Cincinnati, Ohio (Moeller)
36	Parise, Tom Sophomore	F.B., 6'0", 208 Longmont, Colo. (Longmont)
33	Parker, Mike Junior	D.H.B., 5'11", 175 Cincinnati, Ohio (Elder)
16	Payne, Randy Sophomore	D.H.B., 5'9", 175 Palmer Park, Md. (Largo Senior)
44	Penick, Eric Junior	H.B., 6'1", 213 Cleveland, Ohio (Gilmour Academy)
56	Pomarico, Frank Senior	O.G., 6'1", 250 Howard Beach, N.Y. (St. Francis)
40	Potempa, Gary Senior	L.B., 6'0", 227 Niles, Ill. (Notre Dame)
47	Pszeracki, Joe Sophomore	L.B., 5'11", 214 Ambridge, Pa. (Ambridge)
77	Quehl, Steve Junior	O.T., 6'4", 238 Cincinnati, Ohio (St. Xavier)
65	Rohan, Andy Junior	C., 6'1", 234 Cincinnati, Ohio (St. Xavier)
7	Rudnick, Tim Senior	D.H.B., 5'10", 187 Chicago, Ill. (Notre Dame)
24	Samuel, Al Junior	H.B., 6'1", 178 Newport News, Va. (Huntington)
29	Sarb, Pat Sophomore	D.H.B., 6'0", 181 Dearborn, Mich. (Sacred Heart)
76	Sawicz, Paul Senior	O.G., 6'4", 238 Lackawanna, N.Y. (Canisius, Buffalo)
97	Simon, Tim Freshman	S.E., 5'10", 165 Pontiac, Mich. (Waterford-Mott)
11	Slager, Rick Sophomore	Q.B., 5'11", 192 Columbus, Ohio (Upper Arlington)
75	Smith, Gene Freshman	L.B., 6'2", 224 Cleveland, Ohio (Chanel)
55	Smith, Sherm Junior	L.B., 6'2", 210 Chillicothe, Mo. (Chillicothe)
48	Stock, Jim Sophomore	D.E., 6'3", 210 Barberton, Ohio (Barberton)
42	Sullivan, Tim Senior	L.B., 6'3", 227 Des Moines, Iowa (Dowling)
73	Susko, Larry Senior	D.T., 6'1", 262 Sharpsville, Pa. (Sharpsville Area)
69	Sweeney, Bob Junior	O.T., 6'5", 244 Salem, Mass. (Salem)
71	Sylvester, Steve Junior	O.T., 6'4", 236 Milford, Ohio (Moeller, Cincinnati)
67	Szatko, Greg Senior	D.T., 6'4", 241 Western Springs, Ill. (Lyons Township)
98	Thomas Bob Senior	K., 5'10", 171 Rochester, N.Y. (McQuaid Jesuit)
27	Townsend, Mike Senior	D.H.B., 6'3", 178 Hamilton, Ohio (Garfield)
80	Townsend, Willie Senior	S.E., 6'3", 196 Hamilton, Ohio (Garfield)
10	Trosko, Fred Sophomore	Q.B., 6'2", 195 Ypsilanti, Mich. (Ypsilanti High)

SOUTHERN CAL — 1973

9	Adolph, Rob Senior	Q.B., 6'1", 189 Dinuba, Calif.	
55	Anthony, Charles Senior	L.B., 6'0", 230 Fresno, Calif.	
66	Bain, Bill Junior	O.G., 6'4", 273 Pico Rivera, Calif.	
42	Bell, Rickey Freshman	L.B., 6'1", 201 Los Angeles, Calif.	
69	Bohlinger, Tom Senior	L.B., 6'2", 197 Santa Ynez, Calif.	
7	Boulware, Dave Senior	F.L., 6'1", 189 Downey, Calif.	
92	Bradley, Otha Junior	D.T., 6'1", 264 St. Joseph, La., Calif.	
63	Brown, Booker Senior	O.T., 6'3", 267 Santa Barbara, Calif.	
50	Bruce, Kevin Sophomore	L.B., 6'0", 212 LaCanada, Calif.	
82	Byrd, Glenn Junior	D.T., 6'4", 231 Oakland, Calif.	
16	Cantwell, John Junior	F.L., 5'11", 180 San Pedro, Calif.	
5	Carey, Mike Freshman	ROV., 6'1", 191 San Francisco, Calif.	
21	Carter, Allen Junior	T.B., 6'0", 201 San Dimas, Calif.	
24	Cobb, Marvin Junior	D.B., 6'0", 175 Riverside, Calif.	
71	Cordell, Mike Sophomore	O.G., 6'3", 238 Long Beach, Calif.	
28	Davis, Anthony Junior	T.B., 5'9", 190 San Fernando, Calif.	
64	Davis, Joe Sophomore	O.G., 6'3", 244 Claremont, Calif.	
26	Diggs, Shelton Freshman	F.L., 6'3", 190 San Bernardino, Calif.	
72	Doris, Monte Senior	D.G., 6'4", 242 Fresno, Calif.	
67	Flood, Jeff Sophomore	C., 6'2", 228 Escondido, Calif.	
38	Fudge, Bill Sophomore	F.B., 6'0", 225 Santee, Calif.	
37	Gray, Ken Junior	F.B., 6'2", 218 San Pedro, Calif.	
10	Pat Haden Junior	Q.B., 5'11", 180 West Covina, Calif.	
6	Hertel, Rob Freshman	Q.B., 6'3", 174 Hacienda Hts., Calif.	
48	Hogan, Doug Sophomore	D.B., 6'4", 196 San Diego, Calif.	
54	Jackson, Melvin Sophomore	L.B., 6'1", 243 Los Angeles, Calif.	
79	Jeter, Gary Freshman	D.T., 6'5", 250 Cleveland, Ohio	
77	Knutson, Steve Junior	O.T., 6'3", 248 SouthGate, Calif.	
11	Limahelu, Chris Senior	K., 5'5", 135 Covina, Calif.	
86	Lingenfelter, Dean Senior	T.E., 6'3", 226 Pomona, Calif.	
40	Lucas, James Sophomore	P., 6'2", 198 Arcadia, Calif.	
73	Marderian, Greg Junior	D.T., 6'4", 235 Granada Hills, Calif.	
58	McCaffrey, Bob Junior	C., 6'2", 238 Bakersfield, Calif.	
74	McGirr, Mike Senior	O.T., 6'5", 263 Walnut, Calif.	
25	McKay, John Junior	S.E., 5'11", 178 Covina, Calif.	
27	McNeill, Rod Senior	T.B., 6'3", 213 Baldwin Park, Calif.	
60	Miller, Bob Sophomore	L.B., 6'1", 210 Memphis, Tenn.	
44	Moore, Manfred Senior	F.B., 6'0", 187 San Fernando, Calif.	
85	Mitchell, Dale Junior	L.B., 6'3", 204 Carlsbad, Calif.	
89	Obradovich, Jim Junior	T.E., 6'2", 217 El Segundo, Calif.	
45	O'Brien, Bill Sophomore	D.B., 6'2", 198 Montebello, Calif.	
14	Parker, Artimus Senior	D.B., 6'3", 205 Sacramento, Calif.	
65	Patton, Marty Senior	C., 6'2", 227 Downey, Calif.	
49	Phillips, Charles Junior	D.B. Pasadena, Calif.	
87	Powell, Ed Junior	L.B., 6'1", 220 Richmond, Calif.	
88	Powell, Marvin Freshman	T.E., 6'4", 238 Fayetteville, N.C.	
12	Randle, Ken Sophomore	S.E., 6'0", 183 Kansas City, Calif.	
46	Reece, Danny Sophomore	D.B., 5'11", 180 Wilmington, Calif.	
75	Rhames, Tim Sophomore	D.G., 6'2", 222 Fresno, Calif.	
29	Rice, Brad Freshman	S.E., 6'3", 189 Sepulveda, Calif.	
70	Riley, Art Junior	D.T., 6'4", 238 Phoenix, Ill.	
78	Riley, Steve Senior	O.T., 6'5", 248 Chula Vista, Calif.	
47	Roberson, Ted Sophomore	D.B., 5'11", 175 Bakersfield, Calif.	
52	Rodriguez, Ray Senior	L.B., 5'11", 191 Los Angeles, Calif.	
62	Shaputis, Bob Senior	O.T., 6'4", 243 Norwalk, Calif.	
41	Sims, James Senior	L.B., 6'0", 193 Los Angeles, Calif.	
56	Smith, Mike Junior	O.G., 6'3", 244 Montebello, Calif.	
90	Stewart, George Sophomore	D.T., 6'4", 233 Pasadena, Calif.	
22	Swann, Lynn Senior	F.L., 6'0", 175 San Mateo, Calif.	
34	Washmera, Ray Senior	F.B., 6'1", 207 San Francisco, Calif.	
83	Wood, Richard Junior	L.B., 6'2", 213 Elizabeth, N.J.	

1974
CHAPTER 47

"THE WEATHER DIDN'T SEEM TO BOTHER HIM WHEN HE BEAT US 51-0 IN 1966."
. . . John McKay, 1974

Oscar Wilde once noted that a man cannot be too careful in his choice of enemies (he should have heeded his own advice . . . he wasn't even too careful in his choice of friends. But what the hell, if he had been more circumspect we would have been deprived of *The Ballad of Reading Gaol*).

By 1974 it was obvious that the University of Notre Dame and the University of Southern California had chosen well. True, this 48 year old love-hate relationship between the two had clearly established the Irish as the dominant partner, BUT . . . since McKay's first season in 1960, things had evened out a bit. That year the series score stood Notre Dame 21, SC 9 and two ties. In the next thirteen years USC won 6, Notre Dame 5 and they played two more ties. And on this November 30th meeting in the Coliseum, they could hardly have been better matched. The Trojans were favored by four points, but the Irish were rated number one defensively in the country, having allowed only nine touchdowns to be scored against them all season. The Trojans were not far behind, they had yielded only 101 points.

Both had been consistent in their inconsistency. Notre Dame had been picked to maul Purdue, but lost 20-31. USC stumbled before an inferior Arkansas team 7-22. Both had beaten superior teams and struggled to win over weak teams, and both had bowl invitations — the Irish to the Orange Bowl and the Trojans to the Rose Bowl. Their season records were substantially the same. Notre Dame 9-1-0, USC 8-1-1.

For most of the season they had been ranked almost even. At game time UPI ranked USC fourth and Notre Dame fifth. The Associated Press saw it differently, USC sixth and Notre Dame seventh.* An interesting match-up, another hard fought game . . . a tight game, a defensive game with little scoring, right? Well, partly. An interesting match-up it was and it was certainly a hard fought game, but tight it was not.

On a gloomy overcast autumn afternoon, 83,552 incredulous fans watched the Trojans of Southern California bury the Fighting Irish of Notre Dame 55-24 . . . but it wasn't the size of the score that boggled their minds; it as the way it was done. At halftime it was Notre Dame 24, Southern Cal 6, then in the second half . . . but let's not get ahead of the script.

Anthony Davis, USC All American Tailback

*The difference was that AP ranked Oklahoma number one, but since the Sooners were on probation, the coaches who voted in the UPI poll refused to rank them at all and named Alabama to the number one spot.

J.K. McKay makes catch on 10 yard line and goes on in and scores

People who live in Tinsel Town live with fantasy every day. They grow accustomed to it. After a while they begin to expect the same miracles to happen off the silver screen that they produce on it. On November 30, 1974, they were not disappointed. It was pure Hollywood at its 1930's best . . . written and produced by John McKay, directed by Pat Haden, starring himself, J. K. McKay, Anthony Davis and a cast of thousands. DeMille couldn't have done better. In the final two reels the bad guys didn't have a chance.

Opening scene: Quarterback Haden, directing the USC offense, has his confidence shaken by an interception and failure to make a first down with an inches to go gamble on his own 29-yard line. Dissolve to: Irish quarterback Tom Clements coolly, confidently and cleverly completing nine of twelve passes for 134 yards, one touchdown and directing his team to a 24-0 lead early in the first half.

Intercut shots of Wayne Bullock going in on a 2-yard plunge, split end Pete Demmerle catching a 29-yard pass for the second score, Dave Reeve kicking a 20-yard field goal and halfback Mark McLane capping a 79-yard drive with a nine-yard run into the end zone.

Cut to: SC's Anthony Davis fielding an eight yard pass in the end zone from Haden . . . Point after attempt blocked. Ten seconds to go to halftime. Close up of scoreboard: Notre Dame 24, USC 6. Sound effect: single shot from gun signifying end of half.

Not a bad scenario, but so far hardly dramatic enough to win any Academy awards . . .

But the producers of this epic opened the second half with a chase scene that electrified the entire audience and brought the production to a high level of drama. And there it stayed to the final gun.

Pat Haden, USC quarterback

Notre Dame started the second half by kicking off directly to Anthony Davis . . . how quickly they forget. But it seemed safe enough, after all he was two yards deep in the end zone and in the face of Notre Dame's vaunted defense the logical thing to do would be to ground the ball and bring it out to the 20-yard line. However, the roar of temptation almost always drowns out the whisper of logic, and nearly everybody knows the best way to silence temptation is to yield to it. Anthony Davis loves to fun with footballs . . . it is his greatest temptation in life. He yielded. He picked up some blockers, tore through a crowd at the 20, and with a key block from Mosi Tatupu broke free at his own 35, headed for the left sideline and the chase was on. Only one Irish defender had a chance to head him off at the pass and Mario Celotto took care of him at the Notre Dame 35. A. D. galloped the rest of the way unmolested with the Irish posse in futile pursuit.   Pandemonium.

Coach Parseghian tried to call time out, but the stadium had erupted in such deafening noise that he couldn't be heard. A. D. was so excited that he forgot to favor the crowd with his little knee dance.

The two point conversion failed, but A. D.'s performance so shook up the Notre Dame offensive unit that their attack bogged down almost immediately. SC tackle Art Riley forced the Irish to punt when he threw Eric Penick for a five yard loss on third down. Charley Phillips returned it to Notre Dame's 38 yard line and the Trojans were poised to strike again.

On second down J. K. McKay slanted across the field, got a step on Irish strong safety John Dubenetzky. Haden's pass was perfect. J. K. grabbed it on the 10 and made it to the six. A. D. powered over on the next play, Chris Lemahelu's kick was good and suddenly the Irish lead was trimmed to 24-19 and Ara sprouted a few new gray hairs.

Two minutes later, it was grayer still. The Trojans led 27-24. SC cornerback Danny Reese forced Irish wide receiver to fumble Tom Clement's pass and Trojan linebacker Kevin Bruce recovered on the 36-yard line of Notre Dame. Haden completed a 13-yard pass to Shelton Diggs, then a 17 yarder to J. K. McKay who made a spectacular acrobatic catch on the four-yard line right in front of Irish defensive halfback Reggie Barnett. Davis took the pitchout on the next play and drove in for his fourth touchdown of the day. To add insult to injury he also ran in his own two point conversion. The television audience probably thought they were watching an instant replay.

The Irish offense was numb . . . or possibly in pain. If so, it might have been sympathy pain for their defense. At any rate, the offensive unit seemed to have turned to stone before the Medusa-like stares of the Trojan defense.* Of course, Art Riley, Gary Jeter, Kevin Bruce, Marvin Cobb, Richard "Batman" Wood and Charley Phillips could have intimidated almost anyone that afternoon. Certainly Notre Dame. They were forced once more to punt after kickoff and this time it was Marvin Cobb's turn to do it to them. He returned the punt 58 yards to the 19 doing a sort of tightrope dance along the sideline. He very nearly made it all the way. Haden passed to McKay on third down. Eighteen yards down the middle. Irish halfback Randy Payne slipped and fell and left J. K. all alone. Johnny didn't mind being lonely, he simply scampered into the end zone where he knew he would presently be joined by many of his friends. Limahelu's kick was good and the score was now 34-24 and the Trojans were just getting warmed up.

The Notre Dame offense came out of its trance long enough to move the ball to the USC 35, but Phillips intercepted a Clement's pass and returned it 25 yards to the 50. Six plays later, the last play of the quarter, Haden and McKay decided to treat their visitors to an encore. The Irish secondary got mixed up just long enough to allow McKay to get lonely again — this time down the middle on a post pattern. From his own 45 Haden fired a bullet to J. K. on the two for an easy touchdown. The point after kick was good and the third quarter was over. The Fighting Irish of Notre Dame must have thought it would never end. 41-24, USC. The Trojans piled up 35 points in that quarter. In a little over nine minutes, they had scored 28 points.

The Irish just couldn't come out of shock. Remick fumbled again, Bruce recovered again and SC scored again. This time Haden to Diggs, a 16-yard touchdown pass and only *17 seconds* into the fourth quarter. A little over a minute later, Phillips intercepted Clements again with an amazing one-handed catch and loped 58 yards for another touchdown. That did it. The kick was good and the final score . . . USC 55, Notre Dame 24. In 17 minutes of the second half the Trojans scored 7 touchdowns . . . 49 points!

After the game, Irish linebacker Greg Collins sat in the locker room staring at the tips of his shoes. Suddenly he

Steve Niehaus, Notre Dame defensive tackle

looked up. "Say, what *was* the final score, anyway?", he asked.

The stats were amazingly close. Notre Dame had the edge in first downs, yards rushing, offensive plays and in pass completions. Total net yards were fairly close, SC 400, Notre Dame 367. The main difference was in the net yards passing . . . USC 254 to Notre Dame's 180, and the Trojans completed them when they counted.

The Southern Cal students, alumni, and fans were, of course, ecstatic to the point of hysteria. One west coast paper even compared the game to World War II when, ". . . the British after taking an early beating got off the floor to deck Germany." (?) And, ". . . George Washington . . . at Valley Forge turned it around on the British in 1778."

And of course the Trojan team was no less delirious. "We had some magic," said Anthony Davis. "We turned into madmen."

"It was pure fantasy," said Pat Haden. Even Coach McKay, in what for him was an outburst of victorious enthusiasm, said, "Yes, I think it's fair to say that this is probably one of the wildest things that ever happened on a football field."

Coach Parseghian probably agreed, but he wasn't saying much. His explanation for the second half collapse was that the weather in South Bend had been so cold that his team had not been able to train properly. "The cold weather seems to thicken the blood or something," he said.

Said John McKay, "The cold weather didn't seem to bother him in 1966 when he beat us 51-0."

Oddly enough the USC victory over Notre Dame had little effect on the standing in the polls. UPI still saw them fourth, AP did move them up one notch to fifth. Notre Dame dropped to ninth in both polls.

For the third straight year USC met genial Woody Hayes and his Ohio State Buckeyes in the Rose Bowl. This time, however, the game decided the UPI version of the national championship since Notre Dame, still eager to help the Trojans up the ladder, upset number one ranked Alabama in the Orange Bowl. So when USC upset Ohio State in the Rose Bowl, the Trojans were catapulted from fourth to first and won their seventh national championship. AP still had Oklahoma on top, USC second.

Notre Dame's victory over the Buckeyes moved them up to fourth in both polls, but the sting of the 55-24 loss was still there. No other team had ever scored 35 points in one quarter against the proud Irish of Notre Dame.

The 55 points scored against them by Southern Cal was only four short of the all time record of 59-0 perpetrated by Army in 1944. That massacre was engineered by Col. Red Blaik, aided and abetted by Glen Davis and Doc Blanchard. Notre Dame didn't even have a regular coach. Frank Leahy was in the service, as was nearly everyone who could place one foot in front of the other and that of course includes most varsity quality football players. But that sort of evens things up and all in all, for an interim coach, Ed McKeever was having a pretty good year. He had won five by impressive scores and lost only one to Navy when he ran into Army in Yankee Stadium on that terrible November afternoon. The following story is told:

Coach McKeever was no Rockne, and he had no George Gipp . . . he didn't even have his ghost. The spectre of the Gipper had been spot played against Army so many times it had begun to lose yardage. But McKeever did have an aunt, at least on November 11, 1944, he had one . . . and she was ill, very ill, in the hospital, listening to the game, so you know what the coach's halftime request was. A few minutes before the end of the fourth quarter, Irish quarterback Francis "Boley" Dancewicz, later with the Boston Yanks, told his team to concentrate on defense to hold down the score, rathern than take chances trying for touchdowns.

"But Boley," said one of the linemen, "what about the coach's poor old aunt?"

Boley looked up at the scoreboard which read ARMY 59-NOTRE DAME 0. "The hell with it," he growled. "If she ain't dead by now, she's by God immortal."

Ara Parseghian would suffer no more autumn afternoons like that one in November, 1974. He was quitting.

Ara Parseghian

Bowl in 1966 and beat Alabama 35-10 in the 1969 Gator Bowl contest. So Coach Devine was no neophyte college coach and he had had good training. After a short but very successful high school coaching career, he had gone to Michigan State University as Biggie Munn's freshman coach, and had stayed on to serve as Duffy Daugherty's backfield coach before going to Arizona State.

By the time Coach Devine and the Fighting Irish welcomed the Trojans in South Bend on October 25, 1975, the first-year coach of Notre Dame had logged five victories and one defeat. On paper that sort of record doesn't look too bad, but not everyone was happy with Coach Devine's handling of the available talent (although Parseghian, too, had lost one game by this time the previous year and had been plagued by the same inconsistency). The sole loss thus far was an upset win by Michigan State, but it seemed that the Irish were struggling lately to defeat inferior teams.

After defeating highly touted Boston College 17-3 in the first game of the season, and soundly trouncing Purdue 17-0 and Northwestern 31-7, the Irish had been upset by Michigan State 10-3. The following week they squeaked by North Carolina 21-14 on a last minute desperation pass. One week later, just seven days before facing unbeaten Southern Cal, they needed (and got) a 21 point fourth quarter to edge a weak Air Force team 30-31. So Notre Dame had, in the last three weeks, lost one and won two. But the two wins were over inferior teams and the Irish had to labor to beat them by a total margin of only eight points. You could hear the rosary beads clicking all the way to East Chicago.

In the City of Angels, the script was much the same . . . only the cast was different. The Trojans, too, were having another uneven year. Despite the fact that his team was 6-0 in conference play and ranked number three nationally, John McKay was not happy. "We threw poorly and we blocked poorly," said McKay after the Trojan's 17-3 victory over Oregon, then almost as an afterthought, "although I thought we punted well." The California press agreed with the coach. It was the consensus that USC was playing uninspired football and had been toiling to defeat teams that were 28-point underdogs.

"Marvin Powell, an All-American," continued McKay, "made only *three* blocks, and that's a couple more than other people made . . . This is the poorest passing team I've ever been around . . . Our receivers aren't good. Our flanker position is a disaster area; I think between them they've caught four passes all year. Shelton Diggs is the fastest receiver we've got, but every time he hits the ground his shoulder pops out. I'm beginning to think he's physically incapable of playing an entire game."

And so on . . . A litany of doom. It sounded too much like one of Rockne's diversionary tactics to be true, but it was. The

All American Ross Browner — Notre Dame

Trojans had suffered more broken limbs than a clumsy centipede. Dave Farmer had started it off in the second game of the season with a broken leg. Since then it had become endemic or epidemic or both. Vince Evans was next, then Jeff Flood, Ted Roberson, Mario Celotto, Rob Hertel, and then one week before the Notre Dame game Mosi Tatupu's tibia was traumatized. Coach McKay must have felt like Napoleon Bonaparte reviewing the retreat from Moscow.

Whatever hope the Trojans had for a victory over Notre Dame and an unblemished record seemed to be pinned on Heisman Trophy candidate Ricky Bell at tailback. Bell had gone over the 1,000 yard mark rushing in the Oregon game and was physically sound, but when the coach was asked if Notre Dame could be beaten with an offensive limited to ground attacks, McKay said, "No way."

"Because of their big tough defense you won't make a first down that consistently. I've always thought the best way to prepare our young players for their first trip back there would be to take each one down to the basement and have three of our biggest players sit on him. Then, while he's down, a corps of drummers will move in and beat their drums directly over his head."

In 1975 it's doubtful that McKay had enough big men to indulge in such bizarre preparation. Every player on the team was young, his youngest team ever at USC.

USC's Ricky Bell is off and running

In fact, it seemed quite probable that he would never again field a team so young. Rumor had it that this was John McKay's last year in college football . . . that next year he would be in Tampa, guiding the latest NFL expansion team, the Buccaneers. The Iceman, as McKay had come to be called, remained silent. He neither confirmed nor denied the rumor, but the West Coast sportswriters were convinced enough to refer to his trip East as "McKay's last Bend."

Pre-game pep rallies at Notre Dame have been compared with the Draft Riots of 1863 or the Roman slave revolt led by Spartacus in the First Century, B.C. Visiting teams and their coaches, even supporters who dare accompany them on their autumn assaults, refer to the ordeal as "The Notre Dame experience." An apt description; you have to experience it to believe it, and at no time is the madness more unbridled than

when the Trojans of Southern Cal make their biannual crusade to the land of the Golden Dome. This year was no exception. At the steps of the campus chapel were placed eleven mock tombstones inscribed with the names of USC's eleven offensive starters, "Here Lies USC's Offense — October 25, 1975 — R.I.P." Thousands of students and alumni roamed the streets of South Bend chanting, "Never again," or, "Revenge! Revenge!" Mini-buses packed with thirsty students made regular trips to and from Niles, Michigan, only eight miles away, where beer is served legally to eighteen-year-olds. Banners made from any available material were flung from dormitory windows like battle flags from the parapets. "Wring Ricky's Bell," they screamed, "October 25, 1975 . . . The Day the Bell Was Silenced."

But on that chilly overcast Saturday afternoon the Bell rang and rang and rang. Ask not for whom the Bell tolled; it tolled for the University of Notre Dame.

Forty times the slashing 6-2, 215-pound tailback carried the ball for a total gain of 165 yards, a new SC record against the Irish . . . wiping out O. J.'s 1967 effort of 150 yards in 38 carries.

Before the game, McKay had told reporters, "To beat Notre Dame you must make the big plays. Usually when we've beaten them we've passed well; ball control just won't do it for you." Well, it was upside down. Notre Dame made the big plays, USC didn't pass well (3 for eleven and two interceptions), USC controlled the ball, and USC won the game 24-17.

The electric thrill of the come-from-behind 55-24 victory the year before was absent, but the 1975 meeting had its moments. The Irish led three times during the game but couldn't make it stick. The Trojans were behind 6-0 at the end of the first quarter, 14-7 at the half, and early in the fourth period they were down 17-14 . . . as a matter of fact, there were a few moments when it appeared that the USC production company was trying to put together a sequel to the 1974 thriller, but this year they didn't have the all-star cast. They did have Ricky Bell, however, and along with fullback Mosi Tatupu and quarterback Vince Evans it was good enough.

Without a superb performance by the USC defensive unit, it might have been another story. They allowed but one touchdown in the 1st quarter — a 52-yard run around right end by halfback Al Hunter which sent the Irish ahead 6-0 with but two minutes and 37 seconds into the first quarter. Linebacker Kevin Bruce blocked the kick and there was no further scoring in that period.

As if to apologize for the lack of drama in the first quarter, the Trojans managed eventually to (a) lose the ball twice on fumbles, (b) lose the ball twice on interceptions, (c) allow Luther Bradley to block back-to-back punts, the first of which was recovered in the end zone by Irish senior cornerback, Tom Lopienski (a penalty nullified the touchdown), and (d) score two touchdowns and a field goal.

The first Trojan score came just 20 seconds into the second quarter as an indirect result of that first Bradley-blocked punt. Devine had looked to the Heavens for aid (freshman halfback Jerome Heavens, that is), but Heavens fumbled and Trojan linebacker Dave Lewis recovered. The USC drive was halted on the 38-yard line and they were forced to punt. Bradley's beautiful blocking job was nullified by a holding penalty which gave the Trojans a first down on the Notre Dame 31. Seconds later, Vince Evans faked to Bell and threw a 21-yard pass to flanker Shelton Diggs for the first SC touchdown, the point after attempt was good and for the first time the Trojans led 7-6.

But any Catholic team with a coach named Devine and a halfback named Heavens cannot remain out of grace for long.

Ricky Bell breaks into the clear

Shortly before the end of the quarter, USC was forced once more to punt, and once more Bradley blocked it, and once more Tom Lopienski recovered. This time, however, Tom covered the 13 yard distance without incident, halfback Al Hunter passed to Kris Haines for a two point conversion and the Irish led again, 14-7. They came within a few minutes of increasing that lead when Tom Lopienski intercepted a desperation pass by Evans and made it to the USC 27 before Ricky Bell and the clock stopped him. At the half . . . 14-7, Notre Dame.

In the third quarter Trojan roverback Doug Hogan made a diving interception of Joe Montana's pass (it wasn't one of Joe's better days . . . he was three for 11) and Tatupu and Bell worked their way into the end zone with a seven-yard assist from Evans. Bell administered the coup de grace with a two-yard smash for the score. The point after kick was good and the score was tied 14-14.

Up until this time the favored Trojans had played efficient but unspectacular football. It was almost as though they were waiting for a cue to begin the fireworks. At 3:22 in the final quarter after a 14 play, 60-yard drive, Dave Reeve came in to kick a 27-yard field goal to send the Irish ahead 17-14. That was the cue. For most of the afternoon Bell had been sprung

Steve Orsini takes hand off for short gain

off right tackle and around end . . . head-long into the waiting monolithic breasts of tackle Steve Niehaus* and end Ross Browner. Now, Ricky Bell is a strong young man and has all the deceptive moves on an attacking mongoose . . . but after all, Niehaus is 6'5" and 285, and little Ross Browner is 6-3 and 235 pounds of defensive distemper.

By the middle of the fourth quarter, Bell must have felt like the pigeon that got caught in a badminton game. True, he had gained over one hundred yards, but clearly this was not the way to ice a game against the Fighting Irish of Notre Dame . . . not when you're three points behind with minutes to play. Who would know better than the coaching staff of USC? They changed the offense. On the first series of plays they employed the "25 Power play" which gave Bell the option of slamming straight up the middle or sweeping the ends. It confused even the alert Irish defense often enough and long enough to allow the Trojans to march from their 29-yard-line to the end zone and a score in just four minutes. First Bell cutting to the left with SC line blocking straight ahead . . . a gain of 19. Same play, 12 more. Tatupu and Bell to the Irish three and a first down. One play later Bell took the hand-off and dove through . . . no, not through, *to* the middle of the line and was stopped right there without the ball. It had squirted

out of his arms and was bouncing around dangerously close to the end zone. Melvin Jackson, USC's quick offensive tackle, recovered. On the next play, Bell slammed once more into the center of the massive Irish line . . . again without the ball. Vince Evans had it this time and strolled over the goal line to send the Trojans into the lead. Glenn Walker's kick was good and the score was 21-17. It was all over. Walker's 35-yard field goal a few minutes later was just icing on the cake.

Naturally, there was gloom in the Irish locker room and no one was gloomier than Dan Devine. And naturally there was joy in the Trojan locker room and no one was more joyful than John McKay. It *was* his "last Bend," and he was savoring it. And why not? He stood 8-6-2 against the University of Notre Dame; he had beaten them twice in a row at home for the first time since 1932. Since the 51-0 humiliation in 1966 he had lost to the Irish only once, tied twice, and defeated them six times. No one at USC had ever come close to that record. While Dan Devine paced the floor in the room next door and explained that his young team of today would be the winning team of tomorrow, McKay sat and smiled as he puffed his cigar, visions of Tampa Bay and stock options dancing in his head.

"Coach," someone asked, "After this, would you have the

Al Hunter sweeps right end for good yaradage against Trojan defense

heart to leave college football?"

"Heart?" said McKay, "I just had it checked the other day
. . . I haven't any."

*Just another McKay one-liner. Of course he has a heart . . .
a big one and strong. And he needed it all his first year at
Tampa Bay. The Buccaneers, it seemed, couldn't pirate a single
game. Couldn't even beg or borrow one. Expansion teams are not
expected to pull off miracles . . . but maybe just one game? It
was not to be. The Tampa Bay Buccaneers were the only winless
team in the NFL. 0-14. But John McKay is a tough, intelligent
man and a realist, he is also patient. Somewhere, probably in
biology 102, he learned that a 150 ton sperm whale and a three
ounce mouse come from the same size egg. He was willing to
wait for Anthony Davis, Ricky Bell, and a lot of good draft
choices. He got them.*

*Interesting to note that only a few years ago when Bear
Bryant was considering resignation from Alabama, he tried to
interest McKay in the job. "Think of it John," the Bear growled,*

*"you wouldn't have to fight those freeways every morning."
"Paul," answered McKay, "I don't mind driving those freeways
to work."*

*In the spring of 1977, Coach McKay told Los Angeles sports-
writer John Hall after an interview in the Buccaneer office,
"Enough of this office . . . I want you to see the house. It's just
five minutes away. You can't imagine how much time and
energy you save not having to spend two hours every day on the
freeway."*

*He's not a worried man. They shipped his favorite booth from
Julie's restaurant near SC (it came to be called Heretige Hall
East) to Malio's in Tampa. They are so impressed there that
they named a room after him.*

*Tampa is on the west coast of Florida, where the sunsets are
spectacular when viewed across the Gulf of Mexico. But one has
the feeling that one morning John McKay will arise and shout
an order, and the sun will rise in the west over Tampa Bay.*

SOUTHERN CAL — 1975

42	Bell, Ricky Junior	T.B.-F.B., 6'2", 215 Los Angeles, Calif.	52	Martin, Rod Junior	O.L.B., 6'1", 195 Los Angeles, Calif.
69	Bethel, Gary Sophomore	O.G., 6'4", 235 Turlock, Calif.	60	Matthews, Clay Sophomore	I.L.B.-O.L.B., 6'2", 230 Kenilworth, Ill.
50	Bruce, Kevin Senior	I.L.B., 6'0", 215 La Canada, Calif.	70	Miller, Rick Junior	O.T., 6'3", 280 Lakewood, Calif.
44	Burns, Mike Junior	D.B., 5'11", 193 Richmond, Calif.	63	Morris, Pat Senior	O.G., 6'1", 226 Sylmar, Calif.
23	Bush, Ron Junior	D.B., 6'0", 180 San Bernardino, Calif.	93	Nunnally, Larry Senior	D.T., 6'3", 253 Savannah, Ga.
21	Cain, Lynn Sophomore	T.B., 6'1", 207 Los Angeles, Calif.	14	Obradovich, Steve Junior	S.E., 6'2", 185 Manhattan Beach, Calif.
5	Carey, Mike Sophomore	Q.B., 6'1", 199 San Francisco, Calif.	81	O'Brien, Bill Junior	T.E., 6'2", 202 Montebello, Calif.
59	Celotto, Mario Sophomore	O.L.B., 6'4", 230 Manhattan Beach, Calif.	33	Odom, Ricky Sophomore	D.B., 6'0", 180 Los Angeles, Calif.
85	Cobb, Gary Freshman	O.L.B., 6'4", 212 Stamford, Conn.	89	Olivarria, Tony Freshman	O.L.B., 6'2", 190 Grand Terrace, Calif.
17	Connors, Rod Sophomore	T.B., 6'2", 190 Rancho Cordova, Calif.	78	Page, Otis Sophomore	O.T., 6'4", 250 Saratoga, Calif.
68	Cordell, Mike Senior	C., 6'3", 232 Long Beach, Calif.	72	Peters, Ray Sophomore	D.T., 6'3", 235 Tujunga, Calif.
64	Davis, Joe Senior	O.G., 6'3", 244 Claremont, Calif.	76	Powell, Marvin Junior	O.T., 6'5", 268 Fayetteville, N.C.
26	Diggs, Shelton Junior	F.L., 6'3", 195 San Bernardino, Calif.	3	Preston, Rob Freshman	Q.B., 6'2", 200 Vista, Calif.
92	Dimler, Richard Freshman	D.T., 6'6", 260 Bayonne, N.J.	12	Randle, Ken Junior	S.E., 6'0", 180 Kansas City, Mo.
8	Evans, Vince Junior	Q.B., 6'2", 205 Greensboro, N.C.	46	Reece, Danny Senior	D.B., 6'0", 187 Wilmington, Calif.
67	Flood, Jeff Senior	C., 6'3", 240 Escondido, Calif.	97	Rhames, Tim Senior	N.G., 6'2", 236 Fresno, Calif.
56	Fraser, Scott Freshman	L.B., 6'2", 230 Riverside, Calif.	24	Rice Paul Freshman	T.B., 5'11", 193 Lewisville, Tex.
22	Ford, Dwight Sophomore	T.B., 5'11", 180 Bell, Calif.	47	Roberson, Ted Senior	D.B., 6'0", 183 Bakersfield, Calif.
86	Gay, William Sophomore	T.E., 6'6", 215 San Diego, Calif.	43	Robinson, Robin Sophomore	D.B., 6'0", 177 Los Angeles, Calif.
45	Hearne, Gabriel Junior	D.B., 6'2", 185 Bell, Calif.	2	Sanford, Mike Sophomore	Q.B., 6'0", 175 Los Altos, Calif.
6	Hertel, Rob Sophomore	Q.B., 6'2", 185 Hacienda Heights, Calif.	74	Schuhmacher, John Sophomore	O.T., 6'5", 265 Pasadena, Calif.
61	Hickman, Donnie Junior	O.G., 6'3", 258 Flagstaff, Ariz.	82	Shipp, Joe Sophomore	T.E., 6'4", 225 Carson, Calif.
48	Hogan, Doug Senior	D.B., 6'4", 206 San Diego, Calif.	18	Simmrin, Randy Sophomore	S.E., 6'1", 170 Burbank, Calif.
29	Hollmer, Kurt Sophomore	T.B., 6'0", 190 Alamo, Calif.	4	Sorce, Art Freshman	P.K., 6'1", 215 Costa Mesa, Calif.
80	Howell, Mike Junior	T.E., 6'7", 225 Corona, Calif.	71	Steele, Harold Junior	N.G., 6'2", 250 San Diego, Calif.
66	Howell, Pat Freshman	O.G., 6'6", 258 Fresno, Calif.	49	Strozier, Clint Junior	D.B., 6'3", 195 Oxnard, Calif.
65	Jackson, Melvin Senior	O.T., 6'1", 253 Los Angeles, Calif.	10	Studdard, Howard Sophomore	S.E., 6'4", 204 Los Angeles, Calif.
27	Jamerson, Ron Junior	F.L., 6'2", 205 Pacoima, Calif.	36	Tatupu, Mosi Sophomore	F.B., 6'0", 225 Honolulu, Hawaii
79	Jeter, Gary Junior	D.T., 6'4", 240 Cleveland, Ohio	7	Thurman, Dennis Sophomore	F.L.-S., 6'0", 170 Santa Monica, Calif.
88	Johnson, Ricky Freshman	O.L.B., 6'3", 215 Los Angeles, Calif.	95	Underwood, Walt Sophomore	D.T., 6'4", 225 Atlanta, Calif.
96	Lapka, Myron Freshman	D.T., 6'4", 230 Northridge, Calif.	75	Van Dyke, Vinny Sophomore	D.T., 6'5", 225 Greenwich, Conn.
19	Lee, Junior Senior	S.E., 6'2", 180 Long Beach, Calif.	53	Wakefield, Jeff Junior	I.L.B., 6'1", 215 Van Nuys, Calif.
57	Lewis, David Junior	O.L.B., 6'3", 224 San Diego, Calif.	39	Walker, Glen Junior	P.-P.K., 6'1", 220 Gardena, Calif.
54	Logie, Dale Senior	I.L.B., 6'1", 220 Los Angeles, Calif.	55	Williams, Eric Junior	Kansas City, Mo.
83	Lozano, Danny Freshman	I.L.B., 6'2", 215 Los Angeles, Calif.	94	Zoller, James Freshman	N.G., 6'3", 230 Yorba Linda, Calif.

NOTRE DAME — 1975

79	Achterhoff, Jay Senior	D.T., 6'4", 248 Muskegon, Mich.	53	Likovich, John Junior	O.L.B., 6'2", 211 Phoenix, Ariz.
12	Allocco, Frank Senior	Q.B., 6'1", 176 New Providence, N.J.	26	Lopienski, Tom Senior	C.B., 6'1", 176 Akron, Ohio
56	Andler, Ken Senior	C., 6'6", 238 Cleveland, Ohio	81	MacAfee, Ken Sophomore	T.E., 6'4", 251 Brockton, Mass.
17	Banks, Mike Junior	S.S., 6'2", 194 Youngstown, Ohio	91	Malinak, Don Junior	D.E., 6'4", 204 Flemington, Pa.
68	Bauer, Ed (Capt.) Senior	O.T., 6'3", 248 Cincinnati, Ohio	31	Maschmeier, Tom Senior	C.B., 5'11", 180 Cincinnati, Ohio
43	Becker, Doug Sophomore	O.L.B., 6'0", 220 Hamilton, Ohio	71	McDaniels, Steve Sophomore	O.T., 6'6", 264 Seattle, Wash.
44	Bonder, Frank Junior	F.B., 6'1", 199 Niles, Ohio	22	McLane, Mark Junior	H.B., 6'1", 204 Wilmington, Del.
20	Bradley, Luther Sophomore	C.B., 6'2", 198 Muncie, Ind.	99	McLaughlin, Pat Senior	K., 6'0", 225 Santa Barbara, Calif.
4	Brantley, Tony Senior	P., 6'0", 200 Oklahoma City, Okla.	60	Meyer, Howard Freshman	O.G., 6'3", 219 San Jose, Calif.
46	Brown, Ivan Senior	D.E., 6'3", 221 LeRoy, Ill.	3	Montana, Joe Sophomore	Q.B., 6'2", 184 Monongahela, Pa.
33	Browner, Jim Freshman	F.B., 6'3", 207 Warren, Ohio	57	Moore, Elton Junior	O.G., 6'1", 230 Portland, Ore.
89	Browner, Ross Sophomore	D.E., 6'3", 235 Warren, Ohio	1	Moriarty, Kerry Junior	H.B., 5'9", 164 Santa Barbara, Calif.
61	Buck, Dave Junior	O.T., 6'5", 234 Austin, Tex.	70	Niehaus, Steve Senior	D.T., 6'5", 270 Cincinnati, Ohio
18	Burgmeier, Ted Sophomore	S.E.-C.B., 5'11", 179 E. Dubuque, Ill.	38	Novakov, Tony Senior	O.L.B., 5'11", 200 Cincinnati, Ohio
83	Buth, Doug Junior	T.E., 6'5", 228 Green Bay, Wis.	14	Orsini, Steve Sophomore	F.B., 5'10", 199 Hummelstown, Pa.
73	Calhoun, Mike Freshman	D.T., 6'5", 241 Youngstown, Ohio	36	Parise, Tom Senior	F.B., 6'0", 211 Longmont, Colo.
64	Carney, Mike Sophomore	O.G., 6'2", 215 LaMirada, Calif.	88	Pattillo, Reynold Sophomore	O.G., 6'1", 227 Los Angeles, Calif.
28	Christensen, Ross Sophomore	S.S., 6'1", 190 Racine, Wis.	16	Payne, Randy Senior	C.B., 5'9", 170 Palmer Park, Md.
84	Crews, Ron Freshman	D.E., 6'4", 223 Columbia, Mo.	67	Pohlen, Pat Senior	O.T., 6'4", 242 Downey, Calif.
23	Cullins, Ron Sophomore	C.B., 6'0", 190 Warren, Ohio	47	Pszeracki, Joe Senior	M.L.B., 5'11", 212 Ambridge, Pa.
24	DeCicco, Nick Sophomore	O.L.B., 5'10", 188 South Bend, Ind.	77	Quehl, Steve Senior	C., 6'4", 241 Cincinnati, Ohio
72	Dike, Ken Sophomore	D.T., 6'2", 235 Crown Point, Ind.	13	Reeve, Dave Sophomore	K., 6'3", 198 Bloomington, Ind.
32	Doherty, Kevin Senior	S.E., 6'0", 178 Portland, Ore.	7	Restic, Joe Freshman	P.-Q.B., 6'2", 175 Milford, Mass.
87	Driscoll, John Sophomore	T.E., 6'1", 219 Cincinnati, Ohio	93	Rodenkirk, Don Junior	D.T., 6'4", 248 Milwaukee, Wis.
41	Dubenetzky, John Junior	S.S., 6'5", 213 Hobart, Ind.	45	Ruettiger, Dan Senior	D.E., 5'8", 185 Joliet, Ill.
42	Eastman, Tom Junior	M.L.B., 6'1", 229 Elkhart, Ind.	9	Rufo, John Junior	H.B., 5'11", 194 Lansdowne, Pa.
40	Eurick, Terry Sophomore	H.B., 5'10", 190 Saginaw, Mich.	54	Russell, Marv Junior	M.L.B., 6'0", 225 Ford City, Pa.
76	Fedorenko, Nick Senior	D.T., 6'5", 257 Chicago, Ill.	86	Rutkowski, Frank Senior	D.T., 6'4", 220 Middletown, Del.
8	Forystek, Gary Sophomore	Q.B., 6'2", 202 Livonia, Mich.	29	Sarb, Pat Senior	C.B., 6'0", 176 Dearborn, Mich.
94	Fry, Willie Sophomore	D.E., 6'3", 226 Memphis, Tenn.	19	Schmitz, Steve Sophomore	H.B., 5'11", 185 Lakewood, Ohio
96	Galanis, John Senior	D.E., 6'4", 245 Ipswich, Mass.	59	Sharkey, Ed Junior	C., 6'3", 242 Renton, Wash.
55	Golic, Bob Freshman	M.L.B., 6'3", 240 Cleveland, Ohio	27	Simon, Tim Sophomore	F.S., 5'10", 170 Pontiac, Mich.
69	Gullickson, Tom Junior	D.T., 6'2", 243 Joliet, Ill.	11	Slager, Rick Junior	Q.B., 5'11", 188 Columbus, Ohio
82	Haines, Kris Freshman	S.E., 6'0", 174 Sidney, Ohio	90	Smith, Gene Junior	O.L.B., 6'2", 215 Cleveland, Ohio

1976
CHAPTER 49

" I DIDN'T BELIEVE IT WAS McKAY'S TRADITION . . . IT WAS USC'S, AND *IT* WASN'T LEAVING."

USC's new coach was John Robinson, a 41-year old former end from the University of Oregon. After graduation he stayed on as Len Casanova's assistant until 1971 when he journeyed south to USC to become McKay's offensive coordinator for three years. In 1975 he left the Trojans to join the coaching staff of the Oakland Raiders, but in 1976 he was back at the University of Southern California as head coach, replacing John McKay. As we know, replacing a legend is not easy . . . especially if that legend is articulate, witty, and can reel off one-liners like Henny Youngman. Dan Devine was having the same difficulty at Notre Dame, and Ara wasn't nearly as swift with a riposte as The Iceman. It might have been tougher on Robinson if McKay had added another national championship or another Rose Bowl win his last year at SC, but he didn't and in the view of some purists he had sold his soul to the pros. So some of the lustre had been rubbed off of the McKay legend

and it was further tarnished by that 0-14 season at Tampa Bay. Furthermore, every coach in the conference expected Robinson to be a winner, he had inherited a good coaching staff, a team with depth, and a tradition of winning. Yes, the future looked bright for the first year coach of the Trojans of Southern California . . . until the first game of the season. He ran full tilt into the Spoilers, otherwise known as the University of Missouri. Through sheer weight of numbers the Trojans should have crushed Mizzou. They had eighty-eight players suited up, a two hundred piece marching band, with another sixty in reserve, 20 flag bearers, eight song girls, seven cheerleaders and . . . well the only thing they forgot was a partridge in a pear tree. And, their defensive game. The Tiger's offense made monkeys of "Goux's Gorillas," as the defensive unit liked to be called. The final score was 46-25, Missouri . . . the highest score ever run up on a Trojan team in an

New Southern Cal Head Coach John Robinson

Vince Evans, SC quarterback fades back to pass

Freshman Charles White takes off on long gain

opener, the most total points scored against them since the 0-51 Notre Dame debacle in 1966. For John Robinson, hardly an auspicious beginning.

He partly vindicated himself the following week, however, by beating up on some old friends, the Oregon Ducks. The men of Troy vented their frustration to the tune of 53-0. The following week they downed Purdue, and then crushed Iowa, which had upset Penn State the week before. The 55-0 score against the Hawkeyes was the highest number of points scored against an opponent since Howard Jones creamed Georgia 60-0 in 1931. Things began to look brighter in Southern California, by the time they met Notre Dame on November 27 in the Golden Anniversary game, the last game of the season, the loss to Missouri was the only blemish on the Trojan record.

The week before, they had stopped unbeaten UCLA 24-14 for their ninth straight win. The Trojans stormed into the Coliseum ranked number two in the nation and eight point favorites over the Fighting Irish of Notre Dame.*

The Irish came to southern California with an 8-2 record, an opening game loss to powerful Pitt 10-31 and a mid-season stumble against Georgia Tech, 14-23 had been their only faults. They were ranked 11th and 13th in the nation, depending on which poll you like.

The Trojans waited until the second quarter to go to work, moving 67 yards in 10 plays, capped by a six-yard pass from quarterback Rob Hertel to flanker Shelton Diggs. Glen Walker's conversion kick was good, and USC led 7-0.

Vince Evans came back in the third quarter and in less than two minutes set up a 63-yard pass to Randy Simmrin for the second touchdown of the game. Again Walker's kick was good and the Trojans led 14-0.

The Irish scored early in the fourth quarter on a 17-yard pass from quarterback Rusty Lisch, a 6-4, 200 pound sophomore, to split end Kris Haines. Dave Reeve kicked the conver-

273

The two teams are set at line of scrimmage with SC on offense

sion and the Irish were on the scoreboard. The Trojans answered back with a 48-yard drive ending in a 46-yard field goal by Walker to make the score 17-7. Only seconds before the game ended, Lisch sneaked over from the one-yard line, climaxing a 76-yard march in 12 plays. A two point conversion attempt failed and time ran out on the fighting Irish.

Strangely, there were no cries of woe or soul rending lamentations in the Notre Dame dressing room . . . they were already looking to 1977. After all, they had brought to the Coliseum a team with only 12 seniors on the roster. Eleven of the starters were juniors, nine were sophomores, and fullback Vagas Ferguson was a freshman . . . he wasn't the only one. Devine brought with him 14 more, many of whom played. The defense which held Ricky Bell to 106 yards would return intact in 1977. Only two starters, quarterback Rick Slager and wide receiver Dan Kelleher would not be on hand to greet the

Trojans in Notre Dame, Indiana the following year.

No wonder Dan Devine was smiling through his tears . . . of course football coaches learn to do that well.

With a 10-1 record for the season Robinson's confidence seemed to wax while the memory of John McKay began to wane. "I refused to recognize this 'legend' thing," he said, "I didn't really see where there was any conflict with the tradition established before me.

"I don't believe it was John McKay's tradition . . . it was USC's . . . and *it* wasn't leaving."

And so John Robinson showed that underneath that rather casual exterior he too possesses that quality that sets apart a successful man from the pack.

"I strongly believe in my own ability to accomplish things," he said.

"This may sound arrogant as hell, but even after the Missouri

Rick Slager passes for short yardage to Vagas Ferguson

game, I believed we'd turn it around."

Well, he did and went on to defeat Michigan 14-6 in the Rose Bowl . . . the Trojans fourth appearance there in five years.

Dan Devine and his Fighting Irish whipped Penn State in the Gator Bowl, so his season ended also on a positive note . . . and don't forget, all those juniors and sophomores and freshmen . . . and 1977.

SC All American, Gary Jeter

SC All American Marvin Powell

Notre Dame defender, Luther Bradley

Notre Dame's Al Hunter is off and running

USC ROSTER — 1976

NO.	NAME	POS.	HGT.	WGT.	CL.	HOMETOWN (HIGH SCHOOL)
90	Anderson, Daivd	N.G.	6'3"	250	Fresh.	Arcadia (Arcadia)
42	Bell, Ricky	T.B.	6'2"	218	Sr.	Los Angeles (Fremont)
69	Bethel, Gary	C.	6'4"	235	Jr.	Turlock (Turlock)
64	Brooks, Bruce	O.T.	6'2"	257	Jr.	Los Angeles (Washington)
65	Budde, Brad	O.G.	6'6"	250	Fresh.	Kansas City, Mo. (Rockhurst)
88	Burns, Dan	T.E.	6'4"	230	Jr.	Playa del Rey (St. Bernard's)
44	Burns, Mike	D.B.	5'11"	185	Sr.	Richmond (El Cerrito)
23	Bush, Ron	D.B.	6'0"	190	Sr.	San Bernardino (San Bernardino)
5	Carey, Mike	D.B.	6'1"	202	Jr.	San Francisco (Riordan)
91	Catoe, Ed	D.T.	6'4"	245	Jr.	San Bernardino (San Bernardino)
59	Celotto, Mario	I.L.B.	6'4"	230	Jr.	Manhattan Beach (St. Bernard's)
53	Cobb, Garry	O.L.B.	6'3"	220	So.	Stamford, Conn. (Stamford)
17	Connors, Rod	T.B.	6'3"	190	Jr.	Rancho Cordova (Cordova)
26	Diggs, Shelton	W.R.	6'2"	200	Sr.	San Bernardino (San Bernardino)
92	Dimler, Rich	D.T.-N.G.	6'6"	260	So.	Bayonne, N.J. (Bayonne)
67	Evans, Ken	O.G.	6'4"	252	Jr.	Walnut Creek (Ygnacio Valley)
8	Evans, Vince	Q.B.	6'2"	204	Sr.	Greensboro, N.C. (Smith)
15	Farmer, Dave	F.B.	6'2"	210	Sr.	La Puente (Workman)
40	Fisher, Jeff	W.R.	5'10"	170	Fresh.	Woodland Hills (Taft)
62	Foote, Chris	C.	6'3½"	238	Fr.	Boulder, Colo. (Fairview)
38	Galbraith, Jim	F.B.	6'3"	220	Jr.	Burbank (Burroughs)
86	Gay, William	T.E.	6'6"	225	Jr.	San Diego (Hoover)
50	Gutierrez, Ed	O.L.B.	6'0"	216	Jr.	Los Angeles (Salesian)
11	Hartwig, Carter	D.B.	6'0"	195	So.	Fresno (Central)
25	Hayes, Michael	F.L.	5'9"	177	So.	San Diego (San Diego)
6	Hertel, Rob	Q.B.	6'2"	185	Jr.	Hacienda Heights (Los Altos)
61	Hickman, Donnie	O.G.	6'3"	255	Sr.	Flagstaff, Ariz. (Flagstaff)
29	Hollmer, Kurt	T.B.	5'11"	180	Jr.	Alamo (San Ramon)
84	Houghton, Jeff	I.L.B.	6'1"	220	So.	Bakersfield (Foothill)
66	Howell, Pat	O.G.	6'6"	252	So.	Fresno (Fresno)
85	Hunter, James	T.E.	6'4"	220	Fresh.	Santa Barbara (Santa Barbara)
45	Jackson, Vic	F.B.	6'3"	226	Fresh.	Santa Barbara (San Marcos)
27	Jamerson, Ron	D.B.	6'2"	205	Sr.	Pacoima (Sylmar)
91	Janke, Jesse	O.T.	6'6"	255	Jr.	La Mirada (La Mirada)
79	Jeter, Gary	D.T.	6'4½"	255	Sr.	Cleveland, Ohio (Cathedral Latin)
56	Johnson, Dennis	I.L.B.	6'4"	218	Fresh.	Flint, Mich. (Northwestern)
41	Kenlon, Steve	O.L.B.	6'0"	200	So.	Fullerton (Servite)
1	Kerr, Rob	P.K.	6'0"	180	Fr.	San Gabriel (San Gabriel)
98	Lacy, Norm	O.G.	6'3"	230	Sr.	Pacifica (Pacifica)
96	Lapka, Myron	D.T.	6'4"	245	So.	Chatsworth, (Chatsworth)
51	Lawryk, Gene	C.	6'3"	235	Sr.	Bell (Bell)
35	Levy, John	D.B.	5'11"	182	Sr.	Seal Beach (Los Alamitos)
57	Lewis, David	O.L.B.	6'4"	230	Sr.	San Diego (Lincoln)

52	Martin, Rod	O.L.B.	6'2"	195	Sr.	Los Angeles (Hamilton)
60	Matthews, Clay	I.L.B.	6'2"	232	Jr.	Arcadia (Arcadia)
58	McDonald, Mike	I.L.B.	6'2"	215	Fresh.	Burbank (Burroughs)
9	McDonald, Paul	Q.B.	6'2"	180	Fresh.	Covina (Bishop Amat)
54	McParland, Kevin	C.	6'6"	245	Sr.	Oakland (Tech)
70	Miller, Rick	O.T.-O.G.	6'3"	280	Sr.	Lakewood (Lakewood)
4	Moore, Ken	D.B.	6'1"	185	Fresh.	San Fernando (San Fernando)
77	Munoz, Anthony	O.T.	6'6"	260	Fresh.	Ontario (Chaffey)
14	Obradovich, Steve	S.E.	6'1"	195	Sr.	Manhattan Beach (El Segundo)
33	Odom, Ricky	D.B.	6'1"	183	Jr.	Los Angeles (Los Angeles)
97	O'Grady, Steve	O.L.B.	6'3"	220	Jr.	Flossmoor, Ill. (Mendel)
37	Olivarria, Tony	F.B.	6'2"	210	So.	Colton (Colton)
78	Page, Otis	O.T.	6'6"	265	Jr.	Saratoga (Saratoga)
72	Peters, Ray	N.G.-D.T.	6'3"	240	Jr.	Tujunga (St. Francis)
76	Powell, Marvin	O.T.	6'5"	265	Sr.	Fayetteville, N.C. (Seventy-First)
81	Pugh, Allen	D.T.	6'3"	230	Fresh.	Santa Barbara (San Marcos)
28	Randle, Kenny	S.E.	6'0"	185	Sr.	Kansas City, Mo. (Central)
10	Ransom, Walt	Q.B.	6'1"	190	Jr.	South Gate (South Gate)
16	Robinson, Mike	S.E.	6'1"	190	Sr.	Richmond (El Cerrito)
2	Sanford, Mike	D.B.	6'0"	176	Jr.	Los Altos (Los Altos)
74	Schuhmacher, John	O.T.	6'5"	275	Jr.	Pasadena (Arcadia)
82	Shipp, Joe	T.E.	6'4"	230	Jr.	Carson (Carson)
18	Simmrin, Randy	S.E.	6'2"	165	Jr.	Burbank (Burroughs)
63	Sperling, Tyrone	O.G.	6'1"	225	Fresh.	Wilmington (Banning)
34	Spino, Mark	D.B.	6'1"	184	Sr.	Las Vegas, Nev. (Clark)
71	Steele, Harold	N.G.	6'1"	240	Sr.	San Diego (Lincoln)
49	Strozier, Clint	D.B.	6'3½"	190	Sr.	Oxnard (Oxnard)
87	Studdard, Howard	T.E.	6'4"	214	Jr.	Los Angeles (Manual Arts)
19	Sweeney, Calvin	F.L.	6'2"	181	Jr.	Riverside (Perris)
99	Tammaro, Vince	I.L.B.	6'3"	234	Jr.	Burlingame (Serra)
31	Tarver, Bernard	T.B.-F.B.	5'10"	185	Jr.	Bakersfield (Arvin)
36	Tatupu, Mosi	F.B.	6'0"	220	Jr.	Honolulu, Hawaii (Punahoe)
7	Thurman, Dennis	D.B.	5'11"	170	Jr.	Santa Monica (Santa Monica)
95	Underwood, Walt	D.T.	6'4"	220	Jr.	Atlanta (Southwest)
68	Van Horne, Keith	O.T.	6'6"	230	Fresh.	Fullerton (Fullerton)
75	Van Dyke, Vinny	D.T.	6'5"	252	Jr.	Greenwich, Conn. (Greenwich)
93	Wakefield, Jeff	I.L.B.	6'1"	227	Sr.	Van Nuys (Notre Dame)
39	Walker, Glen	P.-P.K.	6'1½"	220	Sr.	Gardena (Gardena)
46	Wiese, Van	F.B.	6'3"	215	Fresh.	Carson (Carson)
12	White, Charles	T.B.	6'0"	180	Fresh.	San Fernando (San Fernando)
55	Williams, Eric	I.L.B.	6'2"	215	Sr.	Kansas City, Mo. (Central)
24	Williams, Kevin	F.L.	5'9"	170	Fresh.	San Fernando (San Fernando)
94	Zoller, Ray	N.G.	6'3"	240	So.	Yorba Linda (Troy)

NOTRE DAME ROSTER — 1976

NO.	NAME	POS.	HGT.	WGT.	CL.	HOMETOWN
37	Allocco, Rich	H.B.	6'2"	196	Sr.	New Providence, N.J.
15	Alvarado, Art	F.S.	6'2"	193	So.	Los Angeles, Calif.
17	Banks, Mike	55	6'2"	198	Sr.	Youngstown, Ohio
43	Becker, Doug	L.B.	6'0"	220	Jr.	Hamilton, Ohio
47	Bonder, Frank	F.B.	6'1"	197	Sr.	Niles, Ohio
20	Bradley, Luther	C.B.	6'2"	198	Jr.	Muncie, Ind.
33	Browner, Jim	S.S.	6'3"	222	So.	Warren, Ohio
89	Browner, Ross	D.E.	6'3"	247	Jr.	Warren, Ohio
24	Browner, Willard	F.B.	6'2"	223	Fr.	Warren, Ohio
15	Bucci, Elvo	F.B.	5'11"	205	Sr.	Chicago, Ill.
69	Buck, Dave	O.T.	6'5"	220	Sr.	Austin, Tex.
68	Bush, Rob	D.E.	6'6"	235	Fr.	Amsterdam, N.Y.
18	Burgmeier, Ted	C.B.	5'11"	187	Jr.	East Dubuque, Ill.
77	Calhoun, Mike	D.T.	6'5"	254	So.	Youngstown, Ohio
64	Carney, Mike	O.G.	6'2"	232	Jr.	La Mirada, Calif.
28	Christensen, Ross	F.S.	6'1"	195	Jr.	Racine, Wisc.
92	Czaja, Mark	D.E.	6'5"	238	Fr.	Lewiston, N.Y.
49	DeCicco, Nick	S.S.	5'10"	196	Jr.	South Bend, Ind.
79	Dike, Ken	D.T.	6'2"	224	Jr.	Merrillville, Ind.
26	Domin, Tom	H.B.	6'3"	208	So.	Villa Park, Ill.
5	Dover, Steve	H.B.	6'1"	205	So.	Kemmerer, Wyo.
41	Dubenetzky, John	L.B.	6'5"	218	Sr.	Hobart, Ind.
47	Duncan, Bob	L.B.	5'11"	218	Jr.	Chicago, Ill.
42	Eastman, Tom	L.B.	6'1"	239	Sr.	Elkhart, Ind.
40	Eurick, Terry	H.B.-F.B.	5'10"	196	Jr.	Saginaw, Mich.
69	Ewald, Mark	O.T.	6'4"	248	Sr.	Palos Park, Ill.
32	Ferguson, Vagas	H.B.	6'1"	194	Fr.	Richmond, Ind.
23	Flynn, Tom	C.B.	6'0"	174	So.	West Palm Beach, Fla.
73	Foley , Tim	O.T.	6'5"	246	Fr.	Cincinnati, Ohio
8	Forystek, Gary	Q.B.	6'2"	207	Jr.	Livonia, Mich.
62	Frericks, Tom	O.T.	6'5"	225	Sr.	Circleville, Ohio
94	Fry, Willie	D.E.	6'3"	242	Jr.	Memphis, Tenn.
46	Gleckler, Ed	L.B.	6'2"	234	Sr.	Bay Shore, N.Y.
55	Golic, Bob	L.B.	6'3"	239	So.	Willowick, Ohio
83	Graziani, Larry	D.E.	6'2"	230	So.	New Castle, Pa.
96	Grindinger, Dennis	T.E.	6'6"	233	So.	Dallas, Tex.
69	Gullickson, Tom	O.T.	6'2"	238	Sr.	Joliet, Ill.
82	Haines, Kris	W.R.	6'0"	179	So.	Sidney, Ohio
85	Hart, Speedy	W.R.	6'1"	201	Fr.	Phoenix, Ariz.
63	Hautman, Jim	C.	6'3"	248	So.	Cincinnati, Ohio
58	Heimkreiter, Steve	L.B.	6'2"	228	So.	Cincinnati, Ohio
66	Horansky, Ted	O.T.	6'3"	251	So.	Cleveland, Ohio
56	Huffman, Dave	C.	6'5"	241	So.	Dallas, Tex.
65	Hughes, Ernie	O.G.	6'3"	257	Jr.	Boise, Ida.
25	Hunter, Al	H.B.	5'11"	195	Jr.	Greenville, N.C.
51	Johnson, Pete	L.B.	6'4"	249	Jr.	Fond du Lac, Wisc.
29	Johnson, Phil	C.B.	6'0"	191	So.	Fond du Lac, Wisc.

80	Kelleher, Dan	W.R.	5'11"	187	Sr.	Ellensburg, Wash.
21	Knott, Dan	H.B.	6'1"	203	Jr.	Chowchilla, Calif.
69	Leon, John	O.G.	6'2"	239	Fr.	Wellsburg, W.Va.
61	Leopold LeRoy	L.B.	6'2"	213	Fr.	Port Arthur, Tex.
53	Likovich, John	L.B.	6'2"	218	Sr.	Phoenix, Ariz.
6	Lisch, Russ	Q.B.	6'4"	208	So.	Belleville, Ill.
81	MacAfee, Ken	T.E.	6'4"	253	Jr.	Brockton, Mass.
84	Malinak, Don	D.E.	6'4"	210	Sr.	Flemington, Pa.
75	Martinovich, Rob	D.T.	6'5"	230	Fr.	Houston, Tex.
52	McCormick Keith	O.T.	6'5"	235	Fr.	Omaha, Neb.
71	McDaniels, Steve	O.T.	6'6"	274	Jr.	Seattle, Wash.
22	McLane, Mark	H.B.	6'1"	199	Sr.	Wilmington, Del.
38	Merriweather, Ron	F.B.-H.B.	6'0"	195	Fr.	San Marcos, Tex.
60	Meyer, Howard	O.G.	6'3"	220	So.	San Jose, Calif.
57	Moore, Elton	O.G.-O.T.	6'1"	240	Sr.	Portland, Ore.
1	Moriarty, Kerry	Q.B.	5'9"	172	Sr.	Santa Barbara, Calif.
9	Morse, Jim	C.B.-P.	6'0"	182	So.	Muskegon, Mich.
38	Muhlenkamp, Chris	L.B.	6'3"	218	Fr.	Ansonia, Ohio
4	Muno, Kevin	Q.B.-P.	6'0"	178	Fr.	Los Angeles, Calif.
50	Murphy, Terry	C.	6'1"	214	Jr.	Saginaw, Mich.
14	Orsini, Steve	F.B.	5'10"	209	Jr.	Hummelstown, Pa.
45	Pallas, Pete	F.B.	6'2"	215	So.	Yakima, Wash.
68	Pattillo, Rey	O.G.	6'1"	241	Jr.	Los Angeles, Calif.
72	Rayam, Hardy	D.T.	6'5"	240	Fr.	Orlando, Fla.
13	Reeve, Dave	P.K.	6'3"	205	Jr.	Bloomington, Ind.
7	Restic, Joe	P.-F.S.-Q.B.	6'2"	188	So.	Milford, Mass.
76	Rodenkirk, Don	D.T.	6'4"	238	Sr.	Milwaukee, Wisc.
2	Rufo, John	H.B.	5'11"	190	Sr.	Lansdowne, Pa.
54	Russell, Marv	L.B.	6'0"	237	Sr.	Ford City, Pa.
19	Schmitz, Steve	H.B.	5'11"	195	Jr.	Lakewood, Ohio
67	Sharkey, Ed	C.	6'3"	239	Sr.	Renton, Wash.
27	Simon, Tim	W.R.	5'10"	187	Jr.	Pontiac, Mich.
11	Slager, Rick	Q.B.	5'11"	188	Sr.	Columbus, Ohio
90	Smith, Gene	D.E.	6'2"	226	Sr.	Cleveland, Ohio
16	Soutner, John	S.S.	6'2"	205	Sr.	Steelton, Pa.
93	Thomas, John	D.E.	6'4"	228	Fr.	Thomasville, N.C.
67	Tull, Bob	O.T.	6'3"	242	Jr.	South Bend, Ind.
38	Uniake, Kevin	H.B.	6'2"	230	Sr.	Hicksville, N.Y.
99	Unis, Joe	P.K.	5'11"	182	Fr.	Dallas, Tex.
36	Unis, Tom	C.B.	5'10"	173	Sr.	Dallas, Tex.
59	Vinson, Dave	O.G.	6'2"	237	Jr.	Liberty, Tex.
34	Waymer, Dave	C.B.-H.B.	6'3"	186	Fr.	Charlotte, N.C.
91	Weber, Robin	T.E.-O.T.	6'5"	239	Sr.	Dallas, Tex.
35	Weiler, Jim	T.E.	6'2"	215	Sr.	Cleveland Hgts., Ohio
62	Whittington, Mike	L.B.	6'2"	220	Fr.	Miami, Fla.
78	Woebkenberg, Harry	O.T.	6'2"	261	Jr.	Cincinnati, Ohio
39	Zappala, Tony	D.E.	6'0"	211	Sr.	Elmwood Park, N.J.

1976 NOTRE DAME FOOTBALL TEAM

FRONT ROW, LEFT TO RIGHT — John Dubenetzky, Doug Buth, Tom Gullickson, Ed Sharkey, Terry Murphy, Don Malinak, Don Rodenkirk, Willie Fry, Mark McLane, Tom Frericks, Dave Buck, Mark Ewald, Vince Klees, Dan Kelleher, Tom Unis, Elvo Bucci.

SECOND ROW, L-R — Tom Eastman, Gene Smith, Ed Gleckler, John Soutner, Rich Allocco, Stan Bobowski, Mike Banks, Luther Bradley, Mike Kafka, Mary Russell, John Likovich, Tony Zappala, Jim Weiler, Kevin Uniacke, John Rufo, Frank Bonder, Kerry Moriarty, Rick Slager.

THIRD ROW, L-R — Ross Browner, Al Hunter, Dan Knott, Ken Dike, Mike Carney, Steve Heimkreiter, Nick DeCicco, Steve McDaniels, Randy Harrison, Terry Eurick, Steve Schmitz, Bob Duncan, Bill Adams, John Driscoll, Bob Golic, Pete Johnson, Doug Becker, Elton Moore.

FOURTH ROW, L-R — Ted Horansky, Ron Crews, Jeff Weston, Ross Christensen, Gary Forystek, Dave Reeve, Harry Woebkenberg, Ralph Miranda, Chris Meagher, Jim Browner, Kenny Harris, Rey Pattillo, Kim Uniacke, Howard Meyer, Terry Murphy, Mike Calhoun, Dave Huffman, Ernie Hughes, Tom Flynn, Phil Johnson.

FIFTH ROW, L-R — Rusty Lisch, Larry Graziani, Steve Dover, Kevin Hart, Dennis Grindinger, Jay Case, Ted Burgmeier, Dave Betlach, Leo Driscoll, Rich Manso, Mike Geers, Joe Montana, Steve Orsini, Jerome Heavens, Tom Domin, Kris Haines, Vince Rachal, Bob Tull, Pete Pallas, Dave Vinson, John Hager, Jim Hautman, Art Alvarado.

SIXTH ROW, L-R — Joe Unis, Hardy Rayam, K. C. Ryan, Pat Boggs, Larry Hufford, Tom Wroblewski, Tex Ritter, Mark Quinn, Keith McCormick, John Thomas, Mark Czaja, John Leon, Scott Zettek, Rob Martinovich, Tim Foley, Mark Thuney, Ian Gray, David Waymer, Tom Van Denburgh, Jim Morse, Mike Whittington.

SEVENTH ROW, L-R — Leroy Leopold, David Mitchell, Willard Browner, Jeff Crippin, Lou Pagley, Chris Muhlenkamp, Ty Dickerson, Kevin Muno, Speedy Hart, Rob Bush, John Scully, Vagas Ferguson, Ron Merriweather.

TOP ROW, L-R — Dan Buck, Head Football Manager, Tom Hackett, Assistant Football Manager, Gene O'Neill, Equipment Manager, Tom Connelly, Part-time Assistant, Ross Stevenson, Part-time Assistant, Ron Toman, Assistant Coach, Hank Kuhlmann, Assistant Coach, Paul Shoults, Assistant Coach, George Kelly, Assistant Coach, Dan Devine, Head Football Coach, Joe Yonto, Assistant Coach, Dan Ruettiger, Graduate Assistant, Francis Peay, Assistant Coach, Merv Johnson, Assistant Coach, Brian Boulac, Assistant Coach, Steve Bossu, Graduate Assistant, John Whitmer, Assistant Trainer, Gene Paszkiet, Head Trainer, Bob Hull, Assistant Football Manager.

MISSING FROM PHOTO — Ken MacAfee, Tim Simon, Joe Restic.

1976 USC FOOTBALL TEAM

FRONT ROW L-R — Asst. Coach Marv Goux, Rob Kerr, Mike Sanford, Art Sorce, Ken Moore, Mike Carey, Rob Hertel, Dennis Thurman, Vince Evans, Paul McDonald, Walt Ransom, Head Coach, John Robinson, Carter Hartwig, Charles White, Steve Obradovich, Dave Farmer, Mike Robinson, Randy Simmrin, Calvin Sweeney, Lynn Cain, Dwight Ford, Ron Bush, Asst. Coach Don Lindsey.

2nd ROW — Asst. Coach Foster Andersen, Kevin Williams, Michael Hayes, Shelton Diggs, Ron Jamerson, Ken Randle, Steve Sourapas, Bernard Tarver, Ricky Odom, Mark Spino, John Levy, Mosi Tatupu, Tony Olivarria, Jim Galbraith, Glen Walker, Jeff Fisher, Ricky Bell, Phil Pugh, Mike Burns, Vic Jackson, Van Wiese, Asst. Coach John Jackson.

3rd ROW — Asst. Coach Paul Hackett, Larry Braziel, Tim Lavender, Clint Strozier, Ed Gutierrez, Rod Martin, Garry Cobb, Kevin McPartland, Eric Williams, Dennis Johnson, David Lewis, Mike McDonald, Mario Celotto, Clay Matthews, Donnie Hickman, Chris Foote, Tyrone Sperling, Bruce Brooks, Brad Budde, Pat Howell, Ken Evans, Part-Time Coach Norval Turner.

4th ROW — Asst. Equipment Mgr. Bill Sutton, Part-Time Coach Mike Haluchak, Keith Van Horne, Gary Bethel, Rick Miller, Harold Steele, Ray Peters, Ed Catoe, John Schuhmacher, Vinnie Van Dyke, Marvin Powell, Anthony Munoz, Otis Page, Gary Jeter, Ricky Johnson, Allen Pugh, Joe Shipp, Danny Lozano, Jeff Houghton, James Hunter, William Gay, Asst. Coach Skip Husbands, Trainer Jack Ward.

5th ROW — Asst. Coach Bob Toledo, Asst. Equipment Mgr. Carl Lundgren, Howard Studdard, Dan Burns, David Anderson, Jesse Jahnke, Asst. Trainer Dave Maurer, Rich Dimler, Asst. Dave Crawley, Jeff Wakefield, Ray Zoller, Asst. Trainer Buck Muir, Gene Lawryk, Myron Lapka, Steve O'Grady, Norm Lacy, Vince Tammaro, Dave Engle, Scott Fraser, Bryon Weissberg, John Perry, Rob Bushman, Joe Jones, Rob Preston, Dan Morovick, Graduate Asst. Coach Pat Morris, Asst. Coach Hudson Houck, Grad. Asst. (Women's) Trainer Debbie Gooden.

BACK ROW — Managers Michael Wong, Cliff Rowe, Brad Green, Kevin Brett, Equipment Manager George Yablonsky, Managers David Rush, Hap Linpock, Manuel Gonzales.

Conclusion

The seasons have come and gone . . . many of them. Fifty to be exact, and still the game goes on. The whispering sycamores of Indiana still glow each autumn with crimson and gold as if to welcome the Trojans of Southern California with their own proud colors, and the California palms answer with a wave of greeting to the warriors of the mid-west, and the ghosts of Rockne, Howard Jones, Layden and Leahy . . . of Jeff Cravath and "Gloomy Gus" Henderson still . . . well, we'd like to think they're looking on.

Morly Drury, "the Noblest Trojan of them All" is with us yet; Gwynn Wilson is too and still recalls vividly that day in 1925 when the Rock called him in Chicago and said, "The game is on."

Chet Grant, who played for Rockne and was Elmer Layden's backfield coach still prowls the campus of Notre Dame in the company of the shades of Gus Dorais, Jess Harper and the "Gipper." He's nearing 80 now and retired but his memory is keen and he's only a few pounds over his playing weight in 1916 when he first fell under the spell of the golden dome. "Moose" Krause is still there . . . he never left.

Irvine Warburton sits at his moviola and edits motion pictures with the same style and grace he once showed on the field, but the curly platinum thatch that gave him his nickname, "Cotton," is gone and the years have slowed the once swift feet and added weight to the small muscular frame. Not far away his teammate Aaron Rosenburg sits in his Hollywood offices still tough, still determined.

The years did to Emil Sitko what no opponent of Notre Dame could ever do . . . they stopped him. He played four years as a starter and never lost a game. He led the Irish in yardage gained and averaged 6.1 yards per carry. On a Saturday morning in 1973 he couldn't get out of bed. He died that day at age 50.

We know what happened to Hornung, Arnett, Garrett, and Hanratty. To Simpson, Bleir, Davis and Bell, Lujack and Gifford. They're still going strong and so is the game.

History tells us that the game of football probably was played by the Greeks in the fifth century B.C. They called it *harpaston* or *phollis*. The Romans took the game when they took Greece and changed the name to *harpastum*. But they didn't have an exclusive. It is said that Julius Caesar came upon some Germanic tribesmen kicking what appeared to be a ball. Ever the sport fan, Julius angled toward a seat on the 50-yard-line. When he got there he found to his mild amazement that it was not a ball, but the freshly severed head of an enemy soldier. Thus giving hundreds of sportswriters over the years an opportunity to make witty allusion to the first man to ever have lost his head over the game of football.

Who knows where it all started, the beginning shrouded by the mists of time.

Author and teacher M. D. Morris researched the subject and doubts the Julius Caesar yarn. He contends that in England, at least the game didn't get started until the eleventh century after the Britons had kicked the Danes off the island. It seems, according to Dr. Morris, that a group of young British stalwarts with nothing to do one afternoon happened on the skull of a hated Dane unearthed by some medieval construction crew. It seemed like a good idea at the time to start kicking the unfortunate Viking's head around as a game. It looked like such fun that another group decided to dig up their own. After all, a little head only goes so far.

The game was great fun, but the wear and tear on the toes was incredible. The English may have been the first to learn what nearly everyone now knows . . . no foot in the world is as hard as a Scandinavian skull. They overcame that in a hurry, some enterprising young Anglo-Saxon inflated a cow, or a sheep, or a pig bladder and kicked the hell out of it with little or no discomfort to the feet. That made it even more fun. So much so that whole villages would compete. Somewhere in between two competitive towns a referee would drop the bladder and the game was on. The object was to kick that bladder all the way to your home town, and do a little looting and pillaging along the way. The size of the team varied as much as the rules. 100 men on a side was not unusual.

Someone, probably the spiritual great-great-great-grandfather of the guy who took the fun out of sandlot baseball by coming up with the Little League organized the game in the middle of the 11th century and named it *futballe*. It was restricted to 20 to 50 men per team and banished to circumscribed fields outside of town.

This did nothing to dampen the enthusiasm or hamper the popularity of the game. As a matter of fact; *futballe* became so widespread King Henry II called time . . . one of the longest time outs on record. It lasted four hundred years. It seems that good King Hal was concerned over absenteeism at compulsory archery practice caused by preoccupation with what was rapidly becoming the national sport (Centuries later, thousands of wives would agree with the King, especially at Super Bowl time). The Normans and the Saxons hadn't been getting along too well since the battle of Hastings in 1066, and King Henry knew he couldn't put down a Saxon uprising with inflated pig bladders.*

The ban against *futballe* was about as successful as the 18th amendment. Naturally the Irish were the first to wink at the law and underground games flourished.

The size of the teams continued to decrease, but there was little change in the basic structure of the game until 1823 when a frustrated football player at the Rugby school in England picked up the ball and ran with it. That of course is against the rules, but on that day William Webb Ellis originated Rugby and American football was only a half century away.

The game has changed since 1926, and so have the players. They're bigger, stronger, faster, and smarter. Gone are the close fitting leather helmets, and the skimpy padding and the *Statue of Liberty play.*

College football is big business now. Teams travel cross country by chartered airplane . . . a far cry from the turn of the century when Cornell president Andrew M. White said, "I will not permit 30 men to travel 400 miles merely to agitate a bag of wind." They travel thousands of miles now with twice that many players and a dozen coaches.

It's a very big business. Since Wilson and Rockne first got together, over three million people have watched Notre Dame and USC do battle every year. And at an average of 7.00 per seat over the years, that's not bad.

College players are signed for astronomical figures by the pros. Ricky Bell reportedly received 1.3 million dollars to sign with the Buccaneers of Tampa Bay.

But there's got to be more than the money that drives an athlete through endless hours of drills from spring until fall . . . the aching muscles, the injuries, the gallons of sweat. Call it pride, call it competitive spirit, or just call it the love of the game.

You'll see it once again this autumn when the Trojans of Southern California thunder through that tunnel of love from the locker room to the playing field of Notre Dame stadium to meet the proud Fighting Irish. Banners will wave, bands will play, the crowd will cheer, and you'd have to be awfully jaded not to experience pick-up in the heartbeat . . . a tightening in the chest when the first whistle blows . . . the kick-off . . . and the game is on.

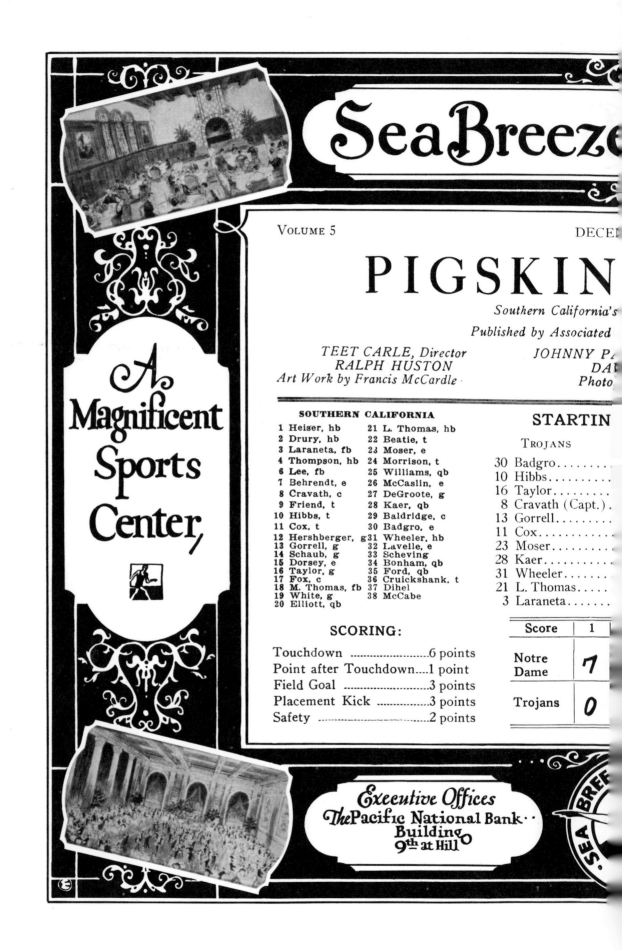

SeaBreeze

VOLUME 5   DECE[MBER]

PIGSKIN

Southern California's

Published by Associated

TEET CARLE, *Director*
RALPH HUSTON
Art Work by Francis McCardle

JOHNNY P[A
DA[
Photo[

A Magnificent Sports Center,

SOUTHERN CALIFORNIA

1 Heiser, hb	21 L. Thomas, hb
2 Drury, hb	22 Beatie, t
3 Laraneta, fb	23 Moser, e
4 Thompson, hb	24 Morrison, t
6 Lee, fb	25 Williams, qb
7 Behrendt, e	26 McCaslin, e
8 Cravath, c	27 DeGroote, g
9 Friend, t	28 Kaer, qb
10 Hibbs, t	29 Baldridge, c
11 Cox, t	30 Badgro, e
12 Hershberger, g	31 Wheeler, hb
13 Gorrell, g	32 Lavelle, e
14 Schaub, g	33 Scheving
15 Dorsey, e	34 Bonham, qb
16 Taylor, g	35 Ford, qb
17 Fox, c	36 Cruickshank, t
18 M. Thomas, fb	37 Dihel
19 White, g	38 McCabe
20 Elliott, qb	

STARTIN[

TROJANS

30 Badgro	. . . .
10 Hibbs	. . . .
16 Taylor	. . . .
8 Cravath (Capt.)	.
13 Gorrell	. . . .
11 Cox	. . . .
23 Moser	. . . .
28 Kaer	. . . .
31 Wheeler	. . . . . .
21 L. Thomas	. . . . .
3 Laraneta	. . . . . .

SCORING:

Touchdown ....6 points
Point after Touchdown....1 point
Field Goal ....3 points
Placement Kick ....3 points
Safety ....2 points

Score	1
Notre Dame	7
Trojans	0

SEA BREE[